Biracial Families

Roudi Nazarinia Roy • Alethea Rollins
Editors

Biracial Families

Crossing Boundaries, Blending Cultures, and Challenging Racial Ideologies

Springer

Editors
Roudi Nazarinia Roy
Department of Family and Consumer Sciences
California State University Long Beach
Long Beach, CA, USA

Alethea Rollins
Child and Family Development Program
School of Human Services
Harmon College of Business and Professional Studies
University of Central Missouri
Warrensburg, MO, USA

ISBN 978-3-319-96159-0 ISBN 978-3-319-96160-6 (eBook)
https://doi.org/10.1007/978-3-319-96160-6

Library of Congress Control Number: 2018958309

This Springer imprint is published by the registered company Springer Nature Switzerland AG
The registered company address is: Gewerbestrasse 11, 6330 Cham, Switzerland

To my parents for crossing racial boundaries at a time when it wasn't always safe to do so. To Ronnie for loving me unconditionally and allowing me to be authentic. Arie and Rocco, you inspire me, challenge me, and motivate me. And you always crack me up with your inside jokes ("What's biracial?!" LOL).

—Alethea Rollins

To my parents for always encouraging me to stand up for what I believed in. To Donovan, for being my number one supporter and confidant. Mali and Maia, your curiosity for the world around you gives me a rich new perspective on life. Your laughter fills our home, and your love for music and dancing is contagious.

Alethea and I met more than 8 years ago as the student/new professional representatives for the Ethnic Minorities Section of the National Council on Family Relations. This book project led to an invaluable friendship filled with support and encouragement. I have learned so much from Alethea. Her wisdom as a mother and an academic who strives to maintain a work-life balance is inspiring. Her genuine ability to listen and to validate so many of my own experiences as a mother of two biracial daughters have made her an irreplaceable friend.

—Roudi Nazarinia Roy

Acknowledgments

When we began this project we had one clear purpose in mind: For the people, by the people. We wanted a diverse group of authors to tell a diverse story. We asked authors to use personal stories and reflections, to share openly and honestly, yet to maintain academic integrity and rigor. We are indebted to each and every author of this book; they pushed themselves personally and professionally. We are delighted with the outcome. There will always be more to say, stories left untold, and research that we missed. Yet we trust that everything written in these pages is genuine and authentic.

> *So long as you write what you wish to write, that is all that matters; and whether it matters for ages or only for hours, nobody can say.*—Virginia Woolf (1882)

We thank each author for their commitment to this project, their patience as we traversed a few challenges to completion, and their ongoing dedication to working with and supporting diverse people and families. We appreciate Karin Horler's hard work and editorial support on the chapters we wrote and the Springer Publishing Company for acknowledging the gap in the literature and a need for this book. Lastly, we are grateful to our families. We could not have completed this work without the support of our loving husbands and inspiring children. Thank you for giving us the space and time needed (even on vacation) to complete this important work.

Contents

Part IV Challenges and Opportunities

Contributors

James E. Brooks Department of Psychology, Tennessee State University, Nashville, TN, USA

Chalandra M. Bryant Department of Human Development and Family Science, University of Georgia, Athens, GA, USA

JahRaEl Burrell Kentucky Community Colleges, Versailles, KY, USA

Annamaria Csizmadia Human Development and Family Studies, University of Connecticut, Stamford, CT, USA

Fabienne Doucet Department of Teaching and Learning, Steinhardt School of Culture, Education, and Human Development, New York University, New York, NY, USA

Jeneé C. Duncan Department of Human Development and Family Science, University of Georgia, Athens, GA, USA

Melissa Giraud EmbraceRace, Amherst, MA, USA

Vanessa Gonlin Department of Sociology, Texas A&M University, College Station, TX, USA

Marcella Runell Hall Division of Student Life, Mount Holyoke College, South Hadley, MA, USA

Henry L. Harris Department of Counseling, University of North Carolina at Charlotte, Charlotte, NC, USA

Katie M. Hrapczynski Department of Family Studies and Community Development, Towson University, Towson, MD, USA

Sean G. Jefferson Department of Family and Consumer Sciences, California State University, Northridge, CA, USA

Katie W. Lamberson Department of Counseling at University of North Georgia, Dahlonega, GA, USA

Leigh A. Leslie Department of Family Science, University of Maryland, College Park, MD, USA

Jeremy Lynch Department of Psychology, Fisk University, Nashville, TN, USA

Clare P. Merlin Department of Counseling, University of North Carolina at Charlotte, Charlotte, NC, USA

Alethea Rollins Child and Family Development Program, School of Human Services, Harmon College of Business and Professional Studies, University of Central Missouri, Warrensburg, MO, USA

Roudi Nazarinia Roy Department of Family and Consumer Sciences, California State University Long Beach, Long Beach, CA, USA

Farrell J. Webb College of Health and Human Development, California State University, Northridge, CA, USA

Susan White Clinical Mental Health Counseling, Southern Connecticut State University, New Haven, CT, USA

Jennifer L. Young Department of Family Science, University of Maryland, College Park, MD, USA

About the Editors

Roudi Nazarinia Roy, Ph.D. is an assistant professor and area coordinator of Child Development and Family Studies in the Department of Family and Consumer Sciences at California State University Long Beach. She is also the 2017–2018 Ethnic Minorities Section Chair for the National Council on Family Relations. She has a B.A. in Psychology and an M.A. in Family Science from the University of British Columbia. She received her Ph.D. in Family Studies from Kansas State University in 2009. She teaches courses related to the transition to parenthood, family life education, families and diversity, and parent education. Her research interest revolves around the transition to parenthood and cultural influences on parental roles. Dr. Roy is also a consultant for community agencies serving diverse populations of families.

Alethea Rollins, Ph.D. earned her M.S. and Ph.D. from the University of North Carolina Greensboro (UNCG). She completed her post-doctoral work at the Center for Youth, Family, and Community Partnerships at UNCG. Alethea is a professor, researcher, wife, and mother. She teaches courses in human development across the lifespan, including child development and adolescence, adulthood, and death, grief, and dying. She volunteers regularly in her children's schools and with the school district at large. Her research focuses on bi-/multiracial individuals and families, parental racial socialization, and racial socialization practices of early childhood educators.

About the Authors

James E. Brooks, Ph.D. is an Assistant Professor in the Counseling Psychology Program at Tennessee State University where he is the Coordinator of the M.S. program and serves as a core faculty member of the Ph.D. program. Dr. Brooks earned his doctorate in the Counseling Psychology program from the University of Illinois at Urbana-Champaign. His research interests include interracial relationships, multiracial families, and multicultural counseling.

Chalandra M. Bryant, Ph.D. is a Professor of Human Development and Family Science at the University of Georgia. Dr. Bryant earned her doctorate from the University of Texas—Austin. She completed a 2-year National Institutes of Mental Health (NIMH) post-doctoral fellowship. She teaches courses in family development, family theories, and intimate relationships. Her research focuses on close relationships and the manner in which social, familial, economic, and psychosocial factors are linked to marital and health outcomes.

JahRael V. Burrell, Ph.D. is an Assistant professor and Program Coordinator for Human Services at Hopkinsville Community College. A graduate of Kansas State University, his work focused on the hegemonic influences among sex, gender, and ethnicities in the United States, sexual identity, social movements, social justice, race/ethnicity, violence, and poverty. His working background includes positions as Instructor/Assistant Professor at Kansas State University Southern University at New Orleans, LA; Murray State University at Murray, KY; and Lindsey Wilson College at Columbia, KY.

Annamaria Csizmadia, Ph.D. is Associate Professor of Human Development and Family Studies (HDFS) at the University of Connecticut. She studies ethnic-racial identity, racial socialization, and social-emotional development in ethnic-racial minority, specifically multiracial and immigrant, children. Her work on these topics has been published in *Family Relations, Social Development, Parenting: Sciences and Practice*, *Journal of Marriage and Family*, *Journal of Black Psychology*, *and Maternal and Child Health Journal*. Additionally, she has published book chapters on interracial families and multi-ethnic and multiracial marriages. She teaches courses on diversity, adolescence, research methods, and early and middle childhood. Dr. Csizmadia is on the Editorial Board of *Journal of Marriage and Family, Journal of Youth and Adolescence, and Journal of Family Psychology*. She earned her Ph.D. and master's degrees from the University of Missouri and her undergraduate degree from the University of Trier, Germany.

Fabienne Doucet, Ph.D. is Associate Professor of Early Childhood Education in the Department of Teaching and Learning at the NYU Steinhardt School of Culture, Education, and Human Development. Born in Spain, raised in Haiti, and migrating to the USA at the age of ten, Doucet embodies a hybrid identity that is mirrored in her interdisciplinary approach to examining how immigrant and US-born children of color and their families navigate education in the USA. A critical ethnographer, Doucet specifically studies how taken-for-granted beliefs, practices, and values in the US educational system position linguistically, culturally, and socioeconomically diverse children and families at a disadvantage, and seeks active solutions for meeting their educational needs. Doucet has a Ph.D. in Human Development and Family Studies from UNC-Greensboro. She was a postdoctoral fellow at the Harvard Graduate School of Education with fellowships from the National Science Foundation and National Academy of Education/Spencer Foundation.

Jeneé C. Duncan, M.S. is a doctoral candidate in the Department of Human Development and Family Science at the University of Georgia. Jenee's research interests include couple and co-parenting relationship processes and functioning, with a particular interest on African American couples and parents. She is also interested in how family life education may promote resiliency with these families.

Melissa Giraud, M.Ed. is the Co-founder/Director of EmbraceRace, a community of adults supporting each other to raise a generation of kids who are brave, informed, and proactive on matters of race and racial justice. Professionally, she has been most interested in supporting learning and life outcomes for underserved students and families, especially immigrant girls and girls of color. Those driving concerns have shaped her work as an educator, radio producer, education strategist, and now as a co-founder of EmbraceRace.

Vanessa Gonlin is a doctoral student and Diversity Fellow in the Department of Sociology at Texas A&M University. Her research interests include analyzing trends in multiracial identity, identity formation, and racial ideology within interracial partners. Gonlin has worked with administrators and peers to design and facilitate discussions intended to enhance campus race relations, and he has served as a mentor and research trainer for underrepresented graduate and undergraduate students.

Marcella Runell Hall, Ph.D. is a mama to two amazing daughters, a wife and partner and an author of essays and curriculum related to social justice education. She is also currently serving as Vice President for Student Life and Dean of Students at Mount Holyoke College. She has a bachelor's degree from Ramapo College of New Jersey, a master's degree from New York University and a doctorate from University of Massachusetts, Amherst. Her next project is called Uncommon Bonds: Women Reflect on Race and Friendship (Peter Lang, 2018) with Kersha Smith.

Henry L. Harris, Ph.D. is a Professor and Chair of the Department of Counseling at the University of North Carolina at Charlotte. He received his master's degree in School Counseling from the University North Carolina at Chapel Hill 1986 and his Ph.D. in Counseling, with a specialization in Sports Psychology, from the University of Virginia in 1996. He is also a Licensed Professional Counselor (LPC), a former high school counselor, and United States Air Force military veteran.

Katie M. Hrapczynski, Ph.D. is an Assistant Professor in the Department of Family Studies and Community Development at Towson University. She received her Ph.D. in Family Science and M.S. in Marriage and Family Therapy from the University of Maryland. Dr. Hrapczynski's research examines family processes conducive to promoting youth and family well-being in adoptive families with a primary focus on transracial adoption. She teaches courses on family relationships, services for children and youth, and family science research methods. Her scholarly and teaching activities are largely informed by her experiences in the human services and practice as a couple and family therapist.

Sean Graham Jefferson, Ph.D. is an Assistant Professor in the Department of Sociology, Anthropology, and Child and Family Studies at the University of Louisiana at Lafayette. He received his Ph.D. in Educational Psychology, with a concentration in human development and family studies, from the University of North Texas in 2017. His research focuses on examining the self-respect of emerging adults, championing interpersonal relationships through addressing issues regarding emotional intelligence, and extinguishing group-level social injustice and social inequality through challenging public policy.

Katie W. Lamberson, Ph.D. is an Assistant Professor in the Department of Counseling at the University of North Georgia. Dr. Lamberson received her Doctorate in Counseling and Counselor Education from the University of North Carolina at Greensboro. She currently teaches courses in addictions, ethics, and family counseling.

Leigh A. Leslie, Ph.D. is an Associate Professor in the Department of Family Science at the University of Maryland. She holds a Ph.D. from the Pennsylvania State University with apre-doctoral internship in clinical-community psychology from Yale University, School of Medicine. She is the author of numerous book chapters and over 40 scholarly articles focusing on family functioning and mental health. Specific foci include social support, gender issues in families, and interracial families. She teaches courses in marriage and family therapy, cultural competency, and gender. Dr. Leslie is a licensed psychologist and a marriage and family therapist.

Jeremy Lynch, Ph.D. is a practicing psychologist in the Nashville and Middle Tennessee area. Dr. Lynch earned his Ph.D. in Counseling Psychology from Tennessee State University. His research interests relate to multicultural competence and quality assurance in an integrated behavioral health settings.

Clare P. Merlin, Ph.D. is an Assistant Professor at the University of North Carolina at Charlotte. A former school counselor, she earned her doctorate in Counselor Education and Supervision from the College of William & Mary. Her primary area of research is focused on school counselors and multicultural education.

Farrell J. Webb, Ph.D. is Professor and Dean of the College of Health and Human Development at the California State University, Northridge. Dr. Webb worked at California State University, Los Angeles, as Professor and Associate Dean and as an Associate Professor at Kansas State University in the School of Family Studies and Human Services for 20 years. He specializes in data analyses and statistics along with the social correlates of well-being, which include race, sex, gender, ethnicity, economics, poverty, and social stratification.

Susan White is currently a graduate student in the Clinical Mental Health Counseling program at Southern Connecticut State University. She earned her B.A. in Psychology and minor in Women's, Gender, and Sexuality studies from the University of Connecticut in May 2017. Her research interests focus on multicultural issues, diversity, and mental health. After completing her master's degree, she plans to further her graduate studies and pursue a doctoral training in psychology.

Jennifer L. Young, M.S., M.A. is a doctoral student in the Department of Family Science at the University of Maryland. She has an M.A. in Chinese Language and Culture from the Ohio State University and an M.S. in Couples and Family Therapy from University of Maryland. Jennifer herself is biracial, and her interests center around interracial couple relationships and developing culturally sensitive mental health interventions. She has a Predoctoral Fellowship at the National Cancer Institute where she conducts psychosocial research on families coping with genetic cancer syndromes. In 2017, Jennifer was named Outstanding Graduate Assistant by the University of Maryland and has previously published on interracial couples in therapy.

Part I
Introduction

Introduction

Roudi Nazarinia Roy and Alethea Rollins

June had recently celebrated her 52nd anniversary with her husband, Rob, when I interviewed her about her experiences as a White woman married to a Black man for over half a century, with three biracial children. June recalls meeting Rob in the school library in the fall of 1964. They were both students at a Catholic college in Buffalo, New York. Their initial conversation over politics turned into a friendship and later a relationship. June was drawn to Rob because he was passionate about things she had not thought about before, and she enjoyed "spending time with him and cared for him." Looking back, she reflected that "he was a better Christian than I was." But she listened to people who tried to give her advice about the relationship. Her parents thought that she was foolish for thinking she could marry Rob in the American racial climate of the time. Her friends and Rob's family were skeptical, too.

She married Rob when they graduated that spring, and her parents did not come to the wedding. Only her paternal uncle came, with his wife. Her uncle and aunt did not have children of their own, and June had a close relationship with them. June was also very close with her maternal grandmother, who did not come to the wedding. After the wedding, Rob joined the army for the educational stipend, and they had children right away. When June gave birth to her first daughter, she recalls her mother and maternal grandmother coming to the hospital to see her. Later, her father came too. The birth of her daughter changed things for her family; they came to like Rob and see him as a

R. Nazarinia Roy (✉)
Department of Family and Consumer Sciences, California State University Long Beach, Long Beach, CA, USA
e-mail: Roudi.Roy@csulb.edu

A. Rollins
Child and Family Development Program, School of Human Services,
Harmon College of Business and Professional Studies, University of Central Missouri, Warrensburg, MO, USA
e-mail: arollins@ucmo.edu

R. Nazarinia Roy, A. Rollins (eds.), *Biracial Families*,
https://doi.org/10.1007/978-3-319-96160-6_1

good man. Chuckling, June said, "Once they got to know him, I think they actually liked him more than they liked me. He was a good man and a good father."

Sarah, their eldest daughter, was 12 months old when June gave birth to their son, and the children were 6 and 18 months old when Rob went off to Vietnam. She begged him to get out of the army when he returned home, so he joined the Air Force, and they moved to Germany for three and a half years. They had their third and final child, a daughter, while stationed in Germany. When I asked June about her experience raising biracial children, she said, "The military was a great place to raise biracial children. There was always lots of diversity." Their children had friends from many racial and ethnic backgrounds. Their family was also very involved in the Catholic church. Their friends from church were mainly White, but the children grew up with diverse groups of friends.

She recalled the first time her eldest daughter, a toddler at the time, was called the N-word. The experience shook June, but of course she wasn't surprised by it. She says her son was called the N-word by a White neighbor's daughter too, when he was a toddler. He would later go around calling little White children the N-word because it "got a rise out of people." June stated that her experiences early on taught her to stay calm and "respond to people, not react to them." She wanted to teach her children not to react to these types of situations but rather to "respond as dignified human beings."

Reflecting back, she said that a nun from her college days once asked her, "Do you follow through with things?" At the time, she didn't understand the question, but years later she understood that "the nun was concerned that if things got difficult I [might] bail on my family." Things did get difficult, and it wasn't always easy. She stressed that she now knows that Christ is the reason her family stayed strong and that she married a good man, a good father, and a good Christian. Those things kept her family together through their early experiences.

June's parents initially disapproved of her marriage to a Black man, and it was only after the birth of her first child that they built a relationship with Rob. Unsupportive family members sometimes become more open to a biracial couple when a grandchild arrives, but even in this scenario they may continue to disapprove of the biracial relationship.

If we are quick to assume that a family member's disapproval of a biracial relationship is guided only by prejudice, we fail to recognize the fear and concern the family members have based on what they know to be real in our society. Our society has an embedded structure of racism in which, as Allan Johnson (2006) writes, we have created categories of race based on skin tone and attributed characteristics to the individuals within these categories in order to emphasize our differences and perpetuate a structure of power and privilege. This embedded structure of our society touches every aspect of our lives, from our pre-K-12 educational system, where young Black and Hispanic boys are more likely to be expelled than their White counterparts, to our healthcare system, which is flooded with racial inequalities in access and opportunity.

June, in the opening story, was raised by parents who taught her to love all members of her society. They had never spoken ill of people from different race groups, and they raised their children with those same values. But when June chose to marry a Black man, she was choosing a very different life than the one she knew. Her choice was seen as naïve by her parents, and they in turn chose not to support her. June did lose privileges she had in our society after she married Rob, but her family's support after the birth of her first child was a source of strength that enabled her to endure the prejudice her new family experienced. Although June's relationship began decades ago, and we would like to think that things are different today, we are only blinding ourselves to the realities of people's lives. Not only are Black and White partnerships still an issue among families, but we have had students and research participants from multiple cultural backgrounds, such as Indian, Vietnamese, and Mexican families, who have been disowned by their parents for choosing to marry a Black partner. Perhaps what has really changed from the time of June's marriage to today is the increase in the number of biracial and multiracial families. Frequently, one of us (R.N.R.) encounters and connects with complete strangers who approach her to share pictures of their grandchildren with pride, because they look like her daughters. Or mothers passing by her in the store with their biracial children will smile at her, sharing a sense of unspoken connection.

Another unspoken experience common among members of a biracial family is the dual reality of their experiences within society—one reality when they are alone and another when they are with their partner or their family. These realities revolve around the daily privileges that come with who we are perceived to be, where we are, and who we are with at the moment. In some ways, the partner who has lived with privilege is, by association, exposed to a life without such privileges. For some upper-middle-class biracial families living in predominantly White suburban communities with good schools, they might find themselves one of only a few families of color in their community. They may see their neighbors greeting other new families, but not theirs, with welcome baskets. They go about their days saying hello to neighbors and trying not to engage in conversations about why athletes should respect the flag. Often, in conversations like these, they find that the neighbors are seeking not dialogue but confirmation of their own viewpoint by a person or family of color—as though being one family of color could make them representative of an entire population of people. Like most parents, they have curious children who ask questions about the world around them, but sometimes their questions are unique to their family: "Mommy, were you Black before, like us?" or "Mommy, why don't I look like you or Daddy?" And again, like most parents, they listen intently when the children talk about their day at school, but they listen because they have seen when other children have called them names targeting their skin color or have refused to play with them in the park. Perhaps they listen more intently because they cannot be with their children every minute of every day.

The number of biracial and multiracial families in the United States has increased (Pew Research Center, 2017) and will continue to increase steadily, and perhaps life today is less difficult than it was for June's biracial family, yet it is not without trials and tribulations. Biracial couples and their families do not live in a social vacuum. Their interactions with family members, their communities, and the larger society can leave a lasting impact. And although we do not dare assume that all biracial families have the same life experiences, we do believe that some common experiences naturally occur when two individuals from distinct socially constructed categories of race come together as a family.

We specifically chose to use the word *biracial* in the title of our book because in the US context it represents the stark differences often thought of between races and connotes clear difference and duality. But we recognize that many whom we consider biracial may be multiracial and/or multiethnic. Many authors throughout this book use *biracial*, whereas others use terms that reflect their own philosophy and preference with regard to naming and racial classifications. Whether we refer to their relationship as biracial, multiracial, or interracial, we are focusing on the experiences of two individuals, who have had uniquely different experiences in society based on their appearances, as they come together to form a family.

As professional women in biracial families, we took on this book project for three main reasons. First, we are all too familiar with the negative outcomes that permeate the literature on biracial children and adults. This negative frame often puts the individual's struggle with identity development at the forefront of the biracial experience, rather than recognizing how interactions within the family and with systems external to the family affect the biracial individual's reality. Second, we wanted to highlight the strengths within biracial families, stemming from the connection between the biracial couple, who are constantly learning and growing with every new experience as partners and as parents. Finally, we wanted to create a resource for families, educators, and practitioners that will validate the experiences of biracial individuals and their families and highlight the need for more research on the experiences of these families.

In bringing together this book project, we wanted to work with a team of researchers and practitioners who not only are professionally invested in the experience of biracial families but in most cases have a personal vested interest because of their own biracial families. We are grateful for the work of our authors and believe that their work will set a foundation for further research and client-centered practice with biracial families.

Although other publications have examined the experiences of biracial children living in the United States, these books focus primarily on individual experiences and are limited in their scope and their understanding of the biracial family as a whole. With such a narrow focus, the current publications on biracial children leave gaps in our understanding of the experiences of living in a biracial family and raising a biracial child or children. This book fills these gaps by taking a life-span perspective from dating to marriage to the onset of parenting. This book not only reviews the current empirical information on biracial families in a way that is relevant to professionals working in the field but also highlights areas of future research for researchers wishing to pursue further investigations.

Our book is divided into four sections. Part 1, the introductory section, explores the history of race in America and the limited theories and practices we have to explore families and race-related matters. Part 2, "Family Formation," examines mate selection, marriage, and transition to parenthood among biracial couples. The third part, "Parenting," explores the experience of parenting biracial children, their racial socialization, and biracial families formed through adoption. The final part, "Challenges and Opportunities," examines the variability among biracial families, and the social context in which biracial families exist.

In the first part of the book, a chapter focused on history, written by Drs. Webb, Burrell, and Jefferson, reviews the past and current definitions of race in the United States. These authors argue that race is a complex concept that is difficult to define but nonetheless is a powerful tool that divides us based on our appearances.

They discuss what it means to be biracial/multiracial in America, and how the increase in this population should cause us to reexamine the existing color lines in our country. The next chapter in this section, written by Dr. Webb and Ms. Gonlin, identifies the elements of family theories and reviews specific theories that have been developed to examine the lives of biracial/multiracial individuals. They discuss the relevance and utility of these theories in evaluating biracial families and conclude with a discussion of how current theories can be improved to guide our understanding of biracial/multiracial families in contemporary America.

The first of three chapters in the second part of this book provides a multidisciplinary review of research related to the process of partnering across race. Drs. Brooks and Lynch explore research in the fields of communication, psychology, sociology, and demographic studies to illustrate the multilayered process of partnering. More importantly, they discuss how individual factors such as beliefs, social networks, geographic location, and communication patterns influence interracial partners' attraction, courting, and relationship initiation. In conclusion, they address how a diverse American population will impact future relationships. Dr. Bryant and Ms. Duncan follow with a chapter on biracial marriage in which they review the history of biracial marriages in the United States and discuss the sociopolitical context in which interracial relationships are embedded. They examine the relationship quality and stability of interracial couples in comparison to same-race couples and highlight the importance of theory in examining such relationships.

The two chapters on relationship formation and commitment are followed by a chapter on the transition to parenthood. Perhaps one of the most life-altering transitions, the transition to parenthood, can be a difficult period for most couples. In this chapter Dr. Roy reviews how this life transition impacts the lives of men and women in common ways, and some key factors that have been identified in the literature as buffers against declines in relationship quality. Throughout this review, she discusses how factors both within and external to the biracial couple can influence their experiences across the transition to parenthood, how these experiences can be unique to the couple, and the importance of having these experiences validated by one's partner.

In the third part of this book, the authors discuss the unique strengths and challenges of parenting within biracial families. In the first chapter in this section, Drs. Doucet, Runell Hall, and Ms. Giraud discuss the unique concerns and challenges faced by the parents of biracial children as they try to blend their cultural beliefs and practices. They also discuss aspects of ethnic identity and racial and cultural socialization within biracial families. In addition, these authors explore the external relationships, pressures, and perceptions faced by biracial families. They conclude their chapter with a review of the gaps in the literature and provide the reader with guiding principles for practice based on the literature they have discussed. In the following chapter, Dr. Rollins explores racial socialization among biracial families using a developmental perspective. She begins with a review of the socialization literature, identifying unique aspects of racial socialization that are important for biracial families across the stages of development. With this focus, she identifies implications for practice among professionals working with biracial families, parents, and children. She highlights important strategies that parents can use as they assist their children in developing a racial identity and emphasizes the importance of the process rather than the label. The final chapter in this section, written by Drs. Leslie, Hrapczynski, and Young, focuses on biracial families formed through adoption. These authors review the current trends in transracial adoption and the prevalence of different types of adoption. They review the literature on transracial adoption, highlighting best practices for promoting resiliency in adoptees. They conclude their chapter by providing clinical implications and recommendations for future research.

In the fourth and final part of this book, the authors focus on the challenges and opportunities that are unique to biracial families. In their chapter on family structures, Drs. Harris, Lamberson, and Merlin examine the population of biracial families in the United States and possible causes of such increases. They explore the diverse family structures among biracial families, which exemplify the fact that biracial families have diverse experiences. They pay particular attention to the strengths within these diverse family forms and make recommendations for clinical practice. Following this chapter, the racial identity chapter, written by Dr. Csizmadia and Ms. White, discusses how macro-level challenges may have disappeared, yet micro-level challenges still exist for contemporary biracial individuals. These authors discuss the existence of different racial identity options today, the factors that affect these options, and the outcomes they create. This chapter highlights the heterogeneous nature of the biracial population, and the authors make specific recommendations for supporting biracial children's racial identity formation and social-emotional development. The authors conclude their chapter by identifying gaps in the literature and specific areas that require attention in future research. The final chapter of this book summarizes the future directions discussed throughout this book and highlights the need for more research on biracial families, whose experiences are constantly changing in our ever-changing society.

This multidisciplinary book is intended not only for educators and practitioners but also for researchers who can take on some of the much-needed future research work and further our knowledge of the diverse experiences of biracial families. We hope that the content of this book is also helpful in validating the experiences of biracial individuals and biracial couples. More importantly, we hope that parents of biracial children see this book as a resource that can assist them in navigating the challenges they may face while at the same time helping them to recognize their own strengths and abilities to meet their children's needs.

References

Johnson, A. G. (2006). *Privilege, power, and difference*. Boston, MA: McGraw-Hill Higher Education.

Pew Research Center. (2017). *Intermarriage in the U.S. 50 years after Loving v. Virginia*. Retrieved from http://www.pewsocialtrends.org/2017/05/18/intermarriage-in-the-u-s-50-years-after-loving-v-virginia/

Social Constitutionality of Race in America: Some Meanings for Bi/Multiracial Families

Farrell J. Webb, JahRaEl Burrell, and Sean G. Jefferson

The authors of this chapter all share some multiracial heritage. However, only one has historical evidence. He has a White father and a Black mother. He grew up in the South and attended predominately Black schools and completed his education at an HBCU. It was his choice. He also says that it was because of the limited exposure and society's expectations that he was not as good as others helped him to form his understanding (or lack there-of) of race and racial identity that has led him to make some of the choices he has made. Upon reflection he might have done things differently if there had been a more clear pathway.

A very simple question such as "what is race?" can lead to a series of very complex answers. Race is often thought of as socially constructed—that is something that is made up of social definitions and exists within different social contexts in different ways. We define race as something referring to physical and sociocultural differences that groups and cultures consider socially significant (adapted and modified from the ASA Website, 2017). The definition is enhanced in most social dictionaries and texts but the essential features remain. When sociologists speak about race they are primarily concerned with examining the causes and consequences of the socially constructed division across groups and how they influence one group versus another. It is also true that in race, when separated from ethnicity—the concept that describes the cultural heritage among groups—there are some issues that become confounded and somewhat contradictory. No matter how one views the concept, it is clear that

F. J. Webb (✉)
College of Health and Human Development, California State University, Northridge, CA, USA
e-mail: farrell.webb@csun.edu

J. Burrell
Kentucky Community Colleges, Versailles, KY, USA

S. G. Jefferson
Department of Family and Consumer Sciences, California State University, Northridge, CA, USA

R. Nazarinia Roy, A. Rollins (eds.), *Biracial Families*,
https://doi.org/10.1007/978-3-319-96160-6_2

race as a social construction has helped to shape much of the structured social inequality that exists in the United States today. This fact was not lost on the so-called forefathers who deliberately and consciously (some will say done without a conscience) used race and basis for a social, economic, and political system that promoted and created differences among groups that shaped the relationships that still persist today. In fact, race and its outcomes are easily explained by the Thomas theorem which states that situations that are defined as real become real in their consequences (Thomas & Thomas, 1928). This is true of race in America and its by-product, racism; even though there is no biological basis for race at all, it is nevertheless a real social construct that has had and continues to have a meaningful impact on the life chances of individuals, especially those whose racial designations are devalued by the current hegemonic structure—what we commonly refer to today as people of color.

It is clear that the history of race in America is not only a very complex issue, but it also remains a highly controversial topic, despite the so-called post-racial epoch. Few Americans are willing to engage in conversations about race (Davis & Boyer, 2013). Still fewer make changes in their behaviors or attitudes even after encountering someone of a different race [Black] (Axt & Trawalter, 2017; Shelton & Richeson, 2006). While what is known about US race-based history cannot be summarized into a few pages, we are all too cognizant that the history is too detailed and too rich to do it justice; it is important that we glean some pivotal moments to help address the topic of this chapter. Therefore, what we intend to do is to select certain events and elements of US racial history that will allow us to address the salience for developing the contemporary position of bi/multiracial families within the context of social history. We are attempting to develop some meaningful context by which bi/multiracial families can position themselves in this highly complex and detailed history of race in America.

In effect, we are using a systemic approach to very briefly describe the racial history of the United States. While the basic ecosystemic paradigm (Bronfenbrenner, 1979, 1993, 1995, 2005) and its subsystems and components are well known to family scholars, the one concept that is often overlooked or just presumed to exist but not really addressed by most is that of the chronosystem—or simply put, time itself (see Fig. 1). It is impossible to discuss any history without the consideration of time and its independent influences on society and its existing systems. The person-process-context-time (PCCT) model is a very useful construct that allows one to see the role historical experiences and policy outcomes played and continue to play in the lives of people—in this case, primarily people of color (Bronfenbrenner, 1979, 1993, 1995, 2005). Therefore, what we seek to do in this chapter is not to repeat the history of Blacks in America—we know that this is an impossible task. Rather we have selected different epochs that seem to have had an important influence over particular systems described by the ecosystemic model vis-à-vis the context of time, process, events, and persons. For example, when we want to show how the micro-system of family is influenced by a macro-system (political and economic systems) change we explored the influence of how race laws defined personhood, citizenship, and marriage rights.

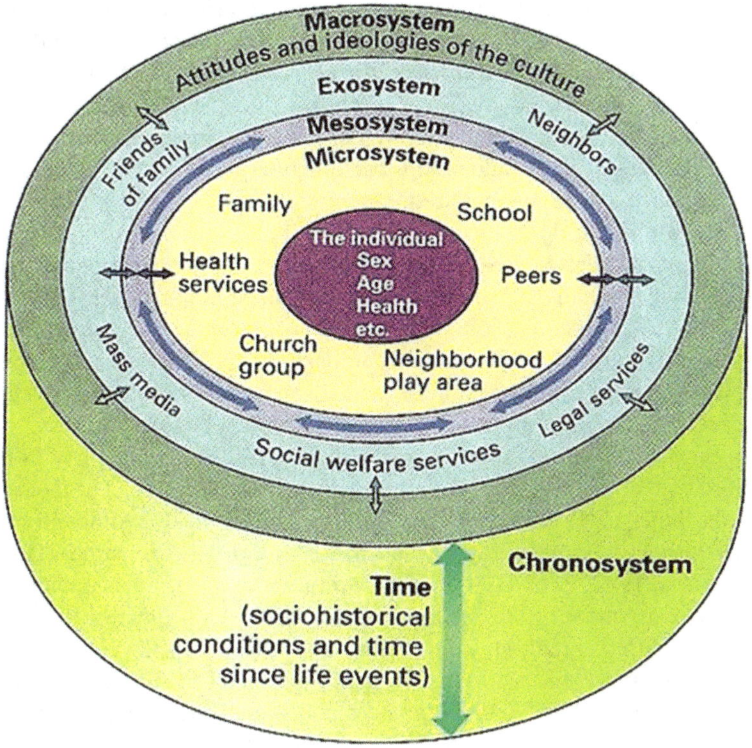

Fig. 1 Ecological model based on Urie Bronfenbrenner's discussion of Ecosystem Influences on Human Behavior

Race Naming as a Process Element

One of the first contexts that we must establish is the idea that multiracial people have existed throughout our early US history. The terms used to refer to these individuals were neither complementary nor polite; they were called a variety of names meant to devalue them and to see them as less than human; for example the terms "mulatto, quadroon, octoroon, slave, niggers, and savages" were used interchangeably and without much formal meaning but really were all meant to suggest that the person was less than a whole person. All of these terms could refer to a variety of color designations all meaning to suggest that the individual was ultimately not White. The socially polite and acceptable term "the Negro or Negro" was introduced by the Census of 1900 to replace the pejorative term of "Colored" which had different meanings depending upon where in the world it was used. All of these expressions morphed into what we have now come to call Black here in the United States where the term has taken on a positive meaning despite the fact that it was the primary group that populated the slave cohort of American society. Only much later, some 450–500 years later, did we begin to see Black become the term used along with other race and ethnic identities which developed into what we now call people of color. The social and political rebirth of race as a construct beyond Black is largely due to an increased awareness on the part of others as to how much the history of Blacks in America has come to shape how all people of color are both reacted to and responded to within this country. This becomes even more relevant when people from different race/ethnic groups become interpersonally involved with each other and produce offspring—children.

What we attempt to do in this chapter is to mix social constructs with relevant historical events in an effort to show how mono- and multiracial people see, prepare, respond, and react to a myriad of racially induced injustices and events proffered by our US history. To that extent it is important to note how the construct of race, as a meaningful paradigm by which social relationships are formed and examined, is viewed. It is clearly a central idea in the social sciences as noted by both early and contemporary thinkers (Allport, 1954; Franklin, 2011). The salience of race becomes enriched and problematic when an individual can be thought of as belonging to more than one race group; in this case, biracial or multiracial as the terms are used (Shih, Sanchez, Bonam, & Peck, 2007; Spickard, 1992). Although there are numerous authors who have argued that race is an artificial construct (Goodman, 2000; Spickard, 1992; Zack, 1995) its known outcomes, e.g., racism and discrimination, and consequences are all too real for those who have been victimized (Bonilla-Silva, 2010; Franklin, 2011; Perry, 2011; Root, 1992; Shih et al., 2007; Smedly, 2007). For people who identify as bi/multiracial the unique consequences of race—including racial stereotyping and racial socialization along with what we are calling "racial diffusion"—serve as important determinants in how bi/multiracial families are able to survive in a hegemonic society that uses race as a very real and valid social construct for determining social, political, and economic status groups. Some of these groups have a parallel structure but always with a decidedly less strong position for those not in the majority group. These subtle distinctions can and do have impacts on social achievement, health, and well-being. Therefore, it is important that when examining issues for bi/multiracial families and their children these dynamics must be considered. In effect the naming process was critical as to how people were allowed to develop within the slave system. This was especially true for those Blacks who were able to pass (*passé blanc*) or those for whom their bi/multiracial status was known. Even within the caste system of slavery there were distinct hierarchies perpetuated by skin type and external features, all of which were used in race naming. The lighter the skin, the more favorable the position within the work duties (Blassingame, 1979; Franklin, 2011; McAdoo, 2007).

Race and Sex: Limiting Interpersonal Relationships

The idea of race has been a part of the American culture since the beginning of our country, although there are some who believe that the most severe racial distinctions only surfaced after the Civil War. In truth, there were many restrictions placed on the earliest of Blacks, the slaves because of their so-called superior bodies and exotic features that were deemed as too dangerous and too enticing for White women (Franklin, 2011; Genovese, 1989). At this point we must point to the important role that the history of anti-miscegenation has played on both children and families. Much of the social residue of prejudice and overt discrimination remains largely in part due to these deep-seeded and misguided beliefs (Blassingame, 1979; Franklin, 2011). So fearful were the colonists of this stereotype that they passed the first laws against interracial relationships in the colony of Maryland, banning interracial marriage in 1664. The intent was to prevent English women from marrying African men. Prior to this law it was not uncommon for White indentured servants and Black slaves to be married. There were also some instances where some slaves were married to some members in the Aristocratic circles. To ensure that this would not be commonplace among the colonies with the great increase in the slave trade interracial marriage was prohibited, first by social practice, and then by law. However, this change did not prohibit interracial relationships from occurring, including some well-known examples, such as Thomas Jefferson and his third slave mistress Sarah "Sally" Hemings (Gordon-Reed, 2008; Thomas Jefferson Foundation, 2017).

This limitation on interpersonal relationships included marriage and had the added economic advantage of supporting industrial development and capitalism by keeping slaves as separate economic units not linked to families of their own. In effect, without the permanent social ties that marriage, relationships, and family mandated (Blassingame, 1979; Franklin, 2011; Genovese, 1989; Williams, 1994) it was easy to view slaves as property with no human rights. These practices continued throughout the colonies, which were now the United States, until 1883 when the US Supreme Court officially sanctioned racial separation with its ruling on *Pace v Alabama* (106 US 583 [1883]) affirming that anti-miscegenation was legal. This ruling would stay in place for some 80 years. Its impact was felt and it embolden states to pass more restrictive laws such as Virginia's "Racial Integrity Act" that said that every person must be recoded at birth and divided into two groups, White and colored. This idea codified into law the *soi-disant* "one-drop rule." It also expanded existing anti-miscegenation laws making it a crime for Whites and non-Whites to be married. To further complicate things the Racial Integrity Act had a clause known as the Pocahontas exception whereby any descendant of one of the first families of Virginia, where they had been some "race mixing" with the indigenous people (Native Americans), could be considered as White if he or she had one-sixteenth Native American ancestry (Maillard, 2005). In 1948, the California Supreme Court became the first to overturn the anti-miscegenation statue on the basis that it violated the XIVth Amendment of the US constitution. In this case, *Perez v. Sharp* (aka *Perez v. Lippold* or *Perez v. Moroney*), Andrea Perez (Mexican-American woman), and Sylvester Davis (African-American man) were refused a marriage license because Perez (classified as White) wanted to marry Davis (a "Negro"). The clerk cited the California Civil Code (CCC) Section 60 which prohibited marriages between Whites and "Negroes, Mongolians, and members of the Malay race, or mulattoes." Furthermore, Section 69 prohibited issuing a license to any of the above groups. The court essentially ruled that laws restricting the right to marriage must not be based solely on prejudice, and as such violated equal protection and due process. In addition, the court held that the CCC violated the XIVth Amendment.

It was not until *McLauglin v. Florida* (379, US 184 [1964]) where the US Supreme Court ruled unanimously that a cohabitation law, that made cohabitation of unmarried opposite sex and race couples illegal, was unconstitutional and the now-famous *Loving v. Virginia* (US 388, US 1 [1967]), that the idea of anti-miscegenation statues overturned. Nevertheless, the State of Mississippi maintained anti-miscegenation laws on their books until November 2000, some 33 years after the US Supreme Court ruling.

One continued testament to the deep-seeded nature of racial prejudice and hostility toward bi/multiracial couples and their families can be seen as recently as 2016. Mississippi, the state that finally removed the anti-miscegenation statues (*de jure change*), was also the same state that did not ratify the XIIIth Amendment, which abolished slavery, until some 148 years later in 2013. It is no wonder that the new-found "religious liberty" laws have been able to flourish. In most Southern states these "religious freedoms" have allowed legal discrimination to continue. In one recent incident involving a biracial couple, a married man and his wife were punished. In this case a Black man and his Hispanic and Native American wife were banned from living in a trailer park by the landlord in Tupelo, Mississippi. Their deposit was returned and the landlord stated that he would not rent to a biracial couple (his language was much less refined). The landlord said that he would close the space rather than rent to a multiracial family (Mitchell, 2016). That this attitude existed is not a surprise given that a recent survey of Mississippi Republicans found that some 29% think that anti-miscegenation policies should be allowed (Smith, 2012).

The plight of interracial couples and their children remains problematic as the social fabric of the United States seems to be unraveling in this new era of intolerance and limited social civility no matter what court rules. The court rulings, nevertheless, have resulted in some positive changes for biracial couples and families. Data from various government and private sources show an overall increase in interracial coupling, marriages, and families (Pew Research Center, 2015, 2016; Wang, 2012).

Race Construction in Post-slave America

For most people race is usually treated as a "visual category," something that can be negotiated by sight. It is an ever-present feature for all bi/multiracial families. However, Allport (1954) noted that race was socially constructed because it could be linked to underlying features—some of these are not verifiable facts—but were linked to social behavior, for example, the belief that Blacks, besides appearing to have darker skin, are often "loud," "lazy," "and "dangerous." Ideas such as these are often reinforced through social mythology and can become the stereotypes that feed prejudice (Allport, 1954; Smith, 2009). Nowhere is the issue of race played out greater for Blacks than in the persistent stereotypes that have been used to vilify and degrade Black people, both now and throughout history.

One of the most problematic and perhaps major difficulties that the history of slavery and the subsequent Jim Crow years produced was a series of long-lived stereotypes and racial "ideal types" that continue even today. Jim Crow refers to a mythical person who represents the epoch where legal segregation was allowed to exist under the pretext of "separate but equal." This allowed for a separation between races reinforcing many of the principles of anti-miscegenation. Jim Crow laws were state and local ordinances enforcing racial segregation. Formal Jim Crowism existed primarily in the Southern United States; however, it was practiced by others throughout the country. The legal form of Jim Crow continued until the civil rights bill ended it in the mid-1960s.

These historically based stereotypes exist and often lead to what Goffman (1963) called stigma. Stigma consists of social processes that occur within the sociocultural environment and whose effects can be observed within the individual. Stigma can take on many characteristics that usually involve a person or group being viewed as negative in some way. This perceived difference can be attached to groups and all who associate with those groups and is usually attached to entire families and is passed through generations. Both mono- and bi/multiracial families have a keen awareness of stigma, since it is likely that they have or know of someone who has experienced this phenomenon. The most important aspect of this is not just awareness of stigma, but the process by which these families equip their members to respond.

It is true that race is a ubiquitous and ordinary construct found throughout the United States (Brown, 2003; Lavender-Bratcher & Dunn, 2016). One of the distinct advantages that bi/multiracial individuals have over their mono-racial counterparts is that, depending upon their phenotype—that is if they appear to more like the majority group—they can either reject or accept the impact of the stereotype—at least on its surface. Research has demonstrated that bi/multiracial individuals, although not often directly impacted by some of the racist stereotypes for themselves, often bear stigma because of their families of origin and its members, some of whom may indeed be mono-racial (Shih et al., 2007; Young, Sanchez, & Wilton, 2016). A recent study by Pew Research Center (2015) using an attitudinal measure to examine if bi/multiracial people considered themselves belonging to more than one race group revealed that 87% of those surveyed indicated that they were not mixed race (Patten, 2015). It is clear that attitudes differ from basic social descriptions. Using the ecological framework it is clear to see how one might develop such a context especially if their experiences over time have revealed to them that their external treatment is that of being seen as one race group over another.

One critical issue in the study of bi/multiracial families is the demographics of the group. As can be seen in Fig. 2 what accounts for bi/multiracial family membership differs from the stereotypic view. Fifty percent of individuals who are bi/multiracial clearly identify as White and American-Indian (Pew Research Center, 2015). This group is most likely to appear as phenotypically White, and as such experiences

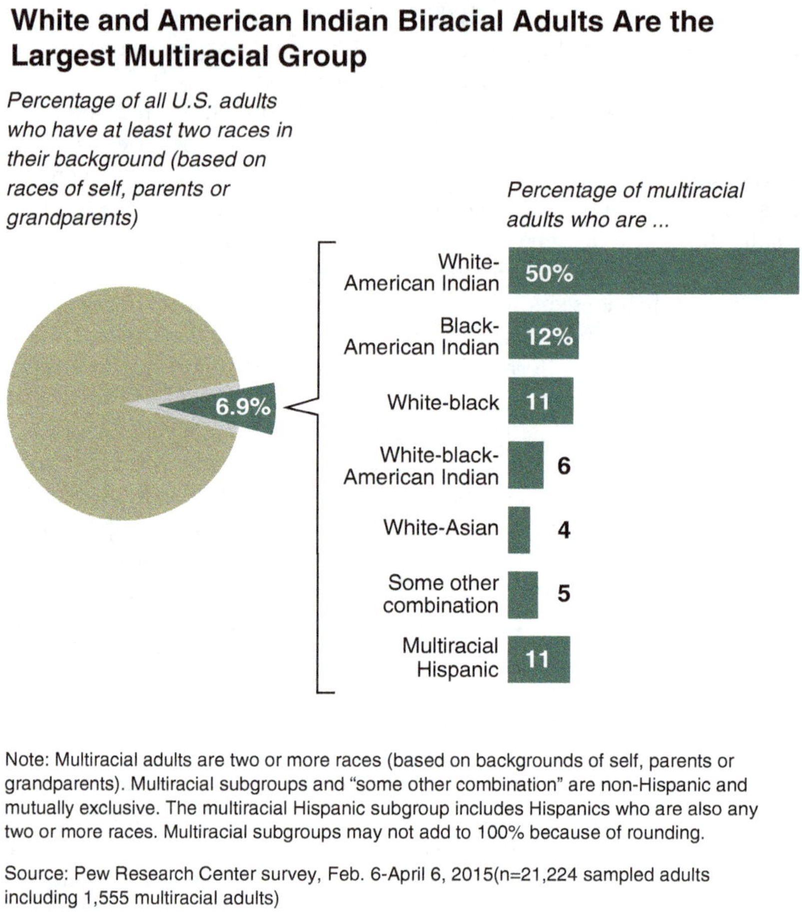

Fig. 2 Biracial and multiracial adults by race and ethnic group designations

the least difficulty of any of the bi/multiracial groups. Despite some reports to the contrary, there is little historical data to support this other than the data that revealed discrimination and prejudice toward Native American people (Iceland, 2017) throughout history, a topic for another book to say the least.

On the one hand, it is clear that children from bi/multiracial homes where parents de-emphasized the importance of race tend to see race as less of a barrier. They were also less likely to believe that their racial identity was less of a determent of their life chances, no matter what message was generated from their families (Pew Research Center, 2016; Shih et al., 2007).

On the other hand, because it is difficult to easily classify bi/multiracial individuals into any mono-racial group of their parents they can often suffer from rejection from both majority and minority groups (Shih et al., 2007). However, because of these problems bi/multiracial children quickly discover that race is a socially constructed ideal (Spickard, 1992) and so too are its outcomes. One outcome of this is that the children may be less inclined to identify with any one racial identity. Their unwillingness to adopt an identity can create a dilemma for parents and others whose own experiences as mono-racial or multiracial individuals, who understand and know that race plays a critical role, must somehow find a way to socialize their children and family members. The dilemma becomes how does one get the message through that whether or not you strongly identify with a race designation; the experience of the social world that exists outside of your family can become problematic—especially in an epoch where racial intolerance, bigotry, and hostility are now becoming norms.

The strength of social stereotypes can and will influence bi/multiracial children, sometimes positively, other times negatively. In fact, the entire categorization of social experiences can be tied to stereotypes. For example, young bi/multiracial males who phenotypically exhibit traits associated with being Black are more likely than not to be treated as a "Black" person in America. In essence, his intelligence is more likely to be questioned, his general demeanor is judged to be problematic, and his attitude toward being treated in this way is considered to be angry, hostile, rude, and inconsiderate—something that most people would feel if they too were prejudged. On the other hand, if the same young man appeared to be phenotypically White, none of these assumptions would be made before he is encountered. Therefore, it is critical that we understand the role perception—from both the perceiver and the perceived—plays in how stereotypes and stigma can influence bi/multiracial individuals.

These stereotypes are linked to the history of slaves in America. For example, our own history is replete with events that allowed social stereotypes to stigmatize large groups of people: the adoption of the US Constitution in 1789 where it allowed slaves to be considered as 3/5th a person, the compromise of 1850 that allowed slavery to be decided upon by popular sovereignty, and the hateful *Dred Scott* decision of 1857 which concluded once again that not only were slaves not people, but they were also not citizens. All of these decision and many more were based on social stereotypes and stigmas of slaves (Blacks) in America.

This pattern continued for many more years culminated in 1896 with *Plessy v. Ferguson* (163 US 537), a case of a Black man, who phenotypically appeared as White—in fact he was what was referred to as an "octoroon. He was one-eight African descent. According to Davis (2017) "the beginning of miscegenation between two populations presumed that others were to be racially pure; quadroons appear in the second generation of continuing mixing with Whites, and octoroons in the third. A quadroon is one-fourth African black and thus easily classed as Black in the United States, yet three of this person's four grandparents are White. *An octoroon has seven White great-grandparents out of eight and usually looks White or almost so*…For example, Booker T. Washington and Frederick Douglass, with slave mothers and White fathers, were referred to as mulattoes."

Under Louisiana law, which used these racial classifications, Plessy was considered Black (colored). Homer Plessy bought a first-class railway ticket and boarded the train in the Whites-only car as he had done before without any problems.

However, this time the railway had been notified of his action in advance and hired a detective to detain and arrest Plessey. The importance of this case is that it legitimated the notion of Jim Crow and allowed the doctrine of separate but equal to flourish. In effect it said that no matter what you looked like, the legal definition of what you were allowed the state to behave as it saw fit. We used this case to illustrate how race as a social construct was and still remains a very powerful element that can have a profound effect on social policy and therefore lives of millions. The notions espoused by Plessey v. Ferguson still have traction among many people today.

Jim Crow and the Irrational Fear of Race

The fear of race and being close to others of a different race remains a deep part of the American psyche regarding race. Although there were many important and significant changes that were occurring in the United States just after the Civil War, perhaps the most salient events were the passage of the XIIIth, XIVth, and XVth Amendments. These amendments abolished slavery, granted rights of citizenship to Blacks, and allowed Blacks to vote as full citizens. However, these rights would be short-lived as Jim Crow laws would soon become part of the fabric of life in the United States. Tennessee became the first state to formally pass Jim Crow laws by segregating state railroads. Other Southern states would follow creating this formally formed informal, illegal, but legal, racial segregation system. These laws were accompanied by the establishment of poll taxes and literacy tests that were given to Blacks who had wanted to vote. The US Supreme Court upheld some of these unfair practices, policies, and laws with their own faulty decisions such as in the case of US v. Stanley (109 US 3, 1883). This case, which was a consolidation of five different cases, allowed rights granted by the XIVth amendment to be abridged by private citizens. The Court ruled that it was unreasonable to force private citizens and businesses to stop discriminating against people they did not like. This led to the concept known as state action doctrine. Although this ruling was overturned with subsequent legislation, the same idea is often used today, e.g., ministers who refuse to marry bi/multiracial couples—even though it is still in violation of the law.

Blacks continued to face the pain of racism, especially in the South—due in part to the large numbers who lived there and the legacy of the Civil War. States such as Louisiana disenfranchised Blacks with the so-called grandfather clause. This ruling restricted Blacks from voting if their fathers or grandfathers had not voted before January 1, 1867—an impossibility for previously enslaved Blacks. Efforts to survive within the Jim Crow South often meant adjusting to the constant barrage of discrimination. In short, people simply tolerated the situation when they had to, but lived their lives as free as possible when not encountering Whites. This separate living system was often fraught with illogical consequences. For example, it was not possible for a Black domestic worker to enter through the front door of the home in which they worked; they had to use the side entrance. However, if the employer wanted them to serve "tea" on the veranda, they would often have to go in and out of the front door to do so as the porch in most Southern homes was located at the front of the house.

One of the prominent leaders of the time, Booker T. Washington, believed that a position of accommodation and self-sufficiency would be the way to survive (Washington, 1999). On the other hand, W.E.B. DuBois called for challenging the existing racial hegemony. He believed that the "color line" was the major problem of the twentieth century (DuBois, 1903, 1935); it turns out that DuBois' belief about how race can be used to perpetuate differences is still prevalent today in the twenty-first century.

One of the most significant and perhaps profound changes to occur in race relations was the Great Migration (1915–1960). This involved the exodus of Blacks from the South to the Northeast, Midwest, and to some extent the Western part of the United States. In 1910 approximately 90% of the Blacks lived in the South; by 1960 that number had dropped to 53%. In effect, over six million Blacks participated in the Southern Diaspora (Gregory, 2005).

This migration was once again greeted by illogical policy changes and procedures on behalf of the Southern White gentry. For example, although Blacks were not valued as members of society, many southern locations would attempt to pass legislation that would make it difficult for Blacks to change residence. Still others were more enlightened and attempted to increase wages to match those in the North. The Southern Metal Trades Association tried to stop Black migration by getting banks to refuse to cash checks sent to finance Black migration. The local railroad clerks were pressured to limit access for Blacks to purchase tickets and local newspapers were pressured to cover and present negative aspects of Black life in the North. All of this was done because the effect of Black labor and its loss would severely cripple the South that relied very heavily upon its agriculture sector (Billingsley, 1992; Gregory, 2005).

Although the migration was life changing for a majority of Blacks, they still faced problems of discrimination and racism in the North. One of the most racist and potentially very damaging groups, the Ku Klux Klan (KKK), had its national origin and headquarters in the industrial Midwest—Indiana to be exact. At one point the Klan in Indiana numbered well over 900,000 members. It was a very powerful group and was responsible for a great deal of trouble for Blacks in the Midwest and South (Fischer, 2016). These organizations and their sympathizers were able to subject Blacks in the Midwest to increased informal isolation and segregation, one of the hallmarks of Jim Crow. The demographic patterns of these effects can be seen in large cities where Blacks migrated, for example the south side of Chicago, or Harlem in New York City.

The great migration had a profound effect on families (Billingsley, 1992). In some cases, the father would leave the home in the hopes of finding work and then send for his family. In other cases, the family might send one of their adult or teenage children "up North" to live with a relative or fictive kin in the hopes of improving the life chances of their child. Often families were able to reunite after some period of time. Most families had some member who made the great migration. This meant that they had links and exposure to other communities. This ability to know others in another geographic location with different customs and histories enhanced the life chances and created positive experiences for Blacks (Billingsley, 1992; Gregory, 2005).

Effects of Oppression

During this same period following the legalization of separate but equal the experiences of Black, bi/multiracial people who identified with their Black relatives experienced a very unique set of circumstances. The proliferation of Jim Crow also gave rise to the idea that Whites as a superior group needed to govern inferior people. Although the *de jure* aspect of Jim Crow was ended the de facto and informal process still exists in many ways today. In her book entitled, *The New Jim Crow*, Michelle Alexander (2010) argued that America's war on drugs disproportionately affects African-Americans and has produced new discrimination comparable to that of the Jim Crow laws by treating Black criminals more harshly than White criminals. The effect has decimated communities of color. In effect, the criminal justice system acts as a method of racial control subjecting people of color to a permanent second-class status despite its principles that call for fairness no matter what the background of the individuals. These practices reinforce the hierarchy of races and continue today (Iceland, 2017). Although not as blatant, to some it has become more problematic since a change in the presidential administration (in the so-called Trump Era). The hegemonic structure of American society has not really changed, witnessing the proliferation of hate speech and the rise of the "*alt-right*." The current changes by the Trump administration to curb rights, the gutting of the voting rights act, and the subsequent election following this action all reveal how the hegemonic structure not only exists, but also maintains its strength. This twisted thinking about race permeated the lives of some groups who today are considered White, e.g., the Italians and Irish. By the time we reached the turn of the nineteenth century new rules and regulations about birthrights and what constitutes Whiteness even among Whites caused greater division. These conversations excluded Blacks who would all but exist in a parallel but unequal world to Whites. The idea that race was somehow a trait by which one could ultimately determine the life chances of an individual became the standard by which Americans lived. The laws that dispossessed Native Americans from their own lands (1830), that prohibited any non-Whites from testifying (1854), as well as those that overtly discriminated against Asians (1913), would persist until addressed by what would become the largest social movement in the history of the country—the civil rights movement.

However, before the civil rights movement we would see the first airborne bombing of a US city by US citizens—Tulsa, Oklahoma. The riots of Tulsa, Oklahoma, in 1921 destroyed the Greenwood neighborhood known as "Black Wall Street." There was resentment on the part of Whites who had seen that the Jim Crow rules could not oppress people as they had intended and who harbored great resentment toward economically successful Blacks. In an effort to quell the violence that had broken out the police commandeered a host of private planes and dropped dynamite on the homes and businesses in the Greenwood community. At least 75 people were killed with that action; another 4000 men, women, and children were detained, arrested, and ultimately placed in concentration camps; and almost three square miles of businesses and homes were destroyed (Oklahoma Commission, 2001). The official death count ranges from 39 to 300 depending upon who is asked. The official Oklahoma Government sought to keep this tragic history from becoming known (Carlson, 2017; Madigan, 2003).

What makes the Tulsa incident so horrendous is that it was precipitated by the arrest of a Black man (Dick Rowland) who allegedly assaulted a White woman (Sarah Page). The allegations were never sustained; however, that did not stop the threats of lynching and subsequent attack upon the Greenwood neighborhood. The end result was the total destruction of some 35 city blocks (Oklahoma Commission, 2001). The situation in Tulsa was emblematic of how simple allegations could cause major social reactions based in part on attitudes toward race issues. The incidents of race riots throughout US history are often caused by some perceived unjust treatment of Blacks by the predominate group. Some of the most well-known of these incidents include the Watts Riots (1965); the LA Riots (1992) based on reaction to the Rodney King verdict; the Ferguson Missouri Riots (2014); and the Baltimore Riots (2015). All of these events occurred because there was a belief that the community had been let down by the jurisprudence system, the only place where people could get justice. Once those systems failed them the frustration often led to a loss of social control.

The changing rules and laws fostered policies that legitimated discrimination in housing programs that benefitted Whites (1934) by offering low-interest loans allowing for greater homeownership while systematically excluding Blacks, Asians, and other people of color. These policies would eventually lead to geographic segregation that would allow for separate but unequal policies to expand. The housing rules were then coupled with changes in social security benefits (1935) and the systematic exclusion form labor unions (1935) ensured the long-term effects of oppression. The Social Security Act of 1935 excluded agricultural and domestic workers from receiving benefits. The Wagner Act of 1935 allowed labor unions to openly discriminate against non-White in effect keeping them from earning benefits. These acts systematically kept Blacks, Asians, Mexicans, and other people of color who made up the bulk of agricultural and domestic workers from being able to fully participate in the labor market and earn the same benefits as White workers.

Much of the social and domestic policies through the 1900s to the 1950s were rooted in the belief and the ideology of racism. In effect, America was thought of as a White-dominated country that tolerated its "colored" citizens. However, the influence of two World Wars, an economic depression, and question of the values by Blacks and Whites alike would come to create a new voice—one that would have long-term consequences and would lead to some fundamental social changes that would have direct effects on families.

Social Change and Retrenchment

The middle of the 1950s saw the country healing from the war, a resurgence in the economy, and a voice demanding an end to the Jim Crow legislation that continued the legacy of slavery, without the institution being visible. The first test of this would come with the Supreme Court's now-famous ruling in *Brown v. Board of Education, Topeka* (347 US 483, 1954). This ruling would overturn *Plessy v. Ferguson* and declared that legal segregation in educational institutions would no longer be allowed. The *de jure* ruling of the Supreme Court would be tested time and time again throughout this period. In open defiance, and the continuation of the now formally declared illegal Jim Crow practices, would continue, especially throughout the South where governors refused to act. It would take the actions of Rosa Parks, a Black woman, refusing to move and give up her seat to a White woman on a bus in the segregated Montgomery Alabama transit system to ignite an uncomfortable national conversation about race which continues today. The coordinated act of defiance, similar to that of Homer Plessy, would lead to a year-long boycott of the bus system, to protest the State's refusal to integrate its public systems, including schools, transportation, parks, and other related agencies. The success of the bus boycott emboldened the organized civil rights movement that was headed up by Reverend Doctor, Martin Luther King Jr.

The end of World War II brought about significant and rapid changes in how the United States was seen by others and how we had to change how we should function as a nation. In fact, the United States had had at least five Civil Rights Acts, one Voting Act, and one Executive Order on Civil Rights in order to bring about a sense of equality across race in the United States.

The Civil Rights Act of 1875 (PL 335-337, 71) argued that all persons in the United States were entitled to equal and full protection and accommodations and that it was granted with regard to every citizen. This Act was followed up by the Civil Rights Cases of 1883 (109 US 3, 1883) in which the US Supreme Court overturned the 1875 Act. The Court, led by Justice Harlan, contended that Congress lacked the authority to regulate private affairs and that no provision or clauses within the XIIIth and XIVth Amendments, which "merely abolishes slavery" and provides citizenship, allowed for any greater expansion of rights that protected the rights of individuals and therefore the law had to be overturned. The elimination of the Civil Rights Act of 1875 virtually insured that de facto discrimination would once again be the law of the land.

It took two World Wars before President Truman issued Executive 9808 to establish a committee on Civil Rights. The job of the committee was to see that law enforcement agencies and other government systems would protect the rights of citizens. This Executive Order was in contrast to the current color line policies that had Blacks more formally involved in the criminal justice system than Whites. Truman followed up with a policy designed to end racial segregation in the US Armed Forces. It is clear from both of these actions that Truman set into motion and imprinted upon the American psyche that race matters and will continue to be a critical part of our history.

The first draft of the modern Civil Rights Act 1957 (PL 85-315, 71) received Congressional approval after Strom Thurmond, an avowed racist and Southern Democratic Senator, ended his filibuster. Essentially this Act served as a voting rights law. The aim was to ensure that all Americans could exercise their right to vote. The 1957 Act was expanded by the Civil Rights Act of 1960 (PL 86-449, 74) which was designed to address the shortcomings of the 1957 legislation. What was important about both of these Acts, although they did not have a very substantial legislative footprint, is that they signaled a readiness on the part of the Federal Government to address the race problem that plagued the country since it began.

These lesser known Acts were overshadowed by the 1964 Civil Rights Act (PL 88-352, 78) and the 1965 Voting Rights Act which served as testaments to Presidents Kennedy and Johnson, and Martin Luther King, Jr and his nonviolent civil rights movement. The 1964 Civil Rights Act outlawed segregation in public places and banned employment discrimination on the basis of race, color, religion, sex, or national origin. Housing discrimination would end with the Civil Rights Act of 1968 (PL 90-298, 82) yet we still have recent examples of its violation such as the example from Mississippi discussed earlier in this chapter.

American Life at the End of the Obama Era

America's long-term report card on race relations reveals a very low grade. Many of the efforts that came about through changes and sacrifices in the 1960s and 1970s were slowed down in the 1980s due largely to a backlash by those in power and a reluctance to share their privileges with others. In today's world the shift in focus has caused the non-European "immigrants" to become the target group of bigotry and hatred. Many of the Black causes and political fights have been subsumed. In terms of progress there seems to be some doubt. Nearly 1 in 15 Black men and 1 in 36 Hispanic men are incarcerated in comparison to 1 in every 103 White men. Essentially although people of color make up 30% of the population they account for 60% of those imprisoned (Kerby, 2012). Students of color also tend to face more difficult punishment than their White counterparts in school. One side effect of these early disciplinary problems may be greater adult incarceration. There are a number of contemporary investigations that explore the school-to-prison pipeline for young men and women of color (Bryan, 2017; Mallet, 2017; Rocque & Snelling, 2017; Simmons, 2017). An ancillary to that is also reduced citizenship rights as voter laws restrict who can vote based on prior convictions, disproportionately affecting men of color. There are still persistent and real differences in terms of educational attainment, income growth, wealth acquisition, wealth transfer, residential segregation, and within-group differences (Bobo, 1997, 1999; Carter, 2005; Conley, 1999; Hacker, 1995; Lockett, Webb, & Chancler, 2013; Massey & Denton, 1998; McAdoo, 2007).

The 1970s was the true beginning of the civil rights movement's influence on contemporary America. This is in part true because there were enforcement mechanisms (for example, the EEOC, Title XI, Affirmative Action, and other programs) and policy shifts that offered some meaningful protections to people as they began the journey of equality or *pseudo-equality* as historians would come to recognize it. But it would appear that for every action there would be an equal and opposite reaction. In truth, there were reactions, but they were not always equal. For example, there were a number of important landmark cases that were focused on eroding some of the very rights finally gained through the recent changes in legislation. One of the most important ones dealt with the role that education played in the advancement of people.

Some of the less obvious issues involving fair practice under affirmative action had to do with the Federal Government insistence and enforcement of Executive Order 11246 (part of the Civil Rights Act of 1964) that required those seeking federal funds for construction projects to submit acceptable affirmative action plans that were measurable and ensured that minority employees would be considered for jobs for which they were qualified. Some companies, for example Home Depot, had insisted that it could not participate in the program because it was not equipped to process vast amounts of paperwork so it would not comply and hence not accept federal contracts. Within two weeks, following public outcry about such a policy Home Depot reversed its decision agreed to all of the povisions of the act. Home Depot went a step further and created its on government solutions group based in Washington, D.C. to address any issues related to its plans.

While some strides were made in the employment sector, the educational arena would experience some major setbacks. In the case of the *Regents of the University of California v. Bakke* (438 US 265 1978) the court held that the University of California had to admit Bakke because rigid racial quotas violated the Equal Protection Clause of the XIVth Amendment. At the same time the court ruled that considering race as part of an admissions decision was in fact constitutional as long as it was not the sole factor in admissions. This ruling was reaffirmed in another case regarding the University of Michigan's school of Law: a 5-4 Supreme Court majority opinion in *Grutter v. Bollinger* (539 US 306, 2003), where Justice Sandra Day O'Connor argued that since the University of Michigan Law school used other criteria for admissions decisions, adding race did not harm those who were nonminority candidates.

Affirmative action practices were challenged again in Texas, in the case of *Fisher v. University of Texas at Austin* (570 US ___, 2013). In this case, Susan Fisher sued the University of Texas on the grounds that their consideration of race violated the XIVth Amendment Equal Protection Clause. The Obama administration had supported the University of Texas system's viewpoint and argued favorably on its behalf. Citing the *Gutter* decision, the second court (5–4) (579 US ___, 2016) concluded that there was no way in which the University of Texas system could improve upon its prior race-neutral practices to achieve its diversity-related goals. However, the court left the door open by suggesting that the University of Texas system should continue to assess its processes to see if the changing demographics have reduced the need for race awareness in their affirmative action goals and policies.

The reactions to some affirmative action decisions have manifested itself in some problematic policy changes, such as California's Proposition 209 (passed in 1997) which amended state's constitution to prohibit public institutions from discriminating on the bases of race, sex, or ethnicity. The ironic fact is that Proposition 209 discriminates by forcing the state to ignore the very standards that federal law says must be considered in hiring and college admissions decisions as affirmed by Supreme Court decisions. The long-term effect is not known, but it is clear that other states are now emulating California. The following states have enacted similar patterns, for example, Arizona (2010), Michigan (2006), New Hampshire (2011), Oklahoma (2012), and Washington (1998).

These policies have also led to a joint action between White and Hispanic employees in hiring decisions. For example, the City of New Haven, CT, was sued for discrimination (*Ricci v. DeStafano,* 557 US 557, 2009). The fire department employees sued after their tests were thrown out because there was not enough diversity in the hiring pool. The court ruled (5-4) in favor of the employees (plaintiffs) stating that their rights had been violated under Title VII (from the 1964 Civil Rights Act) and the XIVth Amendment. This case, and others similar to it, began and were decided on in the era that gave our country our first Black or to some our first biracial President, Barack Obama.

The importance of President Obama's race cannot be overstated. It would be a factor throughout his presidency. He was accused by some of being too pro-Black, while others assailed him as being too neutral, too removed from his racial roots, or just not interested in the issues impacting Black people (West, 2014). Whatever the case the most important factor lies in how President Obama, a biracial man, views himself in the context of his social world. This is an extremely important and critical issue because it is why within this chapter we continued to use the Black-White color line to embrace our discussions. It is why we are still suggesting that the color line will make a difference much in the same way DuBois (1935) suggested.

Recent data from the Pew Research Center (2015) suggested that among biracial adults there is a perception that a majority (61%) are perceived as Black if one of their parents are Black (Fig. 3). When those who are bi/multiracial are asked about themselves 70% admit to having only thought of themselves as one race (Fig. 4). More relevant is the fact that most bi/multiracial people's top reasons for not claiming a bi/multiracial identity are based on the facts that they were raised as one race (47%); look like one race (47%); and identify with one race (39%) (see Fig. 5).

These factors contribute to why we must continue to analyze issues in relationship to race, whether the person is mono-, bi-, or multiracial. Historical, social, political, and economical life chances are all linked vis-à-vis some form of racial designation that has transformed itself across time as was suggested by the ecosystemic model used throughout this chapter.

Fig. 3 Perceptions of racial affiliation by others as reported by biracial White and Black adults

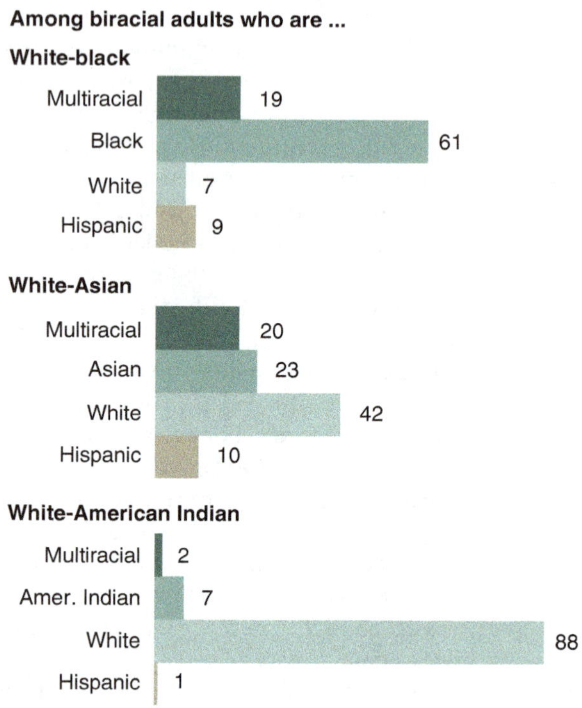

Note: Biracial adults are two races and non-Hispanic (based on backgrounds of self, parents or grandparents). Sample sizes are: 118 white-black, 88 white-Asian, 907 white-Amer. Indian.Some responses not showing(ex: 3% of white-Asian biracial adults said they are seen as Native Hawaiian/Pacific Islander).

Source: Pew Research Center survey, Feb. 6-April 6, 2015

Fig. 4 Perception of multiracial adults who see themselves as one race

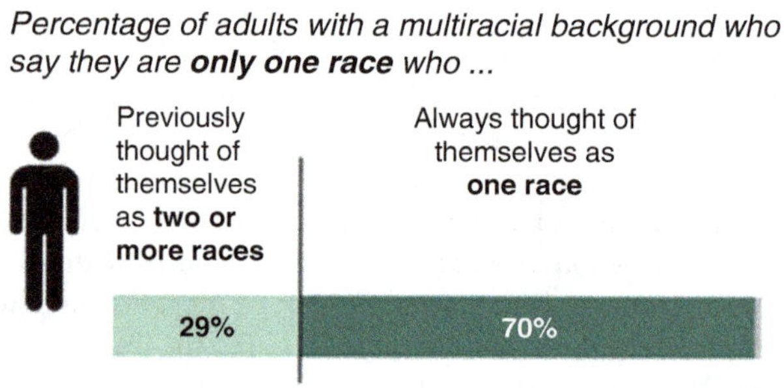

Note: Multiracial adults are two or more races (based on backgrounds of self, parents or grandparents). Those who gave no answer are shown but not labeled.

Source: Pew Research Center survey, Feb, 6-April 6, 2015 (n=1,555 multiracial adults)

Fig. 5 Top reasons that majority of biracial and multiracial adults do not identify themselves as biracial or multiracial

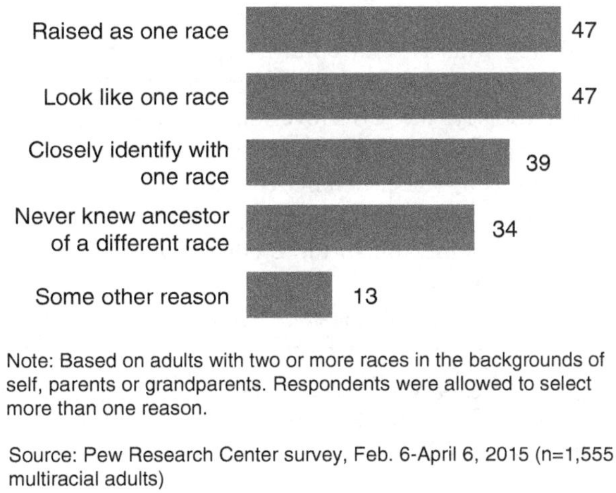

Race as Confounding Factor in the New Era

Despite the negative influences of the social history there has been a fundamental shift in the way different generations view race and its importance in their lives. This can be seen in the growing numbers of interracial relationships. A Pew study in the late 1980s revealed that only 13% agreed that interracial dating was appropriate. Twenty years later that number had jumped to 56% (Pew Research Center, 2015; Wang, 2012). More than just agreeing to interracial relationships in the abstract nine in ten of the Millennials (those born between 1981 and 2000) were fine with a family member being in an interracial relationship. In fact, 43% believed that interracial marriage was good for society. Yet, despite the changes in and projections for more changes, racial boundaries may still be present. For example, Lee and Bean (2010) pointed out that the race boundaries were more fluid for new immigrants than they were for Black Americans. In short, immigrants who were not Black were often not subject to as much historical racism and discrimination that seems to have been reserved for native Black Americans (Burrell, Webb, & White, 2014; Lee & Bean, 2010).

The experience of not being an immigrant most certainly influences the ways Blacks in America are seen and responded to by others both within and outside of the race group (Lockett, 2015; Lockett et al., 2013). For example, Lockett (2015) found that among Blacks, those who were native born were discriminated against more than those who were foreign born. The paradox of immigrants in this sense is the same for bi/multiracial people who live here in the United States should one belong or not belong to a group that has suffered historically if such membership could be avoided. The increasing numbers of interracial marriages and the growing numbers of children from these unions pose a paradox not only for those families, but also for American society in general, particularly since it is so heavily based on a racial hegemony that has always been composed of the simple Black/White dichotomy.

The loss of this dual nature of how people exist within the United States has presented what is referred to as a wicked problem (Conklin, 2005), one to which there is no real solution. Returning to old classifications of race would no longer work. Clearly, the US Government has recognized this problem for years. The struggle by the US Census Bureau to accurately find ways to record race of families has caused a data problem. The now majority minority groupings has exceeded projections. As these groups and their children become more prevalent, racial salience becomes much more complicated and more difficult to define (Webb & Cortez, 2016).

Another factor to consider is that bi/multiracial children who are from nonimmigrant families also face the same issues without the social immigrant history. Some demographers estimate that by 2100, just about 70 years from now, more than one-third (33%) of the country will be bi/multiracial (Farley, 2004; Lee & Edmonston, 2005).

Conclusion: An Observation on the Importance of Race to Bi/Multiracial Families

Despite these important changes, the within-group status of some groups is still less valued than that of others. The growing racism and xenophobia that seem to be gripping the United States is one example of how much work must be done. Moreover, the economic overlay of this resentment must be carefully examined. No matter how much the interracial marriage rate increases, and no matter how many more bi/multiracial families are formed, without a fundamental shift in the powerbase within the country these new family forms will find themselves at the end of an expanded color line—one that just gets wider and long as the country begins to redefine the so-called one-drop rule. The amount of social change and enlightenment that is necessary to move the country from a color-based economic model to one centered on equitable distribution of power and wealth will need to be based on more than just interracial interpersonal relations.

In this chapter we have shown that race remains a powerful concept even for those who we call bi/multiracial. The master status of race, whether one is White or non-White, becomes the defining characteristic especially in a hegemonic society such as ours. In a recent Pew Research Center (2015) survey biracial Whites and Blacks reported being more accepted by Blacks than Whites. For Asians and White biracial adults they indicated greater acceptance by Whites (62%) than from Asians (47%). Among multiracial adults in general, one in six (16%) said that most or all of their close friends were multiracial compared to the rest of society where only 6% of their friends were multiracial. However, even among the multiracial group their friends usually shared their own racial composition (Pew Research Center, 2015); all of this demonstrates that racial hegemony is present and that it continues to influence our relationships with each other, even when its effects should have been reduced. Race as a person, process, and context element remains important across time. Through each of the epochs examined here we see that race, that is being non-White in any variation, remained a basis for differential treatment and outcomes. As we said in the beginning, race is a very complex concept. It is one that has been denied by some, embraced by others, but it is still one concept that cannot be ignored or overlooked, especially in a society whose very existence was built on a color line construct.

References

Alexander, M. (2010). *The new Jim crow: Mass incarceration in the age of color blindness*. New York, NY: The New Press.

Allport, G. W. (1954). *The nature of prejudice*. Reading, MA: Addison-Wesley.

American Sociological Association. (2017). Retrieved from http://www.asanet.org/topics/race-and-ethnicity.

Axt, J., & Trawalter, S. (2017). Whites demonstrate anti-black associations but do not reinforce them. *Journal of Experimental Social Psychology, 70*, 8–18. https://doi.org/10.1016/j.jesp.2016.11.013

Billingsley, A. (1992). *Climbing Jacob's ladder: The enduring legacy of African American families*. New York, NY: Simon & Schuster.

Blassingame, J. W. (1979). *The slave community: Plantation life in the antebellum south*. New York, NY: Oxford University Press.

Bobo, L. D. (1997). The color line, the dilemma, and the dream: Racial attitudes and relations in America at the close of the twentieth century. In J. Higham (Ed.), *Civil rights and social wrongs: Black-white relations since world war II* (pp. 31–55). University Park, PA: Pennsylvania State University Press.

Bobo, L. D. (1999). Prejudice as group position: Micro-foundations of a sociological approach to racism and race relations. *Journal of Social Issues, 55*, 445–472.

Bonilla-Silva, E. (2010). *Racism without racists: Color-blind racism and the persistence of racial inequality in the United States* (3rd ed.). Lanham, MA: Rowman & Littlefield.

Bronfenbrenner, U. (1979). *The ecology of human development*. Cambridge, MA: Harvard University Press.

Bronfenbrenner, U. (1993). The ecology of cognitive development: Research models and fugitive findings. In R. H. Wozniak & K. W. Fischer (Eds.), *Development in context: Acting and thinking in specific environments* (pp. 3–44). Hillsdale, NJ: Erlbaum.

Bronfenbrenner, U. (1995). Developmental ecology through space and time: A future perspective. In P. Moen & G. H. Elder Jr. (Eds.), *Examining lives in context: Perspectives on the ecology of human development* (pp. 619–647). Washington, DC: American Psychological Association.

Bronfenbrenner, U. (2005). *Making human beings: Bioecological perspectives on human development*. Thousand Oaks, CA: Sage.

Brown, T. N. (2003). Critical race theory speaks to the sociology of mental health: Mental health problems produced by racial stratification. *Journal of Health and Social Behavior, 50*(1), 292–301.

Brown v Board of Education, 347 US 483 (1954).

Bryan, N. (2017). White teachers' role in sustaining the school-to-prison pipeline: Recommendations for teacher education. *The Urban Review, 49*(2), 326–345.

Burrell, J. V., Webb, F. J., & White, V. A. (2014). Americans' perceptions of commitment to strong families across race and ethnic groups. *Journal of Marriage and Family Review, 50*(3), 199–215.

Carlson, I. M. (2017). *The Tulsa race riot of 1921*. Retrieved from https://tulsaraceriot.wordpress.com

Carter, P. L. (2005). *Keepin' it real: School success beyond black and white*. New York, NY: Oxford University Press.

Civil Rights Act of 1875. *Pub L 335-337*, 71, *Statute 18* (March 1, 1875).

Civil Rights Act of 1957. *Pub L 85-315*, 71, *Statute 634* (September 9, 1957).

Civil Rights Act of 1960. *Pub L 86-449*, 74, *Statute 89* (May 6, 1960).

Civil Rights Act of 1964. *Pub L 88-352*, 78, *Statute 241* (Oct 3, 1964).

Civil Rights Act of 1968. *Pub L 90-298*, 82 *Statute 73* (April 11, 1968).

Civil Rights Cases, 109 US 3 (1883)

Conklin, J. (2005). *Dialogue mapping: Building shared understanding of wicked problems*. New York, NY: Wiley.

Conley, D. (1999). *Being black, living in the red: Race, wealth, and social policy in America*. Berkeley, CA: University of California Press.

Davis, D. J., & Boyer, P. G. (2013). *Social justice issues and racism in college classrooms: Perspectives from different voices, International perspectives on higher education research* (Vol. 8). Bingley: Emerald Group Publishing.

Davis, F. J. (2017). *Frontline*. Retrieved from January 12, 2017, from http://www.pbs.org/wgbh/pages/frontline/shows/jefferson/mixed/onedrop.html

DuBois, W. E. B. (1903). *The souls of black folks*. New York, NY: Oxford University Press.

DuBois, W. E. B. (1935). *Black reconstruction: An essay toward a history of the part which black folk played in the attempt to reconstruct democracy in America, 1860–1880*. New York, NY: Russell & Russell.

Farley, R. (2004). Identifying with multiple races: A social movement that succeeded but failed. In M. Krysan & A. E. Lewis (Eds.), *The changing terrain of race and ethnicity* (pp. 123–148). New York, NY: Russell Sage Foundation.

Fischer, J. (2016). *The history of hate in Indiana: How the Ku Klux Klan took over Indiana's halls of power*. Retrieved from http://www.theindychannel.com/longform/the-ku-klux-klan-ran-indiana-and-it-can-happen-again

Fisher v University of Texas at Austin, 570 US ___ (2013).

Fisher v University of Texas at Austin, 579 US ___ (2016).

Franklin, J. H. (2011). *From slavery to freedom: A history of African Americans* (9th ed.). Boston, MA: McGraw-Hill.

Genovese, E. D. (1989). *The political economy of slavery: Studies in the economy & society of the slave south*. Middletown, VA: Wesleyan University Press.

Goffman, E. (1963). *Stigma: Notes on the management of spoiled identity*. Englewood Cliffs, NJ: Prentice-Hall.

Goodman, A. H. (2000). Why genes don't count (for racial differences in health). *American Journal of Public Health, 90*, 1699–1702.

Gordon-Reed, A. (2008). *The Hemingses of Monticello: An American family*. New York, NY: W.W. Norton & Company.

Gregory, J. N. (2005). *The southern diaspora: How the great migration of black and white southerners transformed America* (1st ed.). Chapel Hill, NC: The University of North Carolina Press.

Grutter v Bollinger, 539 US 306 (2003).

Hacker, A. (1995). *Two nations: Black and white, separate, unequal, and hostile*. New York, NY: Ballentine.

Iceland, J. (2017). *Race and ethnicity in America*. Oakland, CA: University of California Press.

Kerby, S. (2012). *The top 10 most startling facts about people of color and criminal justice in the United States: A look at racial disparities inherent in our nation's criminal justice system*. Center for American Progress. Retrieved April 24, 2017, from https://www.americanprogress.org/issues/race/news/2012/03/13/11351

Lavender-Bratcher, D., & Dunn, J. L. (2016). Culture, race, and the self: How mixed-race Alaskan people counter micro aggressions, stigma, and identity dilemmas. *Journal of Sociology and Social Work, 4*(1), 134–145.

Lee, J., & Bean, F. D. (2010). *The diversity paradox: Immigration and the color line in 21st century America*. New York, NY: Russell Sage Foundation.

Lee, S. M., & Edmonston, B. (2005). New marriage, new families: US racial and Hispanic intermarriage. *Population Bulletin, 60*(2), 3–40.

Lockett, L. (2015). *Black propinquity in 21st century America*. Retrieved from K-Rex, http//hdl.handle.net/2097/20362

Lockett, L., Webb, F.J., & Chancler, L. (2013). *The effects of black ancestral group on perceptions of blacks*. Paper presented at the National Conference on Family Relations meeting, San Antonio, TX.

Loving v Virginia, 388 US 1 (1967).

Madigan, T. (2003). *The burning: Massacre, destruction, and the Tulsa race riot of 1921*. New York, NY: Thomas Donne, St. Martin's Griffin Press.

Maillard, K. N. (2005). The Pocohontus exception: The exemption of American indian ancestry from racial purity law. *SSRN Electronic Journal*. https://doi.org/10.2139/ssnr.871096

Mallet, C. A. (2017). The school-to-prison pipeline: Disproportionate impact on vulnerable children and adolescents. *Education and Urban Society, 49*(6), 563–592.

Massey, D., & Denton, N. (1998). *American apartheid: Segregation and the making of the underclass*. Cambridge, MA: Harvard University Press.

McAdoo, H. P. (2007). *Black families* (4th ed.). Thousand Oaks, CA: Sage Publications.

McLaughlin v Florida, 379 US 184 (1964).

Mitchell, J. (2016). Mississippi RV park owner evicts interracial couple receives support and criticism. *The Clarion Ledger*. April 5, 2016. Retrieved January 12, 2017 from clarionledger.com

Oklahoma Commission. (2001). *A report by the Oklahoma commission to study the Tulsa race riot*. Retrieved from http://www.ok-history.mus.ok.us/trrc/freport.htm

Pace v Alabama, 106 US 583 (1883).

Patten, E. (2015). *Who is multiracial? Depends on how you ask: A comparison of six survey methods to capture racial identity*. Washington, DC: Pew Research Center. Retrieved November from http://www.pewsocialtrends.org/2015/11/06/who-is-multiracial-depends-on-how-you-ask/

Perez v Sharp, 32 Cal.2d 711, 198 P.2d 17 Oct 1 (1948).

Perry, I. (2011). *More beautiful and more terrible: The embrace of and trancendance of racial equality in the United States*. New York, NY: New York University Press.

Pew Research Center. (2015). *Multiracial in America: Proud, diverse and growing in numbers*. Washington, DC: Pew Research Center. Retrieved June 11, 2015, from http://www.pewresearch.org

Pew Research Center. (2016). *On views of race and inequality, blacks and whites are worlds apart*. Washington, DC: Pew Research Center. Retrieved June 27, 2016, from http://www.pewresearch.org

Plessy v Ferguson, 163 US 537 (1896).

Regents of the University of California v Bakke, 438 US 265 (1978).

Ricci v DeStefano, 557 US 557 (2009).

Rocque, M., & Snelling, Q. (2017). The new displinology: Research, theory, and remaining puzzles on the school-to-prison-pipeline. *Journal of Criminal Research*. Retrieved May 2, 2017, from https://doi.org/10.1016/j-jcrimjs

Root, M. P. P. (1992). *Racially mixed people in America*. Thousand Oaks, CA: Sage Publications.

Shelton, N. J., & Richeson, J. A. (2006). Ethnic minorities' racial attitudes and contact experiences with white people. *Cultural Diversity and Ethnic Minority Psychology, 12*(1), 149–164.

Shih, M., Sanchez, D., Bonam, C., & Peck, C. (2007). The social construction of race: Biracial identity and vulnerability to stereotypes. *Cultural Diversity and Ethnic Minority Psychology, 13*(2), 125–133.

Simmons, L. (2017). *The prison school: Educational inequality and school discipline in the age of mass incarceration*. Oakland, CA: University of California Press.

Smedly, A. (2007). *Race in North America: Origin and evolution of a worldview* (3rd ed.). Boulder, CO: Westview Press.

Smith, G. (2012). *29% of Mississippi republicans still think interracial marriage should be illegal*. Daily Mail.com. Retrieved from http://www.dailymail.co.uk/news/article-2114331

Smith, M. M. (2009). *How race is made: Slavery, segregation, and the senses*. New York, Accessible Publishing Systems, PTY, Ltd.

Spickard, P. R. (1992). The illogical of American racial categories. In M. P. P. Root (Ed.), *Racial mixed people in America* (pp. 12–23). Newbury Park, CA: Sage Publications.

Thomas Jefferson Foundation. (2017). *Thomas Jefferson and sally Hemings: A brief account*. Retrieved February 5, 2017, from https://www.monticello.org/site/plantation-and-slavery/thomas-jefferson-and-sally-hemings

Thomas, W. I., & Thomas, D. S. (1928). *The child in America: Behavior problems and programs*. New York, NY: Knopf Publishing.

United States v. Stanley; United States v. Ryan; United States v. Nichols; United States v. Singleton; Robinson et ux. v. Memphis & Charleston Railroad Company. 109 US 3 (1883).

Wang, W. (2012). *The rise of intermarriage: Rates, characteristics vary by race and gender*. Washington, DC: Pew Research Center, Pew Social & Demographic Trends. Retrieved from http://www.pewsocialtrends.org

Washington, B. T. (1999) [1901]. *Up from slavery*. New York, NY: Modern Library.

Webb, F. J., & Cortez, A. (2016). Creating a program of success for underrepresented students at research institutions. In J. M. Jananagelo (Ed.), *A critical look at institutional mission: A guide for writing program administrators* (pp. 59–74). Anderson, SC: Parlor Press.

West, C. (2014). *Black prophetic fire*. Boston, MA: Beacon Press.

Williams, E. (1994). *Capitalism and slavery*. Chapel Hill, NC: The University of North Carolina Press.

Young, D. M., Sanchez, D. T., & Wilton, L. S. (2016). Biracial perception in black and white: How Black and White perceivers respond to phenotyped racial identity cues. *Cultural Diversity and Ethnic Minority Psychology, 23*(1), 154–164.

Zack, N. (1995). *American mixed race: The culture of microdiversity*. Lanham, MD: Rowman & Littlefield.

Questions and Concerns Regarding Family Theories: Biracial and Multiracial Family Issues

Farrell J. Webb and Vanessa Gonlin

I am mixed, black and white. My husband is black and my children are often assumed to be black. We live in a predominately white Midwest town. I met and became friends with a black parent at my child's school. Because our children were in the same grade we found ourselves thrust together at birthday parties, school programs, and sporting events. We naturally gravitated to one another. As we spent more time together she made comments that made me feel uncomfortable. I initially dismissed them, wondering if maybe I was hypersensitive to racial comments. Yet, the more time I spent with her I felt more and more uncomfortable. I rationalized these comments to be biracial micro-aggressions. But, I wondered whether my feelings were giving me further insight into my current racial identity process. The comments made me more vividly feel my "whiteness."

This same parent once asked me if there were any other black boys in our son's class, I told her yes, there were 2 others. She looked at me puzzled and asked, "who?" I told her. She responded, "oh, I don't know (him) and I didn't count (him), he's biracial." This would not be the last time she referred to this child –

who has a biological white mother and black father—as not-black. When these comments were made I tried to point out that in a police line-up he would be just as endangered as her son; she disagreed. Yet, she identified my son as black. These interactions made me question my own and my children's racial self-identifications and how we are racially identified by others. I often wonder what is the most protective and supportive advice I can give my children about how to identify themselves and our family.

—Anonymous

F. J. Webb (✉)
College of Health and Human Development, California State University, Northridge, CA, USA
e-mail: farrell.webb@csun.edu

V. Gonlin
Department of Sociology, Texas A&M University, College Station, TX, USA

R. Nazarinia Roy, A. Rollins (eds.), *Biracial Families*,
https://doi.org/10.1007/978-3-319-96160-6_3

Theories About Some Families

The role of theory in the study of family is critical to conceptualizing how families work and function within society. These theoretical frameworks provide essential information about the interplay between the social contexts in which these units (families) exist. There are several general family theories that have great import for family development. Some of these perspectives are examined in this chapter.

In general, family scholars rely on theory to help explain the relationship between the social world that we believe we live in and the social reality of how things really are. Sometimes they can contradict each other—such as the case of the role of theory when bi/multiracial families are included. In fact, it is often true when the concept of race becomes part of the conversation. The purpose of this chapter is to discuss the role of theory in family studies, highlighting how these theories have influenced our viewpoint on family, and at the same time address the deficiencies that are present when an important factor such as race is excluded from the design and concepts.

The global nature of most family theories is so broad that these theories are generally thought to be inclusive of most groups, although this assumption is rarely challenged and needs to be examined more carefully. Most of the contemporary family theories used observations of White families as a basis for their development. The social scientists involved in their development collected data primarily from White families, and often use an ideal-type model for family (the so-called nuclear family). This is unfortunate because this family form is not always present in a number of minority group families where such important structures, such as extended and inter-generational families, exist in greater numbers than the "traditional" family model. Yet, there are no mainstream family theories that address these issues in a direct manner.

While the theories of families are broad based, making their general nature and applicability more acceptable, the theories do present with both advantages and shortcomings. One of the essential advantages to existing family theories is that they often use a sociological perspective, focusing on group rather than individual perspectives for understanding behavior. This very advantage leads to one of the shortcomings, that is, they are so broad that they can overlook or subsume particular social characteristics in light of the overall perspective; this is particularly problematic when families of color are considered. For example, in symbolic interaction theory the primary assumption is that individuals have similar kinds of interactions and that policies, procedures, and practices are based on these interactions. What is missing from this is that there are a host of social factors that can and do influence what kinds of interactions a person may have. In other chapters in this volume the authors showed how the social-historical context resulted in different outcomes based on the same interaction and that those outcomes are based on how race was perceived (see Chap. 2 for more information). The implications for those individuals cited were extremely problematic. To overlook such an obvious issue would point to the lack of awareness by the theory progenitors. They too are a part of the social system that has systematically marginalized and overlooked people of color; therefore it is not surprising not to find their voices or presence in the prevailing theories.

This does not mean that many of the theories do not have applicability; they are often not adapted to people of color. In response, there have been a number of important theories that have attempted to address some of these issues as they relate to people of color; however, most of these have used an individualized focus rather than a more broad-based approach as one might need to get a better understanding on how families function and survive in contemporary society.

Theory Primer

In order to understand this discussion it is important to have a general idea of what is theory and more specifically family theory. This information shows that there is a general idea about what theories are and how it is used to guide our understanding of families.

To begin, a theory consists of a set of ideas or concepts that are applied in such a way that it allows us to make certain assumptions about how all of these things seem to help formulate a generalized idea. These elements come together through a series of logical statements or graphical illustrations that purport to provide some "social truth" to a situation. In other words, theories are formed from concepts based on some observable beliefs that are supported through examples that are understood from our own experiences.

The relative importance of theory comes from its ability to help us *understand, clarify, identify, examine, and test* our views about ideas and concepts that we believe are related. Because we are able to do this we can often use theory to help *establish patterns and predict outcomes* with some reasonable certainty. When we are able to empirically verify these "social statements" we are said to have established a theoretical construct or framework. The value from all of this comes from the ability to be able to *revise and refine* these ideas until they become more salient in the lives of those about whom these observations are made.

Another important and very critical idea about theory that is very rarely made is that some theoretical perspectives are *nested* within a larger construct. For example, the ideas surrounding social interaction are generally based on the notion of culture. In effect, interactions are nested within the family, which are in turn nested in the community, and the community is nested within a larger group called society, which is surrounded by or enveloped within a culture. Thus, ideas are nested and understanding the root system of the nesting is helpful for understanding ideas. Global theories, such as systems theory, have become the go-to explanation used by many family scientists. Many believe, mistakenly we might add, that the theory can be used to explain all the problems within a society. However, there needs to be more examination of the elements within the system and that in turn can lead to a better explanation. However, such work requires a great investment on the part of the social scientists that endeavor to address such issues, as is the case with bi/multiracial families in America.

Theoretical Flaws

There are several important theories in the area of family studies. These theoretical constructs have dominated the field for some time. They are the ones taught in most degree programs and they are the ones which most family scientists have some familiarity with. While each of these theories covers important areas of family they are often deficient in some areas. The data in Table 1 examines the problematic areas of several theories across four dimensions of racial identity, a critical element for bi/multiracial individuals and their families.

Personal Theory of Race Identity

Our understanding of biracial and multiracial identity is ever evolving. Identity is fluid in that it may change over time and may change situationally, and an individual's personal racial identification may differ from others' expectations of their racial identification, due to the socially constructed nature of race (Saperstein & Penner, 2012). Race is a social construct with very real consequences for people, especially those for whom their racial designation has been devalued, such as it has been for Blacks, throughout their history here in the United States (Cornell & Hartmann,

Table 1 Typology of racial identities

	Singular identity[a]		Border identity[b]		Protean identity[c]		Transcendent identity[d]	
	Direct	Indirect	Direct	Indirect	Direct	Indirect	Direct	Indirect
Family-based theories								
Exchange	No	Yes	No	Yes	No	No	No	No
Symbolic interaction	No	Yes	No	Yes	No	Yes	No	No
Conflict	No	Yes	No	Yes	No	No	No	No
Bioecological	Yes	Yes	Yes	Yes	No	No	No	No
Individually based theories								
Marginal person	Yes	Yes	Yes	Yes	No	Yes	No	No
Kerwin-Ponterotto	Yes	Yes	Yes	Yes	No	No	No	No
Pan-ethnic identity	Yes	No	Yes	No	Yes	Yes	No	No
Appearance model	Yes	Yes	Yes	Yes	Yes	Yes	No	Yes

[a]Singular identity—sees self as one race even if bi- or multiracial
[b]Border identity—sees self as neither Black or White, views self as a conglomeration of both
[c]Protean identity—sees self as sometimes Black or sometimes White
[d]Transcendent identity—sees self as having no racial identity

2007; Hirschman, 2004; Morning, 2009; Omi & Winant, 1994; Waters, 1990; Webb, Burrell, & Jefferson, 2017; Webb & Cortez, 2016). We see this in variations of racial understanding throughout the world's history. Nevertheless, within this chapter the bi/multiracial families that we will discuss are those formed from minority/White unions, primarily because they are the largest groups and the groups studied most often and hence appear in the extant literature at a greater rate.

In full disclosure, at least one of the authors of this chapter belongs to a biracial grouping. One of the authors identifies as a Black/White Biracial woman. The other as a Black man who has multiracial background historically but is aware of his Black roots most of all, and thus his identification. Both would have been identified as Black during the Jim Crow epoch (1877 to 1965, during which time anyone with known Black ancestry was considered to be Black both by law and social conventions), but through the luxury of some social enlightenment they may now self-identify as White, Black, or biracial in the present-day United States. The second author's personal story follows:

> *Vanessa was born and raised in a racially diverse community in Maryland, and she has traveled to and lived in different states. Her mother is Black and her father is White, and she has a toffee complexion with tightly curled brown hair. Vanessa's parents taught her that she is Biracial, but when she meets people in different places they racially classify her in various ways. In the Northeast, strangers initially think she is Latina but are willing to accept her as Biracial; in the South, most people view her as Black and treat her as such; and on the West Coast, people tend to expect that she identifies as Biracial. ;. With so much variation in how people interact with her, Vanessa questions her racial identity. In her experience, sometimes people reject her asserted racial identity. This means discounting her experiences, informing her that they know her "true" racial identity, and treating her as whichever race they ascribe to her. To add another layer of intricacy, Vanessa's sister has a lighter skin tone than her with long dark brown curls, and people usually assume she is Latina, Arab, or Mediterranean—anything but Black or Biracial. Vanessa reflects on her interracial family, contemplates how people racially identify her, and considers how people racially identify her sister. All of these factors influence Vanessa's racial identity:she identifies as Biracial and as Black, but has not always identified this way, and her racial identity may shift in the future.*

In this chapter, we first identify the major theories of family used by family scientists to aid in our understanding about families. We also identify the specific theories that have been developed to examine the biracial/multiracial individuals. We then map these theories across the typology of biracial identity (Rockquemore, 1999; Rockquemore and Brunsma, 2008) to assess their utility in helping to explicate issues that we have identified as relevant for our discussion. Finally, we offer critiques of these theories and conclude with the idea as to how the theories can be improved to help us in our understanding of biracial/multiracial families in contemporary America. This critical review highlights the existing gaps in our knowledge about biracial/multiracial individuals and families and the ways that these gaps often fall short of providing those with any substantial utility. The ultimate goal of this chapter is to work towards a more complex and dynamic set of theoretical schemas that more closely align with biracial/multiracial familial experiences and processes to provide an equally diverse and complex toolkit of approaches, perspectives, and theories to draw from to more effectively understand how individuals and families navigate their lives within the hegemonic structure of the US society that is principally organized around race.

Racial Identity Typology

The typology of racial identity, developed by Rockquemore (1999), identifies racial identity across four distinct domains. The typology posits the idea that bi- and multiracial individuals have the ability to choose their own racial identity. In other words, they believe that they can define how others in their social world see and react to them in terms of race. There are four identity types identified by this theoretical perspective; they are (1) singular, (2) border, (3) protean, and (4) transcendent. Individuals can have a *singular identity* that is characterized by having a sense of belonging to one racial identity even though they know they are bi- or multiracial. This singularity of identity formation is very common. This identity forms based on a variety of factors; some of these may include family position, community attitudes, hegemonic structure of the society, or just based on phenotypical appearance. Former President Barack Obama would be an example of a singular identity individual. The second identity type is *border identity*. Here the individual can see himself/herself as neither Black nor White; rather they view themselves as a conglomeration of both races. The golfer Tiger Woods is an excellent example. He defines his multiracial family history as "cablinasian" to include his full heritage of Caucasian, Black, Indian, and Asian.

The third form of identity is a *protean identity*. Here the individual is able to shift their racial identity at will. They may move from Black to White and vice versa depending upon the circumstances, their personal needs, or the social issues involved at the time, although he/she might not agree with this characterization. The final identity characteristic is *transcendent identity*. In this formation, the individual does not have any racial identity at all, often referring to self as "human." While the individual may not choose a racial identity the hegemonic structure of the United States, which uses race as a determining factor for most social movement and rewards, will most certainly prescribe the individual to a certain race group.

Family Theories

There are a number of critical theories developed and adapted that center on the social entity of the family. However, the ones that we have selected to examine here find widespread popularity among family scientists. We briefly discuss each selected theory and compare and contrast them with the continuum of racial identity typologies developed by Rockquemore (1999) to see how each perspective addresses the concept of race. We consider a theory as directly related to racial identity if the theory has been (or can be) applied to racial groups by some element contained within the theory. We consider a theory as indirect if the elements contained within the theory have the potential of applying to some aspects of racial identity, but were not. Still there are times when a theory *has no* relevance to racial identity. In examining the theories used for this chapter we found no theory that could not be either directly or indirectly related to racial identity, even if the theory never clearly isolates race as a central element or thesis.

We have examined four family-based theories that are widely used throughout the discipline. Although none of these theoretical approaches address race in a direct fashion, their general applicability to race is what we chose to examine. The four theories that we used are (1) social exchange; (2) symbolic interactionism; (3) conflict; and (4) bioecosystemic approaches.

Social Exchange and Rational Choice

The general principle of social exchange theory is that relationships are balanced by people weighing the costs versus rewards of their actions in an effort to increase their social profits. Each cost and reward is based on three things: (a) how much one desires a reward; (b) how much does the reward cost the individual or group; and (c) what are the actual benefits or rewards for acquiring the goal. The theory postulates that social interaction has implicit cost and reward systems. How individuals are able to balance these elements in their lives is an essential concept of this theory. A basic assumption is that there is an implicit belief in the value of costs and rewards.

A reward is something perceived as beneficial to an actor. A *cost* could be anything perceived as not beneficial to an actor, or as a negative aspect of a reward. *Profit* is the ratio of rewards to costs for any given decision. In short, the general aim of social exchange is to maximize profits and minimize loss. The critical assumptions upon which this theory is based are the following: a) individual actions are often based on social norms and mores; (b) it is possible to predict individual actions by being aware of social costs and rewards; (c) actors are motivated by self-interests; and (d) people act rationally and attempt to maximize rewards, reduce costs, enhance profits, and maintain some balance in their lives.

Issues with race: Among the major critiques of this perspective is the idea that the theory tends to overemphasize the role that individual actor plays. In addition, it tends to overlook the role that the existing culture plays, specifically when it comes to how race is seen and responded to within our society. While there is an implicit *social contract* that binds individuals together it is not always a consideration when certain profits are present. Indeed, some people may act against their own interests if they believe that the profits are well worth the costs no matter how it might be perceived by others. For example, on the one hand, a soldier who acts out of bravery without considering the costs to himself/herself, their families, commanding officers, or others within his/her unit if the ultimate profit is saving the lives of others. On the other hand, the same can be said about the assumption that actors are rational.

It is problematic to verify rationality because the motivation as to why someone acts is only verifiable if we are present to discern their actions. Still, the ultimate motivation may never be uncovered.

Another shortcoming of the theory is that while it could be applied to all types of families and across all groups, there is no explicit assumptions about how this theory can be applied to individuals or groups in terms of race. This is an important fact because the basic assumptions of the theory center on the relationship the individual has to its social systems evidenced by how rewards and profits are calculated. In a culture where some groups are disadvantaged based on some outward social grouping, more specifically measured by race, it is possible that not all groups can gain similar rewards and profits. For example, relationship researchers often use this theory in evaluating relationship commitment, but among biracial partners there may be additional costs to staying in a relationship linked to social experiences related to their partner's race. This assumption is overlooked largely because the basic underlying assumption does not take into consideration the issue of race. Clearly, in a society such as ours, where there is a distinct hegemonic structure that is based on race it is possible to see how some groups would be left out of the essential conversation. We have analyzed this theory and found that it does not have any direct relationships across the racial identity continuum (see Table 1). However, it does have some indirect applicability across the singular and border identity categories.

Symbolic Interaction

Symbolic interaction is a popular theory used in family studies. It focuses on the use of *symbols, words, gestures,* and other *nonverbal* elements that help form patterns of communication, interpretation, and adjustment which are all part of how an individual interacts with others and how they are able to derive meaning from these interactions. It is both *dynamic* and *transactive*. This is demonstrated by the way families reinforce and strengthen bonds via symbolic rituals, such as family meals and holidays. The genesis for symbolic interaction is the works of George Herbert Mead (1934). He argued that the development of what we call "self" occurs in our minds and can be divided into two parts—the "I" and the "Me." These two parts exist simultaneously but can only be referenced one at a time. In effect, the "I" exist for the individual but when seen by others it is known as "me." This is essential because the objective nature of the "I" represented by "me" is known vis-à-vis the symbol manipulation that the "I" performs. Communication is a direct form of symbol manipulation.

The theory works because the basic assumptions are agreed upon by the actors involved. Essentially the theory states that in the day-to-day world of how we behave we are constantly referencing our "I" to that of others via their "me." There is a strong relationship between people and how we come to understand each other. It is based upon our tacit agreement about what we believe are *values, beliefs, roles, norms*, and *mores* about how we should act. In effect, we all influence the actions of others and this process is continuous. We agree upon the symbols and their meanings. We reinforce our meaning through our social actions. For example, while driving we all stop at red lights. While there are no barriers to prevent us from going through the intersection the agreed-upon social contract to stop when the symbol displays a red color is one that we typically respect. These same types of assumptions work within family structures as well. There are agreed-upon roles for mothers and fathers, there are agreed-upon behaviors as to how parents should behave with their children, and there are social structures to support how we interact with each other as family members. All of these social symbols and the roles, rules, and values that support these symbols and our interactions with each other derived from our shared meaning.

An important thing to remember is that there are many facets of an individual's life and that at any time he/she may have to play several roles. Sometimes when the individual is not properly socialized, or when the individual may not understand the social symbols, he/she may make a mistake. The appropriate behaviors associated with each role are acquired by the actors as they navigate the social system. Actors may play roles as expected when they are "onstage" and have a different reality "offstage." Roles are dependent on interactions with others; the expectations of actors vary by social context.

Issues with race: It is easy to see how this theory may have some merit when it comes to addressing issues around race. For example, the same social symbol may mean different things to different people depending upon the group to which they belong. If the individual belongs to two groups at once, such as a biracial person, it may be more problematic to interpret the symbols, or they may simply not identify the symbol as being important. This is particularly true when abstractions such as "words" are used. The terms used suggest that as different set of symbols or meanings appear the interpretation of the rules, values, norms, and mores can change. However, we find that this theory in its current form does not address race directly although it has the ability to do so. This failing occurs not because the theory itself is inadequate, but rather it underscores the prevailing hegemony that overlooks people of color on a regular basis and in most domains of life, including theorizing about them in a positive way.

Conflict Theory

Conflict theory as used by family scientists focuses on the *differences between classes* within society, the competition for *scarce resources*, and the struggle for *political power* and *economic wealth* within *family systems*. These ideas originally appeared in the works of Karl Marx whose central belief was that the root cause of conflict was rooted in economics. However, it was Jetse Sprey (1969) who actually linked the notion of conflict to families. He argued that conflict was not necessarily Marxian, as originally conceptualized, but rather it had more to do with orderly and disorderly social processes. Sprey (1969) believed that competition, conflict, conflict management, and conflict resolution were essential to the growth and development of families. In addition, he believed that *consensus, negotiation,* and *bargaining* were essential to maintaining power—the ability to control the direction or course of action of others. Although these concepts could be applied to most relationships, Sprey believed that the group dynamics of families were different from those of any group. In short, families had unique traits. The first was membership status; people were in families whether they wanted to be or not; these were termed as voluntary versus involuntary membership. The second trait was *intensity* and *proximity*, living together made for intense situations, especially when members were having difficulties. The third trait was the *threat of dissolution* that was extremely problematic.

The fact that conflict was *inherent in social groups* and that it was often *inevitable* made the family dynamic compelling. Conflict was valued because it would generate compromise and in some cases assimilation. These traits would help manage the scarce resources and ensure that people would play their roles appropriately. The key then, for Sprey (1969, 2000) and others, was not that conflict existed, but rather how it was managed within the family. If a family was able to avoid conflict within its ranks, that would not be for very long. The very premise of the theory would suggest that it was not possible to avoid conflict. For families, conflict would be the defining element. Those families that were good at conflict would function well. Those that were bad would function poorly (Sprey, 1969, 2000).

Issues with race: Although the principles of conflict theory centered on dealing with issues of hegemony it is striking that it does not address the issue of race. Since conflict theory centers on the management and maintenance of power within a family it is surprising that the issue of racial hegemony is not raised, particularly because within biracial families race could present as an important power dynamic between the couple. For example, it would be very interesting to examine if conflict was higher or lower in families where there were bi/multiracial family members. We are left with the question of what would the source of conflict be based around race or would it center on other fundamental issues within the family? These questions are never addressed but it is clear that this theory would be one that could offer some insight into these issue. We find that the conflict theory does indirectly address issues of race in terms of singular, border, and protean identity due primarily to the idea that for each of these categories there are elements of conflict that can be identified. The theory does not seem to have any bearing on transcendent identity because there is an absence of conflict.

The Bioecological Family Systems Theory

Family systems theory is a subset of the general systems theory. The notion of systems theory grew out of the early days of cybernetics. In fact, family systems theory has evolved from the early 1920s to the modern bioecological family systems theory that we use today. Each of these theoretical incarnations, based on the simple idea that systems are any set of objects that relate to each other, is characterized by having *boundaries,* has *one-to-one comparisons*, is able to *achieve goals* via *different routes*, and is *hierarchical.* A critical element of human systems is that they are *self-reflexive, interdependent, non-summative, balanced, transactive* (equal and opposite force on behavior), and capable of *change and adaptation.* A system, because of its transactive nature, can *generate feedback* that helps the system adapt. This continuous process is a trait of families where growth and change are fundamental to its existence.

Individuals are part of a family system. It is often difficult to understand individual behavior or beliefs without some understanding of the family unit surrounding and influencing them. In more systemic terms, one can see that a family is a unit distinguished from other units within a similar social environment; this family system is both affected by and affects its immediate environment (White & Klein, 2008). Modern bioecological family systems theory (Bronfenbrenner, 1979) views that there are a number of subsystems that are both interconnected and transactive that contribute to our understanding. The basic assumptions are that people are both biological and social in nature. We are dependent upon the environment and the environment is dependent upon us. We work together in a series of mutual dependencies to maintain a viable environment. Like all systems there are specific roles and these change as individuals grow and adapt. Change is essential and these changes are predicated upon how we interact with each other over time.

The basic bioecological perspective consists of five interrelated subsystems. They are the *microsystem*—the smallest system where the basic activities and interaction patterns can be found. With the microsystem the focus is primarily on the individuals and how they interact with each other. The next level is the *mesosystem*—the concern here is examining connections among microsystems among people and their immediate settings, for example, home, school, church, and clubs. Surrounding these two systems is a third system known as the *exosystem*—these systems usually do not have direct contact with people's immediate life; nevertheless they have an effect on their experiences in their immediate settings. For example, what happens at a parent's workplace can have an overall effect on the family's economic well-being; a student cannot attend school because they did not get a required vaccination—in this case the health system is overriding the education system which is the one directly connected to the individual. In both cases, the exosystem, which is not directly related to the individual, is having an influence on their lives. The fourth system is the *macrosystem*—it consists of all the values, laws, customs, and resources in a given culture. All of these systems are guided by the *chronosystem*—the temporal factor that cannot be controlled or altered and is perpetual. All of these subsystems are connected to each other and are influenced by both individual and group actions.

Issue with race: Although family systems and bioecological theories are very useful to understand the greater picture of how families function, they fall short when it comes to being able to make comparisons across families by groups. When race is considered the concepts fail to distinguish themselves. While we may know that families are influenced by exo- and macrosystems, those who control the scripts for defining what values, laws, customs, and resources are going to be used or considered becomes an important element. Since the theory does not focus on these things it is difficult to see how it can be clearly applied to race in general and more specifically to bi/multiracial individuals who are already challenging many of the assumptions made about people of color. Inasmuch as we find the theory to wanting, we do believe that it can have some practical applicability on identity development specifically in the singular and border identity types, both directly and indirectly. Our interpretation would really depend upon the individual's attitude and belief as regulated by their personal systems.

Theories Specific to Biracial and Multiracial Identity Development

Before any discussion about the individually based theories of biracial and multiracial development begins, it is essential that there be some grounding on some of the social constructs. Just what are the factors that make discussing race a salient component to examine at this time. There are two schools of thought surrounding race and ethnicity in the United States.

Hypodescent

The first concept, *hypodescent*, finds its roots deep in the historical context of our country. This concept is a vestige of slavery, where any one that had any descendant who was Black was considered Black. Hypodescent, commonly referred to as the one-drop rule, refers to the notion that blackness is assigned to any person with "one drop" of Black blood (Davis, 1991; Jordan, 2014; Webb et al., 2017). During slavery, this historical concept was used to determine who was legally Black. Hypodescent could bring Blacks together via a united identity or used to stratify the Black community. The idea of using blood quantum to divide people into groups was widespread during slavery and this unusual idea still exists for American-Indians for tribal membership (Webb et al., 2017). The social construction of blood quantum groups led to distinctions where Black people were referred to as *mulatto* (one-half

Black), *quadroon* (one-fourth Black), *octoroon/terceron/mustee* (one-eighth Black), and even *mustefino* (one-sixteenth Black). This classification system divided the Black community, privileged Whiteness, and stratified by race. Contemporarily, although the "one-drop" rule is sometimes applied to the individuals with White and Asian, Hispanic, or American-Indian heritage, these multiracial individuals tend to have more flexibility and choice in their racial identity than those who are part Black. This is because of the historical categorization of anyone with "Black blood" as Black, which is an experience that individuals of non-Black multiracial heritage did not receive.

*For example: Thomas, who has a Black grandmother, White grandmother, and two White grandfathers, was born in the United States in 1855. Slavery would not be abolished for another 10 years. Since Thomas' grandmother is Black and a slave, Thomas is also considered Black (he would have been a quadroon) and a slave. Even though the majority of Thomas' known ancestry is White, the one drop rule practiced during this time means that Thomas' assigned race is Black and his fate is more similar to Blacks than to Whites (*i.e. *he is enslaved and not free).*

Today, hypodescent is generally denounced. Social scientists tend to agree that people who assert biracial or multiracial identity should be identified as such (rather than be assigned a monoracial category). After rejecting hypodescent, scholars theorized and continue to theorize other possibilities. Hypodescent was important because it influenced the way individuals with complex ancestral racial backgrounds were identified and treated by others (Hollinger, 2003). It also paved the way for social scientists to study other options for individuals who identify as biracial or multiracial.

Genealogy

A newer concept, genealogy, was introduced by Morning (2000) to explain which bi/multiracial people are likely to identify as bi/multiracial. She asserts that those who are the products of an interracial union are more likely to identify as multiracial on the Census rather than those whose multiracial heritage is more distant, such as having grandparents from multiple multiracial backgrounds. Bratter (2007) finds empirical support for this position. Her work reveals that bi/multiracial individuals with two monoracial parents are indeed more likely to identify as multiracial than individuals whose multiracial heritage is a number of generations away; nevertheless her research indicates that the likelihood also varies by racial composition. When one parent identified as either White or American-Indian, their offspring are more likely to claim a multiracial background.

For example: Stephanie knows that her dad is White and Latino, and her mom is Asian American. Stephanie identifies as multiracial. Stephanie has a friend whose grandmother is Latina and Asian, but everyone else in the friend's family is White. Stephanie's friend knows of her multiracial heritage but identifies as White.

These concepts of hypodescent and genealogy inform a host of theories about biracial and multiracial identity. In the next section of this chapter we examine four theories of biracial/multiracial identity development.

Marginal Person Model

The first theoretical model researchers specifically developed to better understand biracial identity development was the marginal person model. Developed by Park (1928) and Stonequist (1935), this model is flawed and outdated but nonetheless provides the foundation for our theoretical understanding of biraciality today. Both Park (1928, 1931) and Stonequist (1935, 1937) assumed that there was conflict when one person has two cultures and actively participates in both. The personality, then, was affected by this conflict. The "cultural hybrids" exhibited "marginal" identity development, as they were associated with multiple cultures but do not fit neatly or wholly into one (Poston, 1990; Stonequist, 1935, 1937).

For example: Jonathan has a White mother and a Black father. He grew up in the United States in the 1930s and was told by Black friends and family members that he wasn't quite Black enough and by White friends and family members that he wasn't White enough. Jonathan experienced conflict, and psychiatrists told him it was because he did not fit into one racial category and had competing cultures. Jonathan was told that being biracial prevented him from finding fulfillment.

Gibbs (1987) expands on the marginal person concept, adding that the problems associated with identity development are exacerbated for people of "mixed race" because they do not follow the "normal" process of identity development. Rather, individuals who identify as biracial face heightened uncertainty about their racial identification, identification with their parents, group identification with peers, and social identification with a specific racial or ethnic group (Gibbs, 1987).

Cheng and Lively (2009), using a nationally representative youth sample to test [what was originally entitled] the marginal man theory, found that individuals who identify as Black/White biracial tended to show more depressive symptoms compared to both Black and White peers. They also experienced more self-deprecation than Blacks but similar amounts as Whites, and felt more alienated in school than Whites but experienced similar levels as Blacks. In addition, Cheng and Lively (2009) tested for variation in six different multiracial groupings and found that bi/multiracial individuals may have better or equal sociability, and poorer or equal psychological health, and believed that the quality of their social relations is more negative than their monoracial peers. Finally, multiracial students exhibited behavior problems equal to the minority group, or are less favorable than both (Cheng & Lively, 2009). These findings emphasized how bi/multiracial students may have experiences more similar to minority groups, yet still are different from minority groups. Although supportive of the marginal person model, these findings revealed that the experiences of bi/multiracial individuals are multifaceted. They are neither better nor worse off; they just have different strengths and challenges associated with their identity than monoracial individuals.

The marginal person model emphasizes that the problem lies with the individual in that being marginal leads to having a marginal personality. Poston (1990) disagrees with the assumption that being "marginal" must lead to a marginal personality. He believed that they may be marginalized: (1) from experiencing prejudice against them and internalizing the messages they are told; (2) from lack of group support from cultures (rather than inherent conflict between cultures); and (3) that individuals seen as marginal are not *destined* to have a marginal personalities. Furthermore, individuals who identify as biracial may not experience the conflict anticipated by the marginal person model; some may even understand biraciality to be an asset, a multicultural rather than marginal lifestyle (Herman, 1970; Poston, 1990).

Social scientists find support for Poston's (1990) assertions. For example, Campbell and Eggerling-Boeck (2006) find that, as a group, bi/multiracial individuals did not consistently report more negative outcomes than peers in other racial and ethnic minority groups. This means that bi/multiracial people tend to do about as well as other racial minority groups, supporting Poston's idea that they are *not* intrinsically flawed and destined to have a marginal personality. In terms of race, the marginal person theory matches well with the singular and border identity domains both directly and indirectly. The theory also had some applicability for the protean identity domain in an indirect manner.

Kerwin-Ponterotto Model of Biracial Identity Development

The Kerwin-Ponterotto model of biracial identity development is a theoretical model intended to predict who identifies as biracial and how they come to this identity. Empirical findings from Kerwin, Ponterotto, Jackson, and Harris (1993) led to the development of the Kerwin-Ponterotto model of biracial identity development, and highlighted the process through which individuals go through to develop a biracial identity. Personal, societal, and environmental factors are introduced as influential in biracial identity development. According to the Kerwin-Ponterotto et al. (1993) there are six stages in which biracial identity may be developed. They are (1) *preschool*—become aware of race but racial salience may vary by person; (2) *entry to school*—classifying others and being classified by others; (3) *preadolescence*—awareness of what constitutes group membership; (4) *adolescence*—a tumultuous time marked by pressure to conform to societal expectations; (5) *college/young adulthood*—further immersion into one culture and rejection of societal expectations; and (6) *adulthood*—includes exploration of multiple cultures, including one's own cultures.

Overall, the assumption with this model is that "successful" completion of the first five stages provides a basis for a biracial identity in adulthood, with the understanding that this identity may continue to be contested and developed.

For example: Michael has an Asian mother and White father. In preschool he noticed that he looked different from other classmates. When he entered school he could tell people apart by races, and White students told him he wasn't really White and Asian classmates said he wasn't really Asian. In preadolescence he became aware of what those students meant when they said White and Asian. He thought being White meant spending time outdoors and being Asian meant being really good at math. During adolescence he tried to conform to societal expectations by camping and hiking, and simultaneously being both good at math. As a young adult he became more immersed in Asian American culture—he was a part of Asian American organizations, had mainly Asian American friends, and listened to diasporic Asian music. As an adult, Michael explored a variety of cultures, including multiple Asian and White cultures. Michael identifies as Biracial.

A strength of the Kerwin-Ponterotto model of biracial identity development is that it emphasizes the social nature of identity development. An individual does not come to identify as biracial on their own. They are influenced first by their family, then by educators and peers, and finally with societal expectations, before coming to their own conclusion. They are undoubtedly affected by the beliefs of others. If family members assert that a child is biracial, the child is more likely to identify as biracial (at least for a time) than if family members assert that a child is monoracial. After first coming into contact with family members, individuals who identify as biracial then come into contact with educators and peers who may agree with or dismiss the identification asserted by family members. Finally, individuals who identify as biracial encounter media, music, news, and other forms of culture that tell them the expectations society has of them and their racial identity. All of these external factors are important in understanding biracial identity development.

The Kerwin-Ponterotto model of Biracial identity development, while acknowledging that identity is a lifelong process, operates from the goal of having people identify as biracial rather than as monoracial or transracial. Importantly, this model asserts that an individual who identifies as biracial should expect to be able to "function effectively in varying situations," such as in predominantly majority *and* predominantly minority spaces. This expectation may not be realistic for some individuals who identify as biracial, particularly those who are identified as monoracial by others (Kerwin & Ponterotto, 1995). Therefore, while this model is useful, it is not the only model that should be used to understand biracial identity development. When race is considered, the Kerwin-Ponterotto model of biracial identity development appears to have applicability to the typology of racial identity on both the singular and border domains. This was expected; what was somewhat surprising was that there does not appear to be any utility in terms of the protean or transcendent identity domains.

Pan-Ethnic Identity/Multigroup Ethnic Identity Measure

Similar to the Kerwin-Ponterotto model of biracial identity development, Phinney's (1989, 1990) pan-ethnic identity model discusses identity as forming in stages, but Phinney looks at ethnic identity in general (rather than biracial identity) and notes that there are stages in identity development that might never be achieved (rather than looking across the life course). Phinney ties together research on racial and ethnic identity in general to determine how ethnic identity is formed: She argued that there are four essential stages; they are as follows: (1) *diffusion*—little exploration of one's ethnicity, and no understanding of one's own ethnicity; (2) *foreclosure*—little exploration of one's ethnicity, but clarity about one's own ethnicity; (3) *moratorium*—exploration of one's ethnicity, and confusion about the meaning of one's own ethnicity; and (4) *achieved*—exploration of one's ethnicity, and a clear, secure understanding and acceptance of one's own ethnicity.

The benefits of Phinney's pan-ethnic identity model are twofold, one that there is no timeframe during which changes in ethnic identity formation occur, and two, not every individual is expected to go through or reach every stage. In this way, her model mirrors reality. Her models' intent is to lead to a better understanding of ethnic identity formation. It has the added advantage that it may be applied to biracial and multiracial identity development as well because these identities are types of ethnic identities, and may occur in the stages discussed above. Expanding on this idea of pan-ethnic identity, Phinney (1992) developed the multigroup ethnic identity measure (MEIM) to test how strongly an individual explores and understands their ethnicity. MEIM merges ethnic identity search and affirmation. Using this measure, researchers have found that having a strong ethnic identity is associated with higher levels of self-esteem and self-affirmation, and stronger family and social ties.

For example: Guadalupe's family has lived in California for multiple generations and she is aware of her Mexican ancestry. As a child Guadalupe did not explore her ethnicity or understand her own ethnicity. As she grew older, Guadalupe interacted with peers and became clearer about her Mexican heritage but did not explore it. Once she met people of different ethnicities, Guadalupe began to explore her ethnicity: she asked her family members about their experiences as Mexican Americans, read stories and books about her history, and formed bonds with other Latinos. Guadalupe was confused about what it meant to be Mexican and Latina, and continued trying to understand. Finally, as an adult, after exploring her ethnic identity and coming to an understanding of how it shapes and guides her life, Guadalupe accepted her ethnic identity specifically as Mexican American and broadly as Latina. Guadalupe feels good about herself and her ethnicity, and interacts well with peers, family, and social interactions in general.

However, since this theory is not specifically intended for biracial and multiracial identity development, the pan-ethnic identity model (which can be measured using MEIM) is more difficult to apply to individuals who identify as biracial and multiracial. For example, although MEIM allows for individuals to identify as more than one race, it may be difficult for these individuals to answer MEIM questions such as "I participate in cultural practices of my own group, such as food, music, or customs" because there are multiple cultures to take into consideration. An individual who identifies as multiracial may be very involved in one culture more than the others. How would they answer such a question? The pan-ethnic identity model may be more useful for individuals who identify as monoracial, leaving us to search for or create a model more applicable to individuals who identify as biracial or multiracial. Although the pan-ethnic identity theory was focused on race it was not surprising that it had direct relevance to both singular and border identity domains.

Additionally, this theory could be used as both a direct and an indirect measure for protean identity. There were no viable connections found to transcendent identity although one might have expected some connection.

Appearance Model

Physical features and appearance influence how individuals understand their racial identities (Stone, 1962). An individual's appearance relays information about how to define that individual (Brunsma & Rockquemore, 2001; Rockquemore, 1999). This is particularly important for individuals who identify as biracial, whose phenotype could be seen as ambiguous. Rockquemore asserts that phenotype, which includes skin color, hair texture, and facial features, is the first means of racial categorization. For example, having identifiably Black physical features may lead people to categorize an individual as Black, regardless of the rest of their appearance. However, an individual who is not visually identifiable as Black may use clothing, jewelry, and language to indicate group membership. Appearance allows individuals to express their own self-identification.

> *For example: Erica has tan skin, curly light brown hair, hazel eyes, and curvy features. When she wears t-shirts and jeans people ask her if she is mixed or Latina, or treat her as White. When she wears earrings in the shape of Africa, a dashiki, and brightly colored shoes people interact with her as if she is Black. Sometimes Erica wears a t-shirt, but usually she wears clothing with West African prints because she wants to assert her Blackness and show her connection to Black culture.*

The appearance model emphasizes phenotype and clothing, but is limited because this is not the sole way of understanding multiraciality. An individual may identify as biracial but choose not to assert their biraciality or multiraciality. This does not make them less "authentic" or "proud" of their heritage. In addition, the appearance model emphasizes the perceptions of others. While identity affirmation is very important in identity construction, it is not the only mechanism involved. An individual may feel comfortable identifying as biracial without garnering acknowledgment from others. Finally, the appearance model highlights singular culture—an individual is identified as or asserts their affiliation with one racial group, rather than multiple cultures. While useful in understanding how individuals are racially identified by others and use personal choice to assert their identity, the appearance model is just one part of the story.

Interactional Validation

In interacting with others, the outward show of identity discussed in the appearance model may be validated or invalidated by others, and this process can influence one's self-identification (Khanna, 2011; Rockquemore, 1999; Rockquemore &

Brunsma, 2008). Proposed by Rockquemore and Brunsma (2008), interactional validation is a social psychological process in which particular racial identities are considered legitimate and accepted by others, or illegitimate and ignored by others. They suggest that interactional validation is a key process influencing identity development, leading Black/White individuals to identify as biracial or as Black depending on the experiences they have with others.

Via in-depth interviews, Rockquemore and Brunsma (2008) and Khanna (2011) find that the Black/White respondents in their studies identify as either Black, White, or biracial. Black/White interviewees who feel rejected by both Blacks and Whites are more likely to identify as biracial, and Black/White biracials who feel rejected by Blacks and believe their asserted biracial identity is accepted by Whites are more likely to identify as biracial (Rockquemore & Brunsma, 2008). These findings are in line with Khanna and Johnson (2010), who find that the majority of Black/Whites identify as biracial, but those who identify monoracially tend to "pass" as Black. They note that this pattern is the reverse of passing in Jim Crow days: rather than passing as White, Black/White individuals tend to pass as Black (Khanna & Johnson, 2010). Black/White respondents tend to have childhood social networks with more Blacks, but they perceive experiencing negative treatment from Blacks in their network, which pushes them away from a Black identity and towards identifying as biracial (Rockquemore & Brunsma, 2008). Finally, Black/White interviewees who feel accepted by Blacks are more likely to identify as Black. Rockquemore and Brunsma (2008) distinguish between these groups as unvalidated and validated in their biracial identity, and some researchers argue that unvalidated biracial people are more likely to receive therapy or counseling (Milan & Keily, 2000). These various types of biracial identity are particularly useful for therapists and clinicians working with individuals who identify as biracial and have disparate experiences.

> *For example: Most of Shanice's friends growing up looked Black to her. Her friends would tell her she wasn't really Black, or say she was White because her mom is White. Shanice noticed she would be treated differently in stores than her Black friends—clerks were nicer to her and did not follow her around. Shanice felt she could not identify as Black because people who she identified as Black did not accept her into their group, and people outside the realm of Blackness* (i.e. *White people) did not treat her as Black. Shanice felt her biraciality was always highlighted. Since White people were relatively nice to her, she began talking to them more. Her White friends did not claim her as White, but accepted her as biracial. Shanice felt close to but simultaneously rejected by Blacks and accepted by Whites, pushing her towards a biracial identity.*

While very useful in clinical and therapy settings, the interactional validation approach is limited in understanding different forms of discrimination, education and health outcomes, and other outcomes that are imposed on groups of people regardless of how individuals self-identify.

The first "others" to validate or invalidate an individual's identity are usually family members since family are usually the first ones in contact with an individual. This individual is developing an identity within the context of their family experience and their society. As such, the previous theories connect the individual's experience to issues of identity. The appearance model is the only theory that seems to have direct applicability to the singular, border, and protean domains of the racial identity typology. It also had the distinction of having indirect applicability on all for domains, including transcendent identity formation (see Table 1).

Conclusion

We have reviewed a number of theories focusing on biracial and multiracial development and how they are measured across a number of perspectives focused on families. Each theoretical overview also includes a brief critique so that highlighted the limitation of each theory as it related to bi/multiracial individuals and families. By highlighting the gaps in our current knowledge about bi/multiraciality, those aiming to work effectively with multiracial individuals and their families are better equipped to do so. These theories highlight that biracial individuals should racially self-identify in the manner that best suits them, recognizing that this may vary from how their siblings identify or how their parents wish to identify them. Hence, practitioners working with biracial individuals must allow them to identify themselves as they see fit.

Future research should consider the self-described experiences of the biracial individual. Rather than imposing expectations, allowing biracial individuals to articulate their own experiences enables researchers and practitioners to have a more accurate understanding of one of the fastest growing racialized groups in the United States. Furthermore, race scholar, counselors, and other practitioners should allow respondents to check more than one box regarding racial categories and avoid reclassifying biracial individuals into a monoracial group. Bi/multiracial individuals have unique experiences that are connected to but different from others, and these experiences may shape how they interpret the world. Finally, theories of biraciality have taught us the nuances in biracial experiences and the impact of one's family and society. A theoretical framework of biraciality must incorporate the society and family in which a biracial individual develops, as this influences their racial identity and how they engage with the world around them. By considering previous theoretical works, we can work towards a more complex and dynamic set of theoretical schemas that more closely align with bi/multiracial experiences and interracial family processes to provide practitioners and scholars alike a diverse and complex toolkit of approaches, perspectives, and theories to draw from in order to more effectively understand bi/multiraciality.

Are These Theories Enough?

The theories presented here provide the groundwork for a cognitive understanding of bi/multiracial identities; unfortunately, none of these theories adequately captures the nuances of contemporary bi/multiracial experiences of individuals and families. Although some may have touched upon various aspects of biracial identity, they all tended to have flaws that rendered their applicability as problematic. Rather than thinking of the theories as obsolete or out of touch, it is preferable to see them as evolving. To that extent, we have attempted to formulate a crude theoretical construct that can be used with bi/multiracial families. We realize that this is only a starting point, but it is a new beginning in the area of family studies. It is time that we acknowledge the need to have theories that cover topics that make some uncomfortable, but at the same time are necessary because we cannot deny the changes that are taking place in the world.

In order to build a theory we must first understand what brings about what, why, and under what conditions these things can occur. The redeeming feature of our theory is that it can be either a proven fact or a contingent fact based on the appropriate circumstances leading to an outcome. Using a model based on Spens and Kovács (2006) we have observed that there are three parts of the research process that will help us in determining the utility of our theory. To begin we made observations about our topic, bi/multiracial families.

We understand and acknowledge that traditional theory building relies on both deductive and inductive approaches. However, there is a third approach known as abduction. In this approach, we establish reasoning from effect to causes or explanation. It produces a more problematic theoretical approach that must use some form of induction to verify the results (Ribeiro, Powell, & Baldwin, 1995). The reason for using an abductive approach in research and theory building is because (1) there is a "puzzling" observation or an anomaly that cannot be explained using established theory or (2) there is the need for a deliberate application of an alternative theory for explaining phenomenon (Andreewsky & Bourcier, 2000; Dubois & Gadde, 2002; Kirkeby, 1990; Kovács & Spens, 2005; Spens & Kovács, 2006, p. 377; Webb & Cortez, 2016).

Acknowledging racial status and its connection to the individual is a deliberate application of alternative theory and must be our first step. It can lead to abductive reasoning between establishing a theoretical framework and generating propositions for a theory. In short, what we are suggesting is that the existing theories observed in box 1 of our figure (known as a review of prior theoretical knowledge) can be both inductive and abductive as we think about ways to incorporate race into our model. The entire process of theory matching has an abductive quality (see Fig. 1). What we are saying in more direct terms is this—constructing theory that uses race as a factor, specifically as it relates to bi/multiracial individuals and families, will be complicated but it is not insurmountable. There has to be careful consideration of the groups, the existing theory, and a deliberate attempt to advance knowledge.

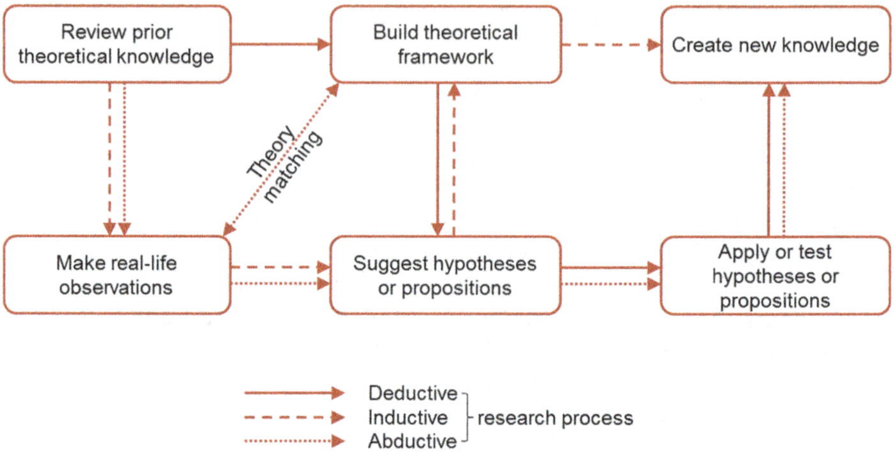

Fig. 1 Elements of theory building using deductive, inductive, and abductive research processes

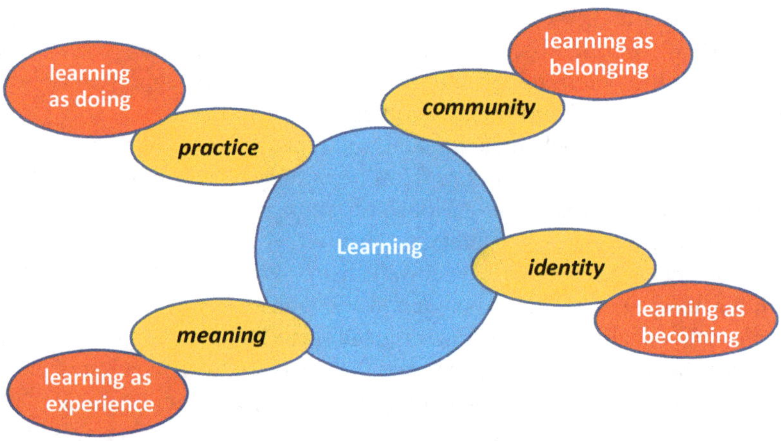

Fig. 2 The social learning theoretical framework using meaning, practice, community, and identity as critical components

As an example we propose to use the general theory of social learning (Wegner, 1999; Wegner, McDermott, & Snyder, 2002) as the theoretical framework by which to test our theory (see Fig. 2). Although used primarily in business we believe that it can have some merit here. There are four postulates that we have juxtaposed to our own postulates (see Table 2).

Figure 2 represents the general social learning model. The components of the model are also essential to our understanding of the idea of learning. The four elements of the model are *meaning, practice, community,* and *identity. These* are interconnected and allow for learning, change, and growth to take place. These elements work in concert to produce what is commonly known as learning.

Table 2 The elements of the social learning and social learning of race theoretical constructs

Social learning postulates	Social learning of race postulates
We are social beings	We are social beings of color
Knowledge is a matter of competence with respect to valued enterprises, e.g., growing up as a boy or girl	We are aware of and acknowledge our racial status—monoracial, biracial, or multiracial heritage
Knowing is a matter of participating in the pursuit of such enterprises that is of active engagement in the world	We acknowledge our racial status and how it can and does influence our social engagement with those who are both like and unlike ourselves
Meaning is our ability to experience the world and our engagement with it as meaningful—it is ultimately what learning is to produce	We learn to experience the world as people of color and that experience helps us to develop more fully

The four components of social learning are described in the following paragraph. *Meaning*—learning as experience is a way of talking about our changing ability—both individually and collectively. In essence, it is the experience to view life as meaningful and desirable. *Practice*—a way of telling about the shared historical and social resource frameworks and perspectives that can sustain mutual engagement. *Community*—a way of talking about the social configurations in which our experiences are defined as worth pursuing and our participation is recognizable as competence. *Identity*—a way of talking about how learning changes who we are and creates personal histories of becoming in the context of our communities. These pragmatic and useful features are elements that can be tested, elements for which hypothesis and propositions can be developed to further our understanding as they are related to individuals and families. The aim of all of this is to create new knowledge whereby we improve our understanding of biracial and multiracial people and families. Because of the utility of this theoretical approach, we could extend it to all families.

Although described here as an abstraction, the theory of social learning of race has considerable application possibilities. We expect that in the near future we will be able to supply some empirical data as to the validity of this approach that we are calling the Social learning of race. We believe that this is just a beginning; nevertheless our approach blends elements from both the family-based and individual-based theories, such as the bioecological and Kerwin-Ponterotto theories, that have important roles in family and individual development. While there is much work to be done in terms of theory development, we believe that we have demonstrated the viability, efficacy, and need for new paradigms for furthering our understanding of race as a critical component that must be included in family theories. In fact, our contribution is to provide analyses of prior research that provides us with an alternative view for explaining social phenomenon.

References

Andreewsky, E., & Bourcier, D. (2000). Abduction in language interpretation and law making. *Kybernetes, 29*(7/8), 836–845.

Bratter, J. (2007). Will 'Multiracial' survive to the next generation? The racial cassification of children of multiracial parents. *Social Forces, 86*(2), 821–849.

Bronfenbrenner, U. (1979). *The ecology of human development*. Cambridge, MA: Harvard University Press.

Brunsma, D., & Rockquemore, K. A. (2001). The new color complex: Appearance and biracial identity. *Identity, 1*(3), 225–246. https://doi.org/10.1207/S1532706XID0103_03

Campbell, M. E., & Eggerling-Boeck, J. (2006). What about the children? The psychological and social well-being of multiracial adolescents. *The Sociology Quarterly, 47*, 147–173.

Cheng, S., & Lively, K. J. (2009). Multiracial self-identification and adolescent outcomes: A social psychological approach to the marginal man theory. *Social Forces, 88*(1), 61–98.

Cornell, S., & Hartmann, D. (2007). *Ethnicity and race: Making identities in a changing world* (2nd ed.). Thousand Oaks, CA: Pine Forge Press.

Davis, F. J. (1991). *Who is black? One nation's definition*. University Park, PA: The Pennsylvania State University Press.

Dubois, A., & Gadde, L. E. (2002). Systematic combining: An abductive approach to case research. *Journal of Business Research, 55*, 553–560.

Gibbs, J. T. (1987). Identity and marginality: Issues in the treatment of biracial adolescents. *American Journal of Orthopsychiatry, 57*, 265–278.

Herman, S. N. (1970). *Israelis and jews: A continuity of an identity*. New York: Random House.

Hirschman, C. (2004). The origins and demise of the concept of race. *Population and Development Review, 30*(3), 385–415.

Hollinger, D. A. (2003). Amalgamation and hypodescent: The question of ethnoracial mixture in the history of the United States. *The American Historical Review, 108*(5), 1363–1390.

Jordan, W. D. (2014). Historical origins of the one-drop racial rule in the United States. *Journal of Critical Mixed Race Studies, 1*(1), 99–132.

Kerwin, C., & Ponterotto, J. G. (1995). Biracial identity development: Theory and research. In J. G. Ponterotto, J. M. Casas, L. A. Suziki, & C. M. Alexander (Eds.), *Handbook of multicultural counseling*. Thousand Oaks, CA: Sage Publications.

Kerwin, C., Ponterotto, J. G., Jackson, B. J., & Harris, A. (1993). Racial identity in biracial children: A qualitative investigation. *Journal of Counseling Psychology, 40*, 221–231.

Khanna, N. (2011). *Biracial in America: Forming and performing racial identity*. Lanham, MD: Lexington Books.

Khanna, N., & Johnson, C. (2010). Passing as Black: Racial identity work among biracial Americans. *Social Psychology Quarterly, 73*(4), 380–397.

Kirkeby, O. F. (1990). Abduction. In H. Andersen (Ed.), *Vetenskapsteori och metodlära. Introduktion, Studnetlittearatur*, Lund. Translated from Danish by Carl G. Liungman: 1994.

Kovács, G., & Spens, K. M. (2005). Abductive reasoning in logistic research. *International Journal of Physical Distribution and Logistic Management, 35*(2), 132–144.

Mead, G. H. (1934). *Mind, self, and society*. Chicago: University of Chicago Press.

Milan, S., & Keily, M. (2000). Biracial youth and families in therapy: Issues and interventions. *Journal of Marital and Family Therapy, 26*(3), 305–315.

Morning, A. (2000). Who is multiracial? Definitions and decisions. *Sociological Imagination, 37*(4), 209–229.

Morning, A. (2009). Toward a sociology of racial conceptualization for the 21st century. *Social Forces, 87*, 1167–1192.

Omi, M., & Winant, H. (1994). *Racial formation in the United States* (2nd ed.). New York, NY: Routledge.

Park, R. E. (1928). Human migration and the marginal man. *American Journal of Sociology, 33*(6), 391–407.

Park, R. E. (1931). Mentality of racial hybrids. *American Journal of Sociology, 36*(4), 534–551.
Phinney, J. (1989). Stages of ethnic identity development in minority group adolescents. *Journal of Early Adolescence, 9*(1–2), 34–49.
Phinney, J. (1990). Ethnic identity in adolescents and adults: Review of research. *Psychological Bulletin, 108*, 499–514.
Phinney, J. (1992). The multi-group ethnic identity measure: A new scale for use with diverse groups. *Journal of Adolescent Research, 7*, 156–176.
Poston, W. S. C. (1990). The biracial identity development model: A needed addition. *Journal of Counseling & Development, 69*, 152–155.
Ribeiro, R. A., Powell, P. L., & Baldwin, J. F. (1995). Uncertainty in decision-making: An abductive perspective. *Decision Support Systems, 13*, 183–193.
Rockquemore, K. A. (1999). Between black and white exploring the 'biracial' experience. *Race and Society, 1*(2), 197–212.
Rockquemore, K. A., & Brunsma, D. L. (2008). *Beyond black: Biracial identity in america* (2nd ed.). Lanham, MD: Rowman & Littlefield Publishers.
Saperstein, A., & Penner, A. (2012). Racial fluidity and inequality in the United States. *American Journal of Sociology, 118*(3), 676–727.
Spens, K. M., & Kovács, G. (2006). A content analysis of research approaches in logistic research. *International Journal of Physical Distribution and Logistic Management, 36*(5), 374–390.
Sprey, J. (1969). The family as a system of conflict. *Journal of Marriage and the Family, 31*(4), 699–706.
Sprey, J. (2000). Theorizing in family studies: Discovering process. *Journal of Marriage and the Family, 62*(1), 18–31.
Stone, G. P. (1962). Appearance and the self. In A. M. Rose (Ed.), *Human behavior and the social processes: An interactionist approach* (pp. 86–116). New York: Houghton Mifflin.
Stonequist, E. V. (1935). The problem of the marginal man. *American Journal of Sociology, 41*(1), 1–12.
Stonequist, E. V. (1937). *The marginal man: A study in personality and culture conflict*. New York, NY: Scribner/Simon & Schuster.
Waters, M. C. (1990). *Ethnic options: Choosing identities in America*. Berkeley, CA: University of California Press.
Webb, F. J., Burrell, J., & Jefferson, S. G. (2017). Social constitutionality of race in America: Some meanings for bi/multiracial families. In R. N. Roy & A. Rollins (Eds.), *Biracial families: Crossing boundaries, blending cultures, and challenging racial ideologies*. New York: Springer.
Webb, F. J., & Cortez, A. (2016). Creating a program of success for underrepresented students at research institutions. In J. M. Janangelo (Ed.), *A critical look at institutional mission: A guide for writing program administrators* (pp. 59–74). Anderson, SC: Parlor Press.
Wegner, E. (1999). *Communities of practices: Learning, meaning, and identity*. Cambridge, UK: Cambridge University Press.
Wegner, E., McDermott, R., & Snyder, W. M. (2002). *Cultivating communities of practice*. Cambridge, MA: Harvard Business School Press.
White, J. M., & Klein, D. M. (2008). *Family theories* (3rd ed.). Thousand Oaks: Sage Publications.

Part II
Family Formation

Partnering Across Race

James E. Brooks and Jeremy Lynch

Opening Story

We begin this chapter on partnering across race by introducing the story of Jeremiah, a 26-year-old Black man, and Caitlyn a 27-year-old White woman, from the same midsize Midwest town in the United States. At the time of their interview, Jeremiah and Caitlyn had been in a romantic relationship for approximately 8 years and were nearing the 4-year anniversary of their wedding. The couple began dating in high school and described a courtship of about 1 year. As Jeremiah and Caitlyn recounted the beginning of their relationship, Jeremiah describes how Caitlyn's blunt challenge about his behavior set him on a path of self-reflection that ultimately led to the decision to go to "the next level." What follows is an excerpt from their longer interview.

Caitlyn: That's when I said, "So you can sleep with a White girl, but you can't date one?"

Jeremiah: Yeah. That really shook me. I had all kinds of thoughts. Am I being racist? Does she have a point? What does that say about me? The truth is, the relationship that I was in when we met was with a White [girl]. But that relationship was secret, anyone who knew about the relationship didn't know she was White, with the exception of Caitlyn and a cousin who was there when we first met. At the time that she asked me that question, I had only been involved with two other people since the first one. One was White and the other was Black. In the moment when she asked, the only legitimate reason I could come up with for the discrepancy between choosing to sleep with White [girls] but not date them was because

J. E. Brooks (✉)
Department of Psychology, Tennessee State University, Nashville, TN, USA
e-mail: jbrook42@tnstate.edu

J. Lynch
Department of Psychology, Fisk University, Nashville, TN, USA

R. Nazarinia Roy, A. Rollins (eds.), *Biracial Families*,
https://doi.org/10.1007/978-3-319-96160-6_4

of how society would respond. How differently we would be treated and the type of racism that we would face. All of the other reasons that I could come up with weren't convincing to me, primarily because they seemed racist or at least would be if they were suggested by a White person. In the end, I knew I wanted more than hook-ups with the other women and I knew that if we were to start dating it would be a public affair. I took a Black female friend to our Senior prom. She helped to give me some courage to ask Caitlyn to start dating. I guess she also knew about my previous relationship and assured me that my experience with Caitlyn's family would probably be different than the one with the previous [relationship]. The day after our prom, I told Caitlyn that I wanted to "try us," through a text message. Just like a true gentleman.

Caitlyn: … Looking back, I think we were both naïve about what exactly we would face in terms of disapproval. Especially regarding how much the little stuff would hurt or annoy us. I had a family member disown me after Jeremiah attended my graduation party after our ceremony. And I am sure there were people who didn't come to the wedding. We respond differently as we have gotten older and are concerned about different things as we raise our biracial children. It has all been worth it.

Introduction

With each passing year, the United States becomes a more racially and ethnically diverse country. The likelihood that an individual will cross paths with someone of a different race continues to increase; thus, the probability that one may enter into a romantic relationship with someone of a different race also increases. In fact, 15% of marriages in the United States were considered interethnic in 2010 (Wang, 2012). If you include cohabiting couples that number would increase (see Chap. 5 for more information). Coinciding with the increased prevalence of interracial relationships has been an increased acceptance of such unions. Public approval of interracial unions has improved since the US Supreme Court ruled that the anti-miscegenation laws that outlawed interracial unions were unconstitutional in 1967. A 2008, Gallup Poll showed that 87% of people polled indicated they approve of marriages between Blacks and Whites compared to 20% in 1968 (Newport, 2013). Interracial couples are a significant faction of romantic relationships, but intraracial relationships are still more typical. Researchers have sought to understand and explain the experiences of partners in interracial relationships. At times, these researchers have investigated interracial relationships as deviant and at other times they have sought to understand their internal processes as well as the resilience and strength that these relationships exhibit.

Historically, research on interracial relationships was informed by the public antipathy for these unions and reified sentiments of interracial relationships as inherently dysfunctional and inferior to intraracial relationships. For example, researchers hypothesized that White men and women who marry Black partners do so out of rebellion against their parents or White partners were characterized as experiencing neurotic conflict and poor self-esteem (Brayboy, 1966; Brown, 1987; Smith, 1966). Other scholars have suggested that people of color marry White partners as a way of "marrying up" in a complex exchange of White social status from one partner for the higher socioeconomic status of another partner; this has been termed the *caste-exchange hypothesis* (Kalmijn, 1993). Still other historical but popular commentary on interracial relationships proclaimed that partners were fueled by lust and that attraction across racial lines was sexually driven and lacked a substantial foundation. Unfortunately, some of these views, or variants of them, are still held by some members of society (Lalonde, Giguere, Fontaine, & Smith, 2007).

Much of the current research on interracial relationships was developed to counter historical explanations of interracial dating that demonized either the relationship or the members in the union. For example, researchers have not found support for the claim that people who engage in interracial relationships are more sexually active than people who do not (Yancey, 2003). It is more likely that partners in interracial relationships enter into their unions for many of the same reasons as those in intraracial relationships, such as shared interests or attractive personalities (Lewis, Yancey, & Bletzer, 1997). The *caste-exchange hypothesis,* that successful people of color trade their socioeconomic status for the social status of a White partner, has had support in some types of interracial unions (e.g., pairings of Black men and White women; Kalmijn, 1993); explicit investigation of this hypothesis found that interracial pairings that appeared to support the *caste-exchange hypothesis* may better be understood as another example of the principle of homogamy in which people seek relationship partners that are similar to themselves. Fu (2008) found that, just as in intraracial relationships, people in interracial relationships were matched on characteristics such as age, education, and socioeconomic status. What has been interpreted as "marrying up" may be marrying the same but across racial lines.

The more recent work of scholars on interracial relationships has moved the field forward in that it no longer demonizes those in interracial relationships and, to some extent, has normalized these unions by comparing them to intraracial relationships. However, some of the research is atheoretical and does not examine the processes within interracial relationships. Furthermore, in an effort to normalize interracial relationships, meaningful differences can be overlooked. Research that focuses on the similarities between intraracial and interracial relationships may miss the reality that, despite their increased prevalence and reported acceptance, interracial relationships can have a very different lived experience than intraracial couples, which include racism, hostile nonverbal behavior, and feelings of unease (Estep, 2011; Forry, Leslie, & Letiecq, 2007; Foster, 2009; Killian, 2013).

Description of Chapter

In this chapter, we explore what is known about partnering across race; who does it, for what reasons, what does it look like, and what are the unforeseen influences. This review is, by nature, multidisciplinary, as capturing the phenomenon of interracial relationships requires a multitude of methodologies and thought. We use the term interracial to describe romantic relationships in which the partners identify as belonging to a different racial group than his/her significant other. We also use the phrase partnering across race to encompass the broad process of choosing to be in an interracial relationship which includes sexual and romantic attraction, relationship initiation, and commitment. We use the opening vignette, disclosures of individuals in interracial relationships, and examples from popular media to demonstrate the broader ideas represented in our review of the literature.

Literature Review

The Influence of Individual Variables

Based on data from a national survey, people of color, Black, Asian, and Latino men and women reported similar rates of having dated someone of a different race (56.5%, 57.1%, and 55.4%, respectively) and White men and women reported significantly lower rates of interracial dating (37.8%; Yancey, 2002). Across these racial groups, there were two characteristics that consistently predicted whether someone had dated a member of a different race, their religious affiliation, and their age. Those who identified as Catholic were less likely to have dated someone of a different race. Religiosity (frequency of attendance at religious services) has been associated with a decreased likelihood of dating a person of a different race (Perry, 2016). It has also been found that participants with Jewish mothers or fathers are more likely than those of other denominations, in particular Protestants, to have dated someone of a different race. As Perry (2016) writes, some have argued that this may be because those of Jewish faith are more liberal, educated, and urban than other religious groups.

Another individual variable that influences some but not all racial groups is gender. In all racial groups except for Asian daters (Asian men and women equally date outside their race), men are more likely to have dated someone of a different race (Yancey, 2002). Generally, women's choices in romantic partners are more highly scrutinized compared to men's (Miller, Olson, & Fazio, 2004). In addition, more liberal political attitudes compared to conservative attitudes have been associated with interracial dating among White and Latino participants and an integrated context, either in racially diverse schools or neighborhoods, was associated with having dated someone of a different race across all racial groups. Several nationwide studies (e.g., Yancey, 2007; Yancey & Yancey, 1998) have found that the prevalence of interracial dating and openness to such relationships vary by geographical region with the Southwestern United States exhibiting a greater prevalence of interracial relationships. For some, the proximity of people of different races may inhibit the opportunity to date someone of a different race. Online dating has removed geographic barriers, that once existed, and researchers have used the opportunity to examine how partnering across race is affected. Yancey (2009) explored the personal ads of 1076 individuals to identify which race's online daters indicated that they were willing to date. He found several demographic influences on interest in partners of different races. Based on the profiles of Asian, Black, Latino, and White users, Asian men and women reported the greatest openness to a member of any race while Latino and White men and women were less likely than Asian daters but more open than Black men and women. Consistent with in-person dating research, it was found that, across race, women were less likely than men to indicate an interest in dating someone of any race. Furthermore, women were less likely to indicate a preference for a partner of a specific race other than their own.

Whereas Yancey (2009) investigated willingness to partner across race, Mendelsohn, Shaw Taylor, Fiore, and Cheshire (2014) examined actual contacts across race in an online context. Their research was limited to the reports of preferences and experiences of Black and White users of an online dating site, but augmented Yancey's study well. They analyzed the number of contacts initiated, with same race and other race users, and the number of initial contacts that users responded to on a popular dating website. The finding of greater interest in interracial dating among men compared to women was supported in this study. They also found that Black daters were over ten times more likely to initiate contact with a White dater than a White dater was to initiate contact with a Black counterpart. To a lesser extent, Black daters were also more likely to reciprocate initial contact from a White dater than vice versa.

By expanding the pool of potential daters, Internet dating may have the effect of increasing the opportunity for people of all races to date someone of a different race; the same may not necessarily be true for in-person contact. Structural diversity (the racial composition of an institution) has a differential impact on White students compared to students of color (Bowman, 2012). The more racially diverse a college campus, the greater the likelihood that a White student has dated someone of a different race; however structural diversity has no effect on students of color in their experience with dating a person of a different race. While one might expect greater structural diversity it does not have a direct and universal implication for interracial dating, regardless of race (Harper & Yeung, 2015). It is likely that structural diversity increases the opportunity to build relationships across race, but that platonic relationship building is most important in increasing the likelihood of partnering across race.

The Intersection of Race and Gender

Thus far, our review has demonstrated that race and gender influence who is more likely to partner across race, but this too is made more complex when considering the implications of the intersection of gender and race as it relates to partnering. In their line of research, Galinsky, Hall, and Cuddy (2013) concluded that there is a gendered nature to racial stereotypes regarding Asian, Black, and White people. That is, by having participants rate various traits associated with stereotypes of

Black and Asian people, the researchers were able to determine that Black people are perceived as being more masculine than White and Asian people, and that Asian people are stereotyped as more feminine than Black and White people. The gendering of race has implications for romantic attraction and interest in dating across race. Galinsky and colleagues went on to demonstrate that, in a heterosexual context, White women reported greater interest in Black men than Asian men and that White men preferred Asian women to Black women. In a sense, Black men are hyper-masculinized because of gendered racial stereotypes and Asian women are hyper-feminized through the same process.

The research of Galinsky and colleagues is also captured in ways in which the intersection of race and gender is explored in mainstream American films. For example, the feminization of Asian men in American films has resulted in the near nonexistence of a lead Asian male as a realistic romantic interest. The 1984 interracial relationship between Long Duk Dong in "Sixteen Candles" (Hughes, 1984), portrayed by Geede Wanatabe, and Lumberjack, portrayed by Debbie Pollack, was a gender role-swapping romance rattled with offensive stereotypes. To be clear, there is nothing problematic with nonconforming gender roles, but the portrayal of the relationship between a small-framed Asian man and taller and more imposing White woman was never meant to be taken seriously by the audience and the scripted absurdity of the movie ensured that it was understood as a comical side story to the protagonists' teenage angst. The 2000 film, "Romeo Must Die" (Bartkowiak, 2000), is an action-packed, martial arts-filled retelling of Romeo and Juliet, in which Chinese actor Jet-Li's reimagined Romeo stars across from Black actress Aaliyah as Juliet. Vargas (2007) recounts that the theatrical ending of the two actors embraced in a tight hug actually replaces the original ending in which the couple share a kiss. The reports are that there was objection to the on-screen romance from communities of color and suggest that the discomfort with some non-White interracial relationships is just as strong as that between non-White and White partners. The result is a film in which the romantic aspect of the relationship is never acknowledged on screen. The struggle to present a realistic romance with an Asian male interest is also prevalent on the small screen.

The television sitcoms *Big Bang Theory* (Lorre, 2017) and *Selfie* (Kapnek, 2014) have also attempted to explore Asian men and romance in an interracial context. Kunal Nayyar's character on Big Bang Theory is an Indian scientist who is utterly inept in building relationships with women, romantic or otherwise. To be fair, this interpersonal difficulty is not limited to his character; the entire male cast has what might be understood as peculiar relationships with women, but Nayyar's character is likely the most debilitated. For the first five seasons of the show, *Raj* was unable to even speak to women unless he was intoxicated. By the time he overcame this hurdle, all of the other male leads had developed a rich romantic life, leaving the impression that he was the least desirable of the otherwise all White cast. As another example, John Cho's character in *Selfie* was a promising departure from portrayals of Asian men as an inept romantic interest in an interracial context. As the first Asian male lead in a romantic sitcom on a major network, many were excited when his character—a successful marketing professional—and the White female lead

(Karen Gillan) in need of a new image and public relations strategy were beginning to entertain a romantic relationship among high sexual tension. Unfortunately, the show was cancelled in its first season before this highly anticipated relationship could come to fruition. Some suspect that the show was not maintained due to the interracial nature of the relationship and that the lead male was Korean.

Though the impact of the intersection of gender and race is strongly indicated in the feminization of Asian men, it is not limited to this demographic. Lalonde et al. (2007) used a measure in their study that examined the stereotypes that people endorse about Black-White interracial relationships. The items on the scale indicate that people perceive the motives for entering into an interracial relationship quite differently based on gender and race. For example, hypothetical Black male partners were perceived to be interested in attaining greater social status while Black female partners who date White men were believed to hold denigrated beliefs about the value of Black men. Furthermore, hypothetical White female partners were almost exclusively motivated by the physicality of Black men whereas White male partners were perceived to be motivated by a "guilt complex" (presumably from the atrocities of slavery) in addition to sexual attraction. These examples underscore the complex intersection of race and gender and reflect the discomfort that continues to exist regarding interracial partnering.

There is an ambivalence that exists among the broader society about partnering across race that can simultaneously allow for intimacy but is also repulsed by it. As such, progress can be seen in the proliferation of interracial representations in television dramas such as *Grey's Anatomy, How to Get Away with Murder,* and *Scandal* (Rhimes, 2017a, 2017b, 2017c) but they also use interracial relationships as a vehicle to expose racial tensions and sometimes presents these relationships as problematic. For example, from 2016 to 2017 two major motion pictures were released that showcased interracial relationships as central to their story. The first, Loving (Nichols, 2016), was a biopic that outlined the relationship, and to a lesser extent the legal journey, of the couple (White male and Black female) at the center of the Loving vs. Virginia decision that struck down the anti-miscegenation laws of the United States as unconstitutional. The other, Get Out (Peele, 2017), was a sort of horror film spin of Guess Who's Coming to Dinner (Kramer, 1967), and featured a Black male who is introduced to the unsuspecting family of his White female partner; mind control, microaggressions, and murder ensue. Both films, Loving and Get Out, received critical acclaim. Loving received several nominations for the Academy Awards and Get Out was something of a cult phenomenon that at the time of this writing had 99% favorability rating of movie critics on rottentomatoes.com (Get Out, 2017).

On the one hand, the diversity of representation of interracial relationships is encouraging; however we would like to argue that the reality the authors could not view Loving because no theatres in the surrounding area played the film and that only one theatre played Get Out suggests that the nature on interracial intimacy still receives an ambivalent response. The Black male/White female pairing has long been identified as the relationship that receives the greatest public opposition, from the motivations of the anti-miscegenation laws to the public outcry at the choice to have this pairing depicted in an Internet commercial for a US-based cereal company. We suspect that it is no coincidence that the US culture would garner great success for a movie that depicts this pairing as problematic and as something that garners suspicion and that is possibly inauthentic.

Ultimately, opportunity to date across race and the development of meaningful interracial friendships, gender, and race are fairly stable predictors of who is willing to and who actually engages in partnering across race. Whether researchers investigate specific pairings (e.g., Black-White partnerships) or interracial pairings more broadly also influences conclusions. Furthermore, understanding the implications of the intersection of race and gender is important not only for who is willing to and does date but how interracial daters are perceived. Outside of demographic variables, there are other influencers of whether someone will partner across race. We now turn our attention to the role of ideologies on interracial romance.

The Impact of Attitudes and Ideologies

When it comes to the role of ideologies or how people think about race, it is an intuitive conclusion to suspect that individuals holding a racial animus toward members of a different race (e.g., racism) would be less likely to partner across race (Schueths, 2015). However, there is an existing and growing body of work that suggests that ideologies, attitudes, and ways of thinking that would not be associated with the propensity to partner across race actually have an influential role. Some of these ideologies (e.g., colorblindness) actually have a counterintuitive relationship with the propensity to partner across race. However, much of the evidence is consistent with expected outcomes.

A group of researchers hosted a speed-dating event to investigate the influence of several character traits in a live action dating environment (Eastwick, Richeson, Son, & Finkel, 2009). Among Black and White speed daters, they found that participants who self-identified as more politically conservative were less likely to want a follow-up date with a speed-dating partner of another race among White daters. In the context of partnering across race, results indicated that greater political conservatism among White participants was associated with less interracial attraction. Conversely, political conservatism had no effect on Black speed daters' interracial attraction. This pattern of results is consistent with Yancey (2007), who found that greater political conservatism was associated with a reduction in willingness to date anyone of another race, not just Black men or women. The conclusion regarding political conservatism for interracial relationships is different than that of racial prejudice. For White people and people of color, greater prejudice is associated with less willingness, interest, or desire to enter into a relationship with someone of a different race. Political conservatism, however, demonstrates a different pattern for White people and people of color.

In theorizing about why some ideologies may have different implications based on group membership, Eastwick et al. (2009) and Yancey (2007) draw on the work of Sidanius and colleagues. Specifically, they indicated that political conservatism is a type of ideology that implicitly reinforces a racial hierarchy that promotes group-based separation by race and dominance of one group over others. To endorse such a system would have different implications for those who occupy a higher place in the hierarchy than those who occupy a lesser place. Ideologies or ways of thought that maintain a racial hierarchy are understood to be hierarchy-enhancing ideologies, and those that challenge the hegemony are considered hierarchy attenuating. Considering the implications of conservatism on interracial dating, it would be considered a hierarchy-enhancing ideology.

Several other researchers have applied this line of reasoning to understanding the dynamics of partnering across race with other ideologies. Social dominance orientation (SDO), the extent to which one desires that their in-group dominates and is superior to out-groups, was used to understand the attitudes toward interracial marriages and relationships among Black and White Canadians (Lalonde et al., 2007). The researchers applied the theory of ideological asymmetry (Sidanius, Pratto, & Rabinowitz, 1994) and concluded that greater SDO was associated with a greater opposition to interracial dating among high-status White participants. They also concluded that SDO had no effect on attitudes toward interracial dating and transracial adoption among individuals who occupy a lower status in the social hierarchy (Black men and women) as there is no group benefit to maintaining a hierarchy that continues to disadvantage one's own group.

Another ideology about intergroup relations, colorblindness, has been described as an ultramodern form of racism that serves to maintain a racial hierarchy (Neville, Awad, Brooks, Flores, & Bluemel, 2013). In the racial hierarchy of the United States, White men and women enjoy privilege and access to power unlike that which is experienced by people of color. In this way, the values, customs, and experiences of people of color are perceived as deviant or inferior as compared to a White (mainstream) standard. Societal narratives suggest that by claiming to not "see color," people are essentially leading a life free of bias in which they cannot be racist. Neville et al. (2013) argue that claiming to ignore race and the system of racism which privileges some, and to dismiss the role of race in people's lived experiences, is to actually reinforce the existing hierarchy. In essence, no race talk means no change. In this way, colorblindness, or as they identify, color-blind racial ideology, is a hierarchy-enhancing ideology.

Color-blind racial ideology (CBRI) poses both an intellectually and practically intriguing conundrum. Colorblindness is sometimes understood to be an ideal approach to race relations, and yet it paradoxically is more likely a detrimental mentality. Grounded by the asymmetrical ideology hypothesis, Brooks and Neville (2016) explored color-blind racial ideology in the context of romantic attraction. They measured Black and White men's level of romantic attraction to both Black and White women. They found that among White men, higher endorsement of color-blind racial ideology was associated with less romantic attraction toward women of a different race and that among Black men it was unrelated to attraction toward women of a different race. Similar to Eastwick et al. (2009), Brooks and Neville found less in-group favoritism among Black men who more strongly endorsed the hierarchy-enhancing ideology than those who agreed less with the ideology. Conversely, the authors also explored a hierarchy-attenuating ideology of multiculturalism, the notion that cultural differences should be acknowledged and appreciated. They found that greater endorsement of multiculturalism was associated with greater attraction to women of a different race regardless of the male's race, adding further evidence of the importance of ideologies to understanding partnering across race.

The opening vignette for this chapter provides an anecdote of how ideologies influence partnering across race. We can see the telling signs of Jeremiah considering thought/ideology on his decision to enter into a romantic relationship with his wife. Certainly, Caitlyn bringing to Jeremiah's attention the hypocrisy in his decision to only engage in sexual relationships with White women touches a bit on what he believes to be an appropriate or even safe level of interracial interaction, but there are more telling signs of the influence of ideology on Jeremiah's decision to enter into a romantic relationship with his wife. Jeremiah states that he struggled with why he has limited his depth of intimacy with White women, but that most reasoning would seem racist if a White person were to espouse them. We would argue that just in this statement Jeremiah has touched on the asymmetry hypothesis, that ideologies can mean something different for an individual based on their position in the racial hierarchy. Perhaps, Jeremiah had concerns about the importance of cultural preservation or about preferences for same-race women or even stereotypes about White women that held him back in his choice to partner across race. Whatever the reservations were, as Jeremiah considered race and the implications of his choice based on social category, he made different choices than what he had made prior to that time.

Research on the impact of ideologies on partnering across race paints a rather complex picture. Some ideologies, such as color-blind racial ideology which enhances the racial hierarchy, influence attraction and willingness to partner across race in the anticipated manner. Other ideologies that, on the surface, would seem to be unrelated to willingness to partner across race, such as political conservatism, have been shown to influence the process. Furthermore, as in the case of CBRI, the impact of an individual's thoughts about race can be rather complex and be influenced by group membership. The framework of understanding ideologies as hierarchy enhancing or attenuating is important in understanding partnering across race. To meaningfully apply such a lens is to require thoughtful investigation into the real implications of each ideology for race relations beyond what it suggests or claims at the surface level. Furthermore, an apt understanding also requires an explanation of the nuances of what it means to hold an ideology based on the position that one's group holds in the socially accepted hierarchy.

Experiences of Interracial Relationships

While current research has challenged early negative hypotheses and normalized interracial relationships, it is clear that experiences of those in interracial relationships are different than those in intraracial relationships. Interracial relationships represent a blatant visual challenge to the societal norm of homogamy and race remains a contentious topic in the United States. As such, partners in interracial relationships are subject to anecdotal and systemic opposition. Despite legal rights, interracial relationships of Black men and White women have recently been denied marriage licenses by state employees and banned from church membership (Estep, 2011; Foster, 2009). Furthermore, the lasting impact of anti-miscegenation laws and institutional practices that are unfavorable toward interracial relationships, such as Bob Jones University's ban on interracial dating (removed in 2000; BJU, 2008), continue to communicate to members of society that interracial relationships are problematic.

Partners in interracial relationships often contend with the negative perceptions of others. A frequent occurrence among interracial couples that emerged from interviews was the assumption of friends and family that difficulties in the relationship were a result of cultural differences (Wieling, 2003). This is not an innocuous assumption, as cultural differences are often cited as concerns for interracial couples. However, the underlying message of such a statement suggests that because the issue stems from differences in culture it is something that cannot be resolved, or rather it is such an ingrained difference that surmounting it would be difficult. In response to interactions with disapproving others, some interracial couples distance themselves from groups or settings they believe will be unwelcoming to their relationship (Hibbler & Shinew, 2002).

In an effort to preserve the cohesiveness of their family, partners in interracial relationships develop tactics to avoid scrutiny. For example, one couple composed of a Black woman and White man described how they sit separate from one another when riding public transportation when traveling in a certain part of their hometown (Killian, 2002). Several couples mentioned that they will send one member of the relationship to test out an environment and assess the likelihood that they will be welcomed, or at least not targeted, prior to going to an unfamiliar place (Hibbler & Shinew, 2002). It is not unheard of for interracial couples to feel isolated, to have more restrictive contact with others (Daneshpour, 2003), or to shut down from parts of the outside world after numerous negative experiences (Henderson, 2000).

However, despite the opposition that they may receive for being a part of a marginalized relationship (Lehmiller & Konkel, 2012), many partners in interracial relationships persevere. As a result of their interracial partnering, successful interracial relationships develop and possess strengths that may not be as essential among their intraracial counterparts. Leslie and Letiecq (2004) found that being in an interracial marriage helped partners to be more aware of their own racial identity as well as that of their partner. The authors posit that racial awareness played a role in marital quality and satisfaction because of tolerance and appreciation of each other's culture and background. Leslie and Letiecq (2004) also found that there were no differences in relationship satisfaction between interracial and intraracial relationships. Partners in interracial relationships are active in their responses to the outside world while also addressing the developmental issues that occur in a romantic relationship. Henderson (2000) noted that interracial couples were more focused on "external issues of influence" than their intraracial counterparts, suggesting that interracial couples were particularly sensitive to potential threats from outsiders. However, they are able to discuss relationship matters with important relatives and friends just as intraracial couples do (Killian, 2001).

Relationship Initiation

The implications of racial difference can be seen at the very beginning of the interracial relationships, even before the relationship has begun, at the point of initiation. The influence of race at the initiation of romantic relationships is made most evident by the work of Harris and Kalbfleisch (2000). Harris and Kalbfleisch asked 120 Black and White men and women to indicate the type of strategies they would employ if they were to meet someone with whom they would like to start a romantic relationship. Within their sample, they found that there were three groups of participants: those who did not change their strategies for securing a date, those that were moderately influenced by race, and those for whom the race of the person of interest had a significant impact on their initiation strategies.

For approximately one-third of the sample, there appeared to be a minimal impact of race. These participants preferred the use of hinting strategies to pursue a date (e.g., discussing mutual interests and related events, flirting with the target by letting him/her know he/she finds the target attractive). Of the 41 participants who did not adjust their relationship initiation tactics based on the race of the other, more than half indicated that there was little possibility that they would date someone of a different race. As such, it is possible that these participants, because of a lack of possibility or interest in dating a person of another race, simply assumed that their actions would be the same since they were removed from the possibility on interracial dating. The lack of change in initiation strategies was demonstrated in some of the interviews conducted by the first author. Kelly, a 19-year-old White woman who had not been in an interracial relationship, best captured the uncertainty of relationship initiation with a person of a different race. She suspected that she would engage in the same behaviors to initiate a relationship with a man of different race as she would to initiate a relationship with a White man. "I would probably, talk about some of the things he was interested in and flirt a little … you know tell him how good he looks or something like that. I'm not really sure, but I guess that is what I would do." Her uncertainty about dating a person of a different race likely impacts her assumption that she would behave in the same manner. On the other hand, Mark, a 23-year-old White man who had been dating a Latina for approximately 7 months, also indicated little change in his initiation strategies. "I've always been pretty good at dating. I'm never really single unless I want to be and when I am ready to start something new, it's always the same thing. Show a little charm, identify shared interests, spend some money to woo them. It sounds kind of formulaic, but honestly there isn't much to it, regardless of who she is."

For the majority of the sample, race of the target did have an impact on how they would initiate the relationship. There was variation in exactly how strategies differed for people in this group. For most of these participants, there was a tendency to use less active and more passive strategies at courting. For example, when interested in a person of their same race, these individuals might explicitly ask whether the other person were available for a dating relationship or express their attraction to the other directly. However, when interested in a person of a different race, the same individuals may, instead, wait for the other person to indicate interest in them or wait for their romantic interest to initiate a discussion of entering into a dating relationship. Some even reported the reverse pattern in which they would become more direct if they were interested in someone of a different race compared to when they were interested in someone of the same race. (For a full discussion of the effects of race on relationship initiation see Harris & Kalbfleisch, 2000.)

We proffer that the participants that indicated no change in their relationship initiation strategies may be operating from a color-blind racial ideology. As noted earlier, this CBRI worldview has proven problematic in that what is espoused is not actually practiced, and that this may often be a manifestation of more socially "acceptable" racial animus. However, it is interesting to note, as in the case of Eric, that individuals with a CBRI can be found in interracial relationships. Qualitatively, the interpersonal dynamics within interracial relationships that minimize race can be different than those that do acknowledge the importance of race. For example, Killian's (2002) interviews with interracial couples provide examples of times when racialized experiences of people of color were negated or discounted by their partners. These microaggressions seem especially salient in couples in which one partner espouses a worldview that endorses silence with regard to race. We also suggest the likelihood of not adjusting initiation strategies or being aware that courting may be different across racial lines is more likely to be endorsed by White partners than partners of color as the former are more likely to espouse a CBRI (Oh, Choi, Neville, Anderson, & Landrum-Brown, 2010).

The Role of Social Support

Once a relationship has begun, the import of social support becomes evident. Societal sentiment, or social support, is often cited as an encourager *and* deterrent to interracial relationships (Clark-Ibáñez & Felmlee, 2004) and has implications for relationship satisfaction (Cox, Wexler, Rusbult, & Gaines Jr., 1997). The social perception around interracial relationships has become more positive since the ban of anti-miscegenation laws and practices across the country beginning in the 1960s (Newport, 2013). Social support that individuals receive for breaking the social norm of dating someone of the same race is influenced by a multitude of factors and has implications for the trajectory of commitment to those relationships (Brooks & Ogolsky, 2016) and satisfaction. The rate of interracial relationships has been used as a barometer of racial relations and implicitly the acceptance and support that partners in these relationships can expect (Yancey, 2002). As previously indicated, gender and race matter in one's willingness to partner, but gender and race also impact the prevalence of received support.

A greater proportion of people of color marry a member of a different race compared to White people (Passel, Wang, & Taylor, 2010). Among people of color, Black men and women are less likely to marry someone of a different race compared to Latinos who are in turn less likely to intermarry than Asian-Americans. A greater occurrence of likelihood to partner across race among one's own racial group can be indicative of greater approval and support; thus the decision to enter into an interracial relationship may be more supported for an Asian woman compared to a White woman, as the former is three times more likely to marry someone of a different race (Passel et al., 2010). Additionally, the race of one's intended partner, and those the racial composition of the couple matter. Lower rates of interracial relationships across groups suggest strong boundaries whereas higher rates of interracial relationships indicate more permeable boundaries. Research supports this assertion as the White–non-White interracial relationship that occurs the least often, unions between a Black partner and White partner (Bratter & Eschbach, 2006), is reported to receive the greatest amount of social opposition (Yancey, 2002) and is less likely to receive the benefit of social support from the broader social world.

Jeremiah and Caitlyn, from the opening vignette, spent some unprompted time discussing the impact of social disapproval on the development of their relationships. They perceived both overt (e.g., being disowned by a family member) and covert (e.g., family members who did not attend their wedding) forms of opposition to their relationship. More negative experiences are implied by Jeremiah via a previous interracial relationship and Caitlyn contests that this is something that the couple has adjusted to and now handles differently since having biracial children. Certainly, not all of the experiences in their relationship are negative, but contesting with social disapproval is common among interracial couples. Ultimately, social support and approval is a great benefit to partners in interracial relationships and the perception of normalcy can be the impetus to partner across race.

Practice Implications

Practitioners working with interracial couples should pay particular attention to the individual ideologies that members of the couple hold. Also, race-conscious therapy may be valuable in work with interracial couples. As discussed earlier a positive racial identity for the individual is a benefit to the couple. Practitioners should foster a healthy exploration of what race means at the individual level as well as within the partnership. In a world in which the dominant narrative tends to be "no race talk" difficulties experienced as a result of a racialized society may be framed as cultural differences. Being aware of the nuances of how race is discussed and a willingness to engage couples of various degrees of comfort and awareness can make for a more transparent therapy experience.

Within such discussion practitioners should pay close attention to the importance of intersectionality of race and gender. Practitioners should call attention to the social messages that may be communicated to the couple and that they may be communicating to each other because of their intersecting identities. Similarly, understanding how negative messages may have been internalized by one or both individuals may be worthy of consideration. Qualitative accounts of partners' experiences in their relationship have highlighted the presence of racial microaggressions within interracial relationships (Killian, 2002) as partners tend to hold onto dominant and marginalized narratives which are likely influenced by their intersecting identities. For example, a woman of color in a relationship with a White man may find it difficult to fully develop trust and intimacy if her partner has fetishized her appearance as exotic. It is also plausible that an interracial relationship comprised of a man of color and a White woman may struggle with the stereotype associated with the *caste-exchange* hypothesis if their socioeconomic backgrounds are very different.

Additionally, it is important to acknowledge existing (or missing) social support, skills (such as navigate racial tensions or discern hostility in new environments), and strengths that partners have developed as a couple. Given the unique nature of their partnership, couples may have developed a sense of interdependence and "we-ness" that may help them fight against negative social attitudes and stereotypes. Interracial partners have to be discerning in regard to whom they socialize with and in what settings. It is likely that they have created a social network that supports their decision to partner across race. Clinicians could help clients identify social groups and multicultural events that might be supportive and enriching for couples. Practitioners should assess what the interdependence looks like for each couple, and acknowledge and encourage the development of a shared identity in order to strengthen the partnership.

Gaps in Our Knowledge and Future Research

Although our knowledge about partnering across race is growing, there is much that is left to learn. In particular, our understanding can be deepened through greater intersectionality among research questions. Further, our understanding of partnering across race is deeply rooted in heterosexuality. Research on the experiences of those in other-sex relationships should be explored. Furthermore, the racial dichotomy of Black-White permeates scholarship in this area. Reliance on the dynamics between Black and White people makes research inapplicable to the majority of romantic partnerships across race. Additionally, we are not clear on the role of intra-personal phenomena such as racial identity on the impact of partnering across race. The exception to this may be the experiences of Black partners as racial identity research has been plentiful among this population. Nonetheless, the role of how individuals think about themselves as racial beings should extend beyond stereotypes of self-loathing people of color and thrill-seeking White men and women that were supported in survey research (Lalonde et al., 2007).

The study of interracial couples could benefit from the application of an appropriate theoretical framework. A special issue of the Journal of Social Issues (Gaines, Clark, & Afful, 2015) explicitly applies interdependence theory to the study of interracial relationships. This is helpful because it uses a well-established and -supported theoretical framework to guide research questions and avoids a haphazard investigation of interracial relationships, much of which is dictated by what is interesting to a researcher or the current zeitgeist. As mentioned earlier, early research on interracial relationships was especially damaging to the science and perception of interracial partnerships as they chiefly reinforced beliefs of poor quality in interracial relationships. The exclusive application of existing theories that do not consider the societal opposition and racialized experiences of those who partner across race could impede our understanding of these couples' experiences. Further, new models grounded in the experience of specific racial pairings would also be advantageous in deepening our understanding and exploring the complexities of interracial partnering experiences.

References

Bartkowiak A. (Director). (2000). *Romeo Must Die* [Motion Picture]. Burbank: Warner Bros.

Bowman, N. A. (2012). Structural diversity and close interracial relationships in college. *Educational Researcher, 41*(4), 133–135. https://doi.org/10.3102/0013189X12439934

Bratter, J. L., & Eschbach, K. (2006). What about the couple? *interracial* marriage and psychological distress. *Social Science Research, 35*(4), 1025–1047. https://doi.org/10.1016/j.ssresearch.2005.09.001

Brayboy, T. L. (1966). Interracial sexuality as an expression of neurotic conflict. *The Journal of Sex Research, 2*, 1797184.

Brooks, J. E., & Neville, H. A. (2016). Interracial attraction among college men: The impact of ideologies, familiarity and similarity. *Journal of Social and Personal Relationships, 34*, 166. https://doi.org/10.1177/0265407515627508

Brooks, J. E., & Ogolsky, B. (2016). The effects of network approval on accounts of commitment trajectories in intraracial and interracial relationships. *Marriage and Family Review, 53*, 347. https://doi.org/10.1080/01494929.2016.1184210

Brown, J. A. (1987). Casework contacts with Black-White couples. *Social Casework: The Journal of Contemporary Social Work, 68*, 24–29.

Clark-Ibáñez, M., & Felmlee, D. (2004). Interethnic relationships: The role of social network diversity. *Journal of Marriage and Family, 66*(2), 293–305. https://doi.org/10.1111/j.1741-3737.2004.00021.x

Cox, C. L., Wexler, M. O., Rusbult, C. E., & Gaines Jr., S. O. (1997). Prescriptive support and commitment processes in close relationships. *Social Psychology Quarterly, 60*(1), 79–90 Retrieved from http://search.proquest.com/docview/619068125?accountid=14553

Daneshpour, M. (2003). Lives together, worlds apart? The lives of multicultural Muslim couples. In *Clinical issues with interracial couples: Theories and research* (pp. 57–71). New York, NY: Haworth Press.

Eastwick, P. W., Richeson, J. A., Son, D., & Finkel, E. J. (2009). Is love colorblind? Political orientation and interracial romantic desire. *Personality and Social Psychology Bulletin, 35*(9), 1258–1268. https://doi.org/10.1177/0146167209338524

Estep, B. (2011). *Pike church takes stand against interracial couples*. Retrieved Kentucky.com November 28, 2012, from http://www.kentucky.com/2011/11/30/1977453/small-pike-county-church-votes.html#storylink=cpy

Forry, N. D., Leslie, L. A., & Letiecq, B. L. (2007). Marital quality in interracial relationships: The role of sex role ideology and perceived fairness. *Journal of Family Issues, 28*(12), 1538–1552. https://doi.org/10.1177/0192513X07304466

Foster, M. (2009). *Interracial couple denied marriage license in Tangipahoa Parish*. Associated Press. Retrieved November 28, 2012, from http://www.nola.com/crime/index.ssf/2009/10/interracial_couple_denied_marr.html

Fu, X. (2008). Interracial marriage and family socio-economic well-being: Equal status exchange or caste status exchange? *The Social Science Journal, 45*(1), 132–155. https://doi.org/10.1016/j.soscij.2007.12.008

Gaines, S. J., Clark, E. M., & Afful, S. E. (2015). Interethnic marriage in the United States: An introduction. *Journal of Social Issues, 71*(4), 647–658. https://doi.org/10.1111/josi.12141

Galinsky, A. D., Hall, E. V., & Cuddy, A. C. (2013). Gendered races: Implications for interracial marriage, leadership selection, and athletic participation. *Psychological Science, 24*(4), 498–506. https://doi.org/10.1177/0956797612457783

Get Out. (2017, March 15). Retrieved from https://www.rottentomatoes.com/m/get_out/

Harper, C. E., & Yeung, F. P. (2015). College student characteristics and experiences as predictors of interracial dating. *College Student Journal, 49*(4), 599–609.

Harris, T. M., & Kalbfleisch, P. J. (2000). Interracial dating: The implications of race for initiating a romantic relationship. *Howard Journal of Communications, 11*(1), 49–64. https://doi.org/10.1080/106461700246715

Henderson, D. A. (2000). Racial/ethnic intermarried couples and marital interaction: Marital issues and problem solving. *Sociological Focus, 33*(4), 421–438. https://doi.org/10.1080/00380237.2000.10571178

Hibbler, D. K., & Shinew, K. J. (2002). Interracial couples' experience of leisure: A social network approach. *Journal of Leisure Research, 34*(2), 135–156.

Hughes, J. (Director) (1984). *Sixteen Candles* [Motion Picture]. United States: Universal Pictures.

Kalmijn, M. (1993). Trends in Black/White intermarriage. *Social Forces, 72*(1), 119–146 Retrieved from http://search.proquest.com/docview/60067634?accountid=14553

Kapnek, E. (2014). *Selfie*. United States: Piece of Pie Productions.

Killian, K. D. (2001). Crossing borders: Race, gender, and their intersections in interracial couples. *Journal of Feminist Family Therapy: An International Forum, 13*(1), 1–31. https://doi.org/10.1300/J086v13n01_01

Killian, K. D. (2002). Dominant and marginalized discourses in interracial couples' narratives: Implications for family therapists. *Family Process, 41*(4), 603–618. https://doi.org/10.1111/j.1545-5300.2002.00603.x

Killian, K. D. (2013). *Interracial couples, intimacy, and therapy: Crossing racial borders*. New York, NY: Columbia University Press.

Kramer A. (Director) (1967). *Guess Who's Coming to Dinner* [Motion Picture]. United States: Columbia Pictures Corporation.

Lalonde, R. N., Giguere, B., Fontaine, M., & Smith, A. (2007). Social dominance orientation and ideological asymmetry in relation to interracial dating and transracial adoption in Canada. *Journal of Cross-Cultural Psychology, 38*(5), 559–572. https://doi.org/10.1177/0022022107305238

Lehmiller, J. J., & Konkel, K. E. (2012). Prejudice and discrimination in relational contexts. In M. Paludi (Ed.), *The psychology of love* (Vol. Vols. 1–4, pp. 75–87). Santa Barbara, CA: Praeger/ABC-CLIO, Santa Barbara, CA.

Leslie, L. A., & Letiecq, B. L. (2004). Marital quality of African American and White partners in *interracial* couples. *Personal Relationships, 11*(4), 559–574. https://doi.org/10.1111/j.1475-6811.2004.00098.x

Lewis, R., Yancey, G., & Bletzer, S. S. (1997). Racial and nonracial factors that influence spouse choice in Black/White marriages. *Journal of Black Studies, 28*(1), 60–78.

Lorre, C. (2017). *Big bang theory*. United States: Chuck Lorre Productions.

Mendelsohn, G. A., Shaw Taylor, L., Fiore, A. T., & Cheshire, C. (2014). Black/White dating online: Interracial courtship in the 21st century. *Psychology of Popular Media Culture, 3*(1), 2–18. https://doi.org/10.1037/a0035357

Miller, S. C., Olson, M. A., & Fazio, R. H. (2004). Perceived reactions to interracial romantic relationships: When race is used as a cue to status. *Group Processes & Intergroup Relations, 7*(4), 354–369. https://doi.org/10.1177/1368430204046143

Neville, H. A., Awad, G. H., Brooks, J. E., Flores, M. P., & Bluemel, J. (2013). Color-blind racial ideology: Theory, training, and measurement implications in psychology. *American Psychologist, 68*(6), 455–466. https://doi.org/10.1037/a0033282

Newport, F. (2013). In U.S., 87% Approve of Black-White marriage vs. 4% in 1958. Gallup Politics. Retrieved May 23, 2014, from http://www.gallup.com/poll/163697/approve-marriage-blacks-whites.aspx

Nichols, J. (Director) (2016). *Loving* [Motion Picture]. United States: Raindog Films.

Oh, E., Choi, C., Neville, H. A., Anderson, C. J., & Landrum-Brown, J. (2010). Beliefs about affirmative action: A test of the group self-interest and racism beliefs models. *Journal of Diversity in Higher Education, 3*, 163–176. https://doi.org/10.1037/a0019799

Passel, J. S., Wang, W., & Taylor, P. (2010). *One-in-seven new U.S. marriages is interracial or interethnic.* PEW Research. Accessed May 23, 2014, from http://www.pewsocialtrends.org/2010/06/04/marrying-out/

Peele, J. (Director) (2017). *Get Out* [Motion Picture]. United States: Blumhouse Productions.

Perry, S. L. (2016). Religious socialization and interracial dating. *Journal of Family Issues, 37*(15), 2138–2162. https://doi.org/10.1177/0192513X14555766

Rhimes, S. (2017a). *Grey's anatomy*. United States: Shondaland.

Rhimes, S. (2017b). *How to get away with murder*. United States: Shondaland.

Rhimes, S. (2017c). *Scandal*. United States: Shondaland

Schueths, A. M. (2015). Barriers to interracial marriage? Examining policy issues concerning U.S. citizens married to undocumented Latino/a immigrants. *Journal of Social Issues, 71*(4), 804–820. https://doi.org/10.1111/josi.12150

Sidanius, J., Pratto, F., & Rabinowitz, J. L. (1994). Gender, ethnic status, and ideological asymmetry: A social dominance interpretation. *Journal of Cross-Cultural Psychology, 25*(2), 194–216. https://doi.org/10.1177/0022022194252003

Smith, C. E. (1966). Negro-White intermarriage: Forbidden sexual union. *Journal of Sex Research, 2*, 169–177.

Statement about race at BJU. (2008). Retrieved from http://www.bju.edu/about/what-we-believe/race-statement.php

Vargas, J. A. (2007, May 25). "Slanted Screen" rues the absence of Asians. *Washington Post*. Retrieved from http://www.washingtonpost.com/wp-dyn/content/article/2007/05/24/AR2007052402573.html

Wang, W. (2012). *The rise of intermarriage: Rates, characteristics vary by race and gender.* Report. Washington, D.C.: Pew Research Center.

Wieling, E. (2003). Latino/a and white marriages: A pilot study investigating the experiences of interethnic couples in the United States. In *Clinical issues with interracial couples: Theories and research* (pp. 41–55). New York, NY: Haworth Press.

Yancey, G. (2002). Who *interracial*ly dates: An examination of the characteristics of those who have interracially dated. *Journal of Comparative Family Studies, 33*(2), 179–190.

Yancey, G. (2003). A preliminary examination of differential sexual attitudes among individuals involved in interracial relationships: Testing "jungle fever". *The Social Science Journal, 40*(1), 153–157. https://doi.org/10.1016/S0362-3319(02)00266-5

Yancey, G. (2007). Homogamy over the net: Using internet advertisements to discover who interracially dates. *Journal of Social and Personal Relationships, 24*(6), 913–930. https://doi.org/10.1177/0265407507084190

Yancey, G. (2009). Crossracial differences in the racial preferences of potential dating partners: A test of the alienation of African Americans and social dominance orientation. *The Sociological Quarterly, 50*(1), 121–143. https://doi.org/10.1111/j.1533-8525.2008.01135.x

Yancey, G., & Yancey, S. (1998). Interracial dating: Evidence from personal advertisements. *Journal of Family Issues, 19*(3), 334–348. https://doi.org/10.1177/019251398019003006

Interracial Marriages: Historical and Contemporary Trends

Chalandra M. Bryant and Jeneé C. Duncan

In June of 1958 Mildred (18 years old) and Richard (24 years old) went to the District of Columbia to get married. They then returned to Virginia to establish their family home. Five weeks later, in the early morning hours, they were awakened in their Central Point, Virginia, home to find that they were being arrested. Their crime: Mildred was a Black woman; Richard was a White man. Both were residents of Virginia, where interracial marriage was prohibited. They were sentenced to 1 year in jail, but the sentence was suspended under the condition that the couple agree to leave Virginia and not return to the state together for 25 years (Pratt, 1998*; Wallenstein,* 1995*). The judge stated that " Almighty God created the races white, black, yellow,... and red, and he placed them on separate continents.... The fact that he separated the races shows that he did not intend for the races to mix." Although the two agreed to leave, living far away from their families left them distraught; dealing with housing discrimination in Washington, D.C. was also challenging for them. On top of all that, they worried about their children living in the city and wanted them to grow up in the country (Pratt,* 1998*). Bottom line: They wanted to return home. So, Mildred decided to write a letter to Attorney General Robert F. Kennedy for help. Through Kennedy, they got in touch with the American Civil Liberties Union. Their case was taken by attorneys Bernard S. Cohen and Philip J. Hirschkop (Martin,* 2008*). In 1967, nine years after their indictment, their case was brought before the US Supreme Court which ruled in their favor. They returned to Central Point, Virginia, where Richard built a home for his family (Curtis,* 2012*). They had two sons, Donald and Sidney, and one daughter, Peggy (Martin,* 2008*). During an interview in 2012, Peggy (52 years old at the time, and the only child alive today) said that she did not know what was going on while growing up until the Ku Klux Klan burned a cross in her maternal grandmother's yard (Curtis,* 2012*).*

C. M. Bryant (✉) · J. C. Duncan
Department of Human Development and Family Science, University of Georgia, Athens, GA, USA
e-mail: cmb84@uga.edu

R. Nazarinia Roy, A. Rollins (eds.), *Biracial Families*,
https://doi.org/10.1007/978-3-319-96160-6_5

The experiences of her parents, Mildred and Richard, are still talked about even today as evidenced by the 2016 release of a movie (aptly titled "Loving") documenting the lives of these spouses. Richard died in 1975 as a result of his car being struck by a drunk driver. Mildred died of pneumonia, years later in 2008. She never remarried.

Introduction

This chapter begins with a focus on history; history provides the sociopolitical context in which interracial relationships are embedded. Without a sound understanding of historical background, one cannot fully understand or even appreciate how interracial relationship trends and attitudes have evolved over time. This chapter begins with the story of Mildred and Richard Loving, which is a part of our historical review; that review also includes an explanation of the Pocahontas exception, Virginia's Racial Integrity Act of 1924, as well as a few US Supreme Court decisions. Demographic data are reviewed, highlighting the proportions of interracial/interethnic couples—both married and unmarried households. Race relations are interweaved throughout—especially in the cross-country comparison. Urie Bronfenbrenner's model, the vulnerability-stress-adaptation model, and interdependence theory are highlighted as frameworks guiding the understanding of interracial unions. We focus on opposite-sex relationships. Interracial relationships are complex enough; adding same-sex unions as another layer of complexity is beyond the scope of this chapter. We also focus primarily on married couples; there is much more information about married couples (compared to cohabiting couples).

Let's begin with a brief history lesson.

Historical Context

Long before Mildred and Richard Loving were arrested, interracial marriage was a particularly tense social issue. In Alabama, around 1883, for example, the state defended its anti-miscegenation law in a US Supreme Court case (Pace v. State of Alabama)—and won. This supported the state's decision to imprison Tony Pace (Black male) and Mary Cox (White female) for engaging in sexual relations (Gaines, Clark, & Afful, 2015; Sollors, 2000). Fast forward four decades and we find that sentiments had not changed in the United States. For instance, Virginia's Racial Integrity Act of 1924 provided a legal definition of White. To be considered White, one must not have any trace of blood other than Caucasian. The "one-drop rule" was an extension of anti-miscegenation laws that already existed; it is the notion that if an individual has even a single drop of Black blood, then that individual is Black. The law provided a special exemption—the "Pocahontas exception," according to which "persons who have one-sixteen or less of the blood of the American Indian and have no other non-Caucasic blood shall be deemed to be white persons" (Section 20-54 of the Virginia Code; see Legal Information Institute (2016), Cornell University Law School). The reason for this exception—to protect Virginia's leading families who happened to be descendants of none other than Pocahontas and John Rolfe. That way, they were not labeled as Black. Walter A. Plecker, who was Virginia's state registrar as well as the official responsible for enforcing the Racial Integrity Act, was against the Pocahontas exception. He argued that Indians in Virginia were using the exception to pass as White (Endo, 2014).

Fast forward again. Even as late as the 1960s many states had anti-miscegenation laws on their books (Barnett, 1964; Moran, 2001). For example, in Delaware marriage was prohibited between Whites and Blacks or Mulattoes—term historically used to refer to individuals who were one-fourth or more Black (Zackodnik, 2001). The penalty was a $100 fine. In Kentucky the penalty for intermarriage was $500 to $5000 in fines and 3–12-month imprisonment if the couple continued living together after conviction (for review see Barnett, 1964). Most laws typically targeted relationships between Whites and Blacks; however, states in the West also targeted relationships between Whites and Asians (Moran, 2004).

Loving vs. Virginia, mentioned in the opening story, is a key case. The Lovings violated two codes—Virginia Code 20-54 which prohibited marriages between "white and colored persons" and Code 20-58 which stated that it was against the law for an interracial couple to marry outside of the state with the intention of returning to cohabit as spouses (see Legal Information Institute, Cornell University Law School). An often-ignored component of the Loving story involves Mildred Loving's claim to be Indian-Rappahannock. While working on her book, *That the Blood Stay Pure: African Americans, Native Americans and the Predicament of Race and Identity in Virginia*, Arica Coleman interviewed Mildred in 2004. During that interview Mildred stated that she had no Black ancestry. (Does this remind you of the Pocahontas exception?)

The Pace v. Alabama case was overturned by McLaughlin v. Florida (1964) and Loving v. Virginia (1967); however, Alabama did not remove its anti-miscegenation law from the books. The law actually remained on Alabama's books until the year 2000—yes, 2000! Although it had not been enforceable for more than three decades, 40% of voters wanted it to remain on the books (Maillard, 2009). In the case of McLaughlin v. Florida, the Court invalidated a statute barring an unmarried interracial couple from living in the same room at night (Koppelman, 2001).

Demographics

Despite the election of Barack Obama, the first Black president of the United States, racism remains systemic in the United States. Although anti-miscegenation laws were ruled unconstitutional, many interracial couples still experience racial discrimination which manifests itself in various forms including, but not limited to, violence, hate speech, and residential segregation (Emens, 2009; Glaser, Dixit, &

Green, 2002; Jones, 1997; Kim, 2013; Leslie & Letiecq, 2004). Discrimination has not reduced the number of interracial unions. In fact, these unions have increased.

Over the past 30 years, the proportion of interracial and interethnic marriages has more than doubled—7% of marriages in 1980 to 15% in 2010 (Wang, 2012). According to US Census Briefs, in 2010 approximately 6.9% of households consisting of married couples included a spouse and householder who were of different races (Census Briefs prepared by Lofquist, Lugaila, O'Connell, & Feliz, 2012). In the Midwest, Northeast, and South, 4–6% of married couples consisted of spouses of different races, while in the West, 11% of married couples consisted of spouses of different races. A relatively high proportion, 17%, of married couples in two states, Alaska and Oklahoma, consisted of spouses of different races. The greatest proportion (37.2%) of married couples was found in Hawaii. The greatest proportion of unmarried, opposite-sex householders with a partner of a different race was also found in Hawaii (56.4%). See Table 1. The aforementioned particular states have large numbers of native populations. When comparing married vs. unmarried households (on Table 1), notice that there is a consistent pattern of more unmarried opposite-sex partners of different races than married partners. For example, in the state of Georgia while 5.2% of married householders had a partner of a different race, nearly twice the proportion (11.0%) were unmarried householders. This pattern is observed in the United States as a whole and not just in certain states; for instance, in 2010, 14.2% of households with unmarried, opposite-sex partners were comprised of partners of different races—compared to 6.9% of married households (Lofquist et al., 2012). Similar to married couples, a relatively high proportion (21%) of unmarried interracial couples resided in the West, with the lowest proportion (11%) living in the Midwest. Cohabitation was most common between White non-Hispanic and Hispanic (of any race) individuals (33.9%), followed by White, non-Hispanic and Black, non-Hispanic individuals (15.9%). This indicates that more interracial couples cohabit rather than legally marry.

As you explore Table 1 more carefully, please note that it consists of three sections: (a) householders with partners of a different race, (b) householders with partners of a different Hispanic origin, and (c) householders with a partner of a different race or origin. Less than 5% of married couples in the United States were comprised of one Hispanic and one non-Hispanic partner, compared to 8.2% of unmarried opposite-sex householders with a partner of a different Hispanic origin (Lofquist et al., 2012).

For those of you who are more visually oriented, you may find this information easier to understand with a map. Figures 1a, b highlight the variations in coupled households with partners of either a different race or Hispanic origin by state. As shown in Fig. 1a, states with the highest percentage of married, opposite-sex couples of different races or Hispanic origin were located in the western and southwestern parts of the United States. Hawaii had the highest percentage of married couples of a different race or Hispanic origin (39%), followed by Alaska, New Mexico, and

Table 1 Percent of households with partners of a different race or Hispanic origin for the United States, regions, and states, and for Puerto Rico: 2010

Area	Householders with partner of a different race				Householders with partner of a different Hispanic origin				Householders with partner of a different race or origin			
		Unmarried partner households				Unmarried partner households				Unmarried partner households		
			Same-sex partners				Same-sex partners				Same-sex partners	
	Husband-wife	Opposite-sex partners	Summary File 1 counts[a]	Preferred estimates[b]	Husband-wife	Opposite-sex partners	Summary File 1 counts[a]	Preferred estimates[b]	Husband-wife	Opposite-sex partners	Summary File 1 counts[a]	Preferred estimates[b]
United States	**6.9**	**14.2**	**12.6**	**14.5**	**4.3**	**8.2**	**8.8**	**10.4**	**9.5**	**18.3**	**17.7**	**20.6**
Region												
Northeast	5.3	12.3	11.0	12.8	3.2	7.1	7.3	8.7	7.5	16.0	15.4	18.1
Midwest	4.4	11.1	9.4	11.1	2.4	5.4	5.1	6.1	6.0	13.9	12.4	14.7
South	6.2	12.7	10.5	12.1	3.9	7.2	7.6	9.2	8.8	16.5	15.3	18.1
West	11.6	20.9	19.1	20.9	7.5	13.4	13.9	15.6	15.9	26.8	26.4	29.2
State												
Alabama	3.9	9.3	6.6	7.8	1.4	2.8	2.3	2.8	4.8	10.5	8.0	9.4
Alaska	17.1	28.4	22.2	22.9	4.8	6.8	7.8	9.0	19.7	31.3	26.1	27.8
Arizona	9.3	18.0	15.2	16.7	8.3	15.1	14.4	16.3	14.3	25.2	23.1	25.8
Arkansas	4.7	11.0	8.6	10.3	2.0	4.0	3.0	3.5	5.9	12.7	10.3	12.2
California	12.8	22.6	21.3	23.4	8.6	14.9	16.1	17.9	17.6	28.9	29.8	32.9
Colorado	8.8	16.1	14.2	15.2	7.7	13.6	13.5	14.8	13.5	23.2	21.7	23.6
Connecticut	5.5	13.8	10.1	11.5	3.7	9.2	7.3	8.7	8.0	18.2	14.6	16.9
Delaware	5.7	13.3	9.6	10.6	2.7	6.1	4.5	4.7	7.3	16.2	12.2	13.4
District of Columbia	10.6	13.8	18.7	19.1	5.1	6.4	12.1	12.7	14.1	17.6	26.8	27.6
Florida	6.5	12.7	10.2	11.3	5.9	10.0	11.0	12.7	10.9	18.8	18.2	20.6
Georgia	5.2	11.0	9.3	11.0	2.7	4.7	5.2	6.2	6.8	13.2	12.6	14.8

(continued)

Table 1 (continued)

Area	Householders with partner of a different race				Householders with partner of a different Hispanic origin				Householders with partner of a different race or origin			
		Unmarried partner households				Unmarried partner households				Unmarried partner households		
			Same-sex partners				Same-sex partners				Same-sex partners	
	Husband-wife	Opposite-sex partners	Summary File 1 counts[a]	Preferred estimates[b]	Husband-wife	Opposite-sex partners	Summary File 1 counts[a]	Preferred estimates[b]	Husband-wife	Opposite-sex partners	Summary File 1 counts[a]	Preferred estimates[b]
Hawaii	37.2	56.4	47.2	49.7	7.6	14.2	11.8	12.6	39.2	58.9	50.1	52.9
Idaho	6.1	12.3	9.3	10.6	4.2	9.0	7.2	8.6	8.6	16.7	13.0	15.1
Illinois	5.2	11.7	11.7	13.8	3.6	7.5	8.2	9.9	7.6	15.6	16.5	19.7
Indiana	4.0	10.2	8.4	9.8	2.3	4.8	4.0	4.4	5.4	12.5	10.5	12.3
Iowa	3.1	9.6	7.1	8.6	1.8	4.7	4.0	5.0	4.2	12.1	9.4	11.5
Kansas	6.4	15.6	11.3	12.9	3.9	8.7	6.7	8.1	8.8	19.9	15.0	17.6
Kentucky	3.3	9.5	7.0	8.4	1.3	2.9	2.3	2.8	4.1	10.8	8.3	10.0
Louisiana	4.3	9.4	7.8	9.0	2.6	3.8	4.6	5.5	6.1	11.4	10.8	12.7
Maine	3.2	6.5	5.2	5.6	1.1	2.0	2.3	2.9	4.0	7.7	6.7	7.4
Maryland	6.9	12.8	12.3	14.0	2.9	4.5	5.3	6.1	8.8	15.1	15.6	17.8
Massachusetts	5.4	12.3	9.9	11.1	2.4	6.5	5.9	6.8	7.0	15.6	13.6	15.4
Michigan	4.7	11.2	8.9	10.5	2.5	5.5	4.3	5.2	6.3	14.3	11.5	13.6
Minnesota	4.4	12.4	10.2	11.7	1.8	4.4	4.3	5.2	5.5	14.6	12.4	14.5
Mississippi	2.9	7.1	5.3	7.3	1.3	2.2	1.8	2.4	3.7	8.1	6.3	8.5
Missouri	4.5	10.4	9.0	10.6	2.1	4.0	4.4	5.4	5.8	12.5	11.6	13.8
Montana	6.1	11.7	11.0	11.8	2.7	5.4	4.7	5.0	7.8	14.8	13.5	14.2
Nebraska	4.4	12.7	9.5	11.1	2.8	7.3	6.0	6.6	6.0	16.1	12.9	14.9
Nevada	13.3	23.6	20.5	22.4	7.9	13.9	14.1	15.8	17.6	29.5	27.4	30.2
New Hampshire	3.6	6.7	5.7	6.5	1.7	3.4	3.4	4.0	4.7	8.6	8.0	9.2

New Jersey	6.2	14.5	11.6	13.5	4.5	10.0	9.1	10.9	9.3	19.8	17.2	20.3
New Mexico	11.1	19.7	17.2	18.8	13.2	20.2	19.4	21.8	19.4	29.7	28.2	31.3
New York	6.6	14.3	13.7	15.9	4.1	8.5	9.7	11.3	9.3	18.7	19.6	22.7
North Carolina	5.2	12.4	9.1	10.5	2.4	4.6	3.9	4.6	6.6	14.4	11.2	13.1
North Dakota	3.8	10.8	9.6	12.3	1.3	3.6	3.6	4.8	4.6	12.7	11.2	14.8
Ohio	3.8	10.4	8.3	9.7	1.7	3.9	3.5	4.2	4.9	12.4	10.4	12.2
Oklahoma	17.2	28.5	21.1	23.1	3.6	7.6	5.4	6.5	19.1	31.4	23.7	26.2
Oregon	8.8	15.7	13.4	14.2	4.4	8.4	8.2	9.0	11.4	19.8	18.2	19.5
Pennsylvania	3.5	9.9	8.3	10.2	1.9	4.8	4.5	5.7	4.7	12.3	10.9	13.5
Rhode Island	5.7	14.1	10.9	11.8	2.5	6.9	4.7	5.1	7.1	17.1	13.4	14.5
South Carolina	4.1	10.5	7.4	9.2	2.0	3.6	3.1	3.8	5.3	12.2	9.2	11.4
South Dakota	4.3	12.8	9.1	12.6	1.5	4.0	3.2	4.1	5.2	14.6	10.7	14.4
Tennessee	3.8	9.9	7.4	8.6	1.7	3.4	3.2	3.7	4.9	11.5	9.2	10.8
Texas	7.6	15.2	12.8	14.8	7.1	13.3	13.8	16.8	12.2	22.0	21.2	25.2
Utah	6.5	15.4	10.8	12.2	5.0	11.6	9.7	11.4	9.4	20.9	16.0	18.3
Vermont	3.3	5.8	6.1	6.7	1.3	2.2	3.2	3.6	4.3	7.1	8.1	9.0
Virginia	7.2	14.3	11.7	13.4	3.2	5.4	5.6	6.6	9.2	16.9	15.1	17.6
Washington	10.9	19.6	17.0	18.5	4.4	8.5	8.3	9.3	13.4	23.4	21.3	23.3
West Virginia	2.6	7.2	5.4	7.3	0.9	1.7	1.8	2.7	3.2	8.1	6.5	9.1
Wisconsin	3.8	10.6	8.6	10.3	2.1	5.4	5.2	6.3	5.1	13.3	11.6	14.1
Wyoming	5.8	11.0	9.9	12.0	5.1	10.3	7.3	9.0	8.9	16.5	14.2	17.2
Puerto Rico	**15.7**	**20.8**	**19.7**	**22.1**	**1.4**	**1.5**	**2.1**	**2.8**	**16.7**	**21.8**	**21.2**	**24.0**

[a]Summary File 1 counts in this table are consistent with Summary File 1 counts shown in the American FactFinder

[b]Preferred estimates remove likely numbers of opposite-sex couples included in same-sex tabulations. *Source*: US Census Bureau, *2010 Census Summary File 1*

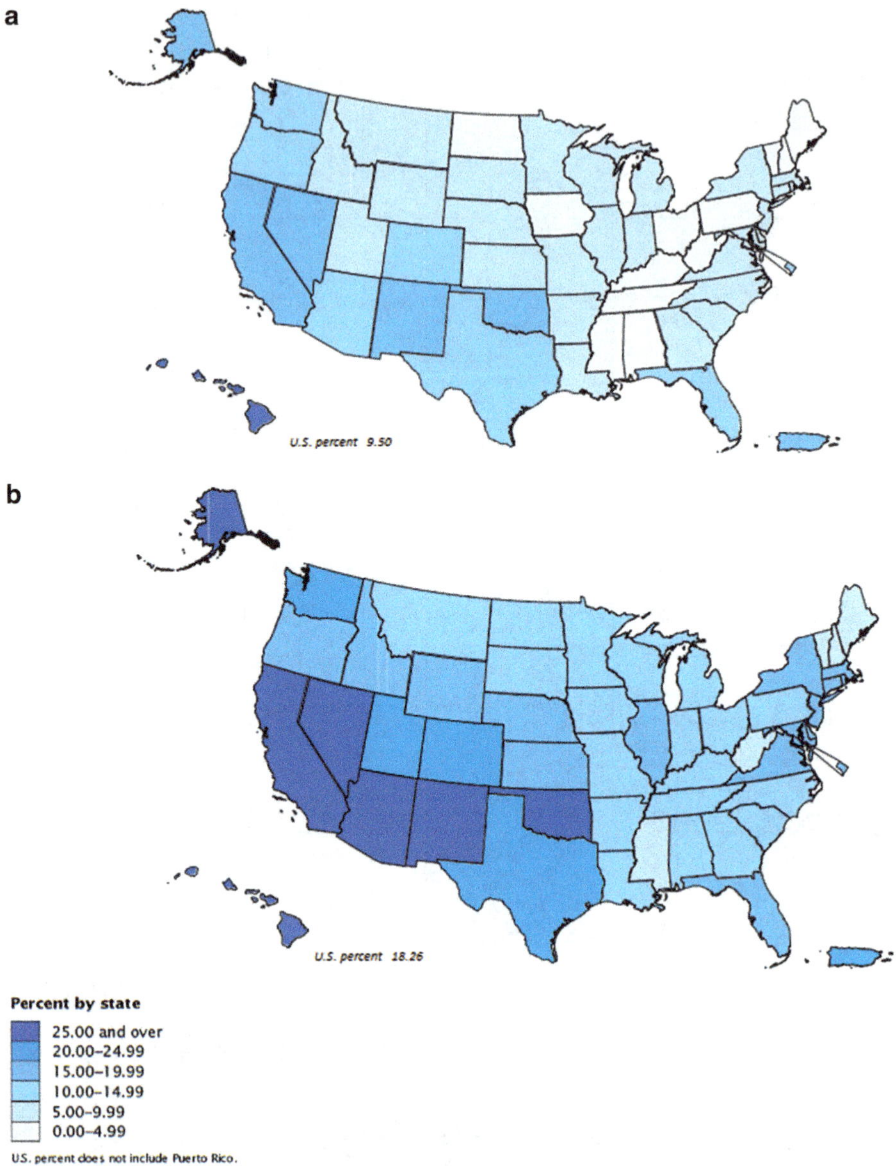

Fig. 1 (**a**, **b**) Households with partners of a different race or Hispanic origin: 2010 (*Source*: adapted from Appendix of Lofquist et al., 2012; US Census Bureau Households and Families: 2010). (**a**) Opposite-sex married couple households. (**b**) Opposite-sex unmarried couple households

Oklahoma (all with percentages around 19%). The low percentage of interracial marriages in states such as Mississippi and Alabama (lower than 5%) reflects the South's history of laws that prohibited marriages between Whites and Blacks. A cluster of states in New England—Maine, New Hampshire, and Vermont—also reported some of the lowest percentages of interracial marriages which may reflect the small proportion of Black or Hispanic individuals residing in these states (1–2%).

Geographic variations in opposite-sex unmarried couples with partners of a different race or Hispanic origin (shown in Fig. 1b) were similar to that of married couples. As with married couples, the highest percentages of opposite-sex unmarried couples with partners of a different race or Hispanic origin were also located in the western and southwestern areas of the country, including Alaska and Hawaii. However, the patterns for married couples and unmarried couples did diverge in some states. For example, states in the Midwest and Northeast reported some of the lowest percentages for interracial or interethnic opposite-sex married couples. However, Kansas, New York, and New Jersey were among the states with above-average percentages of interracial and interethnic unmarried couples.

Which Types of Unions Increased?

Since 1970, non-Hispanic/Hispanic marriages have tripled; in addition, since 1960, Asian/White married couples have increased ten-fold and Black/White marriages have increased five-fold (Qian & Lichter, 2007; Rosenfeld & Kim, 2005). In the United States, for every seven new marriages, one is interracial or interethnic (Taylor et al., 2010). About 9% of White, 17% of Black, 26% of Hispanic, and 28% of Asian newlyweds married someone outside of their race/ethnicity in 2010 (Wang, 2012). Between 2000 and 2010, the number of married as well as the number of unmarried interracial/interethnic opposite sex couples have increased (see Table 2). Table 2 provides information about ten different types of interracial/interethnic couples: (1) White non-Hispanic/Hispanic (any race); (2) White non-Hispanic/Black non-Hispanic; (3) White non-Hispanic/American-Indian and Alaska Native; (4) White non-Hispanic/Asian non-Hispanic; (5)White non-Hispanic/Native Hawaiian and other Pacific Islander; (6)White non-Hispanic/some other race non-Hispanic; (7) both are multiracial (both Hispanic or neither Hispanic); (8) Hispanic/non-Hispanic (excluding White non-Hispanic); (9) other-both Hispanic (spouses different single race, neither White); (10) other-neither Hispanic (spouses different single race, neither White). The number of White non-Hispanic/Asian non-Hispanic married couples increased from 504,119 to 737,493. The number of White non-Hispanic/Black non-Hispanic married couples increased from 287,576 to 422,250. In 2015, there were 11 million intermarried people in the United States. Basically, this means that one out of every ten married people had a spouse of a different race/ethnicity in 2015 (Livingston & Brown, 2017). These growing numbers reflect acceptance of racial/ethnic exogamy (intermarriage). Growing exogamy, in turn, reflects decreasing social distance between racial/ethnic groups, so this is, in essence, a barometer of race relations (Perry, 2013; Platt, 2012; Yancey & Lewis, 2009).

Table 2 Interracial/interethnic households (adapted from Appendix of Lofquist et al., 2012; US Census Bureau Households and Families: 2010)

Type of couple	Opposite-sex married households				Opposite-sex unmarried households			
	2000 total married couple households 54,493,232		2010 total married couple households 56,510,377		2000 total opposite-sex couple households 4,881,377		2010 total opposite-sex couple households 6,842,714	
Total same-race or same Hispanic origin couples	50,452,248		51,141,342		4,146,774		5,593,308	
Total interracial/interethnic couples	4,040,984	100.0	5,369,035	100.0	734,603	100.0	1,249,406	100.0
White non-Hispanic/Hispanic (any race)	1,422,908	35.2	2,020,825	37.6	239,137	32.6	423,496	33.9
White non-Hispanic/Black non-Hispanic	287,576	7.1	422,250	7.9	123,383	16.8	199,016	15.9
White non-Hispanic/American-Indian and Alaska Native non-Hispanic	268,424	6.6	280,780	5.2	46,949	6.4	57,458	4.6
White non-Hispanic/Asian non-Hispanic	504,119	12.5	737,493	13.7	56,502	7.7	94,446	7.6
White non-Hispanic/Native Hawaiian and other Pacific Islanders non-Hispanic	27,264	0.7	33,242	0.6	4849	0.7	6658	0.5
White non-Hispanic/some other-race non-Hispanic	17,948	0.4	29,385	0.5	3660	0.5	5717	0.5
Both are multiracial (both Hispanic or neither Hispanic)	397,766	9.8	341,255	6.4	37,708	5.1	49,983	4.0
Hispanic/non-Hispanic (excluding White non-Hispanic)	253,830	6.3	390,650	7.3	72,060	9.8	138,312	11.1
Other-both Hispanic (spouses different single race, neither White)	16,577	0.4	22,761	0.4	3909	0.5	7599	0.6
Other-neither Hispanic (spouses different single race, neither white)	64,467	1.6	86,233	1.6	13,630	1.9	21,535	1.7

Antecedents

If this is indeed a barometer of race relations, how then does one become more open or accepting of exogamy? What are the antecedents? The old proverb, *familiarity breeds contempt* may not hold true in the case of exogamy. We tend to value what has become familiar to us. That is why we generally tend to feel comfortable around the types of people with whom we grew up. With that in mind, it is not surprising that many studies have found that positive contact with individuals of other races contributes to positive attitudes toward interracial marriage (Emerson, 2006; Emerson, Kimbro, & Yancey, 2002; Golebiowska, 2007). That contact can occur within the context of neighborhoods, schools, or workplaces, to name just a few. This notion is guided by a framework known as the *contact hypothesis*—developed by Gordon Allport (1954), a psychologist (for review, see Perry, 2013). According to this hypothesis "interracial contact will reduce prejudice and promote more harmonious relations between groups" (Perry, 2013, p. 14). Certain conditions need to be met for this to occur:

- Equal status between the groups.
- Absence of competitive interactions between the groups.
- Common objectives shared by the groups.
- Contact that is supported by pertinent powers that be.
- Personal interaction.

These conditions together are antecedents.

Attitudes

United States

In a study of African-American newlyweds (data collected around 2006), 700 couples were asked if they had dated or gone out with someone of a different racial/ethnic background (*A Study of African American Marriage and Health,* funded by the National Institute of Child Health and Human Development*; PI: C. Bryant* (Bryant, n.d.)). All of the study participants resided in a Southern state. Although they were newly married, they ranged in age from 21 to 71 for wives and from 20 to 79 for husbands. Data indicate that men and women under the age of 40 were more likely to have dated someone outside of their race. African-American men were also more likely than African-American women to have dated someone of a different race at all age groups. African-American women aged 61 and older were most likely to respond that they had never dated anyone outside of their race. African-American women were more likely to respond that they had dated someone White, Latino/Hispanic, or biracial, while African-American men were more likely to have dated someone White or biracial. See Table 3.

Table 3 Percent of African-American newlyweds from a southern state that dated outside racial/ethnic group

Age of African-American respondent	Asian or Pacific Islander	Native American/ American Indian	Latino/ Hispanic	White	Biracial/ mixed race
20–30 (n = 642)					
Men (n = 282)	7%	5%	13%	25%	22%
Women (n = 360)	4%	3%	7%	15%	10%
31–40 (n = 416)					
Men (n = 220)	12%	8%	13%	31%	22%
Women (n = 196)	2%	4%	5%	13%	8%
41–50 (n = 208)					
Men (n = 115)	8%	6%	10%	22%	15%
Women (n = 93)	1%	1%	3%	11%	2%
51–60 (n = 91)					
Men (n = 53)	17%	6%	8%	25%	11%
Women (n = 38)	0%	3%	8%	13%	5%
61–70 (n = 25)					
Men (n = 16)	6%	0%	13%	25%	13%
Women (n = 9)	0%	0%	0%	0%	0%
71 and older (n = 7)					
Men (n = 6)	17%	17%	17%	17%	17%
Women (n = 1)	0%	0%	0%	0%	0%

Generally, approval of interracial relationships has increased over time. Findings from the Pew Research Center's report on racial attitudes in the United States (2010), illustrate this change in support across generations. For example, approximately 40% of the "silent" generation (those born between 1928 and 1946) approved of interracial dating in 1987 compared to 68% in 2009. This increase in approval was also seen among baby boomers (those born between 1946 and 1964) and Generation Xers (those born between 1965 and 1980). Nearly all Millennials (those born between 1981 and 1997) reported approval of interracial dating (93%). Interestingly, support for interracial marriage is lower than it is for dating among these groups—85% of Millennials reported supporting interracial marriage (see Fig. 2). In addition to differences in support of interracial dating vs. marriage, there is also a discrepancy seen between global attitudes and personal attitudes toward interracial dating and marriage. For example, in a sample of White men and women, White women were more likely to approve of interracial relationships for others, but not themselves (Herman & Campbell, 2012). Further, both White men and women reported more support for dating someone of another race than cohabiting or marrying someone of another race (Herman & Campbell, 2012). This suggests that, though approval for interracial relationships is on the rise, there remains a discrepancy in terms of support for different types of interracial unions; it seems that attitudes do not necessarily translate into behaviors. Do attitudes expressed in other countries differ from those in the United States?

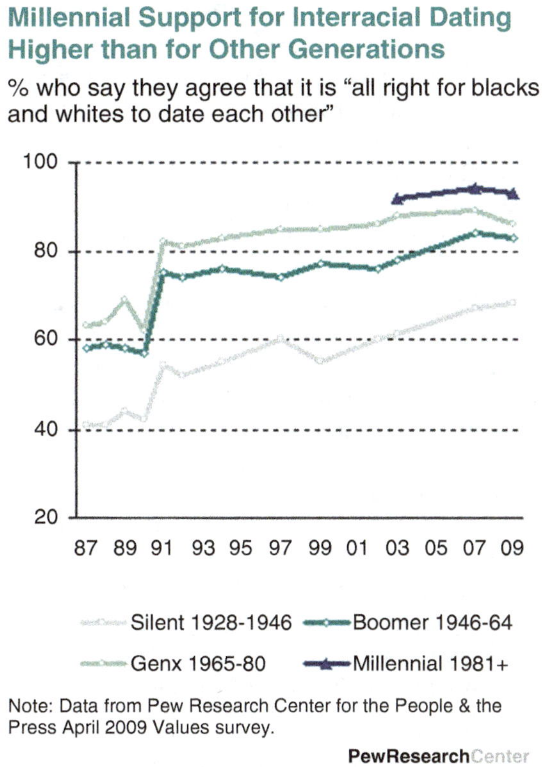

Fig. 2 Change in support for interracial relationships, across generations (*Source*: Pew Research Center, 2010, http://www.pewresearch.org/2010/02/01/almost-all-millennials-accept-interracial-dating-and-marriage/)

A Cross-Country Examination: Britain and Canada

Britain. Although there were no laws in Britain prohibiting interracial marriage that does not mean that race relations were particularly positive, unlike the United States in the 1950s, Britain did attempt to discuss race—often prompted by films to do so. The 1959 crime drama, *Sapphire* (progressive for its time), is a prime example. It is about the murder of a light-skinned Black woman who was attempting to pass as White. Not only were audiences faced with depictions of racial discrimination, but they were also presented with the hope that love could overcome racism. Newspapers proclaimed that "the film would awaken British audiences from their complacent assumption that racism was confined to such countries as South Africa and the United States" (Daily Mail, 1959; Manchester Guardian, 1959; Webb, 2016, p. 10).

This is interesting because in the 1950s when the civil rights movement in the United States was being organized, African-Americans "gained cultural legitimacy for their cause from the apparently more progressive racial politics of Britain" (Webb, 2016, p. 1). An article in the June 9th, 1960, edition of Britain's *Daily Mirror* stressed that it was "bigots in the United States" who were against interracial marriages, unlike "the overwhelming majority of decent people" (Daily Mirror, 1960;

as cited in Webb, 2016, p. 2). An English social anthropologist, Geoffrey Edgar Solomon Gorer professing how tolerant and progressive Britain was with regard to attitudes about race, noted in 1965 that "… we have thanked God that we are not as other men, and particularly not like the white South Africans or Southerners in the United States who are sinners" (as cited in Webb, 2016, p. 2).

Britain may have been more progressive than the United States, but Britain was not necessarily a haven for interracial couples. Britain did not implement sanctions against interracial marriage; however, there were calls for such laws. A constable lobbied for laws banning interracial unions in 1919, shortly after the race riot in Cardiff (Rich, 1986). By the way, Paul B. Rich's book, *Race and Empire in British Politics* (1986), albeit dated now, provides a peek into the racial ideology of the British Empire, in terms of racist attitudes and beliefs, before the 1960s. After World War II, thousands of Caribbean migrants arrived in Britain. Relocating to Britain was a right of all Commonwealth citizens—a right protected under the British Nationality Act (passed in 1948). Black West Indians were characterized as predators undermining the morals of White women. Sexual unions between White women and Black men contributed to the race riots that swept through Nottingham and Notting Hill around 1958 (Pilkington, 1988). White male/Black female relationships were not denounced as much as Black male/White female unions (Webb, 2016). Perhaps the history of White male settlers forming relationships with indigenous women made the former relationship type more acceptable. That attitude sounds somewhat similar to that of the United States. Let's fast forward in time and examine Canada.

Canada. Intermarriage in the United States is rare compared to Canada (Hou, Wu, Schimmele, & Myles, 2015). Of the 25–34-year-old married or cohabiting couples in Canada, 49% of Black women and 62% of Black men have a White partner; however, in the United States, 7% of Black women and 16% of Black men have a White partner (Hou et al., 2015; Hou & Myles, 2013). Two schools of thought explain the differences between the United States and Canada—demographic constraints and social integration.

Demographic Constraints

Personal opportunities in the marriage market are constrained by structural conditions (Blau & Schwartz, 1984). In order for people who desire to marry within their racial group to actually be able to do so, there needs to be enough suitable people in the marriageable pool. Let's focus for a moment on Blacks, Whites, and Asians; the United States is composed of 5% Asian, 13% Black, and 72% White (Humes, Jones, & Ramirez, 2011); Canada is composed of 12% Asian, 2% Black, and 80% White (Statistics Canada, 2008). The United States has a larger proportion of Blacks than Canada, and that may explain the differences in the rates of Black-White interracial marriages between the two countries. Likewise, the smaller percentage of Asians in the United States is the reason Asian interracial marriages are higher in the United States (Hou et al., 2015).

Social Integration

External influences such as families or church, cultural and structural assimilation, as well as personal preferences undergird the social integration perspective (Kalmijn & Van Tubergen, 2010). Cultural similarities, economic inequalities, and social distance between racial groups have a strong impact on personal preferences for endogamy. Increases in intermarriage reflect the merging of racial minorities into mainstream institutions and social networks—known as structural assimilation. As interracial marriages increase, there is typically a decrease in economic inequalities and social distance between racial minorities and Whites (Hou et al., 2015; Lee & Boyd, 2008; Qian & Lichter, 2007). Compared to the United States, feelings about interracial marriage are more positive in Canada. While 77% of Americans have positive attitudes about interracial marriage, approximately 92% of Canadians do (Bibby, 2007). These US-Canada differences in rates of intermarriage and attitudes about intermarriage are a function of historical context. For example, in the United States slavery was much more pervasive; large plantations did not exist in Canada. Moreover, segregation of Blacks is much more prevalent/pervasive in the United States than Canada (Myles & Hou, 2004). Despite more positive attitudes about minorities being held by Canadians, Blacks in Canada (as in the United States) are more likely to experience racial discrimination (Statistics Canada, 2003). According to the social integration theory, a proxy for social equality in any given society is intermarriage, which suggests that Black Americans hold a lower level of social incorporation than do Black Canadians (see Hou et al, 2015 for review).

Understanding demographic trends, attitudes, and behaviors regarding interracial unions can be challenging. Theory-driven models provide frameworks that facilitate that understanding.

Guiding Frameworks

Support for or opposition to interracial unions can come from various levels. Consider Bronfenbrenner's bioecological model which allows researchers to consider the impact of broader societal factors such as the social and cultural milieu (macrosystem) as well as the impact of more direct or immediate environmental factors (microsystem) while also taking into account the impact of time (chronosystem) in both the personal and sociohistorical sense. (Recall, earlier, we stated that interracial unions are embedded within a sociopolitical and historical context. This model helps underscore that notion.) Associations between levels (exosystem, mesosystem) are acknowledged through this model, too. Bronfenbrenner's (1979, 2005) person-process-context-time (PPCT) model is a research design that highlights the powerful nature of these nested elements and the manner in which they influence relationship experiences and outcomes. *Person* factors—race/ethnicity, age, gender, social skills, social ideologies (O'Toole, Hayes, & Mhathuna, 2014; Renn, 2003), to name just a few—may shape the quality of experiences in relationships. Bronfenbrenner (1993) argued that "the attributes of the person most likely to shape the course of development, for better or for worse, are those that induce or inhibit dynamic dispositions toward the immediate environment" (p. 11).

Process factors (interactions with the environment and subsequent responses elicited) can be conceptualized as interactions between spouses and their partners, relationships between spouses and their in-laws, and relationships between spouses and their own family members and friends (MacNeil & Adamsons, 2014; O'Toole et al., 2014); these are relational factors that can shape marital or cohabiting unions. *Context*-based factors such as the social climate or the political climate can also shape these unions. When Bronfenbrenner (1995) spoke of *Time*, he said, "A major factor influencing the course and outcome of human development is the timing of biological and social transitions as they relate to the culturally defined age, role expectations, and opportunities occurring throughout the life course (p. 641). *Time* is a way of acknowledging the changing sociocultural influences. A study exploring conflict among interracial couples used the bioecological model as a guide (MacNeil & Adamsons, 2014). The researchers involved therefore explained that an aspect of the microsystem that may be particularly salient for interracial couples is social support. Because interracial couples may experience lower levels of social support from friends and family members compared to same-race couples, interracial couples may be more likely to experience relational conflict (Killian, 2001; MacNeil & Adamsons, 2014; Zhang & Van Hook, 2009). The researchers further explained that at the macrosystem level (which reflects general societal beliefs), cultural/social stigma influences interracial couples directly and indirectly (through its oftentimes negative impact on social support). Negative societal reactions (manifested in the form of hostility, discrimination, rejection) can generate stress between interracial partners, but that stress does not necessarily lead to poor conflict management; instead, negative societal (macrosystem) reactions may "give interracial couples more experience in navigating societal pressures which subsequently helps them to use more positive conflict management strategies within their relationship" (MacNeil & Adamsons, 2014, p. 254).

Karney and Bradbury's (1995) vulnerability-stress-adaptation model (VSA) is useful in understanding how broad, contextual factors link to microlevel factors to influence the relationship quality and stability of interracial couples. This model suggests that (1) couples possess enduring vulnerabilities that contribute to the stressful events they face; (2) the enduring vulnerabilities that couples possess can affect their ability to adapt to stressful events; and (3) couples' ability (or inability) to engage in effective adaptive processes impacts their marital quality, and in turn stability (Karney & Bradbury, 1995). Interracial couples may experience enduring vulnerabilities at both the individual and dyadic levels. For example, experiencing divorce (either parental divorce or having had a divorce), having children prior to marriage, and low socioeconomic status are all factors that are associated with low marital quality and marital instability. Individuals in interracial unions are more likely to possess all of the aforementioned characteristics (Hohmann-Marriott & Amato, 2008). Discrimination is also an enduring vulnerability that may be experienced at the individual or dyadic level. In marriages where one partner belongs to the dominant group and the other partner belongs to a minority group, the discrimination experienced by the minority partner may also affect the other partner (Leslie & Letiecq, 2004). The couple as a whole, however, may experience blatant or microaggressive discrimination from those that oppose their union (Leslie & Letiecq, 2004; Leslie & Young, 2015). These enduring vulnerabilities may generate stressful events in their lives and/or hinder their ability to successfully adapt to the stress they encounter.

Interdependence theory can be used as a guide facilitating the understanding of interracial relationships—in terms of rewards, costs, investments, and alternatives. Rewards are positive relationship or partner characteristics; while costs are negative relationship or partner characteristics. Rewards promote positive marital outcomes, whereas costs inhibit positive marital outcomes (Rusbult, Agnew, & Arriaga, 2012). Investments are factors individuals put into marriage, that is, factors that would be lost if the relationship dissolved. Alternatives refer to other individuals that could take the place of the current spouse or other options (i.e., divorce and remain single) that could take the place of the marriage.

- Rewards: The most commonly cited reason for embarking upon an interracial relationship is love (Gaines Jr. et al., 1999; Porterfield, 1978). Love facilitates the growth and maintenance of relationships. In interracial relationships, believing that one's partner is using positive relationship maintenance strategies seems to serve as rewards that are associated with turning to social networks for support, applying conflict management techniques, and experiencing greater satisfaction (Dainton, 2015). Rewards may be manifested in several ways. For example, having supportive family members may serve as a buffer against challenges interracial couples may face and that can be rewarding. On the other hand, spouses' bonds to their partners may actually grow stronger if their social network members are unhappy with or critical of the marriage (Leslie & Young, 2015). Rewards may extend far beyond the couple. Think about what could happen at the societal level. Well, interracial marriages may be associated with decreased social distance between racial groups (Wu, Schimmele, & Hou, 2015) as well as improved race relations. Such change is rewarding for society, and not just for the couple (Gaines et al., 2015).
- Social costs: Some individuals intentionally forgo embarking upon interracial marriage because of potential social costs. Some social costs entail having one's own identity challenged. For instance, some African-Americans in interracial relationships reported feeling that other African-Americans questioned their racial identity. They felt that other African-Americans believed that those in interracial marriages did not appreciate their ethnic origins. Whites frequently choosing to initiate anti-Black discussions with African-Americans in interracial marriages are also essentially questioning the racial identities of those individuals (Afful, Wohlford, & Stoelting, 2015). That is a "cost." Costs may occur in another way. In those situations when interracial marriages are driven not by personal choice, but are instead driven by the relative number of marriageable people in each racial group (known as structural constraints), then perhaps

marriage is a cost and that cost may contribute to lower levels of marital quality (Wu et al., 2015).

- Investments: Partners in interracial marriages may feel that they need to work more diligently at investing effort, time, and energy into the relationship in order to earn acceptance from disapproving family members or even to earn social support from family and friends. Perhaps when interracial marriages dissolve, the spouses contend with greater levels of negativity (e.g., *I told you so; I knew this marriage would end; see, it wasn't just a stereotype*) from friends and in-laws than do those individuals who are not in interracial marriages (Clark, Harris, Hasan, Votaw, & Fernandez, 2015).
- Alternatives: There are alternatives for those who are frightened of potential social disapproval: telling no one about the marriage (Lehmiller, 2009), remaining single, or even moving to a more socially accepting community. Of course, moving to a different community would require resources—an investment of resources to identify such communities and an investment of physical, emotion, and financial resources to relocate.

Perhaps, particularly now, a time when the United States is on the brink of changes after a highly contentious 2016 presidential election that was racially/ethically polarizing, and the ensuing divisive social climate, the aforementioned rewards, social costs, investments, and alternatives will change.

Costs and rewards can contribute to marital quality and stability. Let's turn for a moment to quality and stability.

Marital Quality and Stability

As the number of interracial marriages has increased, more attention has been devoted to understanding the relationship quality and stability of these couples. While interracial marriages have consistently been found to be less stable than same-race marriages (Bramlett & Mosher, 2002; Bratter & King, 2008; Fu & Wolfinger, 2011), earlier research has provided mixed results regarding how the relationship quality of interracial couples compares to that of same-race couples. For example, some studies have indicated that couples in interracial relationships are just as happy as same-race couples (Troy, Lewis-Smith, & Laurenceau, 2006), while others have suggested that some interracial couples (i.e., Hispanic/non-Hispanic couples) report greater relationship satisfaction (Negy & Snyder, 2000). In response to the uncertainty of these results, the goal of subsequent research was to further understand the underlying differences in relationship quality and stability between interracial couples and same-race couples, as well as identify unique factors that affect interracial couples.

More recent research has examined the interpersonal and contextual factors impacting interracial couples' relationship quality and stability. A study comparing the relationship quality of same-race and interracial couples found that married and cohabiting interracial couples reported lower levels of relationship satisfaction and higher rates of conflict (Hohmann-Marriott & Amato, 2008). Furthermore, the interracial couples experienced greater complexities (e.g., complex relationship histories, higher likelihood of having children prior to marriage, religious heterogeneity) than did the same-race couples, which accounted for much of the difference in relationship quality between the two groups. Studies have also indicated that the race/gender makeup of interracial couples have implications for their relationship quality and stability. For example, interracial couples that consist of White female/Black male and White female/Asian male were more likely to divorce than White/White couples (Bratter & King, 2008). White/Latino marriages were also at a higher risk for marital dissolution than homogenous Latino marriages, with Latino husband/White wife intermarriages at the highest risk (Fu & Wolfinger, 2011).

Couples face a host of challenges when connecting their lives together. Each individual brings their own background, experiences, and beliefs and each must also learn how to communicate, negotiate, and compromise with their partners. However, in addition to these challenges, interracial couples also experience unique challenges (Bratter & King, 2008; Leslie & Young, 2015; Killian, 2001; McNamara, Tempenis, & Walton, 1999; Tucker & Mitchell-Kernan, 1990; Zhang & Van Hook, 2009). For example, lack of social support, both from the community and family, is a salient challenge faced by interracial couples (Bell & Hastings, 2015; Bertoni & Bodenmann, 2010; Leslie & Young, 2015). Couples often report feeling scrutinized by families and friends, which makes them feel pressured to make the relationship succeed (Wieling, 2003). Lack of paternal support and approval, even if only from one partner's family, creates tension within the couple (Bell & Hastings, 2015). Challenges such as these may explain why married interracial couples report higher levels of psychological distress (Bratter & Eschbach, 2006).

Implications

Future Research

As interracial relationships have become more accepted and numbers of interracial marriages have increased, our knowledge and understanding of these couples grows. However, there is still much to examine. For example, very little is known about the cohabiting relationships of interracial couples. Interracial couples are approximately twice as likely to cohabit than they are to marry (Lofquist et al., 2012). This indicates that, for some reason, interracial couples may be choosing cohabitation either as an alternative to marriage or with an intention to eventually marry; however, the transition to marriage does not typically happen (potentially due to relationship dissolution or other factors). Because cohabitation is a prevalent relationship type among interracial couples, further research is needed to understand the reasons why these couples may choose to "just" live together as opposed to legally marrying.

Another gap in the literature on interracial couples is the examination of a variety of racial pairings. Much of the literature on interracial couples is based on Black/White couples. Due to the social stigma associated with this pairing and their increased likelihood of experiencing discrimination (Leslie & Letiecq, 2004; Zhang & Van Hook, 2009), it is logical that scholars would devote attention to understanding how these relationships succeed (or fail); however, Black/White marriages only make up a small percentage of interracial marriages. For example, in 2010, the highest percentage of interracial marriages were between White non-Hispanic/Hispanic (any race) individuals, followed by White non-Hispanic/Asian non-Hispanic pairings (Lofquist et al., 2012). These couples (that is, those pairings), as well as others, may face different challenges or even have different strengths than Black/White couples. Future research on interracial marriage should include couples of varying racial backgrounds (e.g., Black/Asian, Hispanic/Asian).

Implications for Practice

In addition to the common challenges that couples face (i.e., managing household budgets, learning each other's family traditions), interracial couples also face unique challenges. Previous research has indicated that lack of social support and discrimination—both blatant and microaggressions (Bell & Hastings, 2015; Leslie & Young, 2015)—are common external challenges that interracial couples face. Within the relationship, individuals may struggle with feeling secure in their racial identity or recognizing their racial privilege (Leslie & Young, 2015). Practitioners must understand that the common issues experienced by their interracial couple clients may also be exacerbated by the additional challenges these couples face. Practitioners must be willing and able to allow couples to discuss the role race may play in the lives of their clients. Practitioners must also possess the skills to facilitate such discussions.

The implications of interracial unions are multifold; we will highlight three. First and foremost, the growing number of interracial unions means that there is a growing number of multiracial children (Parker, Morin, Horowitz, Lopez, & Rohal, 2015). Second (and this is related to the first), studying such families is complicated. They are complicated because findings are contingent upon the race and sex compositions of the interracial couples. Various race and sex compositions differentially impact outcomes of multiracial youth. Interracial couples are typically able to provide more educational advantages (i.e., economic resources, cultural resources) to their children than are non-interracial couples. Interestingly, these advantages are not typically observed among Black father/White mother couples (Cheng & Powell, 2007). Also, these advantages do not include social or interactional resources. Perhaps interracial couples/parents are not able to overcome social and structural constraints for their children. This means that interracial couples/parents may face social stigma that hinders their ability to develop social ties at school—ties that would benefit their children. Although multiracial children in kindergarten generally perform better than single-race kindergarteners, that pattern appears to reverse as the multiracial children age and become adolescents. The reasons for these changes are unclear; the change could be associated with negative perceptions of race in the school environment (Aschaffenburg & Maas, 1997; Chenk & Klugman, 2010; Powell, Hamilton, Manago, & Cheng, 2016). The context (context at multiple levels—school, community, nation) in which multiracial families are embedded is critical to their success. That brings us to the third implication. The sociohistorical context in which these families (actually all families) are embedded may shape how they function, where they can safely live, and how they are treated. Recall the story at the beginning of this chapter which underscored a policy designed to prevent and break up interracial unions. If we, as individuals, as citizens, as our brother's keeper, are not watchful, such policies may arise again. During the 2016 presidential election, hate for and distrust of various racial/ethnic minorities surfaced, and that mindset grew after the election. If we are not diligently watchful, the tides may turn, and history may repeat itself.

References

Afful, S. E., Wohlford, C., & Stoelting, S. M. (2015). Beyond "difference": Examining the process and flexibility of racial identity in interracial marriages. *Journal of Social Issues, 71*(4), 659–674.

Allport, G. W. (1954). *The nature of prejudice*. Reading: Addison-Wesley.

Aschaffenburg, K., & Maas, I. (1997). Cultural and educational careers: The dynamics of social reproduction. *American Sociological Review, 62*, 573–587.

Barnett, L. D. (1964). Anti-miscegenation laws. *The Family Life Coordinator, 1394*, 95–97.

Bell, G. C., & Hastings, S. O. (2015). Exploring parental approval and disapproval for Black and White interracial couples. *Journal of Social Issues, 71*(4), 755–771.

Bertoni, A., & Bodenmann, G. (2010). Satisfied and dissatisfied couples: Positive and negative dimensions, conflict styles, and relationships with family of origin. *European Psychologist, 15*, 175–184.

Bibby, R. (2007). *Racial intermarriage: Canada and the U.S. Project Canada Press Release No. 9*. Lethbridge, AB: University of Lethbridge.

Blau, P. M., & Schwartz, J. E. (1984). *Crosscutting social circles*. Orlando, FL: Academic Press.

Bramlett, M. D., & Mosher, W. D. (2002). Cohabitation, marriage, divorce, and remarriage in the United States. *Vital Health Statistics, 23*(22), 1–32.

Bratter, J. L., & Eschbach, K. (2006). 'What about the couple?' Interracial marriage and psychological distress. *Social Science Research, 35*(4), 1025–1047.

Bratter, J. L., & King, R. (2008). "But will it last?": Marital instability among interracial and same-race couples. *Family Relations, 57*(2), 160–171.

Bronfenbrenner, U. (1979). *The ecology of human development*. Cambridge, MA: Harvard University Press.

Bronfenbrenner, U. (1993). The ecology of cognitive development: Research models and fugitive findings. In R. H. Wozniak & K. W. Fischer (Eds.), *Development in context: Acting and thinking in specific environments* (pp. 3–44). Hillsdale, NJ: Erlbaum.

Bronfenbrenner, U. (1995). Developmental ecology through space and time: A future perspective. In P. Moen & G. H. Elder Jr. (Eds.), *Examining lives in context: Perspectives on the ecology of human development* (pp. 619–647). Washington, DC: American Psychological Association.

Bronfenbrenner, U. (2005). *Making human beings human: Bioecological perspectives on human development*. Thousand Oaks, CA: Sage.

Bryant, C. M. (n.d.) Principal Investigator. *A Study of African American Marriage and Health*. Funded by the National Institute of Child Health and Human Development. R01-HD050045-05.

Cheng, S. & Powell, B. (2007). Under and beyond constraints: Resource allocation to young children from biracial families. *American Journal of Sociology, 112*(4), 1044–1094.

Chenk, S., & Klugman, J. (2010). School and racial composition and biracial adolescents' school attachment. *Sociological Quarterly, 51*, 150–178.

Clark, E. M., Harris, A. L., Hasan, M., Votaw, K. B., & Fernandez, P. (2015). Concluding thoughts: Interethnic marriage through the lens of interdependence theory. *Journal of Social Issues, 71*(4), 821–833.

Curtis, M. C. (February 13, 2012). Is "The Loving Story" over, even now? *The Washington Post.* Retrieved October 31, 2016, from https://www.washingtonpost.com/blogs/she-the-people/post/is-the-loving-story-over-even-now/2012/02/13/gIQAkrqECR_blog.html

Daily Mail. (May 8, 1959). *The film that slipped past the faceless ones*, p. 12.

Daily Mirror (June 9, 1960). 'There's NO bar on love', p. 10.

Dainton, M. (2015). An interdependence approach to relationship maintenance in interracial marriage. *Journal of Social Issues, 71*(4), 772–787.

Emens, E. F. (2009). Intimate discrimination: The state's role in the accidents of sex and love. *Harvard Law Review, 122*, 1308–1402.

Emerson, M. O. (2006). *People of the dream: Multiracial congregations in the United States.* Princeton: Princeton University Press.

Emerson, M. O., Kimbro, R. T., & Yancey, G. (2002). Contact theory extended: The effects of prior racial contact on current social ties. *Social Science Quarterly, 83*, 745–761.

Endo, M. (2014). "The word 'mixed' without the 'Indian' would be better": Virginia's Racial Integrity Act and the destruction of Indian race in the early twentieth century. *Native South, 7*, 92–107.

Fu, V. K., & Wolfinger, N. H. (2011). Broken boundaries or broken marriages? Racial intermarriage and divorce in the United States. *Social Science Quarterly, 92*(4), 1096–1117.

Gaines Jr., S. O., Rios, D. I., Granrose, C. S., Bledsoe, K. L., Farris, K. R., Page Youn, M. S., et al. (1999). Romanticism and interpersonal resource exchange among African American/Anglo and other interracial couples. *Journal of Black Psychology, 25*, 461–489.

Gaines, S. O., Clark, E. M., & Afful, S. E. (2015). Interethnic marriage in the United States: An introduction. *Journal of Social Issues, 71*(4), 647–658.

Glaser, J., Dixit, J., & Green, D. P. (2002). Studying hate crimes with the Internet: What makes racists advocate racial violence? *Journal of Social Issues, 58*, 177–193.

Golebiowska, E. A. (2007). The contours and etiology of Whites' attitudes toward Black-White interracial marriage. *Journal of Black Studies, 38*, 268–287.

Herman, M. R., & Campbell, M. E. (2012). I wouldn't, but you can: Attitudes toward interracial relationships. *Social Science Research, 41*, 343–358.

Hohmann-Marriott, B. E., & Amato, P. (2008). Relationship quality in interethnic marriages and cohabitations. *Social Forces, 87*(2), 825–855.

Hou, F., Wu, Z., Schimmele, C., & Myles, J. (2015). Cross-country variation in interracial marriage: A USA-Canada comparison of metropolitan areas. *Ethnic and Racial Studies, 38*(9), 1591–1609.

Hou, F., & Myles, J. (2013). Interracial marriage and status-caste exchange in Canada and the United States. *Ethnic and Racial Studies, 36*(1), 75–96.

Humes, K. R., Jones, N. A., & Ramirez, R. (2011). *Overview of race and Hispanic Origin: 2010.* Washington, DC: United States Census Bureau.

Jones, J. M. (1997). *Prejudice and racism* (2nd ed.). New York: McGraw-Hill.

Kalmijn, M., & Van Tubergen, F. (2010). A comparative perspective on intermarriage: Explaining differences among national-origin groups in the United States. *Demography, 47*(2), 459–479.

Karney, B. R., & Bradbury, T. N. (1995). The longitudinal course of marital quality and stability: A review of theory, methods, and research. *Psychological Bulletin, 118*(1), 3–34.

Killian, K. D. (2001). Reconstituting racial histories and identities: The narratives of interracial couples. *Journal of Marital and Family Therapy, 27*(1), 27–42.

Kim, J. Y. (2013). Postracialism: Race after exclusion. *Lewis & Clark Law Review, 17*, 1063–1139.

Koppelman, A. M. (2001). *Defending the sex discrimination argument for lesbian and gay rights: A reply to Edward Stein*. UCLA Law Review 519. Northwestern University School of Law, Public Law and Legal Theory Series, No. 15-28. Retrieved October 13, 2016, from https://papers.ssrn.com/sol3/papers.cfm?abstract_id=2601762

Lee, S. M., & Boyd, M. (2008). Marrying out: Comparing the marital and social integration of Asians in the US and Canada. *Social Science Research, 37*(1), 311–329.

Legal Information Institute. Cornell University Law School. Loving v. Virginia. Retrieved November 8, 2016., from https://www.law.cornell.edu/supremecourt/text/388/1

Lehmiller, J. J. (2009). Secret romantic relationships: Consequences for personal and relational wellbeing. *Personality and Social Psychology Bulletin, 35*, 1452–1466.

Leslie, L. A., & Letiecq, B. L. (2004). Marital quality of African American and white partners in interracial couples. *Personal Relationships, 11*(4), 559–574.

Leslie, L. A., & Young, J. L. (2015). Interracial couples in therapy: Common themes and issues. *Journal of Social Issues, 71*(4), 788–803.

Lofquist, D., Lugaila, T., O'Connell, M., & Feliz, S. (April 2012). *Households and families: 2010*. 2010 Census Briefs. C2010BR-14. Retrieved November 8, 2016, from https://www.census.gov/prod/cen2010/briefs/c2010br-14.pdf

Livingston, G. & Brown, A. (2017). Pew Research Center, May, 2017, Intermarriage in the U.S. 50 Years After Loving v. Virginia.

MacNeil, T. A., & Adamsons, K. (2014). A bioecological view of interracial/same-race conflict. *International Journal of Conflict Management, 25*(3), 243–260.

Maillard, K. N. (2009). Miscegenation: An American Leviathan. *Human Rights, 36*, 15.

Manchester Guardian. (May 9, 1959). *Spirit of Ealing Persists in "Sapphire": "whodunnit" with topical slant*, p. 5.

Martin, D. (May 6, 2008). Mildred Loving, who battled ban on mixed-race marriage, dies at 68. *The New York Times*. Retrieved November 1, 2016, from http://www.nytimes.com/2008/05/06/us/06loving.html

McNamara, R. P., Tempenis, M., & Walton, B. (1999). *Crossing the Line: Interracial Couples in the South*. Westport, CT: Praeger Publishers.

Moran, R. F. (2001). *Interracial intimacy: The regulation of race & romance*. Chicago, IL: University of Chicago Press.

Moran, R. F. (2004). Love with a proper stranger: What anti-miscegenation laws can tell us about the meaning of race, sex, and marriage. *Hofstra Law Review, 32*, 1663–1679.

Myles, J., & Hou, F. (2004). Changing colours: Neighbourhood attainment and residential segregation among Toronto's visible minorities. *Canadian Journal of Sociology, 29*(1), 29–58.

Negy, C., & Snyder, D. K. (2000). Relationship satisfaction of Mexican American and non-Hispanic White American interethnic couples: Issues of acculturation and clinical intervention. *Journal of Marital and Family Therapy, 26*(3), 293–304.

O'Toole, L., Hayes, N., & Mhathuna, M. M. (2014). A bio-ecological perspective on educational transitions. *Social and Behavioral Sciences, 140*, 121–127.

Parker, K., Morin, R., Horowitz, J. M., Lopez, M. H., & Rohal, M. (2015). *Multiracial in America: Proud, diverse, and growing in numbers*. Report. Washington, DC: Pew Research Center.

Perry, S. L. (2013). Racial composition of social settings, interracial friendship, and whites' attitudes toward interracial marriage. *The Social Science Journal, 50*, 13–22.

Pew Research Center. (2010, February 1). *Almost all millennials accept interracial dating and marriage*. Retrieved from http://www.pewresearch.org/2010/02/01/almost-all-millennials-accept-interracial-dating-and-marriage/

Pilkington, E. (1988). *Beyond the mother country*. London: I.B. Tauris.

Platt, L. (2012). How do children of mixed partnerships fare in the United Kingdom? Understanding the implications for children of parental ethnic homogamy and heterogamy. *The Annals of the American Academy of Political Social Science, 643*, 239–266.

Porterfield, E. (1978). *Black and white mixed marriages: An ethnographic study of black-white families*. Chicago: Nelson-Hall.

Powell, B., Hamilton, L., Manago, B., & Cheng, S. (2016). Implications of changing family forms for children. *Annual Review of Sociology, 42*, 301–322.

Pratt, R. (1998). Crossing the color line: Historical assessment and personal narrative of Loving v Virginia. *Howard Law Journal, 41*(2), 229–244.

Qian, Z., & Lichter, D. T. (2007). Social boundaries and marital assimilation: Interpreting trends in racial and ethnic intermarriage. *American Sociological Review, 72*(1), 68–94.

Renn, K. A. (2003). Understanding the identities of mixed-race college students through a developmental ecology lens. *Journal of College Student Development, 44*(3), 383–403.

Rich, P. B. (1986). *Race and empire in British politics*. New York: Cambridge University Press.

Rosenfeld, M. J., & Kim, B. S. (2005). The independence of young adults and the rise of interracial and same-sex unions. *American Sociological Review, 70*, 541–562.

Rusbult, C. E., Agnew, C. R., & Arriaga, X. B. (2012). The investment model of commitment processes. In P. A. Van Lange, A. W. Kruglanski, & E. T. Higgins (Eds.), *Handboook of theories of social psychology* (Vol. Vol. 2, pp. 218–231). Thousand Oaks, CA: Sage.

Sollors, W. (2000). *Interracialism: Black-White intermarriage in American history, literature, and law*. Oxford: Oxford University Press.

Statistics Canada. (2003). Ethnic Diversity Survey: Portrait of a Multicultural Society. Catalogue No. 89-593-XIE, Ottawa: Statistics Canada.

Statistics Canada. (2008). *Canada's Ethnocultural Mosaic, 2006 Census*. Ottawa: Minister of Industry.

Supplemental Tables. Retrieved November 17, 2016., from http://www.census.gov/population/www/cen2010/briefs/tables/appendix.pdf

Taylor, P., Passel, J. S., Wang, W., Kiley, J., Velasco, G., Dockterman, D. (2010). *Marrying out: One-in-seven new U.S. Marriages is interracial or interethnic*. Report, Pew Research Center, Washington, DC.

Troy, A. B., Lewis-Smith, J., & Laurenceau, J. P. (2006). Interracial and intraracial romantic relationships: The search for differences in satisfaction, conflict, and attachment style. *Journal of Social and Personal Relationships, 23*(1), 65–80.

Tucker, M. B., & Mitchell-Kernan, C. (1990). New trends in black American interracial marriage: The social structural context. *Journal of Marriage and the Family, 52*(1), 209–218.

Wallenstein, P. (1995). The right to marry: Loving v Virginia. *OAH Magazine of History, 9*(2), 37–41.

Wang, W. (2012). *The rise of intermarriage: Rates, characteristics vary by race and gender*. Report. Washington, DC: Pew Research Center

Webb, C. (2016). Special relationships: Mixed race couples in post war Britain and the United States. *Women's History Review*. Published online by Routledge. Retrieved November 17, from http://www.tandfonline.com/doi/pdf/10.1080/09612025.2015.1123027?needAccess=true

Wieling, E. (2003). Latino/a and White marriages: A pilot study investigating the experiences of interethnic couples in the United States. *Journal of Couple & Relationship Therapy, 2*(2–3), 41–55.

Wu, Z., Schimmele, C. M., & Hou, F. (2015). Group differences in intermarriage with White between Asians, Black, and Hispanics: The effects of assimilation and structural constraints. *Journal of Social Issues, 71*(4), 733–754.

Yancey, G., & Lewis, R. (2009). *Interracial families: Current concepts and controversies*. New York: Routledge.

Zackodnik, T. (2001). Fixing the color line: The mulatto, southern courts, and racial identity. *American Quarterly, 53*(3), 420–451.

Zhang, Y., & Van Hook, J. (2009). Marital dissolution among interracial couples. *Journal of Marriage and Family, 71*(1), 95–107.

Transition to Parenthood

Roudi Nazarinia Roy

Sarah and Tony, a biracial couple living in the Midwest, recently celebrated their fifth wedding anniversary. Sarah's family had never indicated disapproval of their relationship; they had attended Tony's college football games and had him over to the house. When Tony asked Sarah's father for his blessing to marry their daughter, things didn't go as well as he had expected. Sarah's family had never questioned their dating relationship, but they had reservations about the marriage. Sarah's father told Tony that he couldn't give his blessing to the young couple because he wanted Sarah to experience life outside of college first. He seemed to be hoping she'd meet someone more like her own family. Although her family questioned Sarah's decision to marry Tony, they attended the ceremony. Sarah's mother paid for the wedding dress, but that was all the support Sarah allowed. She wanted to prove to them that she and Tony did not need their financial support. Tony's mother, too, was skeptical of the marriage; she didn't think it would last without the support of Sarah's family.

After the wedding, Sarah and Tony moved out of state so that Sarah could attend graduate school. Tony worked part-time and completed his teaching credential, and then taught middle school. Two years later, while working on her thesis, Sarah became pregnant with the couple's first child. Her best friend invited Sarah's family to the baby shower. Sarah had kept in touch with her family, but Tony had not accompanied her home since their engagement. Sarah's mother and sister attended the baby shower, which was a very emotional time for Sarah. A couple of weeks later, when they went to the hospital to have their baby daughter, Tony contacted Sarah's family to let them know. This was difficult for Tony because it was hard for him to get past how her family had reacted to their marriage, but he did it for his wife.

R. N. Roy (✉)
Department of Family and Consumer Sciences, California State University Long Beach, Long Beach, CA, USA
e-mail: Roudi.Roy@csulb.edu

R. Nazarinia Roy, A. Rollins (eds.), *Biracial Families*,
https://doi.org/10.1007/978-3-319-96160-6_6

When I asked Sarah about her life as a mother of a 1-year-old, she shared that it was the most amazing gift. She had learned to forgive her father because she and Tony wanted their daughter to know both sides of their family. She was grateful that her husband reached out to her family when she was in the hospital because she needed support from everyone in her new role, and she didn't want to force unwanted relationships on Tony. However, she had found that, even today, ignorance and racism are alive and well in her community. When she was in school, surrounded by friends and like-minded people, she had felt protected. In the real world, people weren't always so open-minded about biracial relationships. She had faced some negative reactions when she and Tony were dating, but when she became a mother she became hypersensitive to the reactions of people around her: the looks, the comments, and the removal of privileges. As a biracial couple and more recently as parents, they experienced discrimination not only from White community members but from African-American members as well. She now has a better understanding of what Tony used to share about his experiences. Having a biracial child who looks more like her father has given her a new perspective. Sarah feels that her daughter's presence makes people see and treat her differently. She lives in a new reality, not just as a new mother, but as the mother of a biracial infant.

In Sarah's story, her pregnancy and the birth of her first child marked a turning point in her relationship with her parents, prompting her husband to reach out to them even though their relationship had been strained. This experience is not uncommon: the birth of a child can enhance relationships with family members who initially did not support a biracial couple's relationship but wish to connect with a grandchild (Kang Fu, 2008; Kibria, 2002). Family members may accept the child, but they may continue to disapprove of the relationship. This disapproval from family, as well as from friends and even complete strangers, can strain any relationship. Biracial couples often turn to each other for the support they need to overcome daily situations that can cause stress, from encounters with strangers to arguments with a parent. When they became parents, Tony's decision to reach out to Sarah's family allowed her to reconnect with her family as a support system, which is often needed and desired by new parents, especially new mothers. Most new parents experience strain across the transition to parenthood as they take on new roles, often learned in their families of origin. During this transition, the couple must turn to each other and often to their extended families for support to maintain their current life roles and successfully add the parenting role.

Millions of children are born in the United States each year (Hamilton, Martin, Osterman, Driscoll, & Rossen, 2017), and we have seen an increase in the percentage of biracial babies over the past 50 years. In 1970, 1% of infants living with both parents were biracial (Livingston, 2017). In 2013, one in ten infants under the age of 1, living with both parents, was biracial (Livingston, 2017). Of the infants living with biracial parents, the most frequent racial pairing (36%) was Black-White, followed by 24% Asian-White and 11% American-Indian–White (Livingston, 2017). With such an increase in biracial infants, greater attention must be paid to how biracial couples' transition to parenthood may differ from that of the general population in order to support them in adjusting to their new roles as parents.

The blending of two family cultures can always be challenging, and biracial couples face the same challenges that monoracial couples do, yet biracial couples face additional challenges that arise from encounters and experiences within and outside their relationship. Considering the fact that biracial couples are not always supported by their families or members of their society (Kang Fu, 2008), this additional strain created by the feelings of rejection from family and society places additional stress on the couple and their relationship. In this chapter, I examine the current multidisciplinary literature on this life event and identify factors that facilitate a less stressful transition to parenthood at the individual, couple, and family levels. Throughout this process I incorporate examples from biracial couples and my own lived experiences to highlight the similarities and differences in the experiences of biracial couples across this important life transition. I then discuss implications for practice and end the chapter with some recommendations for future research.

Literature Review

Transition to Parenthood

The transition to parenthood, the family life stage when a couple becomes parents for the first time, begins at the onset of pregnancy and extends through the first few years of a child's life. This important life transition has a profound effect on multiple domains of an individual's life. From their sense of self to their relationships both within the parental unit and extended family and friend, expecting and new parents experience growth and a multitude of changes. Although people become parents in diverse ways, most of the literature on the transition to parenthood has focused on married couples who become pregnant and parent their first biological child. Although I will draw on this literature, I will also share some of the narratives that parents, mostly mothers, of biracial infants have shared with me that exemplify their experiences across the transition to parenthood. These examples will expose the reader to the raw experience of having a child who has a racial classification different than one's own, and how this experience creates a split reality, a leap into a racial experience beyond that of a biracial relationship—but profound in its experience of parenthood.

When scholars first began to examine the transition to parenthood, it was viewed as a period of great crisis for both the individual parent and the parental relationship (LeMasters, 1957). Over the decades, the work on this important life transition has been guided by several different frameworks. For example, some researchers have focused on the individual experiences of the parent, guided by Belsy's (1984) model of parenting stress, which focuses on the internal and external factors related to an individual parent's life. Others have focused on the multiple domains of family life that are reciprocally impacted by the birth of a child, which Cowan and Cowan (2000) identified as the parent's inner self, their quality of their relationship in the family, stress outside the family, quality of marriage, and the baby itself. Although most of the literature has focused on White, middle-class, married heterosexual couples, the studies that have focused on more ethnically diverse couples have applied a large theoretical framework, such as Bronfenbrenner's ecological theory (1979), to capture the interrelatedness of the contexts within which individual and couples reciprocally interact (e.g., Cao, Mills-Koonce, Wood, & Fine, 2016; Levy-Shiff, 1994).

Although parenthood is a normative life event experienced and celebrated by millions of couples each year around the world, it is also a turning point in the lives of many adults. Understandably, new parents experience a high level of parenting distress (Epifanio, Genna, DeLuca, Roccella, & La Grutta, 2015) as they experience many new and sometimes unexpected challenges (Ronka et al., 2003) and go through a process of renegotiating their roles and priorities (Cowan & Cowan, 2000). The challenges can range from the sudden and often drastic reorganization of daily behaviors and relationships (Belsky & Rovine, 1990) to the creation of new problems and the amplification of preexisting vulnerabilities and inadequacies, partly due to a depletion of existing resources (Cowan & Cowan, 2000). The result is often an increase in relationship conflict (Kluwer & Johnson, 2007) and decline in relationship satisfaction (Gottman & Notarius, 2000; Nazarinia Roy, Walker, Aljayyousi-Khalil, & Dayne, 2016). Yet people have children because at the end of the day, for most parents, the joys and rewards outweigh the costs. More importantly, as parents, we learn that the challenges will pass.

The Individual Parent

The experience of parenthood has many commonalities for first-time parents, from the excitement of anticipating the birth to realizing that they can actually survive with only a couple of hours of sleep each night. Most of the literature on the transition to parenthood has focused on the couple, and because women's lives are found to be more immediately affected by the birth of a child (Belsky et al., 1986; Delmore-Ko, Pancer, & Hunsberger, & Pratt, 2000; Nazarinia Roy et al., 2014a, 2014b; Pancer, Pratt, Hunsberger, & Gallant, 2000) they have become a central focus in the literature. More recently, the experiences of new fathers have gained greater attention as researchers have continuously reported the numerous benefits for child outcomes of having a nurturing, responsible, and involved father (McClain & Brown, 2017). Therefore, in this section I discuss the individual characteristics of mothers and fathers that have been identified in the literature on the transition to parenthood.

Becoming a parent has a profound influence on most mothers and fathers, from the grand shifts in one's life philosophies to the daily shift in their behaviors and routines (Nazarinia Roy et al., 2014a, 2014b). For example, mothers who may have been career focused often pull back and prioritize their time in such a way that allows them more time with their new child, while new fathers report a greater sense of responsibility and accountability and seek safety nets such as life insurance. Generally, we know becoming a parent creates new roles and impacts one's sense of identity and self-esteem (Nazarinia Roy et al., 2014a, 2014b). We also know that the expectations and self-efficacy that a new parent holds about their current and future role can have a dramatic impact on their levels of distress and overall well-being.

Undoubtably the transition to parenthood brings with it a shift in role responsibilities, where new roles such as childcare provider, with all that it encompasses, are created and old roles have to shift. This life transition shifts individuals into predominately traditional gender roles (Katz-Wise, Priess, & Hyde, 2010). These roles are also imposed by the greater society, as men and women are expected to take on traditional gender roles as mothers and fathers (Nazarinia Roy et al., 2014a, 2014b). In traditional gender roles, mothers have a greater responsibility for the housework and childcare, while fathers take on greater responsibility as the family provider and play a greater role in the paid labor force. Generally speaking, younger generations of adults tend to hold more egalitarian gender role attitudes, where the male and female share both household and childcare tasks as well as paid labor force participation (Powers et al., 2003). However, across the transition to parenthood, mothers tend to reduce their labor force participation and become more responsible for the increased household and child-related tasks, while fathers take on a greater role as provider and increase their labor force participation (Baxter, Hewitt, & Haynes, 2008).

For individuals who hold traditional gender role values, this role shift after the baby is born is made with greater ease than it is for their egalitarian counterparts (Cowan & Cowan, 2000). The literature on gender role attitudes and actual role enactments finds that individuals with traditional gender role attitudes are more likely to be married and have children, compared with their egalitarian counterparts (Mickelson, Donahue, & Biehle, 2009). The literature suggests that when there are discrepancies between one's gender role attitudes and the actual roles one holds, these discrepancies are linked to poorer mental and physical health outcomes (Mickelson et al., 2009). This finding holds true for those with both traditional and egalitarian gender role attitudes and is more profound in men. Thus, if a new father holds a traditional gender role attitude and believes that he should be the primary provider for his family, his inability to hold that provider role will result in poorer mental and physical health consequences.

Fathers

Becoming a father can be a stressful time for a man, and men report feeling unprepared for their role as fathers (Boyce, Condon, Barton, & Corkindale, 2007). They are also more likely to experience both psychological and relational difficulties during their partner's pregnancy and after bringing their baby home (Boyce et al., 2007; Matthey, Barnett, Ungerer, & Waters, 2000). Expecting fathers report feeling an increased need to provide financially for their family (Dayton et al., 2016). They also report experiencing an increased level of distress over balancing their roles as the financial provider and an involved father (Kushner et al., 2017). In many ways, a man's financial contribution to his family becomes merged with his identity as a man and provider when he becomes a father. As the importance of the father role has received greater attention in recent years, so too has the important impact of coparenting, as seen in Feinberg's (2003) Ecological Model of Coparenting, where a direct relationship between parental stress, individual characteristics, coparenting support, and couple's romantic relationship is proposed.

Although much of the literature has focused on the economic advantage of having a father in the home, father involvement encompasses much more than just providing financial resources, such as being engaged in a child's daily life and taking on responsibilities related to a child's needs (Lamb, Pleck, Charnov, & Levine, 1987). Fathers' involvement has numerous, well-documented benefits for their children, including positive cognitive, social, and emotional development and mental health (Cabrera, Shannon, & Tamis-LeMonda, 2007; Lamb & Lewis, 2013; Marsiglio, 2000).

Although the experiences of new fathers can be diverse, fathers often see themselves as providers of knowledge, responsible for socializing their children for their future roles as productive members of society (Dayton et al., 2016). Although fathers, especially fathers of color, are often omitted from the literature on parenting, they play a critical role in their children's lives (Coley, 2001). For several of the new African-American fathers in a recent qualitative study I conducted (Nazarinia Roy year) how they socialize their children is often based on their perspective on how society will treat their children. John, an African-American father of a 3-month-old biracial daughter, stated:

> *… a role of a father would have to be leading by example I would also say being a provider as well as someone who is going to be a protector. A provider doesn't necessarily mean with money but just a provider of knowledge and patience, of examples of what a man is to uh your children whether they are a young woman or a young boy and then lead them from there ….*

John's views on how others will perceive and treat his daughter clearly guide his parenting practices. He shared his views:

> *the dream that I have for my child is for her to never question the value that she has as a Black woman, that's also my fear because I fear that society will not allow her to ever reach her full potential cuz she has two strikes against her she's a woman and she's Black and in this society.*

Lamar, a graduate student and father of a 2-year-old biracial daughter, is also keenly aware of how his daughter will be viewed and sees it as his role to educate her on who she is. He stated:

> *… a huge problem I have with the public school system is being that my daughter is Black and Mexican we, me and my wife, refer to her as an Afro-Latina … being that it is that there's a lot of history left out in the educational system I make it a point to introduce her to African-centered books … I want to raise my daughter to be a strong independent culturally competent woman who understands that she is Mexican, she is Black … I'm black and white so she is white … she is a mix of all these cultures, you know, but she's not going to be seen … as that … she gonna be able to be seen as an Afro-Latina … so just educate her in those aspects.*

Fathers of color play a particularly important role in socializing their children, and they are aware of this role early on, as illustrated by Lamar. During his interview, Lamar also talked about his African-American father's important role in his life. Though his parents separated when he was a young boy, his father remained in his life and was ultimately his link to the African-American community, a link his White mother did not have access to. For Lamar, fatherhood was an opportunity to instill racial and cultural pride in his daughter, something he had learned from his own African-American father, although he had not reflected on how important his racial pride was until his wife became pregnant. Lamar stated:

> *Fatherhood make you reflect on the world around you and what you want and don't want for your child. I want her to be proud of her heritage, both her Mexican and Black sides of the family. That is really important to me and my wife ... for our daughter and our future kids.*

Although Lamar's parents separated when he was very young, he had the opportunity to connect with his father. However, many nonresidential fathers do not have the same access to their children. Often a nonresidential father's access to his child is limited by the mother, who plays a gatekeeper role, and access is often linked to the father's ability to provide financially for their child (Pruett, Arthur, & Ebling, 2007). Pregnancy intention also plays an important role in fathers' involvement, such that when the pregnancy is unplanned the father often is less involved (Bronte-Tinkew et al., 2007). The literature on the importance of fathers also indicates that when fathers are involved early, during the pregnancy and early parenting, they are more likely to stay involved in the lives of their children throughout their childhood and later years, resulting in positive child outcomes. Unfortunately for biracial babies, the loss of connection with the other parent can lead to a loss of a connection with an entire community, a valuable resource to a biracial child, as Lamar mentioned in his interview.

Mothers

A woman's role as a mother has always been a focus of the literature on the transition to parenthood. Many women see motherhood as key component of their identity, and researchers have found the parenting role to be important not only for mothers' identity but also for their well-being (Katz-Wise et al., 2010; Maurer, Pleck, & Rane, 2001). The transition to parenthood brings many positive changes in a woman's life, but it can also present challenges. According to the literature, mothers are often the first to report negative impacts, such as a decline in relationship satisfaction (Nazarinia Roy et al., 2014a, 2014b), increased stress (Nomaguchi & Milkie, 2003), anxiety (Warner, 2005), and depression (Evenson & Simon, 2005). This impact on women is mainly due to the fact that their lives are the first to be affected by the onset of a pregnancy and after the birth of their child, as they shift into more traditional female gender roles. Therefore, it is not surprising that women who hold more traditional gender role values, are less career oriented, are more organized (Levy-Shiff, 1994), and have greater confidence in their childcare provider role as a parent (Fillo, Simpson, & Rholes, 2015) show less distress across the transition to parenthood. Although new mothers have higher self-confidence in their caretaker role than new fathers have (Elek, Hudson, & Bouffard, 2003; Fillo et al., 2015; Hudson, Elek, & Fleck, 2001), they are also more likely to face unrealistic exceptions based on an ideology of motherhood that is difficult to attain (Henderson, Harmon, & Newman, 2016).

When expectations of a new role are high, and unattainable, the inability to master them can negatively impact one's self-esteem. A year after giving birth to their first child, parents, especially mothers, report lower levels of self-esteem than their childless counterparts (Bleidorn et al., 2016).

In many ways, our society socializes women at a young age to take on their mothering role. Perhaps this is why so many mothers cherish their roles as mothers and caretakers, seeking to spend as much time as possible with their newborn child. But this new role is exhausting and at times lonely for a new mother. Indeed, motherhood brings an increase in demands and adjustments that can place a mother at risk of experiencing persistent stress. Stress as it relates to parenting is usually "a condition or feeling experienced" when the demands of the parenting role exceed the available resources, creating a state of distress (Cooper, McLanahan, Meadows, & Brooks-Gunn, 2009, p. 2). We know that motherhood is a very demanding role that exposes mothers to feelings of guilt and shame when they are unable to meet these demands (Liss, Schiffrin, & Rizzo, 2013), and the transition period is perhaps the most important time, when mothers are at a heightened level of stress because of all the new demands on them as they take on this new role.

Although motherhood is a universal role, how women experience this role across the transition to parenthood varies. African-American mothers report higher levels of stress than their White and Hispanic counterparts 1 year after having their first child (Cardoso, Padilla, & Sampson, 2010; Nazarinia Roy, Webb, Schumm, & Walker, 2011). This finding may in part be due to the fact that African-American mothers are also less likely than White mothers to seek support from professionals during the postpartum period (Bodnar-Deren, Benn, Balbierz, & Howell, 2017). Similarly, White mothers are more likely to seek both informational and social support from other mothers and professionals than Hispanic mothers are (Pollard, Nievar, Nathans, & Riggs, 2014). Despite these between-group differences, researchers believe that there are greater within-group differences based on contextual factors, such as partner support, social support, and work status (Cardoso et al., 2010; Pollard et al., 2014). Thus, the key to reducing maternal stress across the transition to parenthood is increasing availability of and access to support.

Motherhood not only shifts a woman's role at home with added responsibilities, but it also shifts her role outside the home. New mothers seek more social support from their family (Gjerdingen & Chaloner, 1994) and see shifts in their social networks (Bost, Cox, & Payne, 2002) as they seek new friendships with peers who are parents. Although new parents seek a supportive network, they also meet with unsolicited advice along the way. The encounters with strangers are endless, from the oh's and ah's from strangers who get a glimpse of a sleeping newborn to unsolicited advice such as "don't let them sleep during the day or else they'll keep you up all night" or "make sure you take the pacifier away or else they won't take the breast," to passive-aggressive comments such as "it's awfully cold to have a baby so small out today." These types of comments, which are a common experience for mothers, can reaffirm their efforts or cause more reflection or stress, depending on how they are perceived.

What is unique for some mothers of biracial children is the tendency for not only strangers but even friends and family members to make uninvited comments or be overly curious about their infants. Lisa, a blonde-haired, blue-eyed White mother of a biracial infant son, shared a common daily experience:

> *It just makes me feel like different I guess. That I have a biracial kid and that people … people may look at me and be like wow is that … really yours cause he's dark. But I know it doesn't matter what people think. It's what I think. That's all that matters … Sometime when people stare, smile at me and then stare at him again I want to say 'yes this is my child' and just end their stares.*

Lisa shared that strangers go as far as wanting to touch her son's hair, or they make comments she felt she would never have heard as a mother of a White child. Even her friends' curiosity became annoying.

> *It's just different like my own friends are always touching his hair … I mean would they touch his hair if it was like mine … I just don't like how they all seem to be amused by it.*

For some of the other mothers I interviewed, becoming a mother of a biracial child was a new experience that made them hyperaware of their surroundings. Mothers shared how simple comments had to be analyzed for deeper meaning because they couldn't always tell the commenter's intentions. Take Sue's example: Her 12-month-old daughter was climbing up and down a chair while Sue tried on shoes in a department store. A lady across from her smiled and said, "She is such a little monkey, isn't she?" Sue shared that she froze in the moment, unsure of how to take the comment since her daughter, an Asian and Black toddler, was clearly biracial. She ultimately turned to the lady, smiled, and said, "She definitely has a lot of energy today!" She remembered the incident vividly because it was the first time she had encountered such a comment, but not the last. Mothers of biracial children often experience situations in which they have to reflect on who said what and what was really said (O'Donoghue, 2004). Although they felt they were prepared to handle such circumstances, they were often left in shock for a moment before they could respond. Many of the mothers shared how these types of situations became conversation topics with their husbands and fiancés for weeks at a time. When families share these experiences, they also begin to share a world view, as members of the couple are exposed to the injustices that their partners from different race groups face each and every day.

The Couple

The transition to parenthood is well documented in the literature as a stage in the family life cycle that can be challenging and stressful for most individuals and couples (Doss, Cicila, Hsueh, Morrison, & Carhart, 2014; Doss, Rhoades, Stanley, & Markman, 2009). The new demands of childcare, a common stressor for mothers (Horowitz & Damato, 1999), and changes in the division of household labor, of which mothers often do a greater share (Roy et al., 2016), can place a greater strain on couples' relationships as expectations are violated (Ruble, Fleming, Hackel, & Stangor, 1988) and new responsibilities have to be negotiated (Cowan & Cowan, 2000). Not surprisingly, across this life transition couples report an increase in conflict (Kluwer & Johnson, 2007) and a decline in their leisure time together (Claxton & Perry-Jenkins, 2008), intimacy, and sexual satisfaction (Pacey, 2004). The life changes that accompany parenthood create a steadier decline in the marital satisfaction of new parents compared with that of their childless counterparts (Shapiro, Gottman, & Carrere, 2000). The more successful couples, the ones who demonstrate less decline in their relationship satisfaction, are those in which there is a strong coparenting relationship (Feinberg, 2002) and the individual partners have confidence in their own abilities (Gross & Marcussen, 2017), positive yet realistic expectations (Bouchard, 2009; Curran, Hazen, & Mann, 2009; Harwood, McLean, & Durkin, 2007; Mihelic, Filus, & Morawaska, 2016), and admiration for their partner in their new role as a parent (Shapiro et al., 2000).

When we consider that across the transition to parenthood, proactive coping strategies have the potential to alleviate some of the stressors experienced by new parents (Biehle, 2013), we must also remember that this type of coping is difficult when the couple is unfamiliar with how members of society will react to them or their child. Therefore, for couples in biracial relationships, there is not only the stress of becoming a parent based on their new role demands and adjustments but also the added stress of going against societal norms by being in a biracial relationship in the first place (Kang Fu, 2008).

Expectations

The literature on the transition to parenthood suggests that parents who have realistic expectations of what their lives will be like once they bring a baby home are more likely to make a positive adjustment to parenthood (Biehle & Mickelson, 2012; Delmore-Ko et al., 2000; Flykt et al., 2014; Harwood et al., 2007). Many couples share that in anticipation of their new role they expect that there will be many changes in their individual lives and an increase in responsibility, but they don't necessarily anticipate the changes they will see in their partner or their relationship (Deave, Johnson, & Ingram, 2008). Like many new parents, David, an African-American father with a 1-year-old son, married to a White woman, stated:

> *Motherhood changed her, she was so consumed with our son at the beginning it was like she only needed me when she needed me to get her something. She's six years older than me, so we don't plan on having any more children ... I mean our conversations are always about the baby,*

Later during the same interview, when asked what he would have told himself if he could go back, he recognized some of the family-of-origin differences that can create tension for new parents when they disagree on parenting roles:

> *I wish I knew more about her upbringing ... we just think differently about things and it causes arguments not because she's wrong or I'm right but we are different we were raised differently.*

David is right that we learn a lot about our partners when we become parents, because children create new and unexplored experiences for us as individuals and as couples. Most couples have disagreements based on the different ways they were brought up, but for biracial couples these differences can stem from cultural differences in parenting practices. Unfortunately, when couples have parenting disagreements, mothers act as gatekeepers, restricting access to their child. Essentially this means that the mother decides to do things herself, her way. This gatekeeping essentially tells the father that his way of parenting is wrong or just not good enough, which leads to decreased relationship satisfaction among fathers (Don, Biehle, & Mickelson, 2013; Schoppe-Sullivan, Brown, Cannon, Mangelsdorf, & Sokolowski, 2008) and lower father involvement (Waller, 2012).

Couples often enter parenthood expecting things such as the sharing of household tasks to get better and become more even, when they weren't very even before the children were born (Cowan & Cowan, 2000). We also expect that our partners will take on a more equal share of childcare tasks (Roy et al. 2016), only to find ourselves taking on more traditional gender role tasks when we become parents, as discussed above. The expectations that new parents hold for themselves and their partner during the pregnancy period and after bringing their baby home from the hospital have been linked to both individual well-being and relationship adjustment (Bouchard, 2009; Harwood et al., 2007). We know that positive, realistic expectations result in better adjustment to this important life transition and that negative or unrealistic expectations can be harmful to the individual and their relationship.

Within biracial families, couples not only have to prepare themselves for the adjustment of parenthood and bringing a baby home, but they also have to be aware of how their interactions with others might change. The presence of their child means that their identity shifts as they become not only a parent but also a parent of a biracial child. This identity shift can change their daily interactions with others as they begin to perceive and cope with these new interactions. For example, my husband and I had experienced racism and discrimination during our relationship, within and outside our community. We experienced it from all sides of the primarily White community we lived in and from some African-American members of that same community. Lisa, one of the mothers I have interviewed, shared the fact that while everyone focuses on how White people are racist, through her experiences she had come to know racism from both the White and the Black communities. A new mother can also face an experience that is difficult to accept when their child is considered a member of a group they themselves aren't accepted into. This type of experience is a reality that mothers of biracial babies aren't always aware of or exposed to earlier in their biracial relationships. And the new experiences aren't always discrimination, like the time my husband and I were driving to Kansas from Arkansas and stopped for lunch in a restaurant in Oklahoma City. The waitress started talking to us like she knew who we were. Every time we tried to convince her she didn't know us, she acted like we were joking with her. She had mistaken us for a different biracial couple she knew, showing us that this type of mistaken-identity experience, well known to many minority people in our society, can happen even to couples.

These types of situations led to endless conversations on the topic of discrimination and just simply ignorance. We thought we were prepared for the experiences we might have as parents, until the first experience came. We were at a work-related Halloween party. My 3-month-old daughter was dressed in a little yellow chick costume when one of my husband's acquaintances approached me. This sweet old woman sat down next to me and, with great excitement, introduced herself. She kept complimenting our daughter, who was in my arms, and asked if she could hold her. I felt comfortable with her, so I passed my daughter over to her. Cooing and smiling at my daughter, she looked up at me with a big smile on her face and said, "I've never held a Black baby before." It was an odd statement, one that made me feel uncomfortable. I calmly told her I need to change my daughter and took her back in my arms. I wondered why she thought holding a Black baby would feel any different than holding any other baby.

Later that night, while I was discussing the situation with my husband, he brushed it off and told me she was in her late 80s, grew up during segregation, and had probably never seen a Black baby until she was an adult, let alone held one. He was right. It was a harmless incident compared with other situations we have encountered as a family, but it reaffirmed the fact that my child's race would always be at the forefront of how others see her. No matter how well I thought I had prepared myself to handle race-related situations that might arise, the jolt of having someone refer to my child's race so early was just that: a jolt. I have come to learn that infants of color can be just as mistreated as older children based on the color of their skin. A recent study conducted in California's neonatal intensive care units showed that separation and difference begin from the moment we are born, as findings indicated that a baby's race affects the quality of care, both within and across hospitals (Profit et al., 2017). More specifically, Black and Hispanic infants received lower quality care than their White and Asian counterparts did.

These types of situation are unbelievable or perhaps even deniable for those who have not encountered such experiences. But as biracial couples encounter similar situations of discrimination, these shared experiences shape their world view and are an important part of being able to support and even relate to one another. Take Sarah and Malik, for example, the proud parents of a 4-month-old baby girl. Sarah had contacted a woman selling a stroller and had arranged to pay for and pick up the item that evening. On the drive to their destination, Sarah sat in the back seat, soothing their daughter in her car seat. It was dark out when they reached their destination, and not wanting to upset their baby, Sarah asked her husband if he could go get the stroller by himself. Malik agreed, and as he was getting out of the car, he turned to Sarah and asked, "Does she know I'm Black?" Sarah's initial response was "What?" Malik explained: "We're in a new neighborhood and it's dark. Does she expect a Black man to be knocking on her door?" Sarah's response was a simple "no," and she took out her phone to call the woman, who was kind and brought the stroller out to their car. Sarah shared that it made her angry and sad to have to think about her husband's race every time they encountered new people. Years earlier, when they were dating, she would have told Malik he was overreacting, but experience had taught her that it's better to be prepared than to be blindsided by people's reactions. Now that they had a baby, she felt a heightened sense of awareness of the people around her and their interactions—a defense mechanism she had developed to protect her baby and, in some ways, herself.

On the other hand, Chelsea, a White mother of a 3-month-old biracial son, wasn't always aware of the discrimination her fiancé was experiencing. He would often come home and share what had happened at work: someone had called him a racial slur, or he was passed over for a promotion in favor of someone with less experience. Chelsea had always brushed it off as his way of explaining his own faults. It wasn't until their encounter with the nurses and security staff at the hospital that she began to realize the truth behind his stories. Chelsea had delivered their son just after midnight, and once things had settled down and the baby was resting comfortably, her fiancé stepped out to get some food. He had been gone for over an hour, and Chelsea thought it was odd, so she grabbed her phone. She had missed several calls from him. When she called back, he was irate. When he had come back to the hospital with the food, the security guard stopped him and asked for his identification. When he gave his identification, the security guard contacted the maternity floor and spoke to a nurse, who informed the security guard that they didn't have any African-American infants in labor and delivery that evening. Chelsea quickly contacted her nurse and was frustrated when the nurses acted confused and unaware of such a phone call. Her fiancé was finally allowed upstairs after the matter was cleared up, but the entire ordeal was stressful, and Chelsea would not have believed it if she hadn't lived it. Although her last name didn't match her fiancé's, her son's last name clearly matched, so she didn't understand why the nurse who answered the phone hadn't just checked the last names of the newborns.

Chelsea had, for the first time, shared a microaggression experienced by her fiancé. Microaggressions are the small "daily verbal, behavioral or environmental indignities, whether intentional or unintentional, that communicate hostile, derogatory or negative racial slights and insults towards people of color" (Sue et al., 2007, p. 271). African-American women report microaggressions as a common experience when encountering medical professionals during their pregnancy checkups (Sawyer, 1999). Unfortunately, racial inequalities are so "deeply ingrained in American society" that perpetrators of daily microaggressions sometimes don't even realize how their attitudes and actions discriminate against people of color (Sue et al., 2007, p. 271). For many individuals in biracial relationships, especially White partners, their biracial relationship heightens their awareness of racial injustices. In some ways the individuals in a biracial family become bicultural because their life experiences force them to change the way they view encounters with other people (O'Donoghue, 2004).

These weekly or even daily exposures to small stressors can take a toll on the individuals and their supporting partners. For example, among African-American couples, wives engage in more protective behaviors to support their partners who are exposed to race-related discrimination, which over time has a negative impact on the couple's relationship (Cowdery et al., 2009). Couples in biracial relationships have the added challenges of negotiating cultural differences within their relationship and coping with prejudice from their own family or the larger community (Reiter & Gee, 2008). These types of conflict can put biracial couples at greater risk of relationship dissolution. An increase in exposure to discrimination is associated with an increase in depressive symptoms among wives, leading to less supportive marital interactions (Murry, Brown, Brody, Cutrona, & Simons, 2001). In a recent study, McElroy-Heltzel et al. (2018) assert that culturally based arguing (i.e., repeatedly fighting over the same cultural issue without either partner feeling understood) could lead to lower perceptions of one's partner's cultural humility (i.e., being other-oriented and respectful toward another's cultural background). They suggest that these negative personality judgments could lead to lower commitment and relationship satisfaction among partners. Their results indicated that cultural humility is a key factor in mediating the relationship between arguments and relationship quality (i.e., commitment and satisfaction). Therefore, when an individual feels disrespected by their partner, they become less committed to their partner.

Exposure to discrimination can also lead to less supportive coparenting (Murry et al., 2001). Coparenting is broadly defined as the "ways that parents and/or parental figures relate to each other in the role of parent" (Feinberg, 2003, p. 96). This includes agreement or disagreement on childrearing issues, support for the partner's role as parent, division of childcare, and shared management of family interactions (Feinberg, 2003). Coparenting is essentially about one parent stepping in when the other parent is overwhelmed or stressed: the second parent can give the first parent a break, share in responsibilities, and provide encouragement and reassurance (Feinberg, 2003). When parents agree on how to raise their child, share new responsibilities, respect each other's rules, and offer encouragement and support during times of stress, they feel more connected as partners (Don et al., 2013). When mothers show more support to fathers in their role, fathers' involvement increases (Waller, 2012), and when mothers receive more parenting agreement from their partner, they report greater relationship satisfaction (Don et al., 2013). We know that across the transition to parenthood, mothers are the first to indicate changes in relationship satisfaction, but fathers follow the mothers' lead, so that by the end of the first year mothers and fathers report the same levels of relationship satisfaction (Belsky & Rovine, 1990).

Coparenting enhances the stability of a couple's relationship and the well-being of individual parents across the transition to parenthood (McClain & Brown, 2017). When we consider that at 1 year after the birth of their child, parents in biracial couples indicate less support of their partner compared with their monoracial White, Black, and Hispanic counterparts, it not surprising to learn that these couples are also more likely to be divorced by the time their child is 5 years old (Howard & Brooks-Gunn, 2009). For biracial couples, support must be enacted not only to share in the responsibilities that accompany having a baby, but also to endure the daily hassles of microaggressions and institutional racism that can affect their work, their lives, and their access to opportunities. This is no small task, and there may never be an end to the need for biracial couples to support one another as they face the realities of discrimination in our society.

Family Support

Support received from a partner during the transition to parenthood is an essential part of making a smooth adjustment to the new parenting role (Cowan & Cowan, 2000; Thorp, Krause, Cukrowicz, & Lynch, 2004). New parents, however, also desire greater levels of interaction with their immediate family across the transition to parenthood (Gameiro, Canavarro, Moura-Ramos, Boivin, & Soares, 2010). In fact, family members can serve as an essential support system during the postpartum period (Crinic, Greenberg, Ragozin, Robinson, & Bashman, 1983; Hopkins, Marcus,

& Campbell, 1984; Tinsley & Parke, 1984). Maternal grandmothers in particular play an essential role in supporting a new mother's adjustment to motherhood (Fischer, 1981; Tinsley and Parke, 1984). Extended family members who are close to the new parents can provide hands-on support, such as by providing childcare, an area of great difficulty for many new parents (Gjerdingen & Center, 2004). Family members also provide emotional and material support to new parents (Belsky, 1984; Miller-Cribbs & Farber, 2008) that can be essential when they are not geographically close enough to provide daily help with childcare. During a focus group conducted with seven White, Black, and Hispanic mothers in biracial relationships, we learned that these mothers had relationships with their families and in-laws that varied in closeness (Nazarinia Roy et al., 2014a, 2014b). Mothers who felt supported by their partner and his family were closer to their in-laws, while mothers who had expected a supportive relationship and were let down were less likely to consider themselves close with their partner's family. Although most couples expect some type of support from their families, high expectations for support that are not met have been linked to difficult adjustment to motherhood (Kalmuss, Davidson, & Cuchman, 1992).

Unfortunately, for some biracial couples, support from their families may never be an attainable resource because they "violate prevailing norms" (Kang Fu, 2008, p. 784). Although there are racial differences in kin support practices between African-American, Hispanic, and White families (Haxton & Harknett, 2009), among mothers of biracial infants White mothers with African-American partners found to perceive receiving the least amount of support from family members (Bratter & Whitehead, 2018). Lisa, the mother who shared her experiences of stares from strangers earlier in the chapter, also shared how the lack of support from her African-American mother-in-law had perhaps the most negative effect on her. She stated:

> *his mom [Lisa's mother-in-law] is always making comments about how [the baby] is too fat because he's on formula ... always saying things like none of her babies were this fat ... he's only four months old, he is supposed to be chubby ... it just hurts because I thought she would be more supportive ... I could care less about what strangers think but family is different.*

Although tensions with one's in-laws are not uncommon, Lisa felt especially betrayed by her mother-in-law because she had hoped that her husband's family would have been more supportive. She shared that some of her experiences were hard to share with her own mother, because her mother had not experienced discrimination and couldn't relate to Lisa's stories. Lisa didn't always feel that her husband defended her when issues came up with her mother-in-law, and when she voiced her opinion, he often told her to just let it go.

The types of support received from extended family can often reflect the family culture in which the partners are raised. Even though children increase a couple's interactions with extended family members, parents have to set boundaries as to how involved or uninvolved they want the grandparents, aunts, and uncles to be. When a husband and wife have very different family cultures, the involvement or lack thereof can also create a source of tension for the couple. One partner may have their family over every other night, while the partner would prefer to see them once a month. On the other hand, the extended family may not visit or may not support one parent, and that can also lead to relational conflict between the couple.

Because so much of how we parent is based on what we learned in our own families of origin, how and when we choose to receive support from our families as new parents can create an unexplored area for couples.

Anne, a Chinese-American woman married to a White man shared a different experience of the transition to parenthood. She had moved to the United States after meeting her husband at work in Europe, where they had a great relationship. They decided to get married and move to the United States. Shortly after the move, she became pregnant with their daughter. In her first interview, while in her last trimester of pregnancy, Anne felt confident about her anticipated role as a mother. She did not have many friends, but her husband was supportive, and she had a good relationship with his mother. Although there were not many Asian families in town, Anne felt a connection with the few Asian people she encountered. However, during her postpregnancy interview, 4 months after having delivered her baby, Anne shared some of her struggles as a new mother experiencing motherhood away from her family and culture:

> *In China, as a new mom you don't do anything but rest for the first month ... you have these traditional soups to heal your body ... they are meant to replace the nutrients you lose during childbirth ... I didn't get any of that here ... I don't even think I could find the ingredients here ... it's been really hard because his mom comes over sees the baby and leaves ... I had a C-section so it was especially hard because I didn't have help around the house only childcare ... if I was home [in China] my daughter would have 10 moms, everyone helps out ... it gets annoying [there] because everyone tells you what to do but there is just so much support. I think that's why I got postpartum [depression] ... I just felt so alone ... he [her husband] tries but he works and isn't home during the day ... it not the same ... the medication has helped a lot ... I'm just feeling better about everything now.*

Although Anne faced the added stressor of being in a foreign country, her experience of not having the support of her own family, in terms of both their traditions and their physical support, is not unlike that of new parents who become disconnected with their families when they enter a relationship their families disapprove of. The loss of family support, whether due to geographic location or disapproval of lifestyle, can create additional stress for a new parent on top of the usual stressors of parenthood.

Both Anne and Lisa in the narratives above were married, and although they did not have support from the families in the ways that they had hoped, they did have their husbands' support. For some couples in less committed relationships, the difficulties that accompany the transition to parenthood can lead to dissolution of the relationship. Their primary source of support then becomes their family. Not surprisingly, family support, across the transition to parenthood, is greatest for single mothers who are not involved with their child's father (Mazelis & Mykyta, 2011). This family support can also come at a cost. If the family did not approve of the biracial relationship, the parent who is raising the biracial child may feel a sense of guilt or even shame for not having listened to their family's concerns. This situation is difficult because essentially it is the biracial child who will suffer the consequences if their extended family does not accept their other parent. When single parents are the primary caregiver of a biracial child, they have to recognize the importance of exposing their child to both racial and ethnic groups, as discussed in Chaps. 7 and 8. Single parenting is discussed further in Chap. 10.

Implications for Practice: Preventing and Overcoming Challenges

While the transition to parenthood is an exciting and joyous time for couples, it also presents many challenges. Biracial couples face not just the challenges that accompany the adaptation to new roles and demands, but additional challenges related to stressors from outside the family or a lack of family support due to racial differences or geographical separation. Because the postpartum period is a critical time in the transition to parenthood, especially for mothers, who are undergoing bio-psycho-social changes (Mercer, 2004; Suplee et al., 2014), practitioners working with new parents should engage couples in discussion of potential parenthood challenges in the family planning stages and during the pregnancy, with a focus on prevention through education. Practitioners should guide couples through the challenges that arise when a baby comes home, such as negotiation of responsibilities and setting boundaries with others, including extended family members. The two most important aspects of a smooth transition to parenthood are the same for biracial couples as for monoracial couples. First, couples who are expecting their first child must learn to communicate their expectations and be open to adapting to change. Second, to maintain their relationship quality when faced with all the stressors across the transition to parenthood, couples must engage in coparenting.

Since we know that when couples become parents their roles typically become more traditional, as discussed above, it is essential that therapists, counselors, and family consultants working with couples help them identify the distribution of labor at home, how satisfied they are with this distribution, and what changes they would like to see. Couples should learn that the division of household tasks can impact their satisfaction with these tasks and eventually their relationship. This is especially true for first-time mothers. Couples should also discuss their parenting expectations, and mothers should be made aware that if they restrict access to their baby, consistently indicating that the father's way of parenting is wrong, it will cause him to be less involved and eventually have a negative impact on his relationship satisfaction. Couples should also express their expectations for external family involvement. They should create boundaries for family involvement so that both parents feel supported. At the same time, for couples with distinct cultural practices, the partners should be made aware of the relevance and importance of these practices before the transition to parenthood.

Coparenting, an important topic of discussion and negotiation for all new parents, should be emphasized with biracial couples as a way to support, encourage, and validate each other on a daily basis, supporting their partner through not only the new experiences of parenting but also the negative experiences that can arise from interactions with others who are unsupportive or ignorant. Any professional working with biracial couples expecting their first child should be prepared to acknowledge and validate the reality that their experiences with the daily stressors of microaggressions or perhaps structural racism will influence how they deal with the stress of becoming a parent. Both parents will need to have an opportunity to express and hear how the experiences of discrimination are impacting the other parent. The partner with greater experience with discrimination must support their partner in the same ways that they themselves need support. The couple must understand that once they become parents they are both exposed to discrimination and must learn to cope with and overcome these experiences. Essentially, the couple should work as a team, supporting each other at all times, even when they disagree.

Future Research

Most of the literature on the transition to parenthood has focused on White, middle-class heterosexual couples because they are easily accessible. The literature that has focused on families of color often focuses on low-income and/or high-risk families. Scholars must further examine how biracial couples across multiple socioeconomic classes and geographic locations experience this important life event. The transition to parenthood is a stressful period in the family life cycle, and we must understand how to better support couples in biracial relationships as they experience these challenges. To support the growing population of young biracial families, we must understand the strength of biracial couples who have maintained stable relationships for decades. As the population of biracial families in the United States grows, we must focus our efforts on ensuring that their relationships remain stable and strong, because their children are affected if the relationship dissolves. We know that factors outside the couple's relationship can increase stress and hinder the stability of the relationship. Researchers and practitioners must recognize these factors and work together to support biracial couples as they overcome the challenges of parenthood.

References

Baxter, J., Hewitt, B., & Haynes, M. (2008). Life course transitions and housework: Marriage, parenthood and time on housework. *Journal of Marriage and Family, 70*, 259–272.

Belsky, J. (1984). The determinants of parenting: A process model. *Child Development, 55*, 83–96.

Belsky, J., Lang, M., & Huston, T. L. (1986). Sex-typing and division of labor as determinants of marital change across the transition to parenthood. *Journal of Research in Personality, 50*, 517–522.

Belsky, J., & Rovine, M. (1990). Patterns of marital change across the transition to parenthood: Pregnancy to three years postpartum. *Journal of Marriage and the Family, 52*, 5–20.

Biehle, S. N. (2013). Influences on the utilization of proactive coping during pregnancy and early parenthood. In P. Barberis, & S. Petrakis (Eds.), *Parenting: Challenges, practices and cultural influences* (pp. 213–224).

Biehle, S. N., & Mickelson, K. D. (2012). First-time parents' expectations about the division of childcare and play. *Journal of Family Psychology, 26*, 36–45. https://doi.org/10.1037/a0026608

Bleidorn, W., Buyukcan-Tetik, A., Schewaba, T., van Scheppingen, M. A., Denissen, J. J. A., & Finkenaurer, C. (2016). Stability and change in self-esteem during the transition to parenthood. *Social Psychology and Personality Science, 7*(6), 560–569. https://doi.org/10.1177/1948550616646428

Bodnar-Deren, S., Benn, E. K. T., Balbierz, A., & Howell, E. A. (2017). Stigma and postpartum depression treatment acceptability among Black and White women in the first six-months postpartum. *Maternal and Child Health Journal, 21*, 1457–1468. https://doi.org/10.1007/s10995-017-2263-6

Bost, K. K., Cox, M. J., & Payne, C. (2002). Structural and supportive changes in couples' family and friendship networks across the transition to parenthood. *Journal of Marriage and Family Therapy, 64*, 517–531. https://doi.org/10.1111/j.1741-3737.2002.00517.x

Bouchard, G. (2009). Parents-to-be with overly optimistic expectations of parenthood: Who are they and what should counselors do? *Canadian Journal of Counselling, 43*, 165–177.

Boyce, P., Condon, J., Barton, J., & Corkindale, C. (2007). First-Time Fathers' Study: Psychological distress in expectant fathers during pregnancy. *The Australian and New Zealand Journal of Psychiatry, 41*, 718–725 https://doi.org/10.1080/00048670701517959

Bratter, J. L., & Whitehead, E. M. (2018). Ties that bind? Comparing kin support availability for mothers of mixed-race and monoracial infants. *Journal of Marriage and Family, Advance online publication.* https://doi.org/10.1111/jomf.12485

Bronfenbrenner, U. (1979). *The Ecology of Human Development*. Cambridge, MA: Harvard University Press.

Bronte-Tinkew, J., Ryan, S., Carrano, J., & Moore, K. (2007). Resident fathers' pregnancy intendedness, prenatal behaviors, and links to involvement with infants. *Journal of Marriage and Family, 69*, 977–990. https://doi.org/10.1111/j.1741-3737.2007.00425.x

Cabrera, N. J., Shannon, J. D., & Tamis-LeMonda, C. (2007). Fathers' Influence on their children's cognitive and emotional development: From toddlers to pre-K. *Applied Developmental Science, 7*(4), 208–213. https://doi.org/10.1080/10888690701762100

Cao, H., Mills-Koonce, R., Wood, C., & Fine, M. (2016). Identity transformation during the transition to parenthood among same-sex couples: An ecological, stress-strategy-adaptation perspective. *Journal of Family Theory & Review, 8*, 30–59. https://doi.org/10.1111/jftr.12124

Cardoso, J. B., Padilla, Y. C., & Sampson, M. (2010). Racial and ethnic variation in the predictors of maternal parenting stress. *Journal of Social Service Research, 36*(5), 429–444. https://doi.org/10.1080/01488376.2010.510948

Claxton, A., & Perry-Jenkins, M. (2008). No fun anymore: leisure and marital quality across the transition to parenthood. *Journal of Marriage and Family, 70*, 28–43. https://doi.org/10.1111/j.1741-3737.2007.00459.x

Coley, R. L. (2001). Invisible men: Emerging research on low-income, unmarried, and minority fathers. *American Psychologist, 56*, 743–753.

Cooper, C. E., McLanahan, S. S., Meadows, S. O., & Brooks-Gunn, J. (2009). Family structure transitions and maternal parenting stress. *Journal of Marriage and Family, 71*, 558–574.

Cowan, C. P., & Cowan, P. A. (2000). *When partners become parents: The big life change for couples*. New York: Basic Books.

Cowdery, R. S., Scarborough, N., Knudson-Martin, C., Seshadri, G., Lewis, M. E., & Mahoney, A. R. (2009). Gendered power in cultural contexts: Part II. Middle class African American heterosexual couples with young children. *Family Process, 48*, 25–39. https://doi.org/10.1111/j.1545-5300.2009.01265.x

Crinic, K., Greenberg, M., Ragozin, A., Robinson, N., & Bashman, R. (1983). Effects of stress and social support on mothers and premature and full-term infants. *Child Development, 54*, 209–217.

Curran, M. A., Hazen, N. L., & Mann, T. (2009). Representations of marriage and expectations of parenthood: Predictors of supportive coparenting for first-time parents. *Parenting: Science and Practice, 9*, 101–122. https://doi.org/10.1080/15295190802656794

Dayton, C. J., Buczkowski, R. S., Muzik, M., Goletz, J., Hicks, L., Walsh, T., et al. (2016). Expectant fathers' beliefs and expectations about fathering as they prepare to parent a new infant. *Social Work Research: Special Issue on Social Work with Men and Fathers, 40*(4), 225–236. https://doi.org/10.1093/swr/svw017

Deave, T., Johnson, D., & Ingram, J. (2008). Transition to parenthood: the needs of parents in pregnancy and early parenthood. *BMC Pregnancy and Childbirth, 8*(30). https://doi.org/10.1186/1471-2393-8-30

Delmore-Ko, P., Pancer, S. M., Hunsberger, B., & Pratt, M. (2000). Becoming a parent: The relation between prenatal expectations and postnatal experience. *Journal of Family Psychology, 14*, 625–640.

Don, B. P., Biehle, S. N., & Mickelson, K. D. (2013). Feeling like part of a team: Perceived parenting agreement among first-time parents. *Journal of Social and Personal Relationships, 30*(8), 1121–1137. https://doi.org/10.1177/0265407513483105

Doss, B. D., Cicila, L. N., Hsueh, A. C., Morrison, K. R., & Carhart, K. (2014). A randomized controlled trial of brief coparenting and relationship intervention during the transition to parenthood. *Journal of Family Psychology, 28*, 483–494. https://doi.org/10.1037/a0037311

Doss, B. D., Rhoades, G. K., Stanley, S. M., & Markman, H. J. (2009). The effect of the transition to parenthood on relationship quality: An 8-year prospective study. *Journal of Personality and Social Psychology, 96*, 601–619.

Elek, S. M., Hudson, D. B., & Bouffard, C. (2003). Marital and parenting satisfaction and infant care self-efficacy during the transition to parenthood: the effect of infant sex. *Issues in Contemporary Pediatric Nursing, 26*, 45–57 https://doi.org/10.1080/01460860390183065

Epifanio, M. S., Genna, V., DeLuca, C., Roccella, M., & La Grutta, S. (2015). Paternal and maternal transition to parenthood to parenthood: The risk of postpartum depression and parenting stress. *Pediatric Reports, 7*, 38–44.

Evenson, R. J., & Simon, R. W. (2005). Clarifying the relationship between parenthood and depression. *Journal of Health and Social Behavior, 46*, 341–358. https://doi.org/10.1177/002214650504600403

Feinberg, M. E. (2002). Coparenting and the transition to parenthood: A framework for prevention. *Clinical Child and Family Psychology Review, 5*(3), 173–195.

Feinberg, M. E. (2003). The internal structure and ecological context of coparenting: A framework for research and intervention. *Parenting: Science and Practice, 3*, 95–131.

Fillo, J., Simpson, A. J., & Rholes, W. S. (2015). Dads doing diapers: Individual and relational outcomes associated with the division of childcare across the transition to parenthood. *Journal of Personality and Social Psychology, 108*(2), 298–316. https://doi.org/10.1037/a0038572

Fischer, L. (1981). Transitions in the mother-daughter relationship. *Journal of Marriage and Family, 43*(3), 613–622. https://doi.org/10.2307/351762

Flykt, M., Palosaari, E., Lindblom, J., Vanska, M., Poikkeus, P., Repokari, L., et al. (2014). What explains violated expectations of parent-child relationship in transition to parenthood? *Journal of Family Psychology, 28*, 148–159. https://doi.org/10.1037/a0036050

Gameiro, S., Canavarro, M. C., Moura-Ramos, M., Boivin, J., & Soares, I. (2010). Social nesting: Changes in social network and support across the transition to parenthood in couples that conceived spontaneously or through assisted reproductive technologies. *Journal of Family Psychology, 24*(2), 175–187.

Gjerdingen, D. K., & Center, B. A. (2004). First-time parents' postpartum changes in employment, childcare, and housework responsibilities. *Social Science Research, 34*, 103–116.

Gjerdingen, D. K., & Chaloner, K. (1994). Mothers' experience with household roles and social support during the first postpartum year. *Women & Health, 21(4)*, 57–74.

Gottman, J. M., & Notarius, C. I. (2000). Decade review: Observing marital interaction. *Journal of Marriage and Family, 62*, 927–947.

Gross, C. L., & Marcussen, K. (2017). Postpartum depression in mothers and fathers: The role of parenting efficacy expectations during the transition to parenthood. *Sex Roles, 76*, 290–305. https://doi.org/10.1007/s11199-016-0629-7

Hamilton, B. E., Martin, A., Osterman, M. J. K., Driscoll, A. K., Rossen, L. M. (2017). *Births provisional data for 2016.* Vital Statistics Rapid Release. Report No. 002 Retrieved from https://www.cdc.gov/nchs/data/vsrr/report002.pdf

Harwood, K., McLean, N., & Durkin, K. (2007). First-time mothers' expectations of parenthood: What happens when optimistic expectations are not matched by later experiences? *Developmental Psychology, 43*, 1–12.

Haxton, C. L., & Harknett, K. (2009). Racial and gender differences in kin support: A mixed-methods study of African American and Hispanic couples. *Journal of Family Issues, 30*, 1019–1040. https://doi.org/10.1177/0192513X09333946

Henderson, A., Harmon, S., & Newman, H. (2016). The price mothers pay, even when they are not buying it: Mental health consequences of idealized motherhood. *Sex Roles, 74*, 512–526. https://doi.org/10.1007/s11199-015-0534-5

Hopkins, J., Marcus, M., & Campbell, S. B. (1984). Postpartum depression: A critical review. *Psychological Bulletin, 95*(3), 498–515. https://doi.org/10.1037/0033-2909.95.3.498

Horowitz, J. A., & Damato, E. G. (1999). Mothers' perceptions of postpartum stress and satisfaction. *Journal of Obstetric, Gynecologic, and Neonatal Nursing, 28*, 595–605.

Howard, K. S., & Brooks-Gunn, J. (2009). Relationship supportiveness during the transition to parenting among married and unmarried parents. *Parenting: Science and Practice, 9*, 123–142.

Hudson, D. B., Elek, S. M., & Fleck, M. O. (2001). First-time mothers' and fathers' transition to parenthood: Infant care self-efficacy, parenting satisfaction, and infant sex. *Issues in Comprehensive Pediatric Nursing, 24*, 31–43. https://doi.org/10.1080/014608601300035580

Kalmuss, D., Davidson, A., & Cuchman, L. (1992). Parenting expectations, experiences, and adjustment to parenthood: A test of the violated expectations framework. *Journal of Marriage and the Family, 54*, 516–526.

Kang Fu, V. (2008). Interracial-interethnic unions and fertility in the United States. *Journal of Marriage and Family, 70*(3), 783–795.

Katz-Wise, S. L., Priess, H. A., & Hyde, J. S. (2010). Gender-role attitudes and behavior across the transition to parenthood. *Developmental Psychology, 46*, 18–28.

Kibria, N. (2002). *Becoming Asian American*. Baltimore: Johns Hopkins University Press.

Kluwer, E. S., & Johnson, M. D. (2007). Conflict frequency and relationship quality across the transition to parent- hood. *Journal of Marriage and Family, 69*, 1089–1106.

Kushner, K. E., Sopcak, N., Breikreuz, R., Pitre, N., Williamson, D. L., Rempel, G., et al. (2017). On shifting ground: First-time parents' ideal world of paid work and family time. *Community, Work & Family, 20*(2), 119–141. https://doi.org/10.1080/13668803.2015.1074546

Lamb, M. E., & Lewis, C. (2013). Father-child relationships. In N. Cabrera & C. S. Tamis-Lemomda (Eds.), *Handbook of father involvement: Multidisciplinary perspectives* (pp. 119–134). New York: Routledge.

Lamb, M. E., Pleck, J. H., Charnov, E. L., & Levine, J. A. (1987). A biosocial perspective on paternal behavior and involvement. In J. Lancaster, J. Atmann, A. Rossi, & L. Sherrod (Eds.), *Parenting across the life span: Biosocial dimensions* (pp. 111–142). New York: Aldine De Gruyter. https://doi.org/10.1353/dem.2007.0007

LeMasters, E. E. (1957). Parenthood as crisis. *Marriage and Family Living, 19*, 352–355.

Levy-Shiff, R. (1994). Individual and contextual correlates of marital change across the transition to parenthood. *Developmental Psychology, 30*, 591–601.

Liss, M., Schiffrin, H. H., & Rizzo, K. M. (2013). Maternal guilt and shame: The role of self-discrepancy and fear of negative evaluation. *Journal of Child and Family Studies, 22*, 1112–1119. https://doi.org/10.1007/s10826-012-9673-2

Livingston, G. (2017). *The rise of multiracial and multiethnic babies in the U.S. (Pew Research Center Report)*. Retrieved from http://www.pewresearch.org/fact-tank/2017/06/06/the-rise-of-multiracial-and-multiethnic-babies-in-the-u-s/

Marsiglio, W. , Amato, P. , Day, R. D. and Lamb, M. E. (2000), Scholarship on Fatherhood in the 1990s and Beyond. *Journal of Marriage and Family, 62*, 1173–1191. doi:10.1111/j.1741-3737.2000.01173.x

Matthey, S., Barnett, B., Ungerer, J., & Waters, B. (2000). Paternal and maternal depressed mood during the transition to parenthood. *Journal of Affective Disorders, 60*(2), 75–85. https://doi.org/10.1016/S0165-0327(99)00159-7

Maurer, T. W., Pleck, J. H., & Rane, T. R. (2001). Parental identity and reflected appraisals: Measurement and gender dynamics. *Journal of Marriage and the Family, 63*, 309–321.
Mazelis, J. M., & Mykyta, L. (2011). Relationship and active kin support: The role of need and norms. *Journal of Marriage and Family, 73*, 430–445. https://doi.org/10.1111/j.1741-3737.2010.00816.x
McClain, K., & Brown, S. L. (2017). The roles of father involvement and coparenting in relationship quality among cohabitating and married parents. *Sex Roles, 76*(5–6), 334–345.
McElroy-Heltzel, S.E., Davis, D.E., DeBlaere, C., Hook, J.N., Massengale, M., Choe, E., Ordaz, A., Placeres, V., & Gazaway, S. (2018, March). *Cultural humility in interethnic couples.* Poster presented at the Society for Personality and Social Psychology. Atlanta, GA.
Mercer, R. T. (2004). Becoming a mother versus maternal role attainment. *Journal of Nursing Scholarship, 36*(3), 226–232.
Mickelson, K. D., Donahue, M., & Biehle, S. (2009). Mismatching of gender role attitudes and role status on health. In J. H. Urlich & B. T. Cosell (Eds.), *Handbook on gender roles* (pp. 299–315). Nova Science Publishers, Inc..
Mihelic, M., Filus, A., & Morawaska, A. (2016). Correlates of prenatal parenting expectations in new mothers: is better self-efficacy a potential target for preventing postnatal adjustment difficulties? *Prevention Science, 17*(8), 949–959. https://doi.org/10.1007/s11121-016-0682-z
Miller-Cribbs, J. E., & Farber, N. B. (2008). Kin networks and poverty among African Americans: past and present. *Social Work, 53*(1), 43–51.
Murry, V. M., Brown, P. A., Brody, G. H., Cutrona, C. E., & Simons, R. L. (2001). Racial discrimination as a moderator of the links among stress, maternal psychological functioning and family relationships. *Journal of Marriage and Family, 63*, 915–926.
Nazarinia Roy, R. R., Webb, F. J. Schumm, W. R., & Walker, A. B. (2011, January). *Mothers' expectation fulfillment: Differences across relationship status and race/ethnicity groups.* Poster session presented at the annual meeting of the Society of Personality and Social Psychology, San Antonio, TX.
Nazarinia Roy, R., Mitchell, Y., Hamilton, N., & Lockhart, A. (2014a, November). *Experiences of family and social support during the transition to motherhood among mothers of biracial and monoracial infants.* Paper presented at the National Council on Family Relations, Baltimore, MD.
Nazarinia Roy, R. R., Schumm, W. R., & Britt, S. L. (2014b). *The transition to parenthood.* New York, NY: Springer.
Nazarinia Roy, R., Walker, A. B., Aljayyousi-Khalil, & Dayne, N. (2016). Effects of expected and perceived division of childcare and household labor on mother's relationship satisfaction during their transition to parenthood. *Psychology, 7*(13). https://doi.org/10.4236/psych.2016.713145
Nomaguchi, K. M., & Milkie, M. A. (2003). Costs and rewards of children: The effects of becoming a parent on adults' lives. *Journal of Marriage and Family, 65*, 356–374.
O'Donoghue, M. (2004). Racial and ethnic identity development in white mothers of biracial, black-white children. *Affilia, 19*, 68–84. https://doi.org/10.1177/0886109903260795
Pacey, S. (2004). Couples and the first baby: Responding to new parents' sexual and relationship problems. *Sexual and Relationship Therapy, 19*, 223–246.
Pancer, S. M., Pratt, M., Hunsberger, B., & Gallant, M. (2000). Integrative complexity and the transition to parenthood. *Journal of Personality, 68*, 253–280.
Pollard, S. E., Nievar, M. A., Nathans, L. L., & Riggs, S. A. (2014). A comparison of White and Hispanic women's stories of adjustment to the birth of a child. *Infant Mental Health Journal, 35*(3), 193–209. https://doi.org/10.1002/imhj.21437
Powers, R. S., Suitor, J., Guerra, S., Shackelford, M., Mecom, D., & Gusman, K. (2003). Regional differences in gender-role attitudes: Variations by gender and race. *Gender Issues, 21*(2), 40–54. https://doi.org/10.1007/s12147-003-0015-y
Profit, J., Gould, J. B., Bennett, M., Goldstein, B. A., Draper, D., Phibbs, C. S., et al. (2017). Racial/ethnic disparity in NICU quality of care delivery. *Pediatrics, 140*(3), e20170918. https://doi.org/10.1542/peds.2017-0918
Pruett, M. K., Arthur, L., & Ebling, R. (2007). The had that rocks the cradle: Maternal gatekeeping after divorce. *Pace University Law Review, 27*, 709–739.

Reiter, M. J., & Gee, C. B. (2008). Open communication and partner support in intercultural and interfaith romantic relationships: A relational maintenance approach. *Journal of Social and Personal Relationships, 25*(4), 539–1559. https://doi.org/10.1177/0265407508090872
Ronka, A., Oravala, S., & Pulkkinen, L. (2003). Turning points in adults' lives: The effects of gender and the amount of choice. *Journal of Adult Development, 10*, 203–215.
Ruble, D., Fleming, A., Hackel, L. S., & Stangor, C. (1988). Changes in the marital relationship during the transition to first time motherhood: Effects of violated expectations concerning division of household labor. *Journal of Personality and Social Psychology, 55*, 78–87.
Sawyer, L. M. (1999). Engaged mothering: The transition to motherhood for a group of African American women. *Journal of Transcultural Nursing, 10*, 14–21.
Schoppe-Sullivan, S. J., Brown, G. L., Cannon, E. A., Mangelsdorf, S. C., & Sokolowski, M. S. (2008). Maternal gatekeeping, coparenting quality, and fathering behavior in families with infants. *Journal of Family Psychology, 22*(3), 389–398. https://doi.org/10.1037/0893-3200.22.3.389
Shapiro, A. F., Gottman, J. M., & Carrere, S. (2000). The baby and the marriage: Identifying factors that buffer against decline in marital satisfaction after the first baby arrives. *Journal f Family Psychology, 14*(1), 59–70. https://doi.org/10.1037/0893-3200.14.1.59
Sue, D. W., Capodilupo, C. M., Torino, G. C., Bucceri, J. M., Holder, A. M. B., Nadal, K. L., et al. (2007). Racial microaggressions in everyday life: Implications for clinical practice. *American Psychologist, 62*(4), 271–286.
Suplee, P. D., Bloch, J. R., McKeever, A., Borucki, L. C., Dawley, K., & Kaufman, M. (2014). Focusing on maternal health beyond breastfeeding and depression during the first year postpartum. *JOGNN Journal of Obstetric Gynecologic & Neonatal Nursing, 43*, 782–791.
Thorp, S. R., Krause, E. D., Cukrowicz, K. C., & Lynch, T. R. (2004). Postpartum partner support, demand-withdraw communication, and maternal stress. *Psychology of Women Quarterly, 28*, 362–369.
Tinsley, B. R., & Parke, R. D. (1984). Grandparents as support and socialization agents. In M. Lewis (Ed.), *Beyond The Dyad, Genesis of behavior* (Vol. vol 4). Boston, MA: Springer. https://doi.org/10.1007/978-1-4757-9415-1_8
Waller, M. R. (2012). Cooperation, conflict, or disengagement? Coparenting styles and fathers' involvement in fragile families. *Family Process, 51*(3), 325–342.
Warner, J. (2005). *Perfect madness: Motherhood in the age of anxiety*. New York: Riverhead Books.

Part III
Parenting

Parenting Mixed-Race Children

Fabienne Doucet, Marcella Runell Hall, and Melissa Giraud

> *My eight year-old son, Sebastian, is Guyanese, Japanese and white. Among his nearly all-white classmates, he's perceived as a dark-skinned boy. The color he chooses for self-portraits drawn in school are always 2 or 3 shades darker than his actual skin color. On his all-black basketball team, he's called the light-skinned team member. In our Puerto Rican family (I remarried a Puerto Rican man) he looks Puerto Rican. Sitting next to me, it's clear that he's part Asian.*
>
> *While Sebastian can't fully process these racial identity realities yet, this ambiguity, this fluidity, is a common experience among racially mixed people. To borrow from W.E.B. Du Bois' notion of "double consciousness," many racially mixed people learn to see themselves through their own eyes and through the eyes of others.*
>
> *—Excerpt from "5 things to know if you love a mixed race kid" by Sara-Momii Roberts (Roberts, 2016, June 7)*

Introduction

In recounting her son's experiences navigating the world as a mixed-race child, Sara-Momii Roberts underlines a familiar reality for people of color in the United States—that of walking through the world always conscious of how their bodies are

F. Doucet (✉)
Department of Teaching and Learning, Steinhardt School of Culture, Education, and Human Development, New York University, New York, NY, USA
e-mail: fd30@nyu.edu

M. R. Hall
Division of Student Life, Mount Holyoke College, South Hadley, MA, USA

M. Giraud
EmbraceRace, Amherst, MA, USA

R. Nazarinia Roy, A. Rollins (eds.), *Biracial Families*,
https://doi.org/10.1007/978-3-319-96160-6_7

being read by others. As his mother notes, Sebastian, at 8 years old, may be too young to comprehend the long-term implications of his multiple racial identities, but he is not too young to know that race matters in this society, or that people are treated differently based on the color of their skin (Chang, 2016; Doucet & Adair, 2013). Thus, as he endeavors to find crayons to represent his skin tone or to make sense of being read as dark-skinned among one group of friends and light-skinned among another, his mother's keen awareness of Sebastian's experiences and those that potentially await him is an important protective factor in his development (Rockquemore, Laszloffy, & Noveske, 2006; Stone & Dolbin-MacNab, 2017). As it happens, Sebastian's mother identifies as a mixed-race person herself—she is Japanese and white—and it is perhaps for this reason that she is able to articulate what her son may be feeling so precisely. Scholars of biracial identity have argued that monoracial parents cannot identify with their biracial children's experiences (Csizmadia, Rollins, & Kaneakua, 2014; Rockquemore et al., 2006; Rollins & Hunter, 2013; Snyder, 2012; Stone & Dolbin-MacNab, 2017). However, this should not be taken to mean that many monoracial parents do not recognize the importance of teaching their mixed-race children about race. Indeed, how monoracial parents go about engaging in these conversations is of paramount importance to their children's development of a healthy identity that accounts for both (or all) of their racial and ethnic heritages in their full complexity (Chang, 2016; Collins, 2000; Csizmadia et al., 2014; Nishimura, 1998; Robinson-Wood, 2010; Rockquemore et al., 2006; Rockquemore & Brunsma, 2002a; Rollins & Hunter, 2013; Roth, 2005; Stone & Dolbin-MacNab, 2017).

So, what, if anything, is different about parenting mixed-race children? What are the questions, quandaries, promises, privileges, and joys of parenting children who live and move through the world in ways we, their monoracial parents, may never fully understand? If we are mixed-race parents of mixed-race children, how is our experience different from that of monoracial parents? And if we are white parents of mixed-race children, how do we negotiate conversations about our own race and identity with our children of color? In this chapter, we focus on how parents of mixed-race children can, and do, approach child-rearing in ways that feel responsible, safe, authentic, and grounding. We use the term "mixed race" as a broad umbrella term that encompasses people that might identify themselves or be identified as biracial, multiracial, interracial, or other similar terms, recognizing that the very concept of race is a social construction and thus that there is no such thing as a "pure race." We also narrow the focus of this chapter to biological (or step) parents of mixed-race children since Chap. 9 in this volume speaks to the experiences of adoptive families.

In a white supremacist hegemony, all parents must be vigilant (or "woke," in common parlance) regarding the insidious toxic impact of racism, and parents raising children of color must provide them the psychological and cognitive resources necessary to maintain a healthy sense of self in the face of such racism (Caughy & Owen, 2015). The term "Critical Race Parenting" has been taken up by some schlars interested in an approach to raising children that actively and deliberately acknowledges the role of race in shaping social dynamics. For example, DePouw and Matias (2016), applying the tenets of critical race theory, articulated that "A critical race perspective on parenting includes a critical analysis of systems of oppression, including institutional racism, and is embedded within the lived experiences, knowledge systems, values, and pedagogies (Brayboy & Maughan, 2009) of families and communities of color" (p. 237).

We argue for such "parental wokeness" in this chapter, bringing together (1) the academic literature on mixed-race parenting; (2) the stories and experiences of parents raising mixed-race children and of mixed-race people themselves; and (3) our experiences as mothers of mixed-race children. We engage such topics as racial socialization; negotiating parenting with spouses; navigating relationships with extended family members and in-laws; and what we wish we had known about parenting mixed-race children at the start of our journeys. We conclude by proposing a set of guiding principles for rearing empathic, aware, proud, and self-assured mixed-race children.

It should be noted that as authors of this chapter, we enter the conversation about parenting mixed-race children as mothers of mixed-race children ourselves. Fabienne is a black Haitian immigrant to the United States married to a white American man from North Carolina of Scots-Irish heritage; Marcella is a US-born white American of Irish heritage from New Jersey married to a black man with roots in Barbados on his father's side and St. Kitts and Nieves on his mother's side; and Melissa is a US-born mixed-race American with a white French-Canadian mother and a father from Dominica of African and French heritage; she is married to a black man from Jamaica. In addition to our shared "Caribbean connection," we also all have two children: Fabienne has a 12-year-old son and 9-year-old daughter; Marcella has two daughters, aged 7 and 4; and Melissa also has two daughters, aged 9 and 7. While as cisgender women in heterosexual black-white mixed-race relationships we are by no means a representative sample, the range of experiences we bring to this subject based on our varied adventures walking through the world as immigrant/nonimmigrant, black-white/mixed race, multilingual/monolingual, and Gen X women affords us a rich set of lenses through which to interrogate and speak to the issues we will raise in this chapter. We invite readers to consider their own intersectional identities as they find points of convergence and divergence in their experiences with mixed-race children (or as mixed-race persons), whether as researchers, practitioners, parents, or some combination of the above.

Framing the Chapter

A growing number of "self-help" and children's books, toys, blogs, commercials, and television shows depict mixed-race families. Supermodel Garcelle Beauvais and actor Taye Diggs, who are parents of biracial children, have written children's books about being mixed, while others, like President Barack Obama, singer Mariah Carey, actress and activist Yara Shadidi and her on-camera Mom, Tracee Ellis Ross, and wrestler/actor Dwayne "The Rock" Johnson, by being multiracial public figures, embody, challenge, and push boundaries of race beyond a white racial frame (Chang, 2016; Feagin, 2010). A Google search for "mixed race parenting" yields hundreds of personal testimonies, compilations of "best practices" tips, and even links to organizations where parents of mixed-race children can find one another. Sid the Science Kid, a beloved preschool television character, has parents with different "skin" color; character Princess Pea of *Super Why?* fame has a black mother and white father; Nickelodeon has biracial character Nella the Princess Night; the Disney channel has the new show Andi Mack which portrays the main character as being white and Asian; and American Girl's "Truly Me" dolls have various combinations of skin tones, eye colors, and hair textures and hues that have made them popular among mixed-race families.

Yet in the academic literature, there is a dearth of research on mixed-race parenting (Stone & Dolbin-MacNab, 2017). Further, a disproportionate share of the research that exists focuses on heterosexual white mothers raising black-white children (Caballero, Edwards, & Puthussery, 2008). And while there seems to be more societal acceptance of mixed-race families and their children, the image of the "tragic mulatto" is still alive and well in the popular imagination (Csizmadia, Brunsma, & Cooney, 2012; Gatson, 2003; Johnston & Nadal, 2010), as also evidenced by the number of studies examining the psychological well-being and risk vulnerability of mixed-race people (see, e.g., Barn, 1999; Binning, Unzueta, Huo, & Molina, 2009; Bolland et al., 2007; Jackson, 2012; Jackson, Yoo, Guevarra Jr., & Harrington, 2012; Lusk, Taylor, Nanney, & Austin, 2010; Rauktis, Fusco, Goodkind, & Bradley-King, 2016; Udry, Li, & Hendrickson-Smith, 2003). Indeed, many studies of mixed-race children and families are conducted with clinical samples of some sort, whether they are part of the social welfare system or receiving counseling services (Barn, 1999; Buckley & Carter, 2004; Fusco & Rauktis, 2012; Fusco, Rauktis, McCrae, Cunningham, & Bradley-King, 2010; Jackson et al., 2012; Shih & Sanchez, 2005). This further perpetuates the discourse of distress around mixed-race identity and experience and thus leaves many questions unanswered about what mixed-race parenting looks like in populations that are not clinical, ostracized, or vulnerable.

For this chapter, we take an expanded approach to the "review of the literature," weaving in stories and experiences from the first-person testimonies of parents raising mixed-race children and mixed-race persons themselves, drawing especially from the online support community EmbraceRace.org, co-founded by Melissa and her husband. The EmbraceRace.org website describes it as "a multiracial community of parents, teachers, experts, and other caring adults who support each other to meet the challenges that race poses to our children, families, and communities" (www.embracerace.org). Furthermore, EmbraceRace.org pledges to identify, organize, and create "the tools, resources, discussion spaces, and networks we need to nurture resilience in children of color; to nurture inclusive, empathetic children of all stripes; to raise kids who think critically about the why and how of patterns of racial inequity"; and "to support a movement of kid and adult racial justice advocates for all children" (http://www.embracerace.org/leadership-team). In addition to these stories, the three of us interviewed one another about our experiences raising mixed-race children, and we add our voices to the conversation we will curate here. Based on our search of the literature and our own experiences parenting mixed-race children, we organize this conversation around five central topics: (1) the ethnic identity of mixed-race children; (2) racial and cultural socialization in mixed-race families; (3) navigating extended family relationships; (4) external pressures and perceptions of mixed-race families; and (5) mixed-race parenting beyond the black-white binary.

Ethnic Identity of Mixed-Race Children

Composite Soul
by Kelly Bates

Today, I declare that I will not keep the races separate within me
I will polish off my veneer of black and white, and dare you to see
ALL that is ME,
All that is REAL, and
ALL that is misunderstood, even by the ones that love me the deepest and love the "uniqueness"
Can you handle it?
You'll watch my wild curls spring from my head, every frizz uncovered, every strand untamed, every piece unstraightened
You'll watch me jump, bend, sway, and lift up my fist to fierce soul and hip hop, deep defiant rock and the sounds of steady African drums and off-cue Irish bagpipes
You'll watch me over my lifetime love black men, white men, and women of every hue because I won't fight their beauty or humanness
Can you handle it?
You'll see me wearing big J Lo hoops on my ears with a long Janis Joplin dress hanging from my tan body
You'll hear me talk trash with an urban roots accent, slapping my hands in loud laughter, and next talking quiet with plain words and no inflections, as the freckles rise from my face to yours
Will you accept this freedom and smile with joy?
Watching ME be ME
Watching me discard YOUR images of what you see, or want me to be
And still love me?
I carve up the black and white versions of me
And toss them to the fire
And take back out my true composite soul
Glistening, warm, and never fading
Today, the races are no longer separate within me
And I am ME,
And FREE
Can you handle it?

In the poem above, posted on the EmbraceRace blog, Kelly Bates (2016, June 5) asserts her claim to be both black and white—a composite who is not one thing or another, but two things at the same time. The need for such a declaration is rooted in a long history of the rule of hypodescent in the United States wherein any person with "one drop" of African-American blood was automatically considered African-

American (Anderson, 2015; Blay, 2014; Brackett et al., 2006; Brunsma, 2005; Fusco et al., 2010; Rockquemore & Brunsma, 2002b; Roth, 2005; Shih & Sanchez, 2009; Stone & Dolbin-MacNab, 2017). In demanding to have her whiteness recognized as well as her blackness, Bates defies the rule of hypodescent and other antiquated ways of constructing racial identity. Rockquemore's (1999) groundbreaking work in this area yielded a conceptual model of biracial identity with four options: (1) a singular identity (i.e., just black or just white); (2) a border identity (i.e., just biracial); (3) a protean identity (i.e., shifting between black, white, and biracial); and (4) a transcendent identity ("beyond" race). This model has been used by a number of scholars to examine mixed-race people's self-identification (see, e.g., Coleman & Carter, 2007; Doyle & Kao, 2007; Lou, Lalonde, & Wilson, 2011; Lusk et al., 2010).

Fewer studies have focused on how parents of mixed-race children identify those children, but those that do reveal interesting findings. For example, Qian's (2004) analysis of the 1990 Census (the last year that an interracial option was not available to respondents) revealed that black-white couples were the most likely to identify their children as nonwhite whereas Native American-white couples were equally likely to identify their children as Native American or white, and Asian-American-white couples were the least likely to identify their children as Asian-American. He also found that children were most likely to be racially identified according to their father's race. Brunsma's (2005) analysis of the Early Childhood Longitudinal Study data showed that parents of multiracial children seem to be moving away from the norm of hypodescent and identifying their children as multiracial or white (particularly white-Asian and white-Native American children), rather than automatically defaulting to the ethnic identity of the minoritized group (e.g., black or Latino). Roth (2005), analyzing both 1990 and 2000 Census data, likewise found that some parents in black-white intermarriages were not defaulting to the dictates of the one-drop rule in how they racially identified their children on the 1990 Census. Specifically, although 60.6% of these children were identified as black, about 40% were not, with 25% being identified as white, and 14% being identified as "other," which Roth argued was a stand-in for *interracial*. Once the interracial option was made official in 2000, 53.1% of black-white intermarried couples chose that option to racially identify their children.

Adding another layer of complexity, Bratter (2007) studied how parents who identified themselves as multiracial in the year 2000 US Census identified their children. She reported three main findings: First, when both parents in an interracial couple have an overlapping racial background, the child was more likely to be classified according to the shared background (e.g., white spouse with white-Asian spouse = child identified as white); second, the child was less likely to be classified as multiracial when the father was himself classified as multiracial, particularly if the spouse was black or Asian, suggesting a gendered component to the transmission of a multiracial identity; and third, multiracial parents could be engaging in "a form of reshuffling racial hierarchies" (Bratter, 2007, p. 842) by violating the rule of hypodescent when they identify their part-white-part-something else as simply white. As noted in the first finding, this pattern was most likely when both parents had overlapping white racial backgrounds. Gullickson and Morning (2011) relatedly found that parents of part-white part-Native American children were more likely than parents of black-white or Asian-white children to adopt the rule of *hyper*descent by identifying their children as white only.

Researchers also have looked at mixed family identity in a holistic sense—i.e., not simply how the children are identified/identify, but how a family identity gets built around the ideas that the parents come from different backgrounds (ethnic, racial, religious, etc.) and that their children thus "carry" those diverse backgrounds (Byrd & Garwick, 2004). In their qualitative study of black man-white woman mixed-race couples, Byrd and Garwick (2006) found that most participants developed a family identity around what they called "one interracial voice" developed over time whereby "[t]he Black-White couple incorporated the Black man's view of race and racism with the White woman's racial transformation into an integrated interracial worldview that framed their family life" (pp. 30–31). They identified four primary undertakings in the development of a family identity for mixed-race families: "(a) understanding and resolving family of origin chaos and turmoil, (b) transcending Black-White racial history, (c) articulating the interracial family's racial standpoint, and (d) explaining race to biracial children across the developmental stages" (p. 26). Stone and Dolbin-MacNab (2017) jointly interviewed white mothers and their adult black-white mixed-race children and learned that these mothers felt proud of being in an interracial family and passed that pride on to their children explaining, "In many interviews, mothers and their children expressed the sense that being a part of an interracial family was being a part of something bigger, both culturally and socially" (p. 104; see also Robinson-Wood, 2010).

Root (2003) argued that even though mixed-race children might grow up to identify themselves differently from the ethnic or racial labels their parents use to identify them, it is still important to give children language for talking about their heritage. Indeed, several studies have found that the self-identification of mixed-race people can change over time, prompted by a number of factors (Hitlin, Scott Brown, & Elder, 2006; Root, 2003; Tomishima, 2003). For example, Doyle and Kao (2007) analyzed the National Longitudinal Study of Adolescent Health (AddHealth) for changes in the self-identification of adolescents as they transitioned to young adulthood. They found that while some adolescents who identified as multiracial switched to identifying as monoracial, the reverse was also true—some who identified as monoracial changed to identifying as multiracial. They noted that Native American/white mixed young people were most likely to shift identification and that mixed black and mixed Asian young people were most likely to identify as monoracial. Interestingly, they found that maternal education was strongly associated with stability in self-identification. As a potential explanation, they offered that mothers with higher levels of education may have more choice over neighborhoods and schools for their children, and thus they may be more likely to choose racially integrated communities where children would not necessarily be pushed into rigid categories. The idea that higher social class opens more identity options for mixed-race persons came up in other studies as well (Brunsma, 2005; Herman, 2004; Mahtani, 2002; Qian, 2004; Roth, 2005).

Fhagen-Smith (2003) discussed the experiences of mixed-race children in middle childhood (ages 8–11), proposing that racial salience and racial evaluation could become more important for children at this stage, compared to younger children who tend to use color terminology for self-description (e.g., I am brown). Fhagen-Smith defined racial salience as the degree to which racial markers or characteristics are part of how children describe themselves and racial evaluation as children's feelings (positive, negative, or neutral) about their racial group and physical appearance. As children continue to grow and develop their identities, then, we should expect that factors related to racial identification, such as salience and evaluation, among others, will change in importance over time. Siblings also may identify differently based on their physical appearance and/or other individual differences (Aspinall, 2002; Root, 2003; Tomishima, 2003).

Lived Experience

We have seen such developmental changes and sibling variations play out over the course of our own children's childhoods as well. Fabienne's children, who are read as white or Latinx by most strangers, have shifted their descriptions of themselves over the years. Her son went from describing his color as green as a 3-year old (also asserting that his father was purple and Fabienne was blue) to describing himself as white around ages 5 or 6, to the present day when he calls himself a "black and white milkshake." Fabienne's daughter identified herself as having "skin like dad" or as white when she was a preschooler, to describing herself as "really light" while expressing a desire to have brown skin like Fabienne around age 5, to identifying now as either a "person of color" or as "Haitian and North Carolina [sic]."

Something about which all three of us (authors) have tried to be cognizant is how we react or respond to our children when they share their identities. Fabienne remembers feeling extremely uncomfortable and upset when her children identified themselves as white. She knew rationally that they were not rejecting her or her/their Haitianness or blackness, but she also knew that messages about the undesirability of being black and the desirability of being white are loud, strong, and pervasive, and that children receive and understand those messages from a very early age (see Doucet & Adair, 2013 for an overview of this research). Yet, another important point relative to mixed-race children developing a healthy sense of themselves is that the way parents identify themselves makes a difference in how children perceive themselves. When parents feel shame about their racial or ethnic group, or feel animosity toward other groups, children pick up on it (Root, 2003; Tatum, 2017; Tomishima, 2003). Thus, by continuing to share messages about her pride in being Haitian and being black, Fabienne modeled a healthy racial and ethnic identity for her children, which her husband supported by also expressing respect and love for, and knowledge of, Haitian history and black history.

Ethnic and Racial Socialization

Research has found that the messages parents of color communicate to their children about what it means to belong to a given racial or cultural/ethnic group, known as ethnic and racial socialization (ERS) messages (see Chap. 8 for more information), tend to fall into four categories: (1) ethnic pride, or messages about the positive aspects of belonging to a given group; (2) preparation for bias, whereby parents of color psychologically equip their children to live in a world where they may be discriminated against; (3) egalitarianism, or messages about the equal value and worth of all people, irrespective of their race; (4) warnings that members of other racial or ethnic groups cannot be trusted (Hughes et al., 2006; Lesane-Brown, 2006). Other researchers have added to this list the absence of ERS messages (i.e., *silence* around issues related to race and ethnicity) (Caughy, Nettles, & Lima, 2011; Rollins & Hunter, 2013; Snyder, 2012), as well as messages that are about the individual child's character (Caballero et al., 2008), or what Rollins and Hunter (2013) called "self-development socialization" (p. 146). These forms of ERS have been found in mixed-race families as well, and a number of researchers have provided useful summaries of the literature on racial and cultural socialization in mixed-race families (Csizmadia et al., 2014; Rollins & Hunter, 2013; Snyder, 2012; Stone & Dolbin-MacNab, 2017).

One area of consensus in this body of literature is around the importance of racial and cultural socialization for the psychological health and well-being of mixed-race children (Tatum, 2017). Most parents of mixed-race children seem to understand that their children will encounter messages about race, ethnicity, and culture in the wider world (we expand upon this point further in the section on external pressure) and that, therefore, what their parents have to say about these topics is important (Byrd & Garwick, 2006; Csizmadia et al., 2014; Rollins & Hunter, 2013; Stone & Dolbin-MacNab, 2017; Tatum, 2017).

The literature also demonstrates that a number of factors impact the content, frequency, and timing of racial socialization in mixed-race families, ranging from the age of children to neighborhood and school racial and ethnic composition, to the gender of the socializing parent, to the racial identities parents assign to their children (i.e., as white, nonwhite, or mixed), and to parents' own racial identities (Caballero et al., 2008; Csizmadia et al., 2014; Lesane-Brown, Brown, Tanner-Smith, & Bruce, 2010; Rockquemore et al., 2006; Rollins & Hunter, 2013; Snyder, 2012). For example, mothers tend to take primary responsibility for racial socialization (Caballero et al., 2008; Stone & Dolbin-MacNab, 2017); parents of mixed-race children who are part black are more likely to discuss issues of race, racism, and discrimination than those whose mixed children do not have black heritage (Rollins & Hunter, 2013; Snyder, 2012); and Asian parents are the least likely to actively engage in racial socialization (Chang, 2016; Rollins & Hunter, 2013).

Byrd and Garwick (2006) interviewed eight black-white couples raising school-aged children and found that the couples expressed a great deal of uncertainty about the best way to talk to their children. However, this did not keep them from broaching the topic. Parents seemed primarily anxious about whether they were doing a good job of explaining race to their children—a sentiment to which we as authors can relate. While we wish we always had ready answers for our children's many questions, we are not often prepared to provide a straightforward response and have found, as has been addressed in the literature as well (e.g., Byrd & Garwick, 2006), that race and racial issues are best handled as an ongoing conversation in our households. In this way, our responses to our children's questions are attuned to both their developmental levels and our increasingly refined ways of articulating and explaining these complex issues to our children.

Lived Experience

Melissa remembers how confusing and unsettling it was growing up and being asked often "what ARE you?" or being confidently mislabeled by strangers. She found that it made all the difference to understand that how we're identified racially by others and how we self-identity don't have to be the same and that how we self-identify can change (Tatum, 2017). For example, Melissa proudly identifies as, alternately, multiracial, biracial, or mixed race, but, socially, she is more often perceived as white or of ambiguous ethnicity. Her husband identifies as black and is socially identified as black. Both her daughters currently self-identify as biracial or multiracial. But the 9-year-old is generally socially identified as black and the 7-year-old is socially identified as mixed race or black. Melissa's daughters are accustomed to differentiating between social- and self-identification, and, unlike Melissa at that age, they aren't thrown when those identities don't match.

Colorism is another aspect of racial socialization that Melissa and her partner find important to address early and often with their mixed-race daughters. To be antiracist, kids and adults need to learn to detect and reject white supremacy, anti-blackness, and all racial hierarchies. But when there is a big range of skin colors within a family, as is true for many multiracial families, colorism can not only impact how you value yourself in the world, but also inform a subtle or not-so-subtle color hierarchy within the family. Melissa's immediate family of four has four different skin colors. Melissa and her partner have made it a point to find positive representations of black girls and people of color in books and movies, and to have a diverse friend group in which positive messages about blackness are part of everyday conversations. They talk about skin color with their daughters, notice it aloud, describe it, and delight in the gorgeous range of browns that get significantly less affirmation in popular culture and outside their home.

Melissa's 7-year-old daughter called this approach into question when she asked her, "Mommy, do you not like your [light, white-presenting] skin color?" This question allowed the conversation to evolve. Melissa explained that she says "the blacker the berry, the sweeter the juice" not to put down lighter skin tones but as a corrective to the foundational idea in the United States that the lighter the better, the darker the worse. Melissa and Andrew have taught their daughters that many people push back against that idea and that we must, too. Thus when her daughters saw only white dolls in a toy aisle, push back they did. Melissa wrote about this experience on EmbraceRace in a piece called Why are all white dolls sitting together on the Target shelf? (Giraud,

2016, August 5). She calls it: "the true tale of how my girls pushed back against racial injustice they saw over a month of errands at Target and how I supported them. It is an imperfect on-the-ground example of how to help young kids counter racial injustices and slights they inevitably witness, no matter how curated their lives."

Melissa's story also corroborates assertions in previous research about the importance of intentionality when it comes to the racial socialization of mixed-race children (Chang, 2016; Rockquemore & Brunsma, 2002a; Stone & Dolbin-MacNab, 2017). Indeed, actively and deliberately creating space to work out what it means to be a mixed-race child is one of the most important—and "woke"—parenting practices in which parents of mixed-race children can engage.

Navigating Extended Family Relationships

Extended family relationships can be tricky for all kinds of families. Spouses may not get along well with their in-laws, parents may be concerned about their child's choice of a partner, or a newly married couple can feel pressure from both sides of their family regarding where to spend the holidays. Such issues can feel particularly fraught for mixed-race couples (Byrd & Garwick, 2004; O'Donoghue, 2004), and when children enter the picture, additional tensions may arise (see Chap. 6 for more information), though it is also important to recognize the many strengths multiracial couples report as part of their marital and parenting experiences (Rosenblatt, Karis, & Powell, 1995; Tutwiler, 2016). A number of scholars note a pattern of initial resistance from either/both sides of mixed-race couples' families that is, typically, eventually followed by support (Byrd & Garwick, 2006; Rosenblatt et al., 1995; Tomishima, 2003; Tutwiler, 2016). In her qualitative study of biracial adults, Tomishima (2003) found that all of her black-white biracial participants reported that their white grandparents had rejected them initially, though most grew to accept them with time. On the other hand, intermarriage and arrival of children can actually elicit increasing racism from family members (Chang, 2016; O'Donoghue, 2004). Research has documented the microaggressions that extended family members can inflict, such as showing favoritism for the lighter skinned among biracial siblings, or attempting to measure mixed children's racial makeup, such as pointing out one child as the "more Asian/white/Latino one" (Chang, 2016; Johnston & Nadal, 2010; Tutwiler, 2016; Nadal, Sriken, Davidoff, Wong, & McLean, 2013; Nadal et al., 2011; Nishimura, 1998; Root, 1998).

Lived Experience

A contributor to the EmbraceRace blog, Casey Dupart (2016, October 24), shared painful stories from her childhood. She identifies as Mexican-American and Nigerian, but her older siblings are Mexican and African-American. She wrote,

Any time we watched a television program as a family I would become uncomfortable if the program included any safari-esque wild animals. Because then my siblings might remark, "There are some of your cousins!" It was humiliating, and I hated feeling different.

Among other examples of how her physical appearance was a source of scrutiny and commentary—from her weight to the shade of her skin—Dupart also shared,

My oldest sister was the prize since she was lighter in complexion with a looser wave pattern, according to my maternal grandmother. My hair was thicker, curlier, darker. My sister said I would always "need" a relaxer; I began using relaxers at age 6.

Interestingly, these stories reveal tensions within constructions of blackness as problematic (i.e., too African; "bad hair"), even as such interactions within her family led Dupart to feel she was alternatively too black, not black enough, too Mexican, or not Mexican enough (cf. Chang, 2016; Nadal et al., 2013; Roth, 2005). Chang (2016), Roth (2005), and Snyder (2012) also discussed part-black biracial (e.g., black-Latinx, or black-Asian) children's feelings of exclusion from black communities, adding complex dimensions to our understandings of the experiences of mixed-race individuals. Stories such as these also underscore the importance of "parental wokeness" mentioned earlier, such as that illustrated in Sandra Chapman's (2016, September 8) story on the EmbraceRace blog:

*A practice that caused some controversy for my family was my hard and fast rule that she only receive and play with brown-skinned baby dolls, preferably with no hair, but if there had to be hair it had to resemble her kinky tight curls. Despite my "rule," my daughter received her first peach-skinned Barbie doll from a friend for Christmas when she was six. The next peach-skinned baby doll came from a relative. By the time she was seven she had as many brown-skinned dolls as she had peach-skinned dolls. Every time she reached for a doll that did not resemble her skin tone, I made a frustrating groan and comment about the impact of her choices. My biggest concern was how was she going to feel great about her skin if she choose (*sic*)to play with a doll who had a skin tone she would never have, and came with skin privileges she would never experience.*

In spite of her family's ideas about how she should handle race-related matters with her daughter, Chapman, who identifies as Afro-Latina and describes her daughter as African-American, Dominican, and Puerto Rican, chose to follow her own instincts about how to instill confidence in her daughter about her skin color and hair texture. Chapman's resistance to her family's attempts to marginalize blackness sent an important message to her daughter about the beauty and importance of blackness while also affirming it as an identity her daughter should feel proud of and free to claim.

External Pressures and Perceptions of Mixed-Race Families

Just as extended family members can exert pressure on mixed-race families, messages from the outside world also can impact the experiences of mixed-race children and their parents, especially as children grow older and have increased exposure to the outside world (Byrd & Garwick, 2006; Rockquemore et al., 2006). Root

(2003) called this "community socialization" (p. 38) and also pointed out the importance of identifying hidden factors that impact ethnic and racial identity, such as generation, social class, and regional traditions and variations. Other studies have noted that neighborhood composition seems to have an impact on how children in mixed-race families are racially identified and treated (Caballero et al., 2008; Collins, 2000; Csizmadia et al., 2012; Doyle & Kao, 2007; Harris & Sim, 2002; Herman, 2004; Jackson, 2009, 2012; Lorenzo-Blanco, Bares, & Delva, 2013; Qian, 2004; Townsend, Fryberg, Wilkins, & Markus, 2012). Most of these studies identified the racial and ethnic composition of schools as an important factor as well.

Interracial relationships and the children they produce have long been framed through deficit lenses or with an assumption of inevitable pathology for those involved (Gatson, 2003; Jackson et al., 2012; Jackson & Samuels, 2011; O'Donoghue, 2004). As noted previously, one reason for this in the academic literature is that many studies of mixed-race families or mixed-race people are conducted with clinical populations or people receiving support from social welfare programs. But the US racial hierarchy and accompanying legacy of racism are critical to this history of deficit framing and the anxiety mixed-race children provoke as well (O'Donoghue, 2004). After all, mixed-race children are the product of sexual relations between people of different "races" (Gatson, 2003) and therefore undeniably represent a transgression of the white supremacist construction of racial purity. Indeed, the rule of hypodescent was meant to ensure the enslaved status of the biracial children born from the sexual assault of enslaved African women by their white owners (Rockquemore, 2002; Shih & Sanchez, 2009), and anti-miscegenation laws forbade intermarriage between whites and people of other races (Anderson, 2015).

As a result of these deficit lenses, people who form romantic relationships across racial lines arouse suspicion on all sides, from whites framed as race traitors (O'Donoghue, 2004) to people of color suspected of internalized racism (Chang, 2016). One manifestation of this suspicion is the pervasive assumption in the literature that white mothers of mixed children are unable to teach them about race since for the most part they have not grown up being socialized about their own race and/or they may not have a strong racial or ethnic identification/connection (Harman & Barn, 2005; Lorenzo-Blanco et al., 2013; O'Donoghue, 2004; Stone & Dolbin-MacNab, 2017). However, as will be discussed more thoroughly later in this chapter, this assumption does not account for generational differences or other factors impacting how white mothers of biracial children conceive of their unique parenting role.

Another consequence of the deficit lenses is that mixed-race children experience varying levels of acceptance and rejection from all of the racial or ethnic groups that comprise their backgrounds (Chang, 2016; Herman, 2004; Snyder, 2012). It is thus important for parents of mixed-race children to challenge these problematic frames. Chang (2016) noted that children are watching and noticing disparities, directly experiencing racism, and listening to what people around them—from family members to strangers—say about race. For example, Chang recounted her participants' stories about strangers stopping their children on the street to inquire about their racial makeup, whether because they recognized shared features (as in the case of an Asian older man who was excited to confirm his hunch about the Asianness of some biracial Asian/white children), or because they were surprised to discover a child's mixed parentage. As Chang put it, "The effect of this type of racial commenting is profound. It sends blatant messages to our mixed race children about what others will or will not allow them to be: 'one of us' or 'different than us'" (p. 79). Other scholars have noted the significant role phenotype plays in the identity construction of mixed-race children, particularly with respect to how the outside world interprets the various phenotypic representations of mixed-race people (Chang, 2016; Csizmadia et al., 2012; Johnston & Nadal, 2010; Rockquemore et al., 2006).

These various concerns about, vexations with, and biases toward mixed-race people and families are expressions of *monoracism* or, to use Fhagen-Smith's (2003) terminology, *biracialism*. According to Johnston and Nadal (2010) in their article about the microaggressions faced by mixed-race persons, monoracism is "a social system of psychological inequality where individuals who do not fit monoracial categories may be oppressed on systemic and inter-personal levels because of underlying assumptions and beliefs in singular, discrete racial categories" (Johnston & Nadal, 2010, p. 125), and it can be perpetrated by people of any race (Chang, 2016; Johnston & Nadal, 2010; Snyder, 2012; Stone & Dolbin-MacNab, 2017). Similarly, Fhagen-Smith (2003) used the term biracialism to define "acts of discrimination or racial insults that are unique to the biracial experience. For example … telling someone you are Jewish and being asked what the conversion process was like when in fact you were born to a Jewish mother, or a monoracial person of color thinking that you must think you are better/prettier/smarter because you are part White" (Fhagen-Smith, 2003, pp. 63–64). Variations on monoracism or biracialism can also be perpetrated against parents of mixed-race children who, for example, are being mistaken by strangers for a nanny, babysitter, or nonrelative in general (Murchison-Edwords, 2003).

Lived Experience

Media representations of whites and people of color also represent an external source of socialization that deeply impact (all) children's understandings of race. As Doucet and Adair (2013) wrote, "Even when talk about race and color is absent, children notice that some groups of people seem to be more important or less important than others; that lighter skin and European features are considered more beautiful than dark and African features; and that White people are presented more frequently and often more favorably than darker-skinned people on television, in movies … indeed, all around them (Tobin 2000; Tenorio 2004; Segura-Mora 2008; Dulin-Keita et al. 2011)" (p. 89). Conscious of these issues, Marcella and her husband Dave have worked hard to curate the media content to which their daughters are exposed, as she explains:

> *One challenge for us involves hair, and is very specific to images and ideas of "beautiful" hair. Despite our best attempts to provide counter messages, Aaliyah (7) and Ava (4) experienced various aspects of influence which I equate to pervasive princess culture and even*

many of the pop culture images of women and girls of color (with brown skin) having long straight hair, still adhering to a Barbie-like aesthetic. Both of my girls have short curly hair, but they have different curl types, textures and require different styling. Dave & I (and most of our extended family) have gone out of our way to compliment their hair, especially when it is "out" and curly as opposed to being in a ponytail, which they used to beg us for, until both learned frequent ponytails can slow the growth process for your hair because of breakage, and ultimately they would like their hair to grow. This is a particular challenge for me because my hair is dirty blonde and mostly straight, and I often wear it in a bun or ponytail, so this has felt like a "do as I say, not as I do" moment. Ava will say she doesn't like when her hair looks like a "pumpkin" or "too puffed up" and she will ask when her hair will look like mine. Aaliyah has moved on from any negative feelings about her hair, and is very proud of her skin, hair and that she is a "black girl who rocks!"

I attribute this in part because we had a turning point when she was 4. I took Aaliyah to see the 2014 version of the movie "Annie." An old friend of mine, whose daughter actually has a part in the movie invited us to a friends and family screening. Aaliyah was beyond excited, she dressed up and wore a red "Annie" dress from the Target clothing line and brought her Annie book. But the moment she saw Quvenzhane Wallis come on to the screen, with all her beauty, and talent, and charisma; Aaliyah was transfixed by the immediate identification with and reflection of herself. She walked out of the movie theater proclaiming that it was in fact the best night of her life, has since cajoled multiple friends and family members to see it again and again, and has memorized the soundtrack. Seeing someone so closely resembling herself in such an important role has made a huge impact on her sense of self because Annie reflected a smart, beautiful Black girl, with natural curly hair who was the heroine and center of the story. That resonated with Aaliyah deeply. She even asked my husband and I recently, "Did you know there was a white Annie too?"

We are confident that Ava will have her "Annie moment" sometime soon because race constancy (the idea that racial group membership is fixed) doesn't take hold until about 6 years old (Tatum, 2017*), and we are hopeful that Aaliyah's role modeling is also helpful. But the important take away is that it wouldn't be healthy for me to ignore the questions around hair, or to not acknowledge that in some ways as their Mommy, my own aesthetic is representative of this pervasive standard of beauty. We can have those conversations in authentic ways and function in ways that can disrupt the narrative, without disrupting our connection as a family. Ava recently wanted to win a prize (for me) at a local carnival that involved a Barbie doll; and she tried fervently to win the white Barbie. Aaliyah said, "Mommy wouldn't want the white Barbie anyway; she will want the Brown Barbie because it looks like us." Later Ava said to me in private as we discussed her disappointment about not winning the white Barbie "but Mommy-- you're white!"*

Mixed-Race Parenting Beyond the Black-White Binary

The bulk of literature on mixed-race parenting focuses on black-white families, typically justified by the facts that most mixed-race people are black-white (Jones & Bullock, 2013) and that the black-white color line is still the most divisive and contested (at least in the US context) (Brunsma, 2005; Chang, 2016; Feagin, 2010; Stone & Dolbin-MacNab, 2017). The multiracial population is far more varied than this focus suggests, however, with at least 4.7 million identifying as non-black multiracial (Chang, 2016), and 13 multiple-race groups having at least 100,000 people in 2010, the four largest being black and white (1.8 million), some other race and white (1.7 million), Asian and white (1.6 million), and "American-Indian" or Native

Alaskan and white (1.4 million) (Jones & Bullock, 2013). Furthermore, 1.5 million Census takers in 2010 were counted as "multiple-minority," or identified as mixed race *not* including white (Jones & Bullock, 2013, p. 9). Some researchers include mixed-race individuals from all backgrounds in their samples, or even focus specifically on mixed-race folks who are not black-white, but such studies tend to examine the lived experiences of those individuals through rich qualitative explorations (Caballero et al., 2008; Collins, 2000; Jackson, Wolven, & Aguilera, 2013; Miville, Constantine, Baysden, & So-Lloyd, 2005; Renn, 2003; Roberts-Clarke, Roberts, & Morokoff, 2004; Robinson-Wood, 2010; Rollins & Hunter, 2013; Tomishima, 2003), or to capture a demographic understanding of mixed-race populations through quantitative analyses (Binning et al., 2009; Brunsma, 2005; Campbell & Eggerling-Boeck, 2006; Gullickson & Morning, 2011; Herman, 2004; Hitlin et al., 2006; Shih, Bonam, Sanchez, & Peck, 2007).

A notable exception to these trends in the literature is Chang's (2016) *Raising Mixed Race: Multiracial Asian Children in a Post Race World*, a book based on Chang's qualitative interviews with 68 Asian[1] (monoracial and mixed) parents raising 75 mixed-race children. Chang introduces the topic as one with deep personal relevance: her father is Taiwanese while her mother is white with French Canadian, Slovakian, and German roots; her husband is also mixed with a Japanese mother and a white father of Welsh and British descent; and they are raising their son as a mixed-race child. Chang pointed out that mixed Asians are not relieved from the paradoxical burden of being at once a perpetual foreigner and a model minority, though this varies by "how Asian" these mixed-race individuals look. She also identified three systemic barriers to mixed Asian children's development of a positive racial identity: (1) compounded invisibility as a result of their membership in three demographic groups that tend to be invisible—Asians, multiracial people, and children; (2) racial isolation, or the loneliness that can come from not having family members or peers who can relate to their unique racial identification; and (3) parent indoctrination, defined as "the degree to which parents are indoctrinated into the white racial frame" (p. 101). Consistent with other research addressing racial socialization among Asians (Rollins & Hunter, 2013), Chang found that the majority of her participants did not talk to their children about race and that their own parents had never discussed race with them. Whether these parents were Asian, mixed Asian-white, or white, there was a minimization of the relevance of being Asian among participants that Chang attributed to their acceptance of the racial hierarchy in which Asians have been made honorary whites. She advised parents of mixed Asian children to be concerned, aware, and intentional regarding their children's racial identity development and experiences as a mixed-race person.

[1]Although not explicitly defined, it can be surmised that Chang's definition of Asian is broad, encompassing all people from the large geographic region known as Asia.

Lived Experience

Blogger and writer Thien-Kim Lam, who is a Vietnamese-American woman married to an African-American man, shared her experiences raising two mixed children in an op-ed on NBCNews.com (Lam, 2017, March 14):

> *... I've had strangers stop mid-stride, turn around, and tell me how beautiful my children are.*
>
> *"Mixed babies are the best!" they exclaim, clapping their hands in glee.*
>
> *"Black and Asian babies are the best mix out there," others whisper conspiratorially to me.*
>
> *I'm not even surprised anymore by the strangers who command me to produce more children because my husband and I make such beautiful babies. Apparently, I'm a biracial baby factory tasked to brighten their day with my children.*
>
> *I smile, nod, and continue on my way. It takes energy to discuss racial assumptions, and I have to pick my battles. I've even lied about our family's background because I'm tired of fighting with strangers.*
>
> *I adore that mixed race children are celebrated. There are Facebook pages that proudly celebrate interracial families by sharing photos of mixed race children in every combination imaginable. Interracial and monoracial families alike gush over the children's golden brown skin, luscious curls, and toothy grins.*
>
> *The multiracial children are put on pedestals for their beauty and even for how mixing races will save the United States from all its racism. (Spoiler alert: it won't.)*
>
> *Listen up, people: you can't have it both ways. You can't rhapsodize about the beautiful mix of multiracial babies, then turn around and assume that I'm the nanny. My children aren't memes to make you feel better about the state of race in our country.*
>
> *And don't be offended when someone calls you out on your hypocrisy. You want to be enlightened about interracial families? Stop assuming that we're the nanny.*

This powerful testimony expresses so many layers of the complicated feelings parents of mixed-race children feel, and it is an important voice to add to the conversation on mixed-race parenting that so heavily privileges black-white relationships. It also touches on many of the themes we have discussed already in this chapter.

Gaps in Our Knowledge: Recommendations for Future Research

As noted early on, the academic literature on parenting mixed-race children is limited. More empirical research using multiple research methods is needed to grow our scholarly understandings of people parenting mixed-race children, to broaden our conceptual and theoretical lenses, and to corroborate or challenge anecdotal evidence so that educators, healthcare providers, mental health practitioners, and policymakers can gain knowledge on how best to support the mixed-race children and families they serve. Each of the five focus areas we identified for the current chapter has at least the beginnings of an empirical base of evidence (some certainly more than others), but other dimensions of mixed-race parenting are sorely in need of exploration, including, but not limited to, parents of color raising mixed-race children; fathers of mixed-race children; co-parenting dynamics in mixed-race families; and mixed-race parenting combined with other aspects of the lived human experience, such as socioeconomic status, sexual orientation, and so on—in other words, considering mixed-race parenting through an intersectional lens.

Parents of Color

Given the variation in how parents of color were raised and socialized around race, how they identify themselves racially and/or ethnically, and how comfortable they feel in their identities, it should come as no surprise that there also would be variation in how parents of color of mixed-race children approach and address issues of race with their children (Tutwiler, 2016). However, the dearth of research focusing on parents of color who parent mixed-race children is striking. There are studies of mixed-race parenting that include parents of color in their samples, for example Caballero et al. (2008) and Chang (2016), but there is still much to learn about this population. This gap in the literature parallels a problem in the broader scholarly literature identified 25 years ago by Sandra Graham (1992): "Most of the subjects were white and middle class" (p. 629) and that, as Trainor and Bal (2012) argued, must be addressed by designing culturally responsive research.

What About Fathers?

Very little research on mixed-race parenting considers the experiences of fathers. Notable exceptions include studies in which fathers are included in the sample, such as Brunsma (2005), Byrd and Garwick (2006), Caballero et al. (2008), and Twine (2004). As with the point about parents of color, the lack of focus on fathers also tends to be a problem in the wider scholarly literature, reflected in the self-fulfilling expectation that mothers are responsible for children's care and upbringing (Doucet, 2011) and that anything fathers have to contribute is "extra." As Rollins and Hunter (2013) noted, "Additional research should explore … differences between mothers and fathers, and how parents make decisions about co-socialization of biracial youth …" (p. 151), which leads directly to our next point.

Adventures in Co-parenting

Negotiating parenting with spouses in mixed-race families is another area rarely addressed in literature. Caballero et al.'s (2008) report on mixed families along racial, ethnic, and religious lines suggested that parents in mixed relationships sometimes have different ideas and ideals about how to socialize their children around mixedness, though this did not necessarily lead to conflict. When conflicts did arise, the researchers found that most parents chose not to attribute those differences to culture, race, etc., though they may indeed have reflected different values, such as the Jewish father who wanted his sons to be bar mitzvahed though his wife was hesitant around the religious meaning of the ritual. As a resolution, the mother chose to think of the bar mitzvah as a celebration of their sons' humanity. As Caballero et al. put it, "Reframing cultural difference as difference that stems from the self and choice—such as humanistic, political or personality viewpoints—may offer the mothers and fathers concerned the possibility of resolution of difficulties" (p. 38). Byrd and Garwick (2006) also addressed conflicts within mixed (black man-white woman) couples. In this study, problems arose when the white partner did not believe or accept the black partner's interpretation of the larger society as racist, which naturally led to different and conflicting ideas about how to teach children about race and racism. More studies that explore mixed couples' child-rearing dynamics would broaden as well as deepen current understandings of mixed-race family life.

Raising Mixed-Race Children While …

As noted previously, research on parenting mixed-race children would benefit from intersectional analyses that account for the complexity of people's identities and experiences. For example, aside from Caballero et al.'s (2008) study including a lesbian couple in the interview portion of their study, we were unable to find studies of queer parents raising mixed-race children. Another area that seems to have received limited attention in the literature is the experiences of mixed-race people parenting their own children. Bratter (2007) studied how mixed-race people racially identify their own children, but explorations of parenting processes are also necessary. In Chang's (2016) study of parents raising mixed Asian children, some of the parents in the sample were themselves mixed, as was also the case in Caballero et al.'s (2008) study of mixed-race parenting, but in both cases being mixed while raising mixed children was not an explicit focus of the research. Song and Gutierrez's (2016) in-depth qualitative interview study of how 62 mixed-race people in Britain approach raising their mixed-race children is the first of its kind. These researchers identified four primary approaches to parenting from the interviews: (1) "Raised as British," reported by 8 participants; (2) "Mostly British with ethnic symbolism," reported by 9; (3) "Emphasis on minority heritage," reported by 8; and (4) "Cosmopolitanism," reported by 34 (p. 1135). Song and Gutierrez (2016) used the term cosmopolitanism to "refer to the ways in which these parents spoke of ideals around the appreciation of ethnic and cultural diversity in contemporary British society, in which many different types of people, and hybrid cultural formations, are regarded with mutual respect" (p. 1141). It would be interesting to know how these findings might vary in the United States and other countries with different histories of race relations.

As mentioned previously, social class has been included as a variable in some studies involving parents of mixed-race children. Typically, these are quantitative studies focused on how parents racially identify their mixed-race children (Brunsma, 2005; Qian, 2004; Roth, 2005), and there seems to be an overall consensus in the literature that higher socioeconomic status leads to more choices and greater flexibility in the identity options available to mixed-race people (Byrd & Garwick, 2004; Herman, 2004; Mahtani, 2002). By contrast, Stone and Dolbin-MacNab (2017) found that "the White mothers in this study, specifically the ones most active in educating their children and involved in activism, was that they were from predominantly lower SES backgrounds while raising their children. In fact, it was three mothers in particular, from lower SES, who reported active involvement in the social movement of 1990s for the US Census to include multiple race options for multiracial Americans. This was partially the result of their creation of the [Multi Ethnic Group]. It was also predominantly the mothers from lower SES who created the multiracial organization for their children or strongly encouraged their family's involvement with multiracial networks" (p. 106). This finding corroborates Byrd and Garwick's (2004) point in their literature review of family identity formation among black-white couples raising mixed-race children that there is still much to learn about the perspectives of nonurban, and working-class, and poor parents of mixed-race children. We would add that such studies should address these populations through strength- rather than deficit-based lenses, as much early research on mixed-race families have focused on clinical populations, many in extreme poverty, leading to the problematic stereotypes surrounding mixed-race people we have discussed throughout the chapter.

Another interesting intersection to explore would be that of white women and men who come into mixed-race relationships already having anti-racist attitudes and engaging in anti-racist actions, and/or having complex understandings of racial dynamics, and/or who grew up in integrated neighborhoods (see Twine, 2004). For example, the white mothers of adult biracial children interviewed for the study by Stone and Dolbin-MacNab (2017) all felt it important to hold space in their homes for addressing race and racism, their children's identities, and their children's healthy psychosocial development as mixed-race persons. The extant research seems to focus on white women who were clueless about racial dynamics until they either got with a partner of color or had children of color (see, e.g., Byrd & Garwick, 2006; O'Donoghue, 2004). For example, Byrd and Garwick (2006) stated that the black husbands of the white women in their study "had educated them about Black culture and fostered their knowledge of this ethnicity. Without their husband's presence, the women may have found it difficult to impart this sense of ethnic identity to their children" (p. 75). But this clearly does not represent the experiences of all white women in mixed-race relationships. Writer and psychotherapist Rhea St. Julien, whose husband is Haitian and identifies as black, believes that as the white mother of a biracial black-white child, correcting other white people's misconceptions around race is part of her role. In this excerpt from her article, "That Hair!," St. Julien revealed some of her critically self-reflective ideas, as well as her frustrations with white people's limited understandings around race:

> *The problem I have with questions about my daughter's appearance and our relationship is that they don't go far enough. Why doesn't anyone ever ask me, "Do you worry that as a white woman, a group that has historically oppressed black women, that you are going to fuck up the raising of this young black girl?" Yes, yes I do. I worry that I'm not investigating my own internalized racism enough, that the time I spent researching the best binky clip would have been better used re-reading bell hooks, that my laziness to engage with anti-racist action any further than in my writing is setting the wrong tone for my daughter.*
>
> *Where is the person bold enough to ask not "What product do you use in your daughter's hair?" but "Do you think your daughter will hate you when she goes through her racial identity awakening?" Because I would like to talk about that much more than the merits of shea butter* versus *No Poo. I would be worried if my daughter didn't go through a period of being very angry at all white people. It would mean she was doing a bypass on how messed up things are with race relations in this nation. It would mean she had a less-full picture of her own heritage, and how far we have come.*

While white persons' lack of engagement with their whiteness and their denial about the impacts of racism have been well documented (Britton, 2013; Rauktis et al., 2016), surfacing counternarratives could be an important contribution to research as well, and important to advancing the idea that white parents are also capable of engaging in critical race parenting (DePouw & Matias, 2016). For example, in a study of white parents raising children of African descent, Twine (2004) shared the story of Justine, a white Australian and Dutch woman who had grown up in Ghana, dated only black men, and worked in an African-Caribbean youth community center. Justine had enrolled her teenage daughter in a Saturday School where she could learn about black culture and was concerned that in spite of this her daughter didn't identify herself as black. Justine explained,

> *And I'm quite upset because I've always said to her, "Look, you're black." She goes, "Well, I'm not black because if I say I'm black I'm disrespecting you." And I thought, "You have a good point there." But what I said to her was "Okay, put it this way. Society sees you as black. And it's best that you know that because at the end of the day if it came to one or the other it would be black people that would accept you." The white people don't see you as "mixed with white"... At the end of the day, it's the black people who will look after you. If push comes to shove, it's the black people. I'm not going to tell you any different. I'd rather you be safe, than be in a position where you're not comfortable* (Twine, 2004, p. 891).

Twine has also made many empirical and conceptual contributions to understanding white parents of mixed children, including coining the term "racism-cognizant" (Twine, 2004, p. 881) to describe white parents of mixed-race children who understand racism to be a serious problem that they needed to prepare their children to address and resist, and developing the concept of racial literacy, "an analytical orientation and a set of practices that reflects shifts in perceptions of race, racism, and whiteness" (Twine, 2010, p. 92). Twine (2010) has shown that white parents of mixed-race children are capable of developing racial literacy, which is absolutely essential. Raising race-conscious children is a nonnegotiable for white parents raising children of color. And it is a deep, ongoing, life-altering commitment (Tatum, 2017).

Practice Implications: Guiding Principles for Parents

We end this chapter with ten guiding principles that reflect the practice implications of the research we have presented and discussed here. Given the chapter's focus on parenting, we articulate these as principles for parents, though following Matias (2016), our use of "parents" is broadly construed with parenting defined as "a pedagogical way to engage teaching and learning about race. Therefore, one need not be a biological, legal or foster parent to understand the dynamics between adult and child in the process of teaching and learning about race" (Matias, 2016, p. 4). Critical race parenting of mixed-race children demands knowledge of and, where relevant, commitment to at least the following:

1. **Confronting racism in your sphere of influence (your family, home, community, etc.) should be a salient part of your identity.** Your child is watching to see if what you say and what you do are in alignment. (That is, how diverse is your circle of friends? How well do you interact with family members of different racial backgrounds? How often do you talk about race with people in your sphere?)
2. **Representation matters, and you need to be aware that your consumption patterns have great influence over your children.** This includes books, TV shows, films, and what you value (i.e., which characters do you think are smart, beautiful, or competent). Normalizing the conversation about representation allows children to name race and to express identification in ways that are empowering for them, without fear of disappointing adults. As noted in the introduction, explicit representation of mixed-race people is growing in outlets ranging from children's books to television. Resources such as the EmbraceRace website provide numerous recommendations, advice, and ideas for accessing such materials.
3. **Become a social engineer so that your child engages with people who reflect their identities.** This means playdates, cocurricular choices, and decisions about teachers need to be carefully vetted. It also means that it is your job to do that background work, so your child doesn't have to. This is the case for all parents, but can be especially tricky when parenting across racial lines because it may not come naturally and may even involve becoming invested in communities or playgroups to which you would not normally be drawn.
4. **Get comfortable with the uncomfortable.** It is inevitable to feel vulnerable when crossing boundaries and engaging in activities that can be read as cultural or racial transgression. We acknowledge that even attempting to practice even the first three principles we have outlined can awaken such feelings of vulnerability! Buying a copy of *Latina* magazine when you are a black woman, spending significant time at a hair salon that is in the service of black women when you are Asian, or being the only "white" person in a particular social setting is par for the course. It is likely your child is often the "only one" in majority white environments or the only mixed-race one in a majority person of color environment, and these experiences are not socially neutral. It is okay for you

to be frequently uneasy in order to make life easier for your children. It is a good reminder of the cultural and institutional ways in which racism impacts all aspects of our society.

5. **Racism isn't (just) personal**. Mixed-race children likely live in a vulnerable space most of the time and trust that their love for and loyalty to their parents are real, but they know—consciously or unconsciously—love and loyalty are not enough to combat racism and oppression. Reinforcing dominant culture by making dominant culture "normal" and everything else *other* because that "isn't how you were raised" or you believe that you are actually color-blind is the anthesis to raising healthy, race-conscious children and will likely impede your ability to truly be the teacher, supporter, and parent that you want to be.
6. **Get on the same page**. If you are in relationship with your child's other parent, you should be in regular dialogue regarding language and messaging as it relates to conversations about race. This means explicit conversations about how your child self-identifies, and how you want to talk about everything from Ferguson and Japanese internment camps, to Colin Kaepernick and cultural appropriation.
7. **Intersectionality is not intended to create hierarchies of oppression**. Making intersectional connections to show solidarity for other diverse families can create parallel pathways for liberation. But be careful not to use those differences to reinforce intolerance (i.e., homophobia, religious intolerance, socioeconomic discrimination).
8. **Most parents don't have enough historical context, but it is essential**. The history of people of color in the United States is not add-on information—it is American history, and it is the job of parents to learn it, synthesize it, and then teach it to their children. Don't rely on traditional school curriculum to do that for you. Visiting places like the African-American Smithsonian Museum is a really powerful way to do this together, but can also be painful and confusing for mixed kids, who can feel torn between identities or parents as they try to make meaning of the atrocities committed as a result of white supremacy represented throughout American history.
9. **Special accolades are not part of the agreement**. It may be possible for white people to help raise empowered people of color, but this does not mean white parents who do so should expect to get special acknowledgement or reward for their wokeness: it's your *JOB* as a parent of a child of color. This might seem obvious, but because of the damage that white supremacy has done, there is sometimes an expectation that white people who attempt to engage in anti-racist work (even in their own families) should be treated as exceptions and deserve (or expect) special acknowledgement.
10. **Be mindful of (coded) language**. Children are paying attention to the adjectives used to describe them or people who look like them. They are sponges in the most literal sense—they take in the rhetoric, images, and ideas circulating in the wider world, and without a critical lens these can be damaging. Calling a child's hair "wild" or using animal nicknames, like monkey, for example, can reinforce dominant culture ideas of standards or beauty or behavior.

Beverly Tatum (2017) wrote in the revised and updated version of her classic book *Why are all the Black Kids Sitting Together in the Cafeteria? And Other Conversations About Race* that raising children who are developing critical consciousness is actually a gift, not a burden. In fact, as Tatum put it, we are all "better able to resist the negative impact of oppressive message when we see them coming than when they are invisible to us" (p. 127). Tatum also wrote, "We have the responsibility, and the resources available, to educate ourselves if necessary so that we will not repeat the cycle of oppresson with our children" (p. 129). We believe this to be the paramount opportunity, and perhaps challenge, for mixed-race families.

References

Anderson, C. R. (2015). What are you? A CRT perspective on the experiences of mixed race persons in 'post-racial' America. *Race Ethnicity and Education, 18*(1), 1–19. https://doi.org/10.1080/13613324.2014.911160

Aspinall, P. J. (2002). Collective terminology to describe the minority ethnic population: The persistence of confusion and ambiguity in usage. *Sociology, 36*(4), 803–806.

Barn, R. (1999). White mothers, mixed-parentage children and child welfare. *The British Journal of Social Work, 29*, 269–284.

Bates, K. (2016, June 5). '*Composite soul* [Blog post]'. Retrieved from https://medium.com/embrace-race/composite-soul-being-mixed-means-always-having-to-say-youre-sorry-582d215a5792

Binning, K. R., Unzueta, M. M., Huo, Y. J., & Molina, L. E. (2009). The interpretation of multiracial status and its relation to social engagement and psychological well-being. *Journal of Social Issues, 65*, 35–49. https://doi.org/10.1111/j.1540-4560.2008.01586.x

Blay, Y. (2014). *(1)ne drop*. Philadelphia, PA: BLACKprint Press.

Bolland, J. M., Bryant, C. M., Lian, B. E., McCallum, D. M., Vazsonyi, A. T., & Barth, J. M. (2007). Development and risk behavior among African American, Caucasian, and mixed-race adolescents living in high poverty inner-city neighborhoods. *American Journal of Community Psychology, 40*, 230–249. https://doi.org/10.1007/s10464-007-9132-1

Brackett, K. P., Marcus, A., McKenzie, N. J., Mullins, L. C., Tang, Z., & Allen, A. M. (2006). The effects of multiracial identification on students' perceptions of racism. *The Social Science Journal, 43*, 437–444.

Bratter, J. (2007). Will "multiracial" survive to the next generation?: The racial classification of children of multiracial parents. *Social Forces, 86*(2), 821–849.

Brayboy, B. M. J., & Maughan, E. (2009). Indigenous knowledge and the story of the bean. *Harvard Educational Review, 79*(1), 1–21.

Britton, J. (2013). Researching white mothers of mixed-parentage children: The significance of investigating whiteness. *Ethnic and Racial Studies, 36*, 1311–1322. https://doi.org/10.1080/01419870.2013.752101

Brunsma, D. L. (2005). Interracial families and the racial identification of mixed-race children: Evidence from the early childhood longitudinal study. *Social Forces, 84*(2), 1131–1157.

Buckley, T. R., & Carter, R. T. (2004). Biracial (Black/White) women: A qualitative study of racial attitudes and beliefs and their implications for therapy. *Women & Therapy, 27*, 45–64.

Byrd, M. M., & Garwick, A. W. (2004). A feminist critique of research on interracial family identity: Implications for family health. *Journal of Family Nursing, 10*(3), 302–322. https://doi.org/10.1177/1074840704267189

Byrd, M. M., & Garwick, A. W. (2006). Family identity: Black-white interracial family health experience. *Journal of Family Nursing, 12*, 22–37.

Caballero, C., Edwards, R., & Puthussery, S. (2008). Parenting 'mixed' children: Negotiating differences and belonging in mixed race, ethnicity and faith families.

Campbell, M., & Eggerling-Boeck, J. (2006). "What about the children?" The psychological and social well-being of multiracial adolescents. *The Sociological Quarterly, 47*, 147–173.

Caughy, M. O. B., Nettles, S. M., & Lima, J. (2011). Profiles of racial socialization among African American parents: Correlates, context, and outcome. *Journal of Child and Family Studies, 20*(4), 491–502. https://doi.org/10.1007/s10826-010-9416-1

Caughy, M. O. B., & Owen, M. T. (2015). Cultural socialization and school readiness of African American and Latino preschoolers. *Cultural Diversity and Ethnic Minority Pscyhology, 21*(3), 391–399.

Chang, S. H. (2016). *Raising mixed race: Multiracial Asian children in a post-racial world*. New York: Routledge.

Chapman, S. (2016, September 8). '*Too much or not enough? Racially socializing my Black daughter* [Blog post]'. Retrieved from https://medium.com/embrace-race/too-much-or-not-enough-racially-socializing-my-black-daughter-f5900c057013

Coleman, V. H., & Carter, M. M. (2007). Biracial self-identification: Impact on trait anxiety, social anxiety, and depression. *Identity, 7*(2), 103–114. https://doi.org/10.1080/15283480701326018

Collins, J. F. (2000). Biracial Japanese American identity: An evolving process. *Cultural Diversity & Ethnic Minority Psychology, 6*, 115–133.

Csizmadia, A., Brunsma, D. L., & Cooney, T. M. (2012). Racial identification and developmental outcomes among Black–White multiracial youth: A review from a life course perspective. *Adv Life Course Res, 17*(1), 34–44. https://doi.org/10.1016/j.alcr.2011.10.003

Csizmadia, A., Rollins, A., & Kaneakua, J. P. (2014). Ethnic-racial socialization and its correlates in families of Black-White biracial children. *Family Relations, 63*, 259–270. https://doi.org/10.1111/fare.12062

DePouw, C., & Matias, C. (2016). Critical race parenting: Understanding scholarship/activism in parenting our children. *Educational Studies, 52*(3), 237–259. https://doi.org/10.1080/00131946.2016.1169182

Doucet, F. (2011). Parent involvement as ritualized practice. *Anthropology and Education Quarterly, 42*(4), 404–421. https://doi.org/10.1111/j.1548-1492.2011.01148.x

Doucet, F., & Adair, J. K. (2013). Addressing race and inequity in the classroom. *Young Children, 68*(5), 88–97.

Doyle, J. M., & Kao, G. (2007). Are racial identities of multiracials stable? Changing self-identification among single and multiple race individuals. *Social Psychology Quarterly, 70*(4), 405–423. https://doi.org/10.1177/019027250707000409

Dupart, C. (2016, October 24). *Not "black" enough. Not Mexican enough. Not cool enough. Simply not enough* [Blog post]. Retrieved from https://medium.com/embrace-race/not-black-enough-not-mexican-enough-not-cool-enough-simply-not-enough-1caa99b3d9e6

Feagin, J. R. (2010). *The white racial frame: Centuries of racial framing and counter-framing*. New York: Routledge.

Fhagen-smith, P. (2003). Mixed race youth between 8 to 11 years old. In M. P. P. Root & M. Kelley (Eds.), *Multiracial child resource book: Living complex identities*. MAVIN Foundation: Seattle, WA.

Fusco, R. A., & Rauktis, M. E. (2012). Are Black/White biracial children at higher risk? *Child Welfare, 91*, 55–56.

Fusco, R. A., Rauktis, M. E., McCrae, J. S., Cunningham, M. A., & Bradley-King, C. K. (2010). Aren't they just black kids? Biracial children in the child welfare system. *Child & Family Social Work, 15*, 441–451. https://doi.org/10.1111/j.1365-2206.2010.00690.x

Gatson, S. N. (2003). On being amorphous: Autoethnography, genealogy, and a multiracial identity. *Qualitative Inquiry, 9*(1), 20–48. https://doi.org/10.1177/1077800402239338

Giraud, M. (2016, August 5). *Why are all the white dolls sitting together on the Target shelf?* Retrieved from http://www.embracerace.org/blog/why-are-all-the-white-dolls-sitting-together-on-the-target-shelf-melissa-giraud

Graham, S. (1992). Most of the subjects were white and middle class: Trends in published research on African Americans in selected APA journals, 1970–1989. *American Psychologist, 47*(5), 629–639.

Gullickson, A., & Morning, A. (2011). Choosing race: Multiracial ancestry and identification. *Social Science Research, 40*(2), 498–512.

Harman, V., & Barn, R. (2005). Exploring the discourse concerning white mothers of mixed parentage children. In T. Okitikpi (Ed.), *Working with children of mixed parentage* (pp. 102–112). Dorset: Russell House.

Harris, D. R., & Sim, J. J. (2002). Who is multiracial? Assessing the complexity of lived race. *American Sociological Review, 67*(4), 614–627. https://doi.org/10.2307/3088948

Herman, M. (2004). Forced to choose: Some determinants of racial identification in multiracial adolescents. *Child Development, 75*(3), 730–748. https://doi.org/10.1111/j.1467-8624.2004.00703.x

Hitlin, S., Scott Brown, J., & Elder, G. H. (2006). Racial self-categorization in adolescence: Multiracial development and social pathways. *Child Development, 77*(5), 1298–1308. https://doi.org/10.1111/j.1467-8624.2006.00935.x

Hughes, D., Rodriguez, J., Smith, E. P., Johnson, D. J., Stevenson, H. C., & Spicer, P. (2006). Parents' ethnic-racial socialization practices: A review of research and directions for future study. *Developmental Psychology, 42*(5), 747–770.

Jackson, K. F. (2009). Beyond race: Examining the facets of multiracial identity through a life-span developmental lens. *Journal of Ethic & Cultural Diversity in Social Work, 18*(4), 293–310. https://doi.org/10.1080/15313200903310759

Jackson, K. F. (2012). Living the multiracial experience: Shifting racial expressions, resisting race, and seeking community. *Qualitative Social Work, 11*(1), 42–60. https://doi.org/10.1177/1473325010375646

Jackson, K. F., & Samuels, G. M. (2011). Multiracial competence in social work: Recommendations for culturally attuned work with multiracial people. *Social Work, 56*(3), 235–245.

Jackson, K. F., Wolven, T., & Aguilera, K. (2013). Mixed resilience: A study of multiethnic Mexican American stress and coping in Arizona. *Family Relations, 62*, 212–225. https://doi.org/10.1111/j.1741-3729.2012.00755.x

Jackson, K. F., Yoo, H. C., Guevarra Jr., R., & Harrington, B. A. (2012). Role of identity integration on the relationship between perceived racial discrimination and psychological adjustment of multiracial people. *Journal of Counseling Psychology, 59*(2), 240–250. https://doi.org/10.1037/a0027639

Johnston, M. P., & Nadal, K. L. (2010). Multiracial microaggressions: Exposing monoracism in everyday life and clinical practice. In D. W. Sue (Ed.), *Microaggressions and marginality: Manifestations, dynamics and impact* (pp. 123–144). New York: Wiley and Sons.

Jones, N. A., & Bullock, J. (2013). *The two or more races population: 2010. 2010 census brief series*. Washington, DC: U.S. Census Bureau.

Lam, T.-K. (2017, March 14). *Opinion: We are not just 'the nanny'*. Retrieved from https://www.nbcnews.com/news/asian-america/opinion-we-are-not-just-nanny-n733456

Lesane-Brown, C. L. (2006). A review of racial socialization in Black families. *Developmental Review, 26*, 400–426. https://doi.org/10.1016/j.dr.2006.02.001

Lesane-Brown, C. L., Brown, T. N., Tanner-Smith, E. E., & Bruce, M. A. (2010). Negotiating boundaries and bonds: Frequency of young children's socialization to their ethnic/racial heritage. *Journal of Cross-Cultural Psychology, 41*(3), 457–464. https://doi.org/10.1177/0022022109359688

Lorenzo-Blanco, E. I., Bares, C. B., & Delva, J. (2013). Parenting, family processes, relationships, and parental support in multiracial and multiethnic families: An exploratory study of youth perceptions (Article). *Family Relations, 62*(1), 125–139. https://doi.org/10.1111/j.1741-3729.2012.00751.x

Lou, E., Lalonde, R. N., & Wilson, C. (2011). Examining a multidimensional framework of racial identity across different biracial groups. *Asian American Journal of Psychology, 2*(2), 79–90. https://doi.org/10.1037/a0023658

Lusk, E. M., Taylor, M. J., Nanney, J. T., & Austin, C. C. (2010). Biracial identity and its relation to self-esteem and depression in mixed black/white biracial individuals. *Journal of Ethnic and Cultural Diversity in Social Work, 19*(2), 109–126. https://doi.org/10.1080/15313201003771783

Mahtani, M. (2002). Interrogating the hyphen-nation: Canadian multicultural policy and 'mixed race' identities. *Social Identities, 8*(1), 67–90. https://doi.org/10.1080/13504630220132026

Matias, C. E. (2016). *"Mommy, is being Brown bad?": Critical race parenting in a "post-race" era*. Retrieved from http://soundideas.pugetsound.edu/rpj/vol1/iss3/1

Miville, M. L., Constantine, M. G., Baysden, M. F., & So-Lloyd, G. (2005). Chameleon changes: An exploration of racial identity themes of multiracial people. *Journal of Counseling Psychology, 52*, 507–516.

Murchison-Edwords, M. (2003). Birth to three years: Parental issues. In M. P. P. Root & M. Kelley (Eds.), *Multiracial child resource book: Living complex identities*. MAVIN Foundation: Seattle, WA.

Nadal, K. L., Sriken, J., Davidoff, K. C., Wong, Y., & McLean, K. (2013). Microaggressions within families: Experiences of multiracial people. *Family Relations, 62*(1), 190–201.

Nadal, K. L., Wong, Y., Griffin, K., Sriken, J., Vargas, V., Wideman, M., et al. (2011). Microaggressions and the multiracial experience. *International Journal of Humanities and Social Sciences, 1*(7), 36–44.

Nishimura, N. J. (1998). Assessing the issues of multiracial students on college campuses. *Journal of College Counseling, 1*(1), 45–53.

O'Donoghue, M. (2004). Racial and ethnic identity development in White mothers of biracial, Black-White children. *Affilia, 19*(1), 68–84. https://doi.org/10.1177/0886109903260795

Qian, Z. (2004). Options: Racial/ethnic identification of children of intermarried couples (Article). *Social Science Quarterly (Wiley-Blackwell), 85*(3), 746–766. https://doi.org/10.1111/j.0038-4941.2004.00243.x

Rauktis, M. E., Fusco, R. A., Goodkind, S., & Bradley-King, C. (2016). Motherhood in liminal spaces: White mothers' parenting Black/White children. *Affilia: Journal of Women and Social Work, 31*(4), 434–449. https://doi.org/10.1177/0886109916630581

Renn, K. A. (2003). Understanding the identities of mixed-race college students through a developmental ecology lens. *Journal of College Student Development, 44*(3), 383–403.

Roberts, S.-M. (2016, June 7). '5 things to know if you love a mixed race kid [Blog post]' *EmbraceRace*. Retrieved from https://medium.com/embrace-race/5-things-to-know-if-you-love-a-mixed-race-kid-44943b62b800

Roberts-Clarke, I., Roberts, A. C., & Morokoff, P. (2004). Dating practices, racial identity, and psychotherapeutic needs of biracial women. *Women & Therapy, 27*(1–2), 103–117.

Robinson-Wood, T. L. (2010). Is that your mom? A qualitative investigation of white mothers on non-white children in the United States and in New Zealand. *Journal of Ethnographic and Qualitative Research, 4*, 226–238.

Rockquemore, K. A. (1999). Between Black and Whtie: Exploring the "biracial" experience. *Race & Society, 1*(2), 197–212.

Rockquemore, K. A. (2002). Negotiating the color line: The gendered process of racial identity construction among Black/White biracial women. *Gender and Society, 16*(4), 485–503.

Rockquemore, K. A., & Brunsma, D. L. (2002a). *Beyond black: Biracial identity in America*. Thousand Oaks, CA: Sage Publications.

Rockquemore, K. A., & Brunsma, D. L. (2002b). Socially embedded identities: Theories, typologies, and process of racial identity among Black/White biracials. *The Sociological Quarterly, 43*(3), 335–356. https://doi.org/10.1111/j.1533-8525.2002.tb00052.x

Rockquemore, K. A., Laszloffy, T., & Noveske, J. (2006). It all starts at home: Racial socialization in multiracial families. In D. L. Brunsma (Ed.), *Mixed messages: Multiracial identities in the "color-blind" era* (pp. 203–216). Boulder, CO: Lynne Rienner Publishers.

Rollins, A., & Hunter, A. G. (2013). Racial socialization of biracial youth: Maternal messages and approaches to address discrimination. *Family Relations, 62*, 140–153. https://doi.org/10.1111/j.1741-3729.2012.00748.x

Root, M. P. P. (1998). Experiences and processes affecting racial identity development: Preliminary results from the Biracial Sibling Project. *Cultural Diversity and Mental Health, 4*(3), 237.

Root, M. P. P. (2003). Racial identity development and persons of mixed race heritage. In M. P. P. Root & M. Kelley (Eds.), *Multiracial child resource book: Living complex identities*. MAVIN Foundation: Seattle, WA.

Rosenblatt, P. C., Karis, T. A., & Powell, R. D. (1995). *Multiracial couples: Black & white couples*. Thousand Oaks, CA: Sage Publications.

Roth, W. D. (2005). The end of the drop rule? Labeling of multiracial children in black intermarriages. *Sociological Forum, 20*(1), 35–67.

Shih, M., Bonam, C., Sanchez, D., & Peck, C. (2007). The social construction of race: biracial identity and vulnerability to stereotypes. *Cultural Diversity and Ethnic Minority Psychology, 13*(2), 125–133.

Shih, M., & Sanchez, D. T. (2005). Perspectives and research on the positive and negative implications of having multiple racial identities. *Psychological Bulletin, 131*, 569–591.

Shih, M., & Sanchez, D. T. (2009). When race becomes even more complex: towards understanding multiracial identity and experiences. *Journal of Social Issues, 65*(1), 1–11.

Snyder, C. R. (2012). Racial socialization in cross-racial families. *Journal of Black Psychology, 38*(2), 228–253. https://doi.org/10.1177/0095798411416457

Song, M., & Gutierrez, C. O. N. (2016). What are the parenting practices of multiracial people in Britain? *Ethnic and Racial Studies, 39*(7), 1128–1149.

Stone, D. J., & Dolbin-MacNab, M. (2017). Racial socialization practices of White mothers raising Black-White biracial children. *Contemporary Family Therapy, 39*(2), 97–111.

Tatum, B. D. (2017). Why are all the Black kids sitting together in the cafeteria? In *And other conversations about race*. New York: Basic Books.

Tomishima, S. (2003). When and how families can disrupt mixed race identity. In M. P. P. Root & M. Kelley (Eds.), *Multiracial child resource book: Living complex identities* (pp. 95–101). Seattle, WA: MAVIN Foundation.

Townsend, S. S. M., Fryberg, S. A., Wilkins, C. L., & Markus, H. R. (2012). Being mixed: Who claims a biracial identity? *Cultural Diversity and Ethnic Minority Psychology, 18*(1), 91–96. https://doi.org/10.1037/a0026845

Trainor, A. A., & Bal, A. (2012). Development and preliminary analysis of a rubric for culturally responsive research. *The Journal of Special Education, 47*(4), 203–216. https://doi.org/10.1177/0022466912436397

Tutwiler, S. W. (2016). *Mixed-race youth and schooling: The fifth minority*. New York, NY: Routledge.

Twine, F. W. (2004). A white side of black Britain: The concept of racial literacy. *Ethnic and Racial Studies, 27*(6), 878–907.

Twine, F. W. (2010). *A white side of black Britain: Interracial intimacy and racial literacy*. Durham, NC: Duke University Press.

Udry, J. R., Li, R. M., & Hendrickson-Smith, J. (2003). Health and behavior risks of adolescents with mixed-race identity. *American Journal of Public Health, 93*, 1865–1870.

Racial Socialization: A Developmental Perspective

Alethea Rollins

> *My son Nicholas is 3 years old and attends a predominately White Christian preschool. I was picking him up a little early one day and was chatting with his teacher while he was washing his hands and getting his stuff—and a little girl ran up to me and started chatting and telling me what they did that day and she pointed over where she was playing and there were three other little girls sitting reading books and she started to tell me who each of them were, "that one with the butterfly shirt is Blair, and that one with pink is Anna, and that Black one is Aiyushi." I was caught off guard by her choice to describe this little (what appeared to be) Indian girl as Black; and that she was attempting to identify her racially while describing the other children by their clothing. The other children and the little girl were White. This experience made me wonder how she would identify my biracial son (who looks Black).*
> *A few weeks later I got my answer. I asked Nicholas to pass me a black crayon. He passed me a brown crayon. I said, "This is brown, I asked for the black crayon." Looking puzzled, he replied, "but, that is the color of my skin and I'm Black."*
> *I had never used racial terms to describe him, our family, or anyone. Taking his lead, I had always described him and other people of color as brown or peach or vanilla. He was just learning his colors. I didn't want to confuse him with racial terms. But, I quickly learned that if your child interacts with anyone outside of your home you have to be prepared to talk about race before it is developmentally appropriate.*
>
> —Anonymous

A. Rollins (✉)
Child and Family Development Program, School of Human Services,
Harmon College of Business and Professional Studies,
University of Central Missouri, Warrensburg, MO, USA
e-mail: arollins@ucmo.edu

R. Nazarinia Roy, A. Rollins (eds.), *Biracial Families*,
https://doi.org/10.1007/978-3-319-96160-6_8

Introduction

Similar to parents in other minority groups, parents of biracial children must prepare children to navigate the harsh realities of being a minority, instill pride, and pass on knowledge, traditions, and history. Yet, unlike other minority parents, many parents of biracial children are not minorities themselves and lack firsthand experience with life beneath this veil. Further, they don't know what it means to be biracial, to embody multiple racial (mis)constructions with few examples or role models to lead the way. This chapter provides a review of the racial socialization literature, explicating unique considerations for biracial families as they transmit messages that foster their children's understanding and awareness of race, racism, and cross-race relationships (Hughes et al., 2006). In addition, this chapter provides developmentally appropriate strategies, identifying important considerations for preschoolers, school-age children, and adolescents. This chapter concludes with recommendations for professionals working with biracial children and their families and considerations for future research.

Racial Socialization

In this chapter, the term *racial socialization* is used to encompass what researchers have termed *racial-ethnic socialization* (Hughes et al., 2006). Previously, *racial socialization* was used to describe Black parents' efforts to protect and prepare their children for experiences of racism and discrimination (Bowman & Howard, 1985; Peters, 1985). *Ethnic socialization* was used to describe Latino and Asian parents' efforts to help their immigrant children retain cultural beliefs, traditions, and affiliation; promote their cultural identity; and resist assimilation into mainstream American culture (Knight, Bernal, Cota, Garza, & Ocampo, 1993; Quintana & Vera, 1999). Currently, racial socialization and ethnic socialization have, in many cases, merged into a combination of strategies parents use to inform their children about issues regarding race and ethnicity, and include lessons about group pride and transmission of cultural traditions and values. Given the historical context of racial stratification in the United States, the use of the term *racial socialization* in this chapter signifies the importance of race as a social construction in the lived experiences of people of color. In addition, this centrality of race is integral to the "twoness" biracial people often experience as they cognitively reconcile their unique racial heritage.

Racial socialization consists of verbal and nonverbal, conscious and unconscious, and direct and indirect race-related communication. It includes intentional and unintentional messages and is a by-product of proactive and reactive parenting practices (Hughes & Chen, 1999; Stevenson, 1994). Racial socialization practices reflect one's own racial heritage, received racial socialization, racial identity, class, gender, experiences with racism and discrimination, beliefs, and values (Hughes & Chen, 1997; Thomas & Speight, 1999; Thornton, 1997). Racial socialization is a bidirectional process, influenced by the youth's racial heritage, gender, age, and experiences with racism and discrimination (Hughes, 2003; Hughes & Johnson, 2001; Thomas & Speight, 1999). Furthermore, racial socialization practices depend on the current and historical context and the developmental stage of the child. Scholars have conceptualized racial socialization in varying ways and have identified different dimensions of racial socialization. In this discussion, five synergistic dimensions of racial socialization—minority socialization, cultural socialization, mainstream socialization, egalitarian socialization, and silent socialization—are described to represent the varying ways families of color, including biracial families, employ racial socialization practices.

Minority Socialization

Minority socialization refers to the racial socialization strategies that parents use to prepare their minority children for and buffer and protect them from racial and discriminatory practices of the dominant society. Parents socialize their children toward their future reality (Ogbu, 1982), which is dependent on their historical and contemporary economic, social, and political realities. Although minorities have successfully defeated formal legal barriers, informal remnants persist. People of color continue to experience implicit and explicit racism and discrimination. As a result, parents directly and indirectly socialize their children to deal with the social and economic realities of being a minority in America.

Both parents (Thornton, 1997) and adolescents (Phinney & Chavira, 1995) report experiences of discrimination. In an effort to counter the inevitable discriminatory experiences of their children, most Black parents talk to their children about race (Bowman & Howard, 1985; Sanders Thompson, 1994; Thomas & Speight, 1999; Thornton, 1997). Parents use practical and developmentally appropriate strategies to advise children and adolescents about experiences with personal and institutional racism. The messages include awareness of racism (Phinney & Chavira, 1995; Stevenson, 1994; Thomas & Speight, 1999), direct teaching with regard to racial barriers and blocked opportunities (Bowman & Howard, 1985; Sanders Thompson, 1994; Thornton, Chatters, Taylor, & Allen, 1990), caution about interracial contact and promotion of mistrust of White people (Bowman & Howard, 1985; Stevenson, 1995; Thomas & Speight, 1999; Thornton et al., 1990), encouragement to stand up for one's rights (Thornton et al., 1990), and preparation for bias (Hughes & Johnson, 2001; Stevenson, 1995).

Several authors have posited relations between minority socialization and child outcomes, including the use of more effective coping strategies (Phinney & Chavira, 1995), greater knowledge about one's group and greater understanding of racism and prejudice (Quintana & Vera, 1999), and evidence of advanced stages of racial identity development (Stevenson, 1995). Further, Bowman and Howard (1985) found that adolescents who received messages about racial barriers and who were cautioned about interracial contact had higher grades, and Miller (1999) suggested that minority socialization, along with racial identity, promoted resiliency among Black adolescents.

Scholars suggest a fine line between preparation for bias and promotion of mistrust. A few investigations have found minority socialization practices, including promoting racial mistrust of Whites (Biafora, Warheit, Zimmerman, & Gil, 1993), to be associated with negative outcomes. Parents must carefully negotiate how, when, and to what extent they enact minority socialization. Understanding racism and discrimination and being prepared for bias can help youth deal with inevitable experiences of racial conflict, but to avoid detrimental outcomes parents have to carefully balance those messages with messages of pride and culturally enriching experiences (Hughes & Chen, 1999).

Cultural Socialization

Stevenson (1995) found that minority parents' socialization messages included historical lessons that promote group pride and empowerment. Cultural socialization refers to the cultural conditioning (Boykin & Toms, 1985) that occurs within the family system. This conditioning includes transference within the family context of "modes, sequences and styles of behavior" (Boykin & Toms, 1985, p. 42) that reflect traditions and values directly related to cultural ethos. This type of socialization is empowering and supportive and includes direct teaching and messages of racial pride (Bowman & Howard, 1985; Caughy, O'Campo, Randolph, & Nickerson, 2002; Thornton et al., 1990), historical traditions (Thornton et al., 1990), and religious principles (Stevenson, 1995; Thomas & Speight, 1999; Thornton et al., 1990).

The transmission of cultural beliefs and values is embedded in interpersonal relationships and daily activities. Parents, siblings, extended kin, and the home environment can model and represent cultural ethos to children. Thus, children are inundated with both articulated and unarticulated messages about who they are, how they should behave and interact, and how they are connected to their culture. Although parents may not always consciously make the connection between cultural ethos and their socialization practices, research suggests that parents culturally socialize their children to be proud of their racial heritage (Hughes & Johnson, 2001; Phinney & Chavira, 1995; Thornton et al., 1990).

Cultural socialization is the most often cited racial socialization strategy employed by parents (Hughes & Johnson, 2001), and cross-ethnic findings suggest that it is a normative component of parental socialization for minority parents (Hughes, 2003). Cultural socialization is positively associated with racial identity (Marshall, 1995; McHale et al., 2006; Stevenson, 1995), self-esteem (Constantine & Blackmon, 2002), and anger management (Stevenson, 1997) and is negatively associated with psychosocial problems (Caughy et al., 2002) and depressive symptoms (McHale et al., 2006). Children who are surrounded in their homes by items reflecting their heritage (physical cultural socialization) had a greater wealth of academic factual knowledge and better developed problem-solving skills than other Black children had (Caughy et al., 2002).

Mainstream Socialization

Contrary to minority and cultural socialization, mainstream socialization decenters race. Individuality, as opposed to group membership and solidarity, is encouraged, and discussions of race, racism, and discrimination are avoided (Hughes et al., 2006). Mainstream socialization messages include self-development, positive character traits, and an endorsement of mainstream cultural institutions and values (Constantine & Blackmon, 2002; Sanders Thompson, 1994; Stevenson, Herrero-Taylor, Cameron, & Davis, 2002). Mainstream socialization messages are universal messages with no mention of race or inequalities and aim to prepare children to be successful within the dominant cultural context.

Parents socialize their children to be successful within mainstream society by emphasizing the importance of negotiating the dominant culture and downplaying racial group affiliation. Boykin and Toms (1985) discuss the multiple contexts within which Black socialization occurs and recognize mainstream American society as an important socializing context. Using Boykin and Toms's framework, Thornton et al. (1990) identified several racial socialization messages consistent with mainstream socialization, including achievement and hard work, good citizenship, and moral virtues. Stevenson et al. (2002) found that endorsement of mainstream culture, which highlights the importance of majority culture institutions and values for the advancement of Blacks and deemphasizes racism, discrimination, and African culture, was the racial socialization message most often reported by girls who had not personally experienced racism or discrimination.

Egalitarian Socialization

Similar to mainstream socialization, egalitarian socialization deemphasizes racism and discrimination. Although they often overlap in practice, egalitarian socialization focuses on promoting equality and acceptance of all people, while mainstream socialization avoids or minimizes discussion of race. Parents espousing egalitarian messages encourage their children to look beyond skin color, treat everyone equally, and celebrate all people. Egalitarian socialization messages emphasize the equality of races and minimize or neglect the presence of racial inequalities and discrimination.

Egalitarian socialization subsumes what scholars have identified as the color-blind perspective (Orbe, 1999) and egalitarianism (Bowman & Howard, 1985; Hughes et al., 2006). A color-blind philosophy emphasizes the humanistic similarities among people, maintaining that teaching about race is illogical and perpetuates stereotypes and unscientific falsehoods (Orbe, 1999). Parents who espouse a color-blind approach do not deny the historical consequences of race; however, these parents do not want to perpetuate its significance by referring to their child racially, instead maintaining that their child is human. Few investigations have included color-blind messages; of those that have, findings suggest that the usage of color-blind messages is reported only by White parents (Hamm, 2001) and parents of biracial youth (Orbe, 1999). Rosenblatt, Karis, and Powell (1995) argued that only from a place of privilege can an individual choose not to see race or (attempt) to raise children to be color-blind.

In a national cross-sectional investigation of racial socialization and academic achievement among Black adolescents and young adults, Bowman and Howard (1985) found that 12% reported receiving egalitarian messages, including interracial equality, multiethnic coexistence, and an acknowledgment of the expanded opportunities available for Blacks. Using the National Survey of Black Americans data set, Thornton et al. (1990) found that 6% of Black parents reported egalitarian messages as the most important racial socialization message they impart to their children.

Empirically, very little is known about the influence of mainstream or egalitarian socialization messages on child development. Some scholars suggest that youth who are only socialized within a mainstream and/or egalitarian worldview may be unprepared to handle the complexity inherent in race relations (Hughes & Chen, 1999).

Silent Racial Socialization

Silence may be an attempt to avoid the harsh reality of racism and discrimination or a reflection of the difficult nature of the subject; however, silence speaks volumes. The absence of messages may be just as powerful and important as the transmission of overt messages (Hughes et al., 2006). Nevertheless, investigations of racial socialization have primarily focused on the content, antecedents, and consequences of racial socialization messages and do not report the percentage of parents who do not racially socialize their children (e.g., Marshall, 1995; Quintana & Vera, 1999).

In some cases, one can deduce the percentage of parents who are not reporting any racial socialization from the percentages reporting racial socialization. For example, Stevenson, Reed, and Bodison (1996) found that 49% of Black young adults reported that they had talked in their families about racism and discrimination; thus, one can infer that 51% had not done so. Thornton et al. (1990) found that 63.6% of Black parents reported racially socializing their children; thus, we can assume that 36.4% did not report using racial socialization strategies.

Very few investigations have systematically examined the effects of silent racial socialization. Using data from the National Survey of Black Americans, Bowman and Howard (1985) found that 38% of Black youths reported receiving no racial socialization. Compared with youth who received racial socialization, youth who had not received any racial socialization had lower self-efficacy scores and lower academic achievement. Using the same data set, Demo and Hughes (1990) found that adults who had received egalitarian messages and preparation for bias had stronger feelings of closeness to other Black people and a stronger commitment to Black separatism than those who had not reported any parental racial socialization.

Silent racial socialization is more than an omission; it is an approach to socialization, one that may be more prevalent among biracial families than among other families. More research is needed to explore the impact of the absence, or silence, of racial socialization.

Racial Socialization Among Biracial Families

Historically, the racial socialization literature has focused on the experiences of Black families. Empirical investigations evaluating the racial socialization experiences of other racial/ethnic groups are limited, and few investigations have evaluated racial socialization within a biracial context. Whereas families raising biracial children and adolescents confront some of the same challenges as other minority families, they also face unique challenges inherent in their children's integration of two (or more) distinct heritages. Biracial youth's self-identifications are dynamic and are influenced by socioeconomic status and physical appearance (Davenport, 2016). Often identified as monoracial, biracial people are excluded from the White category and relegated to their minority heritage. Alternatively, they are subsumed by the "other" category, limiting their visibility and opportunity to be recognized as a legitimate group. A challenge for biracial youth is to negotiate inconsistencies between their self-ascribed racial identity and how society, including their parents, chooses to identify them.

Several authors found that open communication in biracial families fosters racial awareness, reduces inconsistent messages, minimizes ambiguity, increases familial interaction, and decreases the effects of conflictual messages (Gibbs & Hines, 1992; Jacobs, 1992; Pinderhughes, 1995; Rosenblatt et al., 1995). Rosenblatt et al. (1995) conducted an ethnographic study of Black/White interracial couples and their children. Parents felt a great responsibility to shield their children from racial injustice and discrimination. Parents believed that in order to rear biracial children without negative psychological effects, they had to socialize their children to have positive, well-adjusted identities. They talked to their children about their racial identities and instructed their children about how to respond in certain situations. Parents also thought it was important to expose their children to appropriate books, films, television programs, and adult role models. These additional socializing agents provide increased opportunities for parents to openly communicate with their biracial children about important racial issues they may confront.

Orbe (1999), summarizing the scant literature available on biracial families, outlined four approaches to racial socialization that biracial families use. First, some parents embrace the Black (or minority) experience, adopting the beliefs and values of one group without recognition of the other (majority) group. Believing they have no other option, these families affirm society's minority appraisal of their children and trust that group affiliation and affirmation will help their children traverse inevitable racism and discrimination. Second, rejecting historical conceptualizations of race, some parents address issues of identity and belonging differently, depending on the current situation, phenotype, and context. For example, a child in a single-parent home, living in a homogenous racial environment and being socialized within that one group, may adopt its traditions, beliefs, and values and singularly identify with that group. Further, the child's physical racial appearance may dictate parental socialization, either by constraining socialization or providing parents with opportunities to "use" their biracial child's ambiguous appearance in situations in which some benefit is gained by choosing one group over another. Third, parents espousing a color-blind perspective consciously avoid the use of race in discussions and descriptions of people in an attempt to transcend the limiting notion of race. Fourth, some parents endorse a "best of both worlds" approach, "affirming the uniqueness of each of the cultures that they represent" (Orbe, 1999, p. 175). This multiracial approach is committed to social consciousness and teaches about both cultures equally. Parents who espouse a multiracial approach support children's individual choices with respect to their racial identity and communicate openly about the prejudice and discrimination that people of color face.

Parents draw on their own experiences and group values to prepare children for experiences with racism and discrimination (Hughes & Chen, 1997; Hughes & Johnson, 2001). Parents of biracial youth have to make a decision about whether to draw from their own intergenerational models of socialization, attempt to socialize their children within the context of the child's other racial heritage, or integrate both heritages in their socialization strategies. This decision can be complicated by the historic relationship between racial groups and varying social positions. White parents were more likely to racially socialize their children by answering questions and teaching equality, whereas Black parents were more likely to emphasize awareness of racial differences and preparation for bias (Katz & Kofkin, 1997). In a qualitative investigation of Black and White parents' socialization beliefs and practices, Hamm (2001) found that in contrast to Black parents who supported and encouraged positive relationships with White peers, White parents were more likely to endorse cross-ethnic contact and exposure, but did not actively support or encourage cross-ethnic relationships. White parents were also more likely to defer socialization efforts to the school, acknowledging their highly segregated lifestyle, living arrangements, and social experiences. For White parents, cross-ethnic relationships are bound contextually and are not integrated into daily life. As a result, their children have little cross-ethnic contact (Hamm, 2001). White parents' lack of racial socialization messages, unsupportive stance with regard to cross-ethnic relationships, and deference of socialization could be attributed to the privileged position of White Americans. Minority parents cannot afford to defer socialization efforts to others, nor can they avoid cross-ethnic contact.

Racial differences in racial socialization messages reflect the differential experiences of each group and suggest that White parents may not inherently possess the knowledge and experience needed to enact minority socialization strategies. Silent racial socialization was used more often by White mothers of biracial youth than by minority mothers of biracial youth (Rollins & Hunter, 2013). White parents may lack the intergenerational modeling that minority parents use as a valuable resource in their child-rearing beliefs and values. Conversations about race can be difficult and uncomfortable for both parents and youth. However, choosing not to communicate about race, racial experiences, and discrimination will influence how biracial youth interpret race and their racial heritage.

In summary, the beliefs and values of parents with respect to their biracial child's racial status within society will influence how racial socialization messages are enacted within child-rearing, including exposure to history, traditions, food, and language; direct teaching and reactive discussions about racism and discrimination; provision of cultural socialization in the home environment; and contact with extended kin and social networks. Ultimately, these racial socialization messages influence how biracial children understand their racial status and how they choose to resolve their "twoness."

Developmental Perspective

Often referred to as the first "R," implicit and explicit lessons about race are often taught before reading, writing, and arithmetic (Lewis, 2003; Van Ausdale & Feagin, 2001). Like other minorities, biracial people face racism, discrimination, and prejudice (Pew Research Center, 2015). As illustrated in the opening example, many biracial youth are ill equipped to handle the complexity of such issues and may be conflicted and overwhelmed by such experiences. It is imperative that parents with biracial children prepare them for the inevitable racial barriers and discrimination they will face. Specifically among biracial youth, racial socialization helps youth explore permeable racial boundaries and learn how to facilitate cross-race relationships. This section considers the primary goals and considerations of parents' racial socialization of biracial youth and briefly explores how to adapt racial socialization goals and strategies to the youths' developmental stage.

Although some aspects of racial socialization are unique to the developmental stage of the child, the foundation for positive racial socialization at all stages of development is a warm and positive parent-child relationship. Throughout childhood and adolescence, parents remain the most significant people in children's lives. Warm and responsive parenting communicates to children that they are competent and worthwhile while also exerting firm, appropriate expectations that help children evaluate their own behavior against reasonable expectations. This foundation is vital as biracial children look to parents for guidance with regard to who they are and how to exist in a world that often devalues and undermines their pride and dignity.

When considering how to broach the subject of race and place with biracial youth, parents have to consider many factors. Maturity, cognitive ability, past experience, and context all influence a child's readiness for certain conversations or ability to handle more advanced and complex discussions. This chapter is meant only to prompt parents and clinicians to think about connecting racial socialization practices to the developmental stage of the child; it is not intended as a blanket guide or prescription of "what to do when your child is 10." Further, for biracial youth, their unique racial heritage and the sociohistorical and sociopolitical climate may lead children and adults toward specific conversations and experiences. Just as there is no universal Latino experience, biracial youth have varying experiences and needs for preparation. Parents must consider the child's racial heritage, contact with extended family, and neighborhood and school environments. Moreover, parents must consider the past, present, and future racial context in which their biracial child will be immersed. Additionally, parents have to examine their own racial beliefs and experiences, and evaluate their interracial relationships, to prepare themselves to discuss these topics with their children.

Early Childhood

During early childhood (2–6 years of age), preschoolers learn about themselves and the world around them through play, observation, and direct teaching. When they encounter unfamiliar topics, are overwhelmed with information, or are confronted with contradictory information beyond their understanding, they may use illogical reasoning. They rely on adults to guide their inferences and help them make sense of the world around them.

Their expanding vocabulary is supported by an ever-increasing ability to categorize. Young children ask questions as they encounter new or contradictory information. Through social interaction, adults translate their insight into language appropriate for young children. Adults do this by scaffolding, or adjusting support to fit the child's current level of understanding. For young children, this support begins with breaking concepts into small bits of information via direct instruction. As the child's capacity expands, adults can provide less support. Thus, picture books and reading allow rich opportunities for growth and development. During these early years, it is important to consider imagery and context. Biracial children should be exposed to books, artwork, and other media that reflect and celebrate their heritage. Obviously if the biracial child is White, that part of their heritage is well reflected, and images are plentiful. However, it is also important to expose children to specific White ethnic groups that reflect their background.

In addition, make-believe play helps children process experiences and social relationships and is associated with increased perspective taking and social abilities. Parents should encourage make-believe play and use it as an opportunity to help young children process experiences or things they may have seen or heard (e.g., news). Parents of biracial children should provide diverse toys, dolls, and props that mirror their family heritage. Parents can observe play to get a sense of what their preschooler is thinking and then use that information to create experiences to support or counter the child's perception as necessary. Parents can also engage in biracial children's make-believe play as a way of discussing race-related issues, passing on cultural knowledge and information, and/or reinforcing familial beliefs and values.

During this developmental period, young children begin to learn about themselves. Early identity development includes self-concept and self-esteem. Self-concept influences their preference for activities and friends and is based primarily on observable characteristics. Early self-esteem is grounded in basic self-judgments related to learning new things, making friends, treating others kindly, and similar actions. Preschoolers do not yet take others' judgments into account when formulating their self-esteem, nor can they integrate the evaluations from multiple domains. Warm and sensitive parental relationships foster positive self-concept and self-esteem. Positive parent-child relationships result in more natural conversations, which can result in a more nuanced understanding of the child's biracial heritage. Further, positive interactions between parents and biracial children provide personal meaning that can facilitate racial identity development and greater cultural knowledge.

Increased capacity to understand emotions, both one's own and others', helps young children better manage negative emotions and experience empathy, which is the precursor to moral development. Young children begin to infer others' feelings based on their behavior but have difficulty interpreting more complex situations, especially when conflicting cues are present (e.g., laughing and crying). When parents talk about emotions, appropriately express emotions, and explain emotions to young children, children become more adept at understanding and expressing emotions. Preschoolers look to parents for guidance about how to respond emotionally. Warm and responsive parenting encourages emotional expressiveness and helps preschoolers develop empathy. Parents do this by modeling appropriate emotional responses and by intervening when children display inappropriate reactions.

Early friendships in this developmental stage are based on pleasurable play and sharing of toys. When parents frequently arrange informal peer-play activities, preschoolers tend to have larger peer networks and be more socially skilled. Further, secure parent-child attachment is associated with more harmonious peer interactions, larger peer networks, and warmer relationships with friends. Parents and caregivers should carefully evaluate the context in which the biracial child is embedded. In addition to relationships with extended family, the child's social networks, peers, neighbors, and religious institutions provide opportunities to surround children with reflections of themselves and to pass on culture, traditions, and values. Parents can foster diverse peer relationships by intentionally arranging diverse playgroups and developing their own diverse peer groups that reflect the racial heritage of their biracial child.

Children develop bias and form opinions about racial groups, their own and others, prior to having the developmental capacity to understand socially constructed racial categories. Despite what many believe, preschoolers are not color-blind (Katz, 2003), and as their natural capacity to categorize allows them to sort people and environments their immature cognitive abilities often lead to stereotyping (Winkler, 2009). Further, preschoolers are prone to in-group favoritism (Patterson & Bigler, 2006), which may lead to feelings of inferiority and inaccurate assessments of other groups. During these young years, as preschoolers' attitudes are forming, it is important to remember that they are amenable. Parents of biracial children should talk to them about their racial heritage, answer their queries in developmentally appropriate ways, and counter in-group favoritism by perpetuating and affirming positive characteristics of members of diverse racial groups. When they see or hear something that creates cognitive dissonance or unease, it is the adult's responsibility to step in and help the child make sense of the experience.

Middle Childhood

In middle childhood (6–11 years), brain development continues to increase, resulting in rapid vocabulary growth and faster, more efficient information processing. Advances in emotional and social development occur as children develop a more realistic sense of self and a more finely tuned moral compass. Children at this age slowly gain independence just as their peer groups become more important and friend choices more nuanced. During this time, children move from a rudimentary understanding of race and space to a more complex and abstract idea of race as a social construct. However, even at the end of this developmental period, children still need considerable guidance and scaffolding as they grapple with what it means to be biracial in a racially divided America.

Rapid growth in vocabulary results in more precise and flexible understanding of word meanings. During this stage, children increasingly grasp subtleties of language, including nuances of meaning, irony, and sarcasm. Their narratives increase in organization, detail, and expressiveness. Children move from egocentrism to more awareness of others' thoughts and feelings. They also see time more holistically and are capable of processing the past, present, and future simultaneously. Thus, scaffolding is especially important as children process race-related language and experiences. Experiences may be personal but may also include fictional and nonfictional accounts of race, racism, prejudice, and discrimination. Scaffolding might include providing definitions and explaining nuances of race-related language. Parents and teachers should help biracial youth explore their own narratives and help them process racial terminology as a means of identifying themselves within the larger cultural context. Adults can help youth understand the difference between the color of one's skin and socially accepted (or assigned) racial categories, as well as give them multiple ways of describing themselves.

Increases in brain development lead to more organized and flexible thinking. In the earlier years of this period, thought is logical, organized, and flexible when dealing with concrete information. As the brain matures and experiences increase, children gain the ability to focus on several aspects of a situation at once, think through a series of steps and reverse direction, sustain attention, view a situation from more than one perspective, and engage in more abstract thinking (Berk & Meyers, 2016). With this expanded cognition, children begin to understand race as a social construct beyond skin color. However, experience and exposure are crucial. Parents can direct growth by purposively choosing experiences, conversations, books, and other influences that promote cultural learning and racial awareness and understanding.

At this stage of social and emotional development, children describe themselves and others in terms of physical and psychological traits; they compare themselves to their peers and speculate about their strengths and weaknesses. Their cognitive gains allow children to process feedback from others, which results in a more realistic sense of self. Thus, parent-child conversations can help construct a rich, positive narrative about self, which can lead children to a more complex, favorable, and coherent self-concept. Self-esteem remains high but becomes more realistic as children receive more feedback and become more capable of social comparisons. Children with more positive self-esteem tend to be more well adjusted, sociable, and conscientious, whereas children with low levels of self-esteem are more likely to experience anxiety, depression, and antisocial behavior (Berk & Meyers, 2016). For minority children, racial socialization has been associated with higher levels of self-esteem (Constantine & Blackmon, 2002). Children who live in diverse neighborhoods and attend schools where their ethnic group is represented feel a stronger sense of belonging and report more positive levels of self-esteem (Gray-Little & Carels, 1997; Scott, Wallander, & Cameron, 2015). Thus, families should carefully consider the racial context of their neighborhoods and schools in order to bolster self-esteem among their biracial children. Finding diverse neighborhoods isn't easy for any family; finding a neighborhood that reflects the racial heritage of a biracial family may be even more difficult. Parents will need to carefully weigh their options. Many families may opt for a predominately minority neighborhood, while others may settle in less diverse neighborhoods and seek other diverse contexts (e.g., religious groups, youth activities) for their family.

As emotional understanding increases, children become capable of understanding and experiencing nuanced and contradictory emotions. They are increasingly able to reconcile facial and situational cues and to more accurately predict how others might feel. These advances result in greater capacity to recognize situations that spark mixed emotions. For example, children may have to reconcile their affinity for a friend who makes a racist joke that feels offensive. Adults should be sensitive to these changing emotional abilities and be willing to engage in supportive dialogue to help biracial children process their growing emotional awareness and the many contradictions they will need to reconcile.

Toward the end of middle childhood, children begin to better understand others' intentions within a broader context and become capable of evaluating moral implications and social conventions. They have the capacity to understand that higher principles should prevail when people's rights and welfare are at stake. However, they often still lack sociohistorical understanding that would help them understand complex, and often disheartening, injustices. Thus, they benefit from guidance and support recognizing and countering pervasive bias and discrimination, especially when it seems counter to (obvious) logical and moral social justice. A growing number of books available for this age group address the history and experiences of diverse people. Adults can use literature, especially historical fiction, as a tool to help biracial youth gain valuable knowledge and insight about their heritage and historical relationships among racial groups. It may be important to help biracial youth process the negative historical relationship between groups represented within their racial heritage. This exploration may also allow for conversations about family members who may not support interracial relationships and the impact of that reality on biracial youth. Open and honest conversations might help them understand how to navigate the juxtaposition of Granny's racist remarks and her loving embrace.

As children mature, their peers become increasingly important, and they develop a strong desire to be a part of a group. At this age peers are largely chosen based on availability (e.g., neighbors and classmates) and similarity, including gender, academic achievement, personality, and, of course, race. Younger children tend to be more inclusive and have more friends, while older children become more exclusive and choose friends that resemble them more closely. Friendship and peer groups can be complex, and inclusion and exclusion can vary greatly. Peer exclusion can lead to social anxiety, peer avoidance, and isolation. As previously discussed, diverse neighborhoods and schools can give biracial children more options and can lead to more affinity and belonging. Group belonging can also be fostered intentionally via group membership, such as 4-H, religious groups, scouting, and sports. As the importance of friends and peer groups increases, time spent with parents begins a slow decline. Children want and need greater independence and freedom but still need parental guidance and support.

Middle childhood offers many opportunities to provide racial socialization. Exposure to cultural knowledge and information is essential. Literature (books, plays, and media) continues to be influential and can be used as a catalyst for critical analysis and discussion that will lay the foundation for later development of beliefs, values, and worldview. In addition, adults should seek to provide literature and experiences that normalize the child's life. Literature isn't only a means to pass on history and teach lessons; it can be used to justify and acknowledge the lived experience among biracial children and families. Sharing everyday images of biracial people experiencing the joys, struggles, and triumphs of life communicates to biracial children they are not an anomaly.

As children mature, greater social experiences and increasing racial awareness necessitate intentional dialogue about race, racism, and social justice. In middle childhood, biracial youth are at a point where they begin to see and feel their "other"-ness. They may find themselves being fawned over, ignored, or misunderstood. They might need adults to help them navigate the racial land mines set for them. Friends, family, and media have opinions about who biracial youth are, how they should identify, and with whom they should align themselves. Adults should look for opportunities to help biracial youth develop their own ideas about their unique racial heritage and what it means in their everyday lives.

Adolescence

As the brain continues to mature in adolescence, the prefrontal cortex becomes more effective, which enables more complex, flexible, and adaptive thought. Adolescents are better at hypothetical-deductive reasoning (Berk & Meyers, 2016) and are capable of thinking both logically and more abstractly. The biggest gains in abstract and logical thinking can be seen in situations where adolescents have had extensive guidance and experience and have practiced using reasoning skills. Here, exposure during the preschool age and conversations and experiences during middle childhood come together with a greater depth of understanding. Biracial adolescents begin to more fully comprehend sociohistorical and present-day experiences and how they and their social location are influenced by cultural and institutional practices and policies.

However, cognitive control networks are still developing, and inhibition, planning, and future orientation are still maturing. It is important for adults to help adolescents think about how to respond in hypothetical scenarios, how to avoid potential dangerous and discriminatory situations, and how to react when faced with inevitable racism, discrimination, and bias. Further, adolescents' decision-making lags behind that of more mature and experienced adults. Adolescents are more likely to focus on short-term rather than long-term outcomes and to experience extreme emotions. Thus, in emotionally charged situations, they are more likely to take greater risks without considering alternatives and weighing all the pros and cons (Huizenga, Crone, & Jensen 2007, as cited in Berk & Meyers, 2016). Adolescents sometimes have difficulty distinguishing between their own and others' perspectives. They can be self-conscious and have an inflated sense of personal importance, which often leads to feeling misunderstood. Adults can assist biracial adolescents by helping them see the range of possible solutions and outcomes, assessing various options relative to long- and short-term goals, and helping them see connections between past mistakes (personal or otherwise) and less favorable outcomes. Adults can model appropriate responses and reactions amid difficult circumstances and racially unjust situations. It is the adult's responsibility to help adolescents understand how they can feel outraged yet not react in ways that could harm themselves or others.

During adolescence, identity development is a key aspect of maturation. Adolescents experiment with alternative identities as a way to explore characteristics and behaviors before committing to their personal ideals and goals. It is important to allow them to explore without judgment, understanding that as they express themselves and receive feedback they will make adjustments and refine their identity. As adolescents progress through identity formation they may take many paths, and the patterns may vary among their many identities (e.g., religion, work).

Identity development is a process for all adolescents, and it continues to be refined well into adulthood as individuals reevaluate their commitments and choices. For biracial adolescents, ethnic identity is central to the identity development process, as it is for other minority youth. It is often assumed that biracial youth struggle with identity formation and commitment (see Chap. 11 for more information). But research has clearly documented that biracial youth resolve their "other" status (Root, 1990; Stephan, 1992), albeit in ways that others may not readily understand or accept. Biracial youth negotiate varying ethnic contexts with a unique capacity to shift their identity, aligning themselves with group norms and values, as a normal part of their identity development and commitment process. For them, racial boundaries are permeable, and identity is fluid. This fluidity is adaptive and supportive for biracial youth who have many options as they decide how to identify themselves within a system that often pressures them to choose a single box.

Adolescents, more so than younger children, are aware of and sensitive to how race and ethnicity influence one's choices, options, and treatment. Biracial adolescents may feel caught between cultural expectations, societal assumptions, and their own burgeoning sense of self. Experiences with racism and discrimination can influence their ethnic identity formation and commitment. Understanding oneself as part of a group that is consistently and systematically devalued and undermined can be painful and confusing. Lower ethnic identity has been associated with lower self-esteem (Hughes et al., 2006). It is vital that adults support minority adolescents in developing a healthy racial identity. Biracial youth are in an especially precarious position; they report similar levels of racism and discrimination and report lower levels of ethnic identity as they regard race as less central to their identities (Herman, 2004). Adolescents coming of age in the Black Lives Matter movement may have very strong opinions and feelings about the world and their place in it. They may also have very different experiences with diversity, White peers, and mixed media messaging. Having grown up during Obama's presidency, which was then countered by Trump's, biracial adolescents are grappling with who America is and who Americans are.

It is important for adults to understand the fluid nature of identity development among biracial adolescents and support their exploration without judgement or interference. However, adults should initiate discussion regarding the antecedents and consequences of biracial adolescents' choices to ensure that they make informed and thoughtful decisions about how to racially identify themselves. Biracial youth may also need permission to avoid racial identification and reassurance from adults that it is acceptable to not racially identify themselves. Resisting classification may help adolescents process racial ideologies as they consider their unique heritage. Biracial people's identity changes over time, varies by context, and may be inconsistent with how other people identify them (Rollins & Hunter, 2008). Further, it may vary depending on the individual's specific combination of heritage. Adults should give biracial adolescents freedom to fully explore their heritage and the varying options available to them. Helping biracial adolescents understand the socially constructed nature of race might facilitate their identity process and aid them in developing strategies and responses to deal with racial comments (e.g., queries, jokes) from peers and others, including family. Adults must help biracial youth explore the boundaries, intersections, and fluidity of race as they deconstruct race as a social construct.

With adolescents' gains in cognitive, emotional, and social development and increased freedom beyond the watchful eyes of adults, it is important for adults to foster an environment that allows adolescents to communicate openly and honestly. Continuing to define terms and concepts, provide contextual understanding, and share historical perspectives helps adolescents process the world around them and develop their own perspectives about how to cope, counter, and cooperate in a racially unjust society. Adults should encourage adolescents to share their perspective; asking open-ended questions helps them process their thoughts and integrate previous teaching and exposure. Adults should provide supportive and loving responses that validate the adolescents' feelings while maintaining a judgment-free atmosphere. When adults disagree or want to provide counter perspectives, they should do so without shaming or negating the adolescents' thoughts or feelings. As children become teens, adults transition into the role of facilitator, allowing teens to freely explore their ideas and emotions. While it is still appropriate for adults to plan experiences and share cultural knowledge, the teenage years are also a time to facilitate critical interrogations around race and social location.

Conversations about race, racism, and discrimination can be emotionally difficult for everyone. Parents should reflect on their own beliefs and experiences before engaging in conversations with young people. It is particularly important for parents to process their own feelings and become clear about their goals when conversing with teens. Inevitably, difficult conversations or situations will arise. It is acceptable, and preferable, to say "I don't know" and promise to find out together. Our racially divisive world can cause fear, confusion, and frustration. The ability to recognize these feelings and withstand the discomfort will allow parents to successfully navigate racially charged conversations. Most importantly, parents must keep the conversation alive. There is no single "race talk" that parents can have and then move on. An ongoing conversation fosters new understanding, allows for further questions, makes room for clarification, and enables parents to reinforce important messages. The accumulation of smaller discussions and diverse experiences allows teens to retain information, assimilate new experiences, and amend their understanding.

Racial socialization practices (e.g., preparation for bias, history lessons, practice of traditions) have been associated in adolescence with greater likelihood of exploring and progressing toward higher levels of ethnic identity achievement. However, similar to immigrant parents whose adolescent children often rebel against their ethnic heritage, parents of biracial or minority youth have to be careful that racial socialization practices don't push adolescents too hard or too fast. As youth grapple with numerous issues related to adolescence, dealing with race, racial identity, and countering bias may be lower on their list of priorities. At a time when they are focused on fitting in and being accepted, they may be less open to direct teaching and experiences that remind them of the stark differences between them and their peers. Forced participation may prove counterproductive. Planned cultural exposure and experiences may leave adolescents feeling "required" to enjoy activities (or people, books, etc.) simply because they belong to or reflect their racial heritage. As one minority adolescent reflected, "I knew these activities would only feed into the stereotypes I had already been handed by the world" (Schaffer, 2018). Further, adults have to be careful not to perpetuate stereotypes. As one mom of a Black-White biracial son suggested, "I don't want my son to think of his blackness as a caricature of Black culture" (D. Means, personal conversation, January 15, 2017). Adults have to weigh many factors as they seek to provide developmentally appropriate racial socialization during adolescence.

The parent-child relationship is the foundation on which racial socialization is cemented. Especially in adolescence, when puberty is often associated with distancing and independence, and when advances in cognitive development are accompanied by increased autonomy and larger social networks, adolescents still need guidance and protection. Parenting that is warm and responsive provides developmentally appropriate monitoring, supervision, and consistent discipline; engages in democratic decision-making; and models effective relationship and communication skills that fosters adolescent competence and will more likely succeed in passing on racial socialization messages, cultural traditions, and familial beliefs and values.

Implications for Practice

As our society becomes increasingly multiracial, it is imperative that human service workers, teachers, counselors, and researchers consider the complex processes associated with crossing racial boundaries and occupying a biracial social location. While working with biracial families, there are a few things to consider. First and foremost, practitioners must take an honest look in the mirror and identify their bias, evaluate their racial awareness, and explore personal experiences with racism and discrimination. It is especially important to consider personal and family history regarding interracial contact and biracial people. Further, it is helpful to interrogate personal connection to oppression: participation in or recipient of. An exploration of personal biases and racial ideology will aid practitioners as they seek to provide compassionate and authentic support for biracial families.

Practitioners should enhance their knowledge of biracial people and interracial relationships. There are many documentaries, books, and movies that capture these experiences. Greater awareness of diverse experiences will help practitioners avoid stereotypes and myths about biracial families. Just as there is no universal Black experience, there is no universal biracial experience. Race is only part of one's story. It informs experience and shapes values, but it cannot definitively define an individual. A person is Korean because their family heritage includes Korean people. Race doesn't make the person; people make up a racial group. A racial group includes all the people with ancestral links to that group. Thus, the individuals, and not the group, define—and redefine—what it means to be Black (or Irish, or Jewish, or biracial). When your ancestry includes multiple groups you embody those groups equally. You make up that group *and* you make up a new group. When researchers say that biracial people blur the racial lines, it's an acknowledgement that biracial people are beyond groupings, yet a part of many groups. Whereas DNA tests may tease out one's racial heritage as 35% this and 22% that and 43% something else, an individual cannot be parsed out this way. What does it mean to be 35% Mexican? It's challenging enough to ascribe to social constructions of racial groupings. It is unreasonable to ask a person to deconstruct their ancestry and choose. Biracial individuals and biracial families should be themselves, free to define and redefine themselves. It is important for practitioners to allow biracial individuals and families to explore themselves and define their own cultural expectations and values.

Practitioners working with parents of biracial youth should help them think critically about the racial heritage of the biracial child. Some racial groups have complicated historical relationship that may impact the type of racial socialization that is most important for their biracial child. The child's unique racial pairing, phenotype, and community context may necessitate specific lessons, cultural experiences, and identity development opportunities. For many parents, race is a four-letter word. However, it is imperative that parents process their racial experiences, beliefs, and values so they can be prepared to help their biracial children develop a positive sense of self and navigate racial experiences. Color-blind approaches do not work (Pahl and Way, 2006). Parents should be educated about types of racial socialization strategies and encouraged to identify specific racial socialization goals. Racial socialization strategies should be intentional and deliberate. Parents should be reminded that when talking about race with their biracial child they will inevitably make mistakes and uncover more bias. Racial socialization is a bidirectional process. Parents will lead and be led by their biracial child's experiences. The most important thing a parent can do is to continue to keep the lines of communication open and be honest and authentic.

As our society is increasingly multiethnic and multiracial and our personal and professional lives become more integrated it may be harder to tease out, and pass on cultural heritage and traditions. As biracial families spread further from their families of origin and create diverse social networks, they encounter diverse cultural experiences and develop new traditions and expectations. This can be a supportive and empowering opportunity for biracial families. It is important to respect and encourage this type of exploration and expression. However, it is also important to pass on important cultural beliefs and practices. When families find themselves isolated, yet desiring to provide cultural experiences and exposure, they should be encouraged to establish a lifestyle that includes groups of people that reflect their family's heritage as a way to provide authentic experiences and foster intimate relationships.

Racial socialization has been positively associated with biracial college students' ethnic identity exploration and resolution, and identity resolution has been associated with higher self-acceptance and self-esteem (Brittian, Umana-Taylor, & Derlan, 2013). Practitioners should familiarize themselves with the racial identity development process of biracial youth and be prepared to discuss the inconsistencies between biracial people's self-identifications and how others (e.g., parents, peers) might racially identify them. For biracial youth, it is normal and protective for racial identity to shift contextually and over time. The self-ascribed racial label is less important than the process of understanding one's social location and accepting a self-identification that feels authentic.

It is also important to educate parents about the racial identity process and think critically about the messages (intentional and unintentional) they are reinforcing. In an attempt to help biracial youth develop a positive racial identity and move beyond racial boundaries, some biracial families espouse a "best of both worlds" philosophy with regard to their biracial children's racial heritage. While this may be well intentioned, this approach may reinforce racial hierarchies, further alienating biracial youth, heightening difference, and inserting a disconnect between the biracial child and their racial groups. Racial identity development can be supported by (1) warm and open communication with adults; (2) discussions that promote critical thinking about race and identity; (3) role models and contact with peers who share similar racial heritage; (4) opportunities to learn about cultural distinctions in an atmosphere of respect; and (5) allowing biracial youth the space to freely choose their own racial self-identity and labels.

Future Research

In the racial socialization literature we often assume that racial socialization practices are in direct correlation with racial groups. However, biracial families push us beyond current conceptualizations to consider how crossing boundaries is related to our beliefs and practices. It has been suggested that instead of relying on racial group membership, it is our racial ideologies that define our racial socialization practices (Rockquemore, Laszloffy, & Noveske, 2006). Thus, investigations of biracial families may be uniquely positioned to challenge assumptions about the antecedents and consequences of racial socialization.

More research is needed to further understand the extent to which racial socialization strategies are used in biracial families. Ethnographic observations would provide more information about the nuances of racial socialization, including the inadvertent, unspoken socialization that often goes unmeasured. This work could be used to develop a qualitative measure of racial socialization for empirical investigation of biracial youth and families. Further exploration of biracial family processes and biracial adolescent development could potentially be used to create race-specific parenting education curricula for parents with biracial children, both biological and transracially adopted.

In addition, children are not merely recipients of racial socialization; they are active participants in a bidirectional process (Hughes & Chen, 1999). Future research should include the childs' perception and/or receipt of racial socialization as an important factor in evaluations of racial socialization. Further, racial socialization is imparted by both parents and the extended family (Fatimilehin, 1999; Sanders Thompson, 1994). Future investigations of racial socialization should examine the impact of these additional socializing agents. These influences are especially relevant given the multiple heritages of biracial adolescents. This additional socialization may be complementary or contradictory to what the primary caregiver provides and may account for differences in racial identity development. Furthermore, the role of siblings, peers, neighborhoods, and school and classroom context should also be considered important socializing agents.

Many investigations of biracial people (and families) limit their sample to individuals of the same mixed-race heritage (e.g., Black/White only), arguing that biracial experiences differ as a result of varying racial mixes (Fatimilehin, 1999; Rockquemore & Brunsma, 2002). While these investigations are useful for identifying unique experiences within a specific biracial population, investigations of multiple racial mixes could identify universal phenomena related to being biracial. Regardless of what the specific racial mix is, there may be something uniquely different and influential about having multiple heritages as opposed to a singular heritage. Thus, the inclusion of diverse biracial people and families may add to our understanding of universal biracial family socialization messages. Ideally, it would be beneficial to conduct large-scale investigations that allowed for examinations of specific mixed-race heritages and universal biracial family processes.

Biracial people challenge the legitimacy of racial boundaries, shattering the myth of racial categorization. They face racism and discrimination as they negotiate a racially segregated society and work to resolve their dual-racial heritage. Their duality sometimes positions them as members of, yet separate from, the very racial group with which they self-identify. This unique existence requires that parents of biracial youth provide developmentally appropriate racial socialization practices that will help their children navigate the racially contentious US context.

References

Berk, L. A., & Meyers, A. B. (2016). *Infants, children, and adolescents* (8th ed.). Boston, MA: Pearson.

Biafora, F. A., Warheit, G. J., Zimmerman, R. S., & Gil, A. G. (1993). Racial mistrust and deviant behaviors among ethnically diverse Black adolescent boys. *Journal of the American Academy of Child Psychiatry, 24*, 134–141.

Bowman, P. J., & Howard, C. (1985). Race-related socialization, motivation, and academic achievement: A study of Black youths in three-generation families. *Journal of the American Academy of Child Psychiatry, 24*(2), 134–141.

Boykin, A. W., & Toms, F. D. (1985). Black child socialization: A conceptual framework. In H. P. McAdoo & J. L. McAdoo (Eds.), *Black children: Social, educational, and parental environments* (pp. 33–51). Newbury Park, CA: Sage.

Brittian, A. S., Umana-Taylor, A. J., & Derlan, C. L. (2013). An examination of biracial college youths' family ethnic socialization, ethnic identity, and adjustment: Do self-identification labels and university context matter? *Cultural Diversity & Ethnic Minority Psychology, 19*(2), 177–189.

Caughy, M. O., O'Campo, P. J., Randolph, S. M., & Nickerson, K. (2002). The influence of racial socialization practices on the cognitive and behavioral competence of African American preschoolers. *Child Development, 73*, 1611–1625.

Constantine, M. G., & Blackmon, S. M. (2002). Black adolescents' racial socialization experiences: Their relations to home, school, and peer self-esteem. *Journal of Black Studies, 32*(3), 322–336.

Davenport, L. D. (2016). The role of gender, class, and religion in biracial Americans' racial labeling decisions. *American Sociological Review, 81*(1), 57–84. https://doi.org/10.1177/0003122415623286

Demo, D. H., & Hughes, M. (1990). Socialization and racial identity among Black Americans. *Social Psychological Quarterly, 53*, 364–374.

Fatimilehin, I. A. (1999). Of jewel heritage: Racial socialization and racial identity attitudes amongst adolescents of mixed African-Caribbean/White parentage. *Journal of Adolescence, 22*, 303–318.

Gibbs, J. T., & Hines, A. M. (1992). Negotiating ethnic identity: Issues for Black-White biracial adolescents. In M. Root (Ed.), *Racially mixed people in America* (pp. 223–238). Newbury Park, CA: Sage.

Gray-Little, B., & Carels, R. A. (1997). The effect of racial dissonance on academic self-esteem and achievement in elementary, junior high, and high school students. *Journal of Research on Adolescence, 7*(2), 109–131.

Hamm, J. V. (2001). Barriers and bridges to positive cross-ethnic relations: African American and White parent socialization beliefs and practices. *Youth and Society, 33*, 62–98.

Herman, M. (2004). Forced to choose: Some determinants of racial identification in multiracial adolescents. *Child Development, 75*(3), 730–748.

Hughes, D. (2003). Correlates of African American and Latino parents' messages to children about ethnicity and race: A comparative study of racial socialization. *American Journal of Community Psychology, 31*(1–2), 15–33.

Hughes, D., & Chen, L. (1997). When and what parents tell children about race: An examination of race-related socialization among African American families. *Applied Developmental Science, 1*, 200–214.

Hughes, D., & Chen, L. (1999). The nature of parents' race-related communications to children: A developmental perspective. In L. Balter & C. S. Tamis-Lemonda (Eds.), *Child psychology: A handbook of contemporary issues* (pp. 467–490). Philadelphia: Psychology Press.

Hughes, D., & Johnson, D. J. (2001). Correlates in children's experiences of parents' racial socialization behaviors. *Journal of Marriage and the Family, 63*, 981–995.

Hughes, D., Smith, E. P., Stevenson, H. C., Rodriguez, J., Johnson, D. J., & Spicer, P. (2006). Parents' ethnic-racial socialization practices: A review of research and directions for future study. *Developmental Psychology, 42*(5), 747–770.

Jacobs, J. H. (1992). Identity development in biracial children. In M. P. P. Root (Ed.), *Racially mixed people in America* (pp. 190–206). Newbury Park, CA: Sage.

Katz, P. A. (2003). Racists or tolerant multiculturalists? How do they begin? *The American Psychologist, 58*(11), 897–909. https://doi.org/10.1037/0003-066X.58.11.897b

Katz, P. A., & Kofkin, J. A. (1997). Race, gender, and young children. In S. S. Luthar, J. A. Burack, D. Cicchetti, & J. R. Weisz (Eds.), *Developmental psychopathology: Perspectives on adjustment, risk, and disorder* (pp. 51–74). Cambridge, NY: Cambridge University Press.

Knight, G. P., Bernal, M. E., Cota, M. K., Garza, C. A., & Ocampo, K. A. (1993). Family socialization and Mexican American identity and behavior. In M. E. Bernal & G. P. Knight (Eds.), *Ethnic identity: Formation and transmission among Hispanics and other minorities* (pp. 105–129). Albany: State University of New York Press.

Lewis, A. E. (2003). *Race in the schoolyard: Negotiating the color line in classrooms and communities*. New Brunswich, NJ: Ruggers University Press.

Marshall, S. (1995). Ethnic socialization of African American children: Implications for parenting, identity development, and academic achievement. *Journal of Youth and Adolescence, 24*(4), 377–396.

McHale, S. M., et al. (2006). Mothers' and fathers' racial socialization in African American families: Implications for youth. *Child Development, 77*(5), 1387–1402.

Miller, D. B. (1999). Racial socialization and racial identity: Can they promote resiliency for African American adolescents? *Adolescence, 34*(135), 493–501.

Ogbu, J. U. (1982). Socialization: A cultural ecological approach. In K. M. Borman (Ed.), *The social life of children in a changing society* (pp. 253–267). Hillsdale, NJ: Lawrence Erlbaum Associates.

Orbe, M. P. (1999). Communicating about "race" in interracial families. In T. J. Socha & R. C. Diggs (Eds.), *Communication, race, and family: Exploring communication in Black, White and biracial families* (pp. 167–180). Mahwah, NJ: Lawrence Erlbaum Associates.

Pahl, K., & Way, N. (2006). Longitudinal trajectories of ethnic identity among urban Black and Latino adolescents. *Child Development, 77*(5), 1403–1415.

Patterson, M. M., & Bigler, R. S. (2006). Preschool children's attention to environmental messages about groups: Social categorization and the origins of intergroup bias. *Child Development, 77*(4), 847–860.

Peters, M. F. (1985). Racial socialization of young Black children. In H. P. McAdoo & J. L. McAdoo (Eds.), *Black children: Social, educational, and parental environment* (pp. 159–173). Newbury Park, CA: Sage.

Pew Research Center. (2015). *Multiracial in America: Proud, diverse and growing in numbers*. Washington, DC. Retrieved from http://www.pewsocialtrends.org/2015/06/11/multiracial-in-america/

Phinney, J. S., & Chavira, V. (1995). Parental ethnic socialization and adolescent coping with problems related to ethnicity. *Journal of Research on Adolescence, 5*, 31–53.

Pinderhughes, E. (1995). Biracial identity—Asset or handicap? In H. Harris, H. Blue, & E. Griffith (Eds.), *Racial and ethnic identity: Psychological development and creative expression* (pp. 73–94). New York: Routledge.

Quintana, S. M., & Vera, E. M. (1999). Mexican American children's ethnic identity, understanding of ethnic prejudice, and parental ethnic socialization. *Hispanic Journal of Behavioral Sciences, 21*, 387–404.

Rockquemore, K. A., & Brunsma, D. L. (2002). Socially embedded identities: Theories, typologies, and processes of racial identity among Black/White biracials. *The Sociological Quarterly, 43*(3), 335–356.

Rockquemore, K. A., Laszloffy, T., & Noveske, J. (2006). It all starts at home: Racial socialization in multiracial families. In D. Brunsma (Ed.), *Mixed messages: Multiracial identities in the "color-blind" era* (pp. 203–216). Boulder, CO: Lynne Rienner Publishers.

Rollins, A. & Hunter, A. G. (2008, November). *Deconstructing race: biracial adolescents' fluid racial self-labels*. Poster presented at the annual conference of the National Council on Family Relations, Little Rock, AR

Rollins, A., & Hunter, A. G. (2013). Racial socialization of biracial youth: Maternal messages and approaches to address discrimination. *Family Relations, 62*(1), 140–153.

Root, M. P. P. (1990). Resolving "other" status: Identity development of biracial individuals. *Women and Therapy, 91*(1–2), 185–205.

Rosenblatt, P., Karis, T., & Powell, R. (1995). *Multiracial couples: Black and White voices*. Thousand Oaks, CA: Sage.

Sanders Thompson, V. L. (1994). Socialization to race and its relationship to racial identification among African Americans. *Journal of Black Psychology, 20*, 175–188.

Schaffer A (2018, January 31). Life as the token Asian girl. *Dart News Online*. Retrieved from https://dartnewsonline.com/81054/uncategorized/life-as-the-token-asian-girl/

Scott, S. M., Wallander, J. L., & Cameron, L. (2015). Protective mechanisms for depression among racial/ethnic minority youth: Empirical findings, issues, and recommendations. *Clinical Child & Family Psychology Review, 18*, 346–369. https://doi.org/10.1007/s10567-015-0188-4

Stephan, C. W. (1992). Mixed-heritage individuals: Ethnic identity and trait characteristics. In M. P. P. Root (Ed.), *Racially mixed people in America* (pp. 50–63). Newbury Park, CA: Sage.

Stevenson, H. C. (1994). Validation of the scale of racial socialization for African American adolescents: Steps toward multidimensionality. *Journal of Black Psychology, 20*, 445–468.

Stevenson, H. C. (1995). Relationship of adolescent perceptions of racial socialization to racial identity. *Journal of Black Psychology, 21*, 49–70.

Stevenson, H. C. (1997). Managing Anger: Protective, proactive, or adaptive racial socialization identity profiles and African-American manhood development. *Journal of Prevention and Intervention in the Community, 16*, 35–61.

Stevenson, H. C., Herrero-Taylor, T., Cameron, R., & Davis, G. Y. (2002). "Mitigating Instigation": Cultural phenomenological influences of anger and fighting among "big-boned" and "baby-faced" African American youth. *Journal of Youth and Adolescence, 31*, 473–485.

Stevenson, H. C., Reed, J., & Bodison, P. (1996). Kinship social support and adolescent racial socialization beliefs: Extending the self to family. *Journal of Black Psychology, 22*(4), 498–508.

Thomas, A. J., & Speight, S. L. (1999). Racial identity and racial socialization attitudes of African American parents. *Journal of Black Psychology, 25*, 152–170.

Thornton, M. C. (1997). Strategies of racial socialization among Black parents: Mainstream, minority, and cultural messages. In R. J. Taylor, J. S. Jackson, & L. M. Chatters (Eds.), *Family life in Black America* (pp. 201–215). Thousand Oaks, CA: Sage Publications.

Thornton, M. C., Chatters, L. M., Taylor, R. J., & Allen, W. R. (1990). Sociodemographic and environmental correlates of racial socialization by Black parents. *Child Development, 61*, 401–409.

Van Ausdale, D., & Feagin, J. R. (2001). *The first R: How children learn race and racism*. Lanham, MD: Rowman & Littlefield.

Winkler, E. N. (2009). Children are not colorblind: How young children learn race. *PACE: Practical Approaches for Continuing Education, 3*(3), 1–8. Retrieved from http://citeseerx.ist.psu.edu/viewdoc/download?doi=10.1.1.621.9728&rep=rep1&type=pdf

Biracial Families Formed Through Adoption

Leigh A. Leslie, Katie M. Hrapczynski, and Jennifer L. Young

Biracial Families Formed Through Adoption

After having a daughter, Mike and April were unable to conceive a second child to build the two-child family they had always wanted. When their daughter, Lauren, turned 6 they accepted that the second birth child might never come and it was time to consider adoption. Wanting to bring a second child into their family as quickly as possible they focused on domestic adoption. They soon realized that if they wanted an infant, their best opportunity was to adopt transracially. Living in a fairly integrated neighborhood on the West Coast and having a social network that included friends of many races and nationalities, they thought becoming a biracial family would be something they could handle. While they knew there would be unique challenges they believed their placement in a diverse community and their racially aware attitudes would facilitate the development of a healthy adoptive biracial family. Months later they were thrilled when their infant son, Jackson, joined the family. While they felt supported by friends and family in their decision they were surprised at the curiosity and questions from friends, particularly White friends, about their decision and parenting challenges, questions they were not asked when their daughter was born. What they were not prepared for were the stares from strangers, sometimes accompanied by a smile, sometimes a frown, and the uninvited questions and comments they received from African-Americans they knew or past on the street: questions such as "Is that your child?" or "Who are the Black people in your child's life?" They were surprised when a childcare provider at Jackson's nursery became

L. A. Leslie (✉) · J. L. Young
Department of Family Science, University of Maryland, College Park, MD, USA
e-mail: lleslie@umd.edu

K. M. Hrapczynski
Department of Family Studies and Community Development, Towson University, Towson, MD, USA

R. Nazarinia Roy, A. Rollins (eds.), *Biracial Families*,
https://doi.org/10.1007/978-3-319-96160-6_9

upset with them for cutting his hair when he was 9 months of age because "Everyone knows you shouldn't cut a Black child's hair until after they've turned one." As Jackson aged they made sure that he had age-appropriate books about African-American heroes and African-American dolls and action figures, but they began to realize that although their neighborhood and social circle were integrated it was largely with Latinos and Asians, with very few African-Americans. This was punctuated for them by an event that happened after their daughter's soccer game when Jackson was 5. Two parents were handing out juice boxes and snacks to the players and their siblings, and when Jackson reached to get a snack he was told, "No, these are just for the team and their brothers and sisters. You need to run along now." It was then they realized that though there were children of color on Lauren's soccer team, there were no African-Americans. This crystalized for them that it wasn't enough to just live in a diverse community; they needed a community filled with African-Americans where Jackson would grow up knowing people like him and where others thought he belonged. At that time Mike and April became much more intentional about structuring their lives so that Jackson interacted with racially similar adults and peers. They chose to move to another part of town where the mix of families and the schools included more African-Americans; they sought out African-American professionals such as doctors and actively made friends with the parents of other African-American children in the school. As Jackson grows older they know the coming teen years will bring additional challenges and they are more aware of what they do not know about raising an African-American teenage male. But they now have African-American friends in their network and have joined an integrated church with a large African-American population. April has decided to join the local chapter of the NAACP, because even though she is White she is very invested in the success of African-American youth. Mike and April are proud of their family and hopeful for bright futures for both of their children, but they recognize in retrospect how little they really knew when they adopted transracially and how many additional parenting challenges there are when parenting someone racially different from yourself.

Introduction and History of Transracial Adoption in the United States

The majority of biracial families in the United States are formed by adults coming together as partners. In these families, adults of different races choose to become a biracial family. However, biracial families also result from adults of one race adopting children of another race, a process referred to as transracial adoption. Overwhelmingly, transracial adoptive families consist of White parents adopting racial minority children. As the example above demonstrates, in these families, only the members of one race, the White parents, choose to become a biracial family, yet neither of them has a racial minority status or heritage. While the history of transracial adoption is relatively recent, it has, almost from its inception, been controversial.

Concerns regarding White parents' ability to successfully prepare their children for life as a racial minority have been weighed against the importance of children having a permanent family.

While transracial adoption began in earnest in the United States following WWII with the advent of international war orphans, it grew dramatically following the Korean and Vietnam Wars when the number of war orphans and biracial children fathered by American service men increased substantially (Evan B. Donaldson Adoption Institute, 2008). The late 1950s and 1960s also saw an increase in domestic transracial adoptions, first with the Indian Adoption Project which sought to integrate Native American children into mainstream society, and later with programs to find homes for African-American orphans and minority children in state care (Lee, 2003). This increase in the placement of racial minority children into White homes in the 1960s and 1970s also corresponded with a drop in the number of healthy White infants available for adoption (Hollingworth, 2000).

This period of increased domestic transracial adoption was met with vocal opposition, with opponents expressing alarm at children, particularly African-American children, being removed from their culture, and voicing serious doubt that White parents could provide minority children the upbringing they needed to develop a strong racial identity and successfully navigate a racist society. This resistance reached its peak in 1972 when the National Association of Black Social Workers (NABSW) issued a position paper on transracial adoption and took a "vehement stand against the placement of Black children in White homes for any reason" (Transracial Adoption Position Statement, 1972). Following the stance taken by NABSW, transracial adoptions decreased throughout the United States as public and private adoption agencies changed their policies to pursue primarily same-race adoptions (Hollingsworth, 2000).

While the number of domestic transracial adoptions decreased in the late 1970s and 1980s, a counter push grew, arguing that minority children, particularly African-Americans, were languishing in foster care without permanent placement and that research had not established a negative effect of transracial adoption on children (Feigelman & Silverman, 1983).While the accuracy of, or reasons for, poor placement rates for African-American children was debated (and is beyond the focus of this chapter) (Hollingsworth, 1997), the federal government stepped in and in 1994 passed the Multiethnic Place Act (MEPA) which forbid the delay in placement of a child due to race and encouraged the recruitment of minority adoptive parents. In other words, agencies involved in the placement of children into foster care or adoptive homes could not, under penalty of federal law, consider race in their decision-making (Evan B. Donaldson Adoption Institute, 2008).

Although the legal status of transracial adoption has been resolved and the emphasis on permanent placement has prevailed, concerns continue to be raised as to the competency of White parents, and the primarily White communities in which they live, to promote healthy identity development in minority children and to prepare them to manage the bias and discrimination they may encounter in life. Throughout this ongoing debate, research on transracial adoption has reflected the pressing questions of the day. When the debate centered on whether or not to allow transracial adoption, research focused on comparative outcome studies, examining whether or not transracially adopted children differed from other adoptees or from racial minority children living with their biological parents. Once transracial adoption became legally established, research attempted to identify family processes and parenting practices that promoted healthy racial identity development and overall adjustment in transracial adoptees (Lee, 2003). It should be noted that because the controversy over transracial adoption has been cast in terms of the welfare of children, very little research exists examining the experience of parents or family interaction patterns in general.

In this chapter, we first examine the demographic characteristics of transracial adoptive families today. In other words, who are the parents who adopt transracially and who are the children being adopted? We then address the question of how children are faring psychologically and behaviorally in transracial adoptive families, followed by an examination of parenting practices related to positive adjustment for these adoptees. Next, we explore the aspects of transracial adoptive families that are not well understood and directions for future research. Finally, we conclude with the clinical and service implications for working with biracial families formed through adoption.

Prior to proceeding, we want to clarify three parameters we have set for the material covered in this chapter. First, although transracial adoptive families can include families in which the two parents are of different races, we will limit our review to what is known about families in which both parents (or one parent in single-parent families) are White and the adoptee is a racial minority. We do this because the parent-child dynamics in families in which no parent has any experience being a racial minority is likely to be quite different from families in which one parent has lived experience as a racial minority in the United States. Second, we will limit our research to that done on families in the United States. While there is a substantial amount of research on transracial adoptees in Europe and Canada, those countries differ from the United States in the racial homogeneity of their populations, their social attitudes regarding race, and their laws and practices regarding adoption. Because of the importance of context, it is not clear to what extent findings from one country will transfer to another. Finally, a problem throughout some of the transracial adoption literature is a conflation of race and nationality. While many international adoptees are of a different race than their parents, this is not always the case. We will therefore include only those studies of international adoptees that clearly specify the interracial nature of the adoption. Research which focuses on international adoptees without specifying the race of the children and parents in the samples will be excluded.

Who Are Adoptive Biracial Families?

Until recently, the United States lacked adequate records on adoption nationally and internationally (Brumble & Kampfe, 2011). It was not until 2000 that "adopted son/daughter" was included as a category in the national census. Conservative estimates suggest that five million Americans alive today are adoptees, 2–4% of all families have adopted, and 2.5% of all children under 18 are adopted. Out of that five million, 40% of all adopted children were of a different race, culture, or ethnicity than both adoptive parents (Vandivere, Malm, & Radel, 2009).

According to a report on the 2007 National Survey of Adoptive Parents, transracial adoptions are most commonly seen in families who adopted internationally, with 84% of international adoptions in 2007 being transracial (Vandivere et al., 2009). Among the adoptions occurring within the United States, 28% of foster-care adoptions are transracial adoptions, meaning that 28% of all children adopted out of the foster care or who were involved with child protective services were adopted by parents of a different race. Additionally, 21% of private domestic adoptions, which are independently arranged or through private adoption agencies, involve adoptive parents of a different race from their child.

So who makes up this group of transracially adoptive families? First, we will explain the demographic characteristics of parents who adopt transracially and then we will describe the children who are adopted by racially different parents.

Who are the parents who adopt transracially? In general, adults who adopt have higher educational attainment levels and are more affluent than the general population. The same levels of higher education and economic standing exist for adults who adopt transracially. One study of international transracial adoption found that the sample was almost entirely made up of White, well-educated, middle-class parents (Ishizawa, Kenney, Kubo, & Stevens, 2006). Over 97% of the adoptive parents in this study were White, and 60% had a college degree. Another 25% had attended some college. Interestingly, parents with lower levels of education were more likely to adopt children of their own race from abroad than were more highly educated parents. Given the expense of international adoption, most of the families were well off financially, with a mean family income of over $110,000 and a median family income of $85,100.

In addition to having more wealth and education than both the general population and adults who adopt children of the same race (Kreider & Lofquist, 2014), adults who adopt transracially become parents at a later age. Older parental age at adoption is, in part, associated with the societal change of women pursuing careers over family formation (Hollingsworth, 2000). This prioritization of professional careers often results in delayed childbearing and subsequent fertility problems associated with older age. Thus, increasingly, older women with high education and professional attainment and their partners look to adoption, particularly transracial adoption, as an alternate route to family formation (Jacobson, Nielsen, & Hardeman, 2012).

Who are the children being adopted transracially? According to a report on the US Census Bureau's American Community Survey, out of the 438,000 children who were transracially adopted in 2009–2011, 30% were Hispanic, 28% were Asian, 16% were two or more races, 15% were African-American, 7% were White, and 2% were American-Indian or Alaska Native (Kreider & Lofquist, 2014). In the group of transracial adoptees identified as biracial or multiracial, over half were White-Black (59%), and White-Asian and "other" multiracial were the next largest groups (15% for both). Unfortunately, beyond this racial breakdown, very little information is available about the experiences of biracial or multiracial children who are transracially adopted for two reasons. First, regardless of the racial composition, most researches group the children together and categorize them as "other." However, in some cases when a biracial child is White and a minority race, they will be counted in their minority group.

As stated earlier, international transracial adoptions occur at a higher rate than domestic transracial adoptions. However, after peaking in 2004 they have declined dramatically in the last decade (U.S. State Department, 2015). There are several contributing factors to the decrease in international adoptions, the most significant being the Hague Convention on the Protection of Children and Co-operation in Respect of Intercountry Adoption, which was designed to ensure ethical standards in the adoption process. This Convention went into effect in the United States in 2008 and disqualified many countries that did not have clear procedures in place to regulate intercountry adoptions. For example, the number of intercountry adoptions in certain Asian countries such as India, Vietnam, and Nepal has declined due to allegations of irregularity and corruption that have raised concerns about the intercountry adoption process. Children who are transracially adopted internationally come from all over the world, but the countries contributing the most children to these adoptions since 2000 are China, Guatemala, and Ethiopia (Selman, 2012). However, as a result of the Hague Convention (n.d.), the United States banned new adoptions from Guatemala in 2008.

Characteristics of the children adopted tend to vary based on their country of origin. For example, a large majority of the children adopted from China are girls, while the gender distribution is more balanced from other countries. The availability of infants for adoption is greater in Asia or Latin America than from Europe or Russia; therefore White parents seeking to adopt younger children are more likely to adopt transracially from those countries (Ishizawa et al., 2006).

While international adoptions have declined, there has been a movement towards adoption within the United States and the number of adoptions out of the foster-care system has shown small increases (U.S. DHHS, 2014). Among domestic adoptions, there are slightly more transracial adoptions occurring through the foster-care system compared to private adoptions. Nonetheless, among the children who are adopted out of the foster-care system, racial disparities persist despite policies such as the Multiethnic Placement Act (MEPA) of 1994 designed to deter racial preference in adoptions (Smith, McRoy, Freundlich, & Kroll, 2008). Specifically, the number of African-American children in foster care that are awaiting adoption is higher than other racial groups, and the number of African-American children who are being adopted out of the foster-care system, although increasing slightly, is proportionally lower than other minority groups (U.S. GAO, 2007).

Research on Transracial Adoptive Families

As addressed previously, the practice of interracial adoption, particularly domestic adoption of African-American children by White parents, has long been controversial (Transracial Adoption Position Statement, 1972). Thus, much of the research on interracial adoptive families has focused on the well-being of the adoptee, with much less attention to the functioning of the family as a whole, or any other family members. As Frasch and Brooks (2003) point out, in contrast to studies of families in general, which are theoretically grounded in the developmental tasks of family life and the needs of all family members for nurturance, support, and connection, studies of transracial adoptive families are notably atheoretical and targeted on adoptee outcomes. Ignored in much of the research is the fact that the normative tasks and challenges faced by all families, including transracial adoptive families, are further complicated by the lack of a biological or racial connection among members. For example, all families must develop a family identity, a sense of who we are in the world. While this identity is grounded in the connection among members, it is also based on how the family is perceived by others. For transracial adoptive families, not only must they work to incorporate the obvious physical differences into their definition of family ("Mommy, why am I the only one in the family with brown skin?"), but they must also find a way to project family when their mere presence together may, at worst, be denied as family, and at best says "adoption." After an incident when people thought she was trying to kidnap her young African-American son as she tried to carry the screaming child from a store when he did not want to leave, one of the participants in de Haymes and Simon's (2003) study reported carrying a family picture with her everywhere she went for proof of her relationship to her son. Unlike same-race adoptive families who can choose when and where to make adoption part of their identity as a family, racial differences between parents and children make this aspect of family life constantly visible to all (Grotevant, Dunbar, Kohler, & Esau, 2000).

Acknowledging that existing research on transracial adoptive families is limited in scope, existing work seems to fall into two overlapping categories. Early work addressed the question of how transracial adoptees were doing on a host of psychological and behavioral variables. This work typically compared transracial adoptees to other groups such as same-race adoptees or minority race children in homes with biological parents. The second, and more recent, body of work looks deeper into family processes and parenting practices that promote the well-being of adoptees.

How Are the Children Doing? Outcome Studies

Lee (2003) points out that the underlying assumption of outcome studies comparing transracial adoptees to other groups is that if no significant group differences are found, adoptees are doing fine and experiencing no negative effects of being raised by parents of a different race. From this vantage point, research findings would suggest that on the whole transracial adoptees are doing fine and experience few, if any, negative consequences of being raised outside their race. A host of studies and meta-analyses from the late 1970s to the present suggest that transracial adoption is not a risk factor for adoptees and that there are no substantive differences in transracial adoptees and either same-race adoptees or non-adoptees in areas such as behavioral and emotional problems, self-esteem, general health, and school performance (Burrow & Finley, 2004; Juffer & Van IJzendoorn, 2007; Lee, 2003). While a handful of studies found group differences, such as interracial adoptees performing better academically, or African-American males experiencing more behavioral problems than other transracially adopted youth (Burrows & Finley, 2004), most of these differences were attributable to factors such as age at adoption or previous placement in foster care, and not to interracial adoption itself (Weinberg, Waldman, van Dulmen, & Scarr, 2004).

What the outcome research does not do, however, is focus on the unique experiences transracial adoptees may have that are not comparable to same-race adoptees, most notably the experience of discrimination and the development of a racial or ethnic identity (Lee, 2003). In other words, while the comparison-based outcome research might provide an encouraging picture that, in general, transracial adoptees are doing fine, it provides no insight into the lived experiences and possible challenges of racial minority children who are growing up in White families. For example, while Jackson from our opening story and his friend Adam, who is a White adolescent adopted by White parents, both have to face issues of what being adopted may mean for their sense of self, only Jackson has to resolve identity issues related to being of a different race than the rest of his family. While research can examine how the two compare on their academic work or self-esteem, there is no way to assess racial identity issues or a sense of racial belongingness since these are not same thing for the two young men. While Adam may have friends of many different races, he will never struggle with questions of "What race am I?" or "What racial group do I belong to" in the same way that Jackson may have to. Further, this comparison research approach does not provide a window into the experiences and challenges of White parents trying to raise well-adjusted and happy minority children. The questions Jackson's parent must face concerning what to teach their son about racism and how it may impact how he is treated at school, in stores, and by police will never be faced by Adam's parents.

Starting in the early 1990s, the second wave of outcome research began to ask questions concerning the unique challenges faced by transracial adoptees, and in some cases their parents. This work was largely guided by the research on minority youth in general which had clearly established an important link between an individual's strong racial-ethnic identity and psychological well-being (Wakefield & Hudley, 2007). Racial or ethnic identity refers to the extent to which individuals identify with and experience pride in their racial or ethnic group (Phinney, 1990). It is this area of experience with which critics of transracial adoption have long been most concerned. They question whether White parents can really help their minority children develop a full understanding of identification with their race, as well as prepare them for life as members of their minority race. To some extent, the research does support the notion that the development of a healthy racial identity is a complicated and sometimes difficult process for minority children being raised by White parents.

Being "different" than their parents is something that transracially adopted children are aware of from a very young age. The visibility of both their adoptive status and their racial dissimilarity is not only noted but often commented on in public (de Haymes & Simon, 2003). So while transracial adoptees may experience a sense of belonging and family identity at home, that sense of belonging can become more tenuous in public as they face strange looks or awkward questions such as "Is that your Mom?" or "Who's the White lady you are with?". While most transracial adoptees identify with their parents' race, ethnicity, or culture as young children, concerns or questions about one's racial-ethnic identity increase with age, becoming more pronounced around middle childhood and early adolescence and continuing through adulthood (Freundlich and Lieberthal, 2000). In one study, almost half of the young adult adoptees in the study reported having experienced some discomfort with their racial appearance, with the level of discomfort being higher for those who lived in primarily White communities and those who had experienced more discrimination (Feigelman, 2000). Not surprisingly, the process of racial-ethnic identity development seems to happen more slowly for transracially adopted youth than for non-adopted racial minority youth (Lee & Quintana, 2005). And while research suggests that most transracial adoptees do develop a solid racial-ethnic identity, this does seem to be challenging and problematic for some (DeBerry, Scarr, & Weinberg, 1996). And like their non-adopted counterparts, racial-ethnic identity has largely been found to be related to psychological well-being and self-esteem for both adolescents (Yoon, 2001) and adults (Mohanty, Keokse, & Sales, 2006). It should be noted, however, that in a recent review of the racial-ethnic identity literature for transracial adoptees, Castle, Knight, and Watters (2011) point out that this positive association is not consistent with some studies finding no relationship and a few finding a negative relationship. Growing out of this review, Mohanty (2015) proposed and tested a curvilinear relationship between racial-ethnic identity and both self-esteem and psychological well-being for international transracial adoptees. Her results supported a curvilinear relationship such that the highest levels of self-esteem and well-being were found at moderate levels of racial-ethnic identity. Mohanty suggests that it is possible that international transracial adoptees who integrate both their racial/cultural heritage with their adoptive culture feel better about themselves and show fewer symptoms of psychological distress than do those who deny either their racial heritage or their adoptive culture.

While there may be some variation in what is considered the healthiest level of racial-ethnic identity for transracial adoptees, there is uniform agreement among researchers and clinicians that feeling comfortable with one's race and having a strong identification with one's racial group are important to the overall adjustment of transracial adoptees. The research is also very clear that a healthy racial identity does not develop in a vacuum. It is greatly affected by the families and communities in which the children grow up, as will be examined in the next section.

Racial Socialization in Transracial Adoptive Families

White parents adopting across racial boundaries must not only facilitate a healthy family environment by engaging in general parenting behaviors that promote positive outcomes, they must also engage in specific parenting behaviors found to be essential in ethnic minority families for raising well-adjusted racial minority children. The literature on ethnic minority families repeatedly points to the value of parents engaging in racial socialization to promote their same-race child's well-being (Evans et al., 2012; Hughes et al., 2006; Supple, Ghazarian, Frabutt, Plunkett, & Sands, 2006). Racial socialization involves the transmission of information and perspectives about race from parents to children (Hughes et al., 2006). Although there is some variation regarding what behaviors are thought to comprise racial socialization (see Chap. 8 for more information), two distinct categories of parental behaviors are consistently discussed, namely cultural socialization and preparation for bias. Parents engage in cultural socialization when they instill racial or ethnic pride in their child by connecting them to the culture, heritage, customs, and history of their culture of origin (Boykin & Toms, 1985; Hughes & Chen, 1997). Examples of cultural socialization in transracially adoptive families include celebrating the holidays of their child's birth culture, taking their child to cultural events that reflect their child's racial or ethnic group, and traveling to the birth country of their child. Preparation for bias refers to parenting behaviors intended to teach their child about the meaning of race and existence of racism in the United States, in addition to strategies for how to cope with discriminatory experiences (Hughes et al., 2006; Hughes & Chen, 1997). This type of racial socialization includes talking openly and honestly about race and oppression, being sensitive to their child's experiences of discrimination, helping their child recognize that being discriminated against is not due to their personal shortcomings, and developing strategies for responding to microaggressions and discrimination (Hughes & Chen, 1997; Vonk, 2001).

Yet, White parents' ability to engage in racial socialization may be compromised due to the parents' privileged status in the racial majority, lack of access to the racial and cultural community of their child, and/or limited understanding of the meaning of race in society and for their child (Samuels, 2009; Vonk, 2001). When reflecting on their childhood, transracially adopted adults often describe their desire to have been exposed to their racial community and to have been prepared to proactively handle racial discrimination (Samuels, 2009). However, many adoptees, including preadolescents, adolescents, and adults, indicate that their White parents exposed them more often to White cultural orientations, frequently did not recognize the significance of race in their life, and offered little preparation for dealing with experiences of racism (de Haymes & Simon, 2003). Berquist, Campbell, and Unrau (2003) found that White transracial adoptive parents downplayed the racial difference between themselves and their adopted children, with two-thirds stating that adopting an Asian child did not change the racial characteristics of the family.

While many transracially adopted children acknowledged parental attempts to foster their racial identity and connect them to their birth culture, others described a family environment which minimized or even ignored race and experiences of racial discrimination. As one respondent in Samuels' (2009) qualitative study reports, "You know my parents never discussed race with me … EVER. I think they felt that if they ignored my ethnicity, it would kind of go away" (p. 87). As Smith and his colleagues (Smith & Juarez, 2015; Smith, Juarez, & Jacobson, 2011) point out in their qualitative study of transracial adoptive parents, even when parents are mindful of the need to engage in racial socialization and want to promote both their children's pride in their race and their ability to handle the racism they experience, parents do it using a White frame of reference based on their privileged racial status. In particular, they point out how White parents' efforts at instilling pride are typically couched in an individualistic, achievement-orientated framework which one works towards (e.g., "I want my child to learn to be proud of who he is"), instead of a more collectivist-oriented framework one experiences as a member of a minority racial group (e.g., "I want my child to feel connected to the shared struggle and survival of African Americans in general"). Further, one's culture is more likely to be framed as a resource one can tap into for strength as opposed to a way of living in which one is immersed. In terms of preparing their children to address racism and racist events, Smith and his colleagues point out that White parents often emphasize the importance of their children understanding the other's perspective and responding in a way that is mindful of the White perpetrator's feelings, taking a subservient "care-taking" role towards Whites. Additionally, the emphasis in managing racism is frequently on finding a way to not let it upset you instead of resisting and confronting it. As one parent described the message he gives his minority child when experiencing discrimination:

> *You gain more anger when you give out anger, and you get back what you give, so if you do it from a peaceful heart and trust that all. people really want to be good, and that all people are and. intrinsically can see truth, that's the way I handle it* (Smith et al., 2011, p. 1218).

While such efforts by parents may be well intentioned, they are likely to leave a child feeling invalidated, unsupported, and responsible for personally managing the situation.

While most White parents have limited engagement in racial socialization, they do tend to engage in cultural socialization more than preparing their racial minority children for bias (Berbery & O'Brien, 2011). Cultural socialization may include sharing books and stories about one's culture or people of one's race, participation in culturally or racially oriented events or camps, or visits to birth countries, and as discussed later can promote pride and cultural competence in children. However, Quiroz (2012) cautions against what she terms "cultural tourism," an approach which appropriates cultural or racial symbols as something an adoptee can access, but is not a part of his or her lived experience. In order to avoid the sense of marginalization that can result from cultural tourism, it is important that the process of cultural socialization involve integrating aspects of one's culture or race into the family's life instead of mere accessing them periodically or having them merely as decorations in one's life. While cultural socialization is strongest when children are young, it wanes in most families as children age (Berbery and O'Bien, 2011; DeBerry et al., 1996).

On the other hand, preparation for bias occurs at lower rates in transracial adoptive families. While work from the late 1990s indicated that almost three-quarters of White parents adopting African-American children deemphasized (35%) or felt ambivalent about (40%) discussing race and race-related issues with their teenagers (DeBerry et al., 1996), more recent data suggest that parents show slight increases in discussions about racism and how to cope with it as their children get older, although such discussions only happen, on average, one or two times a year (Johnston, Swim, Saltsman, Deater-Deckard, & Petrill, 2007). In other words, White parents seem to pay little, and potentially less, attention to race as their minority children age, even though children's likelihood of experiencing discrimination and racist events increases as they approach and enter the teen years (see Chap. 8 for more information).

Racial socialization and transracial adoptee outcomes: Transracial adoptive parents may engage in limited levels of racial socialization; however it nonetheless is a valuable contributor to their children's development and adjustment. When White parents actively promote their children's racial and ethnic background, transracial adoptees endorse greater racial-ethnic pride and lower feelings of marginality, and experience lower aggression and acting out behaviors, lower distress, higher levels of self-esteem, and better psychological adjustment (Johnston et al., 2007; Lee & Quintana, 2005; Mohanty et al., 2006; Yoon, 2001). Clearly, the extent to which parents provide opportunities for their transracial adoptee to be involved in their birth heritage, through either cultural traditions or interacting with people of the same racial background, is related to the development of their children's racial-ethnic identity (Friedlander et al., 2000; Huh & Reid, 2000; Lee & Quintana, 2005). The co-participation of parents in these cultural endeavors also seems to be a valuable contributor (Huh & Reid, 2000). The benefits of joint cultural participation on transracial adoptees may in part be attributed to enhanced feelings of belongingness to their adoptive family and decreased feelings of marginality (Mohanty et al., 2006). For example, when parents work to learn about their child's cultural history and actively discuss it with the child, rather than just sending the child to classes or providing books, it communicates a deeper valuing of who the child is.

Cultural socialization is consistently associated with positive outcomes for transracially adopted youth; however the influence of preparation for bias is less clear and examined less often. One study found that parenting behaviors, such as educating their racial minority youth about prejudice and racism, positively impacted psychological well-being and self-esteem in Asian adoptees by decreasing their sense of marginality (Mohanty & Newhill, 2011). However, Johnston et al. (2007) found an association between mothers' engagement in preparation for bias and a slight increase in their children's externalizing, or aggression and acting out behaviors, particularly for older children. The authors suggest that a causal relationship cannot be established given that information about these two variables was collected in the same wave of the study. Therefore, this relationship may be attributed to mothers' amplifying their use of preparation for bias in response to their child demonstrating problem behaviors, as opposed to it having a negative influence on the child.

Leslie, Smith, Hrapczynski, and Riley (2012) examined the impact of racial socialization on transracially adopted adolescents' experience of discrimination and the stress it caused them. Discriminatory experiences included being treated unfairly by people, such as teachers or school administrators, fellow students or coworkers, strangers, friends, and neighbors because of their race, and being accused/suspected of doing something wrong, insulted or called a racist name, or made fun of or physically threatened due to their race. Not surprisingly, the frequency with which adoptees experienced discrimination was strongly linked to their stress levels. Interestingly, transracially adopted adolescents whose parents engaged in higher levels of racial socialization did report experiencing more discrimination. However, they were less likely to find this discrimination stressful compared to adolescents exposed to lower levels of racial socialization. Thus, although racial socialization may play a sensitizing role, making adolescents somewhat more aware of or likely to label discrimination, overall it played a highly protective role in minimizing the stressfulness, particularly for those adoptees exposed to higher levels of discrimination. One can speculate that having parents who prepared their children to effectively identify and respond to racism empowered adolescents in ways that increased their confidence in how to handle racist situations they encountered.

Why do some parents engage in racial socialization and others do not? As discussed previously, many White parents engage in the racial socialization of their racial minority child, while others facilitate a familial environment that minimizes racial difference within their family and lacks cultural competence. In order to support families in creating a healthy family environment for their racial minority child, it is important to understand what accounts for differences in racial socialization practices.

Parental attitudes and beliefs: Adopting a racial minority child can force many White parents, sometimes for the first time, to really examine their internalized attitudes about race and recognize their own racial privilege. Several studies have demonstrated the link between these racial attitudes and beliefs and their racial socialization practices with their children. Early work acknowledged that many adoptive parents may promote a color-blind attitude; this perspective refers to the "belief that race should not and does not matter" (Neville, Lilly, Duran, Lee, & Browne, 2000, p. 60). There are many reasons why adoptive parents might choose to deemphasize racial difference among family members. First, in their effort to develop a strong family identity parents may want to focus on the connection among family members, and minimize things that separate them. Second, parents may adhere to a dominant cultural narrative that it is what is "inside" the person not "outside" that should matter. Parents also truly know and love the person that is their child and may not think of them in racial terms.

Although raising their child using a color-blind perspective may be well intended, ignoring racial difference and minimizing racism is, in and of itself, a contemporary form of racism (Neville, Awad, Brooks, Flores, & Bluemel, 2013). Within families, this may communicate lack of acceptance to the child and may inhibit parental beliefs in the value of, and their engagement in, racial socialization practices (Kallgren & Caudill, 1993). Lee et al. (2006), for example, found that White parents who did not endorse a color-blind perspective were more likely to provide their child with cultural opportunities and make their child aware of racism and how to cope with it. It may be that parents who are racially aware engage in an active process of self-examination of their beliefs associated with race and develop cultural empathy, thereby promoting their use of culturally sensitive parenting when raising a racial minority child. As reviewed earlier in this chapter, parental racial socialization practices have important benefits for transracial adoptee development. When White parents are color-blind they are less likely to foster a family environment that nurtures the healthy development of their racial minority children and to provide them with the skills to successfully navigate relationships in a highly race-conscious society. Being raised by parents who are color-blind, therefore, may be harmful to the adoptee.

Recent research, however, has shown that parental attitudes regarding race are more nuanced than simple color-blindness or racial awareness. In her study of White mothers who recognize the unique challenges of raising a minority child and are "trying to do the right thing" (p. 1273), Barn (2013) found three different attitudes towards race which led to different orientations towards racial socialization. Those with a humanitarianism orientation focused on the common humanity and decency of all people, minimizing the significance of the race, ethnicity, or culture of their child. While acknowledging the existence of racism, they chose to respond to it by emphasizing the goodness of their child and expecting the world to see their child for the person the child is. Any racial insults such as name-calling were simply responded to through general reassurance of the value of their child without examining it in a context of race or discriminatory behavior. While meant as a supportive stance, such beliefs on the mothers' part left their children unprepared to manage racism. Additionally, it presented difficulties for children in reconciling how they thought about themselves and how they were seen by the outside world. One mother reported the distress and confusion her daughter experienced when people referred to her as Hispanic, an identity she did not hold for herself because it had never been acknowledged by the family. A second group of mothers had a more ambivalent attitude towards race, knowing that it was important in their children's lives, but experiencing uncertainty and indecision regarding how and if to address it. While wanting to embrace racial diversity, these mothers acknowledged their own discomfort with it and their hesitancy to do so, unless initiated by their child. Further, they were likely to attribute any problems their children encountered to factors other than race or ethnicity. While making some attempts to provide racially or culturally based experiences for their children, the lack of embracement of their child's minority identity also, like the humanitarianism mothers, left their children with limited skills to navigate life as a minority. Finally, mothers with a transcultural orientation acknowledged and embraced the role of race in their family life. They worked hard to create a life that reflected the membership of their family, choosing to live in predominantly minority neighborhoods, belonging to multicultural social or advocacy organizations, or creating multiracial networks. In addition they embedded their child's culture of origin into their lives by doing things such as including cultural artifacts in their home and attending cultural classes and workshops.

Community characteristics: The ability of parents to engage in the racial socialization of their child may be facilitated or thwarted by the family's geographic location. Parents who describe their community as homogenous, nondiverse, or White find it difficult to connect their children with their culture of origin (de Haymes & Simon, 2003; Scroggs & Heitfield, 2001; Vonk, Yun, Park, & Massatti, 2007). Living in a more integrated neighborhood and enrolling their child in a more integrated school facilitate parents' ability to engage in racial socialization and connect with people of the same race as their child. Parents can more easily locate same-race role models for their children and expose them to same-race peers, thereby increasing the potential for interactions and friendships with people who share their racial or cultural background. For example, the White mothers in Barn's study with a transculturalism attitude reported moving to predominantly African-American or highly integrated neighborhoods so their children's doctors, babysitters, friends, etc. would be racially similar. Further, Chinese adoptees living in a community with a higher percentage of Asian people have higher levels of Chinese cultural competence in part due to this cultural exposure (Thomas & Tessler, 2007).

However, even when living in a diverse community, parents of children from different ethnic backgrounds may have differential access to the specific cultural community of their child. For example, it is speculated that mothers with children adopted from China engage in more cultural socialization than mothers who adopted from other Asian countries, like Korea, Vietnam, and Cambodia, due to greater accessibility of Chinese culture in the United States, including Chinese restaurants, Chinatowns, and China-adoption family support groups (Johnston et al., 2007; Scroggs & Heitfield, 2001).

Race of child: The level of visible differences in physical characteristics and skin color between adoptive parents and their children may be related to whether White parents recognize the need for or prioritize racial socialization. While there is limited research in this area, Leslie and Riley (2010) did find the highest level of racial socialization among parents who had adopted African-American children. Additionally, the lowest level of racial socialization and the highest adherence to color-blind attitudes were found among parents who had adopted Latino children. Further, Barn (2013) found that mothers with a humanitarianism attitude which downplayed the significance of race were more likely to have light-skinned Latino or biracial children. It is possible that the race of the child may impact a parent's level of racial socialization in two ways. First, to the extent that a child has an identifiable race that could be the basis of discrimination and mistreatment, parents may be more likely to work to develop racial pride and prepare the child to handle racism. Second, the more the child's physical features make it possible for the child to be assumed to be the parent's biological child, the less inclined parents may be to engage in racial socialization which emphasizes the difference between parent and child. In both of these scenarios, African-American and Asian children may receive more racial socialization because their race could clearly be the basis for stereotypes, bias, and discrimination. These children are less likely to be seen as biologically related to their parents, and parents may be more poignantly aware of the differences in their experiences and their child's experiences. Latino, on the other hand, is an ethnicity which includes a range of races. Therefore, based on the physical features of both the parent and child it is more likely that parents may "see" themselves in their children and be less likely to see race as a critical feature in the child's life. Of course, the race of the child is likely to interact with the community the family lives in to amplify or diminish the parent's perception of the need for racial socialization.

Future Research

While much has been learned about the adjustment of interracially adopted children over the last several decades, there are still many important questions about life in biracial families formed through adoption that that have not been examined. The examination of these questions is vital, not simply as a matter of sociological interest, but because gaining this knowledge can serve to improve the quality of life for all members of these families. Building on the work that has been done on transracially adopted children's well-being, there are several notable gaps that future research should address. First, the vast majority of research in transracial adoption has been done on children internationally adopted from Asian countries, and often the issues of birth culture (or country of origin) and race are intertwined. More effort is needed to disentangle these two important areas of life for internationally adopted racial minority children. Specifically, the ways in which cultural identity and racial identity each separately impacts a child's well-being must be clarified. Further, work should be expanded beyond the primary focus on children adopted from Asian countries, particularly considering the growing number of children adopted from African countries.

Second, because of the focus on international adoptions, much less is known about the adjustment of domestically adopted children. A research focus on the well-being of this group of children is sorely needed, particularly those children adopted out of foster care, who may have had multiple hardships in life prior to their adoption. Further, given that most of the controversy and concern over transracial adoption has centered on the ability of White parents to effectively raise African-American children in our racist society, it is critical that a more intense focus be given to identifying the factors that enhance and inhibit White parent's ability in this area. There is also a significant lack of research that takes into consideration the experiences of biracial children and their adoptive parents' views of their racial identity. Given the racial fluidity of biracial or multiracial individuals, they undergo distinct identity development processes compared to monoracial children, and the complexity of this process and what it means for racial socialization practices for adoptive parents must be explored.

Two other groups of transracial adoptees that we know little to nothing about are White children who are transracially adopted and minority parents who adopt transracially. The focus of the literature on transracial adoption has been on the steadily increasing numbers of non-White children adopted by White parents, whereas the number of White children transracially adopted has remained around 7% (Kreider & Lofquist, 2014). Some of the possible reasons why fewer African-American parents adopt White babies/children are related to practical issues of adoption; for example, fewer African-American families adopt in general, more African-Americans adopt or informally obtain guardianship of children in their extended family, there is sometimes a longer wait to adopt a White baby or child, and proportionately there are more African-American children in foster care in need of families. Other reasons for the low number of African-American families adopting White children may be related to social stigma such as not wanting the risk of being thought of as the nanny or kidnapper of the child, not wanting to expose the child to prejudice and racism that African-American families face, and hostility or questions from other African-Americans as to why they did not adopt a black child (Davenport, 2015). There is virtually no empirical research on this population however, and the low numbers of minority families adopting transracially reflect an important social dynamic that merits further exploration.

Third, the bulk of the research on transracially adopted children is retrospective, told from the perspective of adoptees as adults. Increased attention should be given to studying children throughout the life course, to better understand their needs and challenges at different developmental stages.

Finally, as previously stated, the vast majority of research has been focused on the child's well-being. Very little attention has been paid to other family members or family processes that occur within the family system beyond racial socialization. Future research should give more attention on the functioning of the family as a whole, including more information about the parents pre- and post-adoption, as well as the outcomes of other family members such as the siblings of the adoptee. Family processes such as relationship quality, family boundaries, social support, sibling relationships, and child socialization beyond racial socialization also need to be explored in this population to identify strengthening family patterns.

Implications for Practice

Professionals working with biracial families formed via adoption fall into two broad categories with involvement at different points in the family's adoption journey. Adoption caseworkers' efforts primarily center on finding suitable matches when placing a child into an adoptive home. Their work includes assessing the needs of the child and the capacity of the prospective adoptive parents to meet those needs. Family therapists, on the other hand, intervene after the adoption has taken place to help adoptive families transition, address challenges that arise, and facilitate a family environment that meets the needs of all family members with a specific focus on the well-being of the adopted child. Both adoption caseworkers and family therapists have a responsibility to put into practice what is known to be in the best interest of the child when working with transracial adoptive families. This section elaborates on the implications for these professionals in their practice.

Adoption professionals must first acknowledge that transracial adoption is a viable option for the placement of racial minority youth given the substantial evidence that children tend to fare well in the context. However, this is not enough. Both adoption case managers and family therapists must be aware of the family processes present in these biracial families and the unique challenges they may face. Professionals can then take action to aid families in overcoming them. Education and support regarding racial socialization are primary ways adoption case managers and family therapists can facilitate the well-being of racial minority youth being raised by White parents. Adoption professionals do a great service to biracial families and to the children being raised in them when they challenge White parents to become racially aware and give them the tools to engage in racial socialization.

Adoption caseworkers should assess prospective adoptive parents' comfort, or rather discomfort, with race and racial difference as part of the process of assessing their capacity to provide a healthy and supportive home for this child. As a biracial family, racial difference would be their reality and issues regarding race are likely to arise as they are raising their child. Therefore, it is of value to have clear and candid conversations about the implications of raising a racial minority child as White parents. It is the role of the caseworker to open up this conversation to provide parents the opportunity to navigate their thoughts and feelings about raising a racial minority child and to consider actions they must take to prepare themselves to engage in the racial socialization of their child once he or she joins their family. It is particularly important that these conversations challenge potential adopting parents to think not only about raising a minority child, but also about raising a minority teen and the particular challenges that this stage of life might pose. Given the research indicating that parents pull away from discussions of race often just at the time it is becoming more poignant in their child's life, parents must understand the necessity of engaging in developmentally appropriate racial socialization (see Chap. 8 for more information) over the course of a child's life. After the adoption, family therapists can continue to model an awareness of race and its influence by helping White parents develop racial awareness, challenge their color-blind attitudes, and reflect on the meaning of racial difference within their family.

Adoption professionals should encourage the development of a bicultural home which reflects the racial and ethnic makeup of the family. A bicultural home is one in which the culture of all members of the family is integrated into the family's routines, traditions, and space. This does not mean an abandoning of the White parents' customs, but rather an integration of these with those of their child's culture of origin. For example, a family with a Latino son might choose to speak English but also learn Spanish, a family with an African-American daughter may choose to include paintings in their home that portray African-Americans or read age-appropriate books together about the African-American experience in this country, or a family with a Chinese daughter may also celebrate Chinese holidays. By adapting family life in these ways, parents not only are connecting their child to their birth culture, but they are also communicating a recognition and validation of their family's bicultural identity. Adoption caseworkers and family therapists serve as important resources for families. They should help families think about how they will create a bicultural home and help them to accomplish this task.

What takes place within the home is a critical start to facilitating an environment conducive to raising a healthy racial minority child. However adoption professionals should also be mindful of the community context in which the child is being raised. Racial minority children need to be linked to same-race role models and to engage with same-race peers. Therefore, adoption caseworkers can help prospective adoptive parents plan for how they will fill this need. Living in or relocating to an integrated neighborhood clearly facilitates a family's ability to connect with people of their child's culture of origin. When relocating is not possible for a family living in a predominately White community, adoption professionals can help parents consider alternative ways to proactively link their child to members of their race or culture of origin. For example, parents can foster relationships between their child and members of their birth family (if feasible and deemed safe). Parents can locate nearby or distant diverse communities, and take their family into these communities to engage in routine tasks (e.g., grocery shopping, going to the park, attending religious services, playing on sports teams) or to attend adoption-related or cultural events. For some families, this may require traveling a distance, limiting their ability to engage in these communities frequently. As indicated earlier, periodic engagement in the child's culture of origin is superficial and may not be sufficient to aid in the development of a healthy racial-ethnic identity (Quiroz, 2012). Therefore, parents should attempt to make these encounters a stable part of family life and supplement infrequent engagement with the integration of birth culture in the home.

Caseworkers and family therapists working with transracial adoptive families should facilitate discussion about race and racial issues within the family. Just as it is important for parents to openly discuss adoption in a developmentally appropriate way early in the child's life and continue this conversation as the child gets older, it is necessary for the biracial quality of the family to be on the table for discussion, and recognize that the nature of these discussions will change as the child ages. This opens the door for valuable discussions about racial difference and acceptance within the family. It also serves as a foundation for future dialogue about the realities of discrimination and preparation for how to recognize and cope with racism. Professionals working with transracially adoptive families can equip parents with strategies to help their child cope with discrimination and to validate their child's feelings regarding racial difference in the family and experiences of racism.

Conclusion

The policy question of whether transracial adoption should be allowed has long been answered, and the numbers of biracial families formed through adoption are growing. The goal of our research and our social service practice should be to identify the factors and family processes that can enhance the functioning and well-being of all members of these families, but particularly the children.

References

Barn, R. (2013). 'Doing the right things': Transracial adoption in the USA. *Ethnic and Racial Studies, 36*(8), 1273–1291.

Berbery, M., & O'Brien, K. (2011). Predictors of white adoptive parents' cultural and racial socialization behaviors with their Asian adopted children. *Adoption Quarterly, 14*, 284–304.

Bergquist, K. J. S., Campbell, M. E., & Unrau, Y. A. (2003). Caucasian parents and Korean adoptees: A survey of parents' perceptions. *Adoption Quarterly, 6*(4), 41–58.

Boykin, A. W., & Toms, F. D. (1985). Black child socialization: A conceptual framework. In H. P. McAdoo & J. L. McAdoo (Eds.), *Black children: Social, educational, and parental environments* (pp. 33–51). Newbury Park, CA: Sage.

Brumble, K., & Kampfe, C. M. (2011). The history of adoption in the United States: A focus on the unique group of intercountry transracial special needs children. *Counselling Psychology Quarterly, 24*(2), 157–162. https://doi.org/10.1080/09515070.2011.586413

Burrow, A. L., & Finley, G. E. (2004). Traansracial, same-race adoptions, and the need for multiple measures of adjustment. *American Journal of Orthopsychiatry, 74*(4), 577–583.

Castle, H., Knight, E., & Watters, C. (2011). Ethnic identity as a protective factor for looked after and adopted children from ethnic minority groups: A critical review of the literature. *Adoption Quarterly, 14*, 305–325.

de Haymes, M. V., & Simon, S. (2003). Transracial adoption: Families identify issues and needed support services. *Child Welfare, 82*, 251–272.

Davenport, D. (2015, August 12). *Black families adopting white children.* Retrieved from https://creatingafamily.org/adoption-category/black-families-adopting-white-children/

DeBerry, K. M., Scarr, S., & Weinberg, R. (1996). Family racial socialization and ecological competence: Longitudinal assessments of African-American transracial adoptees. *Child Development, 67*, 2375–2399.

Evan B. Donaldson Adoption Institute. (2008). *Finding families for African American children: The role of race & law in adoption from foster care.* New York, NY. Retrieved from http://www.adoptioninstitute.org/wp-content/uploads/2013/12/MEPApaper20080527.pdf

Evans, A. B., Banerjee, M., Meyer, R., Aldana, A., Foust, M., & Rowley, S. (2012). Racial socialization as a mechanism for positive development among African American youth. *Child Development Perspectives, 6*(3), 251–257.

Feigelman, W., & Silverman, A. R. (1983). *Chosen children: New patterns of adoptive relationships*. New York: Praeger.

Feigelman, W. (2000). Adjustments of transracially and inracially adopted young adults. *Child & Adolescent Social Work Journal, 17*(3), 165–183.

Frasch, K. M., & Brooks, D. (2003). Normative development in transracial adoptive families. An integration of the literature and implications for the construction of a theoretical framework. *Family in Society: The Journal of Contemporary Human Services, 84*(2), 201–212.

Freundich, M., & Lieberthal, J. K. (2000). *The gathering of the first generation of adult Korean adoptees: Adoptees' perceptions of international adoption.* New York: Evan B. Donaldson Adoption Institute.

Friedlander, M. L., Larney, L. C., Skau, M., Hotaling, M., Cutting, M. L., & Schwam, M. (2000). Bicultural identification: Experiences of internationally adopted children and their parents. *Journal of Counseling Psychology, 47*, 187–198.

Grotevant, H. D., Dunbar, N., Kohler, J., & Esau, A. M. (2000). Adoptive identity: How contexts within and beyond the family shape developmental pathways. *Family Relations, 49*, 379–387.

Hague Convention. (n.d.). Retrieved from https://travel.state.gov/content/adoptionsabroad/en/hague-convention.html

Hollingsworth, L. D. (1997). Effect of transracial/transethnic adoption on children's racial and ethnic identity and self-esteem: A meta-analytic review. *Marriage & Family Review, 25*, 99–130.

Hollingsworth, L. D. (2000). Who seeks to adopt a child? Findings from the National Survey of Family Growth (1995). *Adoption Quarterly, 3*(3), 1–23.

Hughes, D., & Chen, L. (1997). What and when parents tell children about race: An examination of race-related socialization among African American families. *Applied Developmental Science, 1*, 200–214.

Hughes, D., Rodriguez, J., Smith, E. P., Johnson, D. J., Stevenson, H. C., & Spicer, P. (2006). Parents' ethnic-racial socialization practices: A review of research and directions for future study. *Developmental Psychology, 42*, 747–770.

Huh, N. S., & Reid, W. J. (2000). Intercountry, transracial adoption and ethnic identity: A Korean example. *International Social Work, 43*, 75–87.

Ishizawa, H., Kenney, C. T., Kubo, K., & Stevens, G. (2006). Constructing interracial families through intercountry adoption. *Social Science Quarterly, 87*(S1), 1207–1224. https://doi.org/10.1111/j.1540-6237.2006.00424.x

Jacobson, C. K., Nielsen, L., & Hardeman, A. (2012). Family trends and transracial adoption in the United States. *Adoption Quarterly, 15*(2), 73–87. https://doi.org/10.1080/10926755.2012.681591

Johnston, K. E., Swim, J. K., Saltsman, B. M., Deater-Deckard, K., & Petrill, S. A. (2007). Mothers' racial, ethnic, and cultural socialization of transracially adopted Asian children. *Family Relations, 56*, 390–402.

Juffer, F., & Van IJzendoorn, M. H. (2007). Adoptees do not lack self-esteem: A meta-analysis of studies of self-esteem of transracial, international, and domestic adoptees. *Psychological Bulletin, 133*, 1067–1083.

Kallgren, C. A., & Caudill, P. J. (1993). Current transracial adoption practices: Racial dissonance or racial awareness? *Psychological Reports, 72*, 551–558.

Kreider, R. M., & Lofquist, D. A. (2014). *Adopted children and step children: 2010 population characteristics*. U.S. Census Bureau.

Lee, D. C., & Quintana, S. M. (2005). Benefits of cultural exposure and development of Korean perspective taking ability in transracially adopted Korean children. *Cultural Diversity and Ethnic Minority Psychology, 11*, 130–143.

Lee, R. M. (2003). The transracial adoption paradox: History, research, and counseling implications of cultural socialization. *The Counseling Psychologist, 31*, 711–744.

Lee, R. M., Grotevant, H. D., Hellerstedt, W. L., Gunnar, M. R., & The Minnesota International Adoption Project Team. (2006). Cultural socialization in families with internationally adopted children. *Journal of Family Psychology, 20*, 571–580.

Leslie, L. A. & Riley, D. (2010). *The role of family factors in the adjustment of transracially adopted adolescents*. Paper presented at the annual meeting of The Joint Council on International Children, Baltimore, MD.

Leslie, L. A., Smith, J. R., Hrapczynski, K. M., & Riley, D. (2012). Racial socialization in transracial adoptive families: Does it help adolescents deal with discrimination stress? *Family Relations, 62*, 72–81.

Mohanty, J. (2015). Ethnic identity and psychological well-being of international transracial adoptees: A curvilinear relationship. In E. E. Pinderhughes & R. Rosnati (Eds.), *Adoptees ethnic identity and social contexts, New directions for child and adolescent development* (Vol. 150, pp. 33–45).

Mohanty, J., Keokse, G., & Sales, E. (2006). Family cultural socialization, ethnic identity, and self-esteem: Web-based survey of international adult adoptees. *Journal of Ethnic and Cultural Diversity in Social Work, 15*, 153–172.

Mohanty, J., & Newhill, C. E. (2011). Asian adolescent and young adult adoptees' psychological well-being: Examining the mediating role of marginality. *Children and Youth Services Review, 33*, 1189–1195.

Neville, H. A., Awad, G. H., Brooks, J. E., Flores, M. P., & Bluemel, J. (2013). Color-blind racial ideology: Theory, training, and measurement implications in psychology. *American Psychologist, 68*, 455–466.

Neville, H. A., Lilly, R. L., Duran, G., Lee, R. M., & Browne, L. (2000). Construction and initial validation of the Color-Blind Racial Attitudes Scale (CoBRAS). *Journal of Counseling Psychology, 47*, 59–70.

Phinney, J. (1990). Ethnic identity in adolescents and adults: Review of research. *Psychological Bulletin, 3*, 499–514.

Quiroz, P. A. (2012). Cultural tourism in transnational adoption: "Staged authenticity" and its implications for adopted children. *Journal of Family Issues, 33*(4), 527–555.

Samuels, G. M. (2009). "Being raised by white people": Navigating racial differences among adopted multiracial adults. *Journal of Marriage and Family, 71*, 80–94.

Scroggs, P. H., & Heitfield, H. (2001). International adopters and their children: Birth cultural ties. *Gender Issues, 19*, 3–30.

Selman, P. (2012). Global trends in intercountry adoption, 2000–2010. *Adoption Advocate, 44*, 1–17.

Smith, D. L., & Juarez, B. G. (2015). Race lessons in Black and White: How White adoptive parents socialize Black adoptees in predominantly White communities. *Adoption Quarterly, 18*(2), 108–137.

Smith, D. L., Juarez, B. G., & Jacobson, C. K. (2011). White on Black: Can White parents teach Black adoptive children how to understand and cope with racism. *Journal of Black Studies, 42*(8), 1195–1230.

Smith, S. L., McRoy, R., Freundlich, M., & Kroll, J. (2008). *Finding families for African American children: The role of race & law in adoption from foster care.* New York: Evan B. Donaldson Adoption Institute.

Supple, A. J., Ghazarian, S. R., Frabutt, J. M., Plunkett, S. W., & Sands, T. (2006). Contextual influences on Latino adolescent ethnic identity and academic outcomes. *Child Development, 77*, 1427–1433.

Thomas, K. A., & Tessler, R. C. (2007). Bicultural socialization among adoptive families: Where there is a will, there is a way. *Journal of Family Issues, 28*, 1189–1219.

Transracial Adoption Position Statement. (1972). National Association of Black Social Workers. Retrieved from http://c.ymcdn.com/sites/nabsw.org/resource/collection/E1582D77-E4CD-4104-996A-D42D08F9CA7D/NABSW_Trans-Racial_Adoption_1972_Position_(b).pdf

U.S. Department of Health and Human Services (2014). *The AFCARS report.* (Report No. 21). Retrieved from https://www.acf.hhs.gov/cb/research-data-technology/statistics-research/afcars

U.S. Government Accountability Office. (July, 2007). *African American children in foster care: Additional HHS assistance needed to help states reduce the proportion in care.* GAO-07-816. Retrieved from www.gao.gov/new.items/d07816.pdf

U.S. State Department, Bureau of Consular Affairs, Intercountry Adoption. (2015). *Annual report on intercountry adoption.* Retrieved from https://travel.state.gov/content/adoptionsabroad/en/about-us/publications.html

Vandivere, S., Malm, K., & Radel, L. (2009). *Adoption USA: A chartbook based on the 2007 National Survey of Adoptive Parents.* Washington, D.C.: The U.S. Department of Health and Human Services, Office of the Assistant Secretary for Planning and Evaluation.

Vonk, E. M., Yun, S. H., Park, W., & Massatti, R. R. (2007). *Transraical adoptive parents' thoughts about the importance of race and culture in parenting. International Korean adoption: A fifty-year history of policy and practice* (pp. 99–112). New York: The Haworth Press.

Vonk, M. E. (2001). Cultural competence for transracial adoptive parents. *Social Work, 46*, 246–255.

Wakefield, W. D., & Hudley, C. (2007). Ethnic and racial identity and adolescent wellbeing. *Theory Into Practice, 42*(2), 147–154.

Weinberg, R. A., Waldman, I., van Dulmen, M. H., & Scarr, S. (2004). The Minnesota transracial adoption study: Parents reports of psychological adjustment at late adolescence. *Adoption Quarterly, 8*(2), 27–43.

Yoon, D. P. (2001). Causal modeling predicting psychological adjustment of Korean-born adolescent adoptees. *Journal of Human Behavior in the Social Environment, 3*, 65–82.

Part IV
Challenges and Opportunities

Diverse Family Structures Within Multiracial Families

Henry L. Harris, Katie W. Lamberson, and Clare P. Merlin

Opening Story Illustrating Topic

Diana is a 32-year-old single White female with a 7-year-old Black/White biracial son from a previous relationship with John, an African-American male. They dated for 3 years and had planned on marriage. However, due to conflicts they experienced, their relationship dissolved. Their son Michael was born during the final year of their relationship. Diana holds her family partially responsible for the breakup because they initially did not approve of the relationship. Her family believed that her life would be too difficult if she married John. They had concerns about the reaction of family and friends. When she informed them of her pregnancy they were cautiously supportive, yet conveyed concerns that her biracial son would have a negative impact on her career as an accountant. Diana is not married and lives alone with Michael. She spends time with her family but is always concerned that some family members are going to make racially insensitive statements around Michael about Blacks or other racial groups. She's overheard things like "Skin color doesn't really matter, but I hope Michael does not get any darker," and "some minority people can be so sensitive, kind of like John sometimes."

John's family was not fully supportive of the relationship either. His parents initially questioned why he would want to bring the additional burden of a White woman into his life. They were concerned about how an interracial relationship and/or marriage would impact John's career, the possible negative reactions the couple would receive from society, and the challenges their future children might encounter. However, when his parents learned of the couple's pregnancy, their attitudes

H. L. Harris (✉) · C. P. Merlin
Department of Counseling, University of North Carolina at Charlotte, Charlotte, NC, USA
e-mail: hharris2@uncc.edu

K. W. Lamberson
Department of Counseling at University of North Georgia, Dahlonega, GA, USA

R. Nazarinia Roy, A. Rollins (eds.), *Biracial Families*,
https://doi.org/10.1007/978-3-319-96160-6_10

became more positive and supportive of the relationship. However, as stated, John and Diana's relationship eventually dissolved. John is a bank executive and married to his wife Monica, who is biracial (Black and Puerto Rican), but identifies as Black. John has always been involved in Michael's life and spends time with him every other weekend.

Michael is an average-size child with curly brown hair and light brown eyes. When in public some have asked Diana if she is Michael's adopted mother. She dismisses this as ignorance; however one area that concerns Diana is how John identifies Michael. She firmly believes that they should simply identify him as a human being and not solely with his Black heritage. She has chosen to live in a racially diverse neighborhood and Michael attends a racially diverse school. John, on the other hand, believes that Michael should identify as Black, regardless of the neighborhood or school that he attends, because he believes that is how society is going to perceive Michael. John believes that Diana's color-blind attitude is naïve and Diana believes John thinks too much about race.

Introduction

Historically, traditional families in the United States have been viewed as intact nuclear families that include a heterosexual man and woman with biological children; however, this perception no longer represents the norm for American families (Goldenberg, Stanton, & Goldenberg, 2017). For example, in 1960, 37% of homes consisted of a married couple and their children and in 2014 that number had decreased to 16% (Pew Research, 2016). Shifts in societal values have impacted family structures; they are differently constructed and more complex. As a result of this transformation, a more broad definition of families is necessary. Interracial coupling (see Chaps. 4 and 5 for further discussions of interracial partnering and marriages) and existence of single-parent households are now examples of the norm among contemporary families.

Biracial families represent a growing segment of families in the United States. Like other monoracial families, biracial families take many forms, represent numerous constellations of structure, and vary in structure. Various social attitude changes have led to an increase in couples living together, divorce rates, single-parent homes, and interracial relationships. For example, in 1980, only 7% of all marriages were between individuals from different racial or ethnic groups (Wang, 2012). However, in 2013, the number of newlywed couples married to someone from a different race had increased to 12%. In addition, the number of individuals claiming a multiracial heritage increased from 2.4% in 2000 to nearly 3% in 2013 (Pew Research Center, 2015a). Furthermore, there has been a significant increase in the number of individuals having children with multiple partners. Some estimates indicate that 23% of fathers and 28% of mothers have children with more than one partner (Vanorman & Scommegna, 2016). Although the races of the partners are unknown, it is safe to assume that taken together with improved social attitudes towards interracial relationships and increased numbers of multiracial people, biracial families represent many diverse family forms. These diverse family structures include married couples, blended families, cohabiting families, single-parent families, gay and/or lesbian families, grandparent-headed families, and adoptive families. Because these families are unique, they have been the focus of very few research investigations. As the number of biracial families and biracial people continues to increase there is much research to be done.

This chapter addresses unique strengths and challenges encountered by diverse biracial families (DBFs). Despite the many forms biracial families can take, this chapter specifically explores single-parent biracial families, biracial stepfamilies, grandparents raising biracial grandchildren, and gay and lesbian biracial families. Appropriate supportive practice implications will be offered for professionals working with this unique segment of the population and we will provide suggestions for future research.

Review of Literature on Biracial Families

Single-Parent Biracial Families

According to the most recent US Census, single-parent households comprised approximately one-third of households with children, with 9.9 million being headed by single mothers and 1.8 million being headed by single fathers (U.S. Census Bureau, 2011a). The number of children living in two-parent households decreased from 87% in 1960 to 69% in 2014. In addition, the number of children raised in single-parent households has increased from 9% in 1960 to 26% in 2014 (Pew Research Center, 2015b). Explanations regarding reasons for the rise in single-parent families include an increase in divorce rates, an increase in individuals choosing to raise a child alone (either through birth or adoption), temporary circumstances that lead to single parenthood (e.g., as a result of military deployment), and single parenthood as a result of death (Gladding, 2015; Harris, 2013). Regardless of the circumstances leading to single parenthood, single-parent households experience a host of unique strengths and challenges.

In a summary of research focused on single-parent families, Chapman (2014) stated that some of the challenges encountered by single-parent families are related to poverty; homelessness; socio-emotional, physical, and cognitive delays among some children; childcare; and work-family conflicts. These outcomes have contributed to perceptions that have described single-parent homes as abnormal, deviant, or broken environments comprised of unmotivated parents that lacked education (Haleman, 2004; Stanley, Richardson, & Prior, 2005). The negative outcomes, particularly the ones focused on children, represent a small sample of single-parent homes. Most children from single-parent households tend to become well adjusted and psychologically healthy adults (Chapman, 2014). Barajas (2011) further noted that much of the research on single-parent families had numerous problems such as

(1) lack of diverse racial populations in research studies, (2) exclusions of different life experiences or other cultural factors, and (3) questionable sampling and statistical procedures (Barajas, 2011).

With regard to biracial children living in single-parent homes, Bratter and Damaske's (2010) analysis of the 2000 Census data indicated that the number of biracial children in single-female-headed households was higher than that in two-parent households. In addition, single White moms represented the largest group of parents with biracial children. These moms also had the lowest rates of poverty among all single moms. Compared to single White moms of monoracial children, single White moms of biracial children were more likely to live in poverty. Bratter and Damaske (2010) suggest "Given the importance of social networks to the livelihoods of single-parent families, women who cross racial lines in ways that are undesirable to friends and family may be cut off from those networks and thus more vulnerable to poverty" (p. 34).

Similar to other single-parent families, biracial families may experience stereotypes due to being viewed as "outside the norm." Despite the legality of interracial marriage, interracial couples do not experience the same privilege as monoracial couples because "interracial mixing continues to be regarded as an unconventional practice" (Bratter & Damaske, 2013, p. 488). For example, biracial families are less likely to be portrayed in the media, a privilege of which monoracial couples may not even be aware (Onwuachi-Willig & Willig-Onwuachi, 1990). Much of this is due to the assumptions and perceptions society holds about interracial couples and biracial children. Despite numerous studies that refute these early findings, biracial people have a controversial history and encounter many preconceived stereotypes. Early research on biracial people asserted that biracial people have a marginal identity and low self-esteem, and experience social isolation as a result of their heritage (Park, 1928; Stonequist, 1937). As a consequence, many in society believe that biracial people have blurred perceptions of their racial identity and assume that they struggle to develop a strong sense of self-worth. In addition, biracial families may struggle to experience cultural sensitivity and acceptance from others (Gladding, 2015). In contrast, biracial families possess high levels of cultural sensitivity, a strong sense of acceptance, strong family bonds, significant adaptability, and resiliency (Powell, Hamilton, Manago, & Cheng, 2014).

Because they often take on additional roles (e.g., breadwinner, caretaker, nurturer, disciplinarian), some single parents experience difficulty when defining and redefining roles and boundaries within the family. This can sometimes be challenging for children and result in additional complexity as biracial children seek to define themselves in relation to others. Further, due to limited parental contact and potentially fewer daily role models, some children from single-parent biracial families may experience additional struggles as they develop their racial identity. Regardless of their race, typical emotions children may experience as a result of the change in their family structure include guilt, sadness, and anger (Gladding, 2015).

Despite the challenges, single-parent families demonstrate important strengths that should be acknowledged. For example, for some single-parent families more flexibility in the family roles and rules can be seen as a strength, allowing for positive interactions within the family system. This flexibility may improve family bonds. Children in single-parent households learn responsibility and maturity as they may take on more adult roles throughout their development. This flexibility of roles and dispersing of responsibilities often lead single-parent families to interact more democratically than two-parent families, allowing the voices of each member to be a part of decision-making process and encouraging positive conflict resolution. Finally, single-parent families demonstrate high levels of learned resourcefulness (Gladding, 2015; Harris, 2013). According to Meichenbaum (1977) learned resourcefulness is a process that centers around developing certain behavioral attitudes that helps individuals successfully manage external stressors and gain control over stressful life circumstances. Single-parent biracial families encounter the typical problem and challenges as other monoracial families, yet have other cultural factors such as race and gender that may impact their family differently.

Reich (2002) discovered in a qualitative analysis of nine single White females raising Black/White biracial youth that all experienced significant losses in the personal lives. Five reported that they were disowned by their family and seven indicated that their family had racist attitudes about their relationship with Black men. In a more recent study, Rauktis, Fusco, Goodkind, and Bradley-King (2016) explored the lived experiences of 18 White moms. One mother was married and the others were separated, divorced, or cohabiting with biological father of their biracial child. All of the mothers experienced some level of social isolation and estrangement from family. However, after the birth of their biracial child, many indicated that their relationships with their White family improved (Rauktis et al., 2016). All the moms provided examples of how they and their biracial children received strange looks from strangers, were asked rude questions, and were called names. Similar to Diane (in opening story) most of these women held a color-blind worldview. However, their beliefs were often challenged by the racism their biracial children experienced.

In these unique families, it is not enough to only consider the experience of single-parent families or biracial families, but rather the intersection of these two experiences. Intersectionality refers to the idea that our different identities intersect to impact our identity as a whole (Crenshaw, 1991). In other words, the experience of being part of a single-parent family and a biracial family interacts to create an even more unique experience, and when it comes to family experiences external forces, such as culture and societal perceptions, can have a strong impact on family resiliency (Goldenberg et al., 2017). For example, if children in single-parent families have more difficulty developing a family identity due to having fewer parental role models, and children in biracial families are perceived to struggle to develop racial identity due to lacking a clearly defined racial culture, one could assume that this experience may be heightened for biracial children from single-parent families because they may only have access to part of their racial heritage. These children may not be exposed to their full heritage, and as a result may only identify culturally with the single parent raising them. This could be problematic if this identification is inconsistent with how they are viewed by the larger society. Similar to John (in opening story), many people believe that biracial children should identify with the parent of color because society will view them that way (Kerwin & Ponterotto, 1995); however this assumes that the child has access to a parent of color.

The confluence of being both biracial and from a single-parent household could impact internalized feelings about the self. These examples highlight the importance of raising knowledge and awareness of the experience of diverse biracial families (DBFs) because these families have unique challenges, experiences, and needs. The significance of the need for single parents to help their biracial children incorporate a biracial identity was succinctly articulated in the Silences documentary. This film, produced by Octavio Warnock-Graham (2006), was based on Octavio's life as a biracial person growing up in a small, predominantly White town in Ohio. Octavio's White mother moves back to her hometown pregnant and unwed, and although she later marries a White man and has two more children, Octavio's racial identity is never a topic of discussion among his family members. It is only when Octavio received hurtful comments from his elementary school classmates that he begins to question why he is different than everyone else in his family. His mother continues to keep his biological father's racial identity a secret throughout his childhood often stating that his father was Native American or Puerto Rican. Even though Octavio experienced love and support from his family, his biracial heritage was completely ignored because his mother and other family members failed to acknowledge, embrace, and incorporate his identity. Even though his White stepfather, extended family, and friends attempted to model a color-blind approach, Octavio wanted someone to acknowledge his racial heritage. As an adult he searches for his biological father. The documentary ends on a positive note when Octavio meets his Black biological father and half-sister, who have an amazing resemblance to him. The impact of undisclosed family secrets, the family's refusal to acknowledge and discuss racial issues, and challenges developing a biracial identity were articulated in the riveting stories throughout the documentary. The documentary further demonstrated the need for single parents of biracial children to embrace and incorporate a biracial identity, live in a diverse neighborhood, and have their children attend racially diverse schools.

Biracial Stepfamilies

Recent data suggests that approximately 16% of children live with a stepparent, stepsibling, or half-sibling, a number that has remained consistent since 1990. Additionally, approximately 63% of women who are remarried are in blended families (Pew Research Center, 2015b). These numbers are significant because of the myriad of ways in which stepfamilies may be created and the diversity in their composition. Furthermore, stepfamilies may include a stepfather or a stepmother, stepchildren (biological children from the mother, father, or both), or half-siblings. Additionally, one or all of these members may be present in the home full or part-time (Dunn, 2002; Gladding, 2015). In the case of biracial stepfamilies, the unique racial pairing adds an additional layer of complexity to our understanding of stepfamilies.

Some families experience several stressors prior to the blending of families and these transitions may cause negative emotions, such as stress, fear, anger, and guilt (Gladding, 2015). Transitioning into a blended family while already experiencing these negative emotions could make this type of family even more difficult. In addition, another stressor that may arise is financial hardship (Dunn, 2002; Jensen et al., 2015). Forming new relationships and bonds is an additional stressor for stepfamilies, as certain members may experience different levels of bonding with different members and may struggle to incorporate new members. It may take up to 5 years for stepparents to establish strong relationships with stepchildren. Navigating differing levels of adaptability and cohesion can be an additional challenge (Gladding, 2015). Perceptions of positive parent–child relationships may be of particular importance in successful family functioning, specifically the mother–child relationship (King, Boyd, & Thorsen, 2015). Adjustment to the blended family may be difficult for some members. This could also be further impacted by when the transition occurs and the racial pairing. For example, one researcher found that children who enter stepfamilies at younger ages have an easier time adjusting than those who are older (Dunn, 2002).

Some of the issues experienced by monoracial stepfamilies may be more intense for biracial stepfamilies as a result of the racial makeup of the stepparent, monoracial children, and biracial children. For example, adjustment may be particularly difficult in biracial stepfamilies as these families will need to learn to blend their individual ways of managing family tasks while also learning to blend their differing cultures. On the other hand, biracial stepfamilies may be at a unique advantage in their ability to remain open and flexible with family roles and rules. These families have a wide range of life and cultural experiences that offer options for how to manage family tasks. Unique perspectives from each family, based on previous experiences and culture, allow the family to work together to creatively navigate conflict and family dynamics.

This perspective was reflected in Mitchell's (2014) qualitative study that explored the life experiences of three African-American stepfamilies that included four Black/White biracial stepdaughters and one stepdaughter of Black/White/Mexican decent. Results indicated that all three families identified themselves as an African-American family as a result of cultural traditions and skin tone. Stepparents also reported that they observed behavioral changes in how their biracial daughters acted when they were with their Black extended family members compared to their White family members (Mitchell, 2014). For biracial children, this behavioral change is known as code-switching and is a normal process (Root, 2003).

Grandparents Raising Biracial Grandchildren

The number of grandparents raising grandchildren in the United States is more than 2.7 million (Ross, Kang, & Cron, 2015; U.S. Census Bureau, 2011), an increase of 500,000 since 2001 (Minkler & Fuller-Thomson, 2005; U.S. Census Bureau, 2002).

This increase appears to be in response to state and federal policy changes that mandate preference be given to relatives in foster children placement decisions (Minkler & Fuller-Thomson, 2005). Given simultaneous increases in multiracial children in the United States, it is likely that the number of multiracial children being raised by their grandparents has also increased in recent decades.

Although estimates of multiracial children raised by grandparents are not available, data suggest that an increasing number of children are part of grandfamilies, or families with grandparents as the sole caregivers (Kaplan & Perez-Porter, 2014). More than 10% of all children in the United States live with caregivers who are grandparents or other relatives (AARP, 2011; Bachay & Buzzi, 2012). Forty-nine percent of children raised by their grandparents are cared for by both grandparents, 46% are raised solely by their grandmother, and 5% solely by their grandfather (Dunifon, Ziol-Guest, & Kopko, 2014; Pilkauskas & Dunifon, 2016).

Grandparent-led families are often either a three-generational or skipped generational household. Three-generational home environments typically include the grandparents, grandchildren, and adult children. This household is often created as a result of numerous factors that included financial hardship, divorce, illness, and a desire for grandparents to help their children and grandchildren (Scommegna, 2012). The skipped generational households consist of only the grandparent(s) and grandchildren. The primary causes for the creation of this home included parental mental illness, incarceration, substance abuse, and or child neglect. Grandparents often become primary caretakers of grandchildren to keep them from being placed in welfare agencies or foster care (Scommegna, 2012).

There are a number of challenges that grandparents may encounter when raising grandchildren, including (1) concerns about their ability to be an effective parent again as a result of their age, (2) their future health, (3) whether or not their grandchildren will make responsible decisions as they mature, and (4) concerns that the grandchildren could be taken from them at any moment if they do not have legal custody (Bachay & Buzzi, 2012). Poverty is another primary concern as grandparents parenting grandchildren are disproportionately poor. Nearly 30% of Black grandparents that live below the poverty line are raising grandchildren (Minkler & Fuller-Thomson, 2005).

General research on the needs of children raised by grandparents suggests that this population faces many challenges. Researchers have found higher rates of behavior problems and lower rates of academic achievement among grandchildren raised by grandparents than those raised by parents (Kelley, Whitley, & Campos, 2011; Pilkauskas & Dunifon, 2016; Smith & Palmieri, 2007). Despite these documented outcomes, it is important to note that children being raised by grandparents fare better behaviorally and academically than children in foster care (Pilkauskas & Dunifon, 2016).

Although no research has provided data on the number of grandparents parenting biracial grandchildren, grandparenting monoracial grandchildren has been cited more often in the African-American community (Minkler & Fuller-Thomson, 2005; Ross et al., 2015). For example, 4% of White children, 5% of Hispanic children, and 9% of African-American children live in grandfamilies (Fields, 2003; Minkler &

Fuller-Thomson, 2005; Ross et al., 2015). The increase for African-Americans is not surprising because the extended family often plays an important role in the African-American community, where the grandmother is often perceived as the protector of their grandchildren and the stabilizing force in the family. White grandparents play an active role in the lives of their grandchildren; however African-American grandparents tend to have a more substantial role in the racial socialization of their grandchildren (Chancler, 2014). Racial socialization is a significant factor in the development of biracial children (Root, 2003) and includes cultural socialization and preparation for bias (see Chap. 8 for more information).

Research on the unique needs of biracial grandfamilies is lacking. However, Chancler's (2014) research on seven African-American grandmothers raising their Black/White grandchildren revealed some intriguing results. First, the African-American grandmothers believed that it was necessary for them to justify their child's decision to procreate a biracial child. Second, even though grandmothers indicated that they recognized their grandchildren as being both Black and White, they racially socialized them as if they were Black. Third, grandmothers were keenly aware of how physical appearance would impact societal treatment of their biracial grandchildren, and thus wanted their grandchildren to feel loved and secure in a safe environment (Chancler, 2014).

Challenges faced by biracial grandfamilies may be more intensified given generational differences related to racial attitudes. Many grandparents were raised in a more racially segregated time, when negative attitudes towards interracial relationships and biracial children were prevalent. For example, in Chancler's study one African-American grandmother reflected on her distrust of White people and indicated that her feelings towards them had become mixed after the birth of her biracial grandson. While she indicated that she was supportive of her grandson having contact with both sides of his family, she was going to socialize him as Black because that is how society would perceive him. Future research should explore how the race of the grandparents and the gender of biracial grandchildren may impact the family environment. Further, more research is warranted to understand the context of identity formation for children in biracial grandfamilies, particularly if grandparents are raising other monoracial grandchildren.

Same-Sex Biracial Families

Like multiracial grandfamilies, little research has been published on same-sex biracial families. An emerging body of research is focusing on same-sex parenting and many of these findings may be applicable to multiracial families. The percentage of households in the United States headed by same-sex couples has historically been challenging to estimate. Due to fear of discrimination, many same-sex partners conceal their sexual orientation (Lambert, 2005). Likewise, many same-sex parents choose to conceal their identities due to fears over losing custody of children because of their sexual orientation (Lambert, 2005; Patterson, 2000). It is clear, though, that same-sex parents have become increasingly more common in the past decades (Lambert, 2005; Richards, Rothblum, Beauchaine, & Balsam, 2017). In a 2002 survey of parenting among gay men and lesbian women, 33% of lesbians and 17% of gay men reported having children (Gates, Badgett, Macomber, & Chambers, 2007). But in a similar survey conducted in 2008, researchers found that 49% of lesbians/bisexual women and 19% of gay/bisexual men reported having children (Gates, 2011; Richards et al., 2017). The Pew Research Center (2015b) estimates that 1% of households are headed by same-sex couples. They further estimate that approximately 130,000 of these couples are raising children (Pew Research Center, 2015a, 2015b) .

Same-sex families come in several forms. For example, same-sex parents may have children from a prior heterosexual relationship. If parents are sharing custody of the children they may become blended and/or stepfamilies. In addition, same-sex individuals may also become parents by adopting or fostering children. Alternatively, lesbian and bisexual women may have children via donor insemination, and gay men may do the same with surrogate mothers (Richards et al., 2017). The variations in these family structures and the potential biracial nature of these families have implications for the children being raised in them.

Due to historic discrimination towards same-sex parents, much research on these families has focused on exploring unfounded harmful differences in the upbringing of children in same-sex families. To date, the overwhelming majority of research on this topic has found that children raised in same-sex families have the same cognitive, social, and behavioral skills as children raised in heterosexual families (Chan, Brooks, Raboy, & Patterson, 1998; Patterson, 2000). The development of children raised in these families appears no different from the development of children in heterosexual families (Lambert, 2005; Patterson, 2000). Moreover, Gartrell et al. (2000) found that children with lesbian mothers had reportedly higher academic and social competence than children from heterosexual families, as well as less frequent social problems and externalizing behaviors. Only one significant difference among these populations has emerged. In a study of children with gay fathers or lesbian mother, Ray and Gregory (2001) found that nearly half of the children reported teasing about their parents' sexual orientations. This teasing may take its toll on children over time and is a concern that needs to be monitored. Being biracial may deepen the emotional burden because of the stereotypes historically associated with this unique segment of the population.

Same-sex biracial families will likely encounter unique challenges related to the juxtaposition of race and sexuality. Despite greater acceptance of interracial relationships and same-sex partnerships, gay and lesbian biracial families may still be confronted with myths specifically associated with their sexual orientation and race. These myths may include the following: (a) gay and lesbian parents are more likely to molest their children and be involved in appropriate sexual behavior in front of their children, (b) gay and lesbian individuals are emotionally unstable and not capable of being good parents, (c) children raised by lesbian mothers are more likely to develop psychological problems, (d) children will develop homosexual preferences as a result of living with gay and lesbian parents (McIntyre, 1994), (e) children will be confused about their racial heritage, and (f) children will experience negative psychological consequences due to difficulties with their racial identity. However, many research investigations have refuted these claims. In a summary of research findings on same-sex parents, Patterson (2005) debunked these myths and further revealed that there was a great level of diversity among same-sex parents.

Extended Family

The extended family of DBFs plays a significant role in creating a healthy family environment and could help alleviate some of the stress and challenges associated with DBFs. The extended family may consist of relatives from both sides of the family and include grandparents, aunts, uncles, cousins, and close friends that parents and children share a special connection with. It is important to be mindful of how the racial makeup of DBFs may impact the level of extended family support. Some extended family members of DBFs may provide warm, supportive, and nurturing relationships, while others may yield a family climate that is cold, and disowning (Dhooper, 2003). Outcomes from Pew Research Center (2015a) indicated that while only 10% of multiracial adults indicated that they had been unfairly treated by extended family members or at times made to feel like an outsider, for Black-White biracial adults that number increased to 21%. For multiracial adults that were American Indian, Black, and White, the numbers were similar at 19%, further highlighting the impact of race.

Often without conscious intention, DBFs may be subjected to microaggressions at the hands of their extended family. Microaggressions are defined as "brief and commonplace daily verbal, behavioral, or environmental indignities, whether intentional, or unintentional that communicate hostile, derogatory, or negative racial slights and insults towards people of color" (Sue et al., 2007, p. 271). According to Johnston and Nadal (2010), microaggressions that multiracial individuals experience are placed into six categories. The categories are as follows: (1) denial of multiracial identity which happens when monoracial individuals invalidate the experiences of multiracial persons, (2) exoticization and objectification occur when a multiracial person is treated like an object rather than a person, (3) assumption of mistaken or monoracial identity happens when a multiracial person is assumed to be from a different racial group, (4) exclusion and isolation typically happen when a multiracial person is made to feel excluded or isolated because of their racial heritage, (5) pathologizing of experiences and identity microaggressions take place when the identity of the multiracial person is perceived as abnormal, and (6) stereotypical microaggressions happen when multiracial individuals experience prejudicial behaviors that monoracial individuals also experience based upon others' biased attitudes. As a result, some biracial persons experience isolation within their family, particularly within their extended family. In addition, biracial people report feelings of distress as a result of being treated both less favored and more favored than monoracial family members (e.g., cousins). Racial microaggressions may be more common in the lives of biracial persons, compared to monoracial peers, and have a significant impact on identity and mental health (Johnston and Nadal, 2010). More research is needed to identify microaggressive commonalities among DBFs.

Practice Implications

There are a number of strengths and challenges that should be taken into consideration when working with DBFs. Biracial children should be encouraged to openly discuss their racial heritage and explore identity options. Biracial children should be encouraged to develop friendships with individuals from diverse racial backgrounds by attending racially diverse schools and living in racially diverse neighborhoods. Parents should acknowledge that their biracial child's racial background is different from their own and should make efforts to incorporate their child's multiple heritages. Parents should help biracial children make contact with positive role models reflective of their multiple heritages. Families may self-identify as a biracial, multiracial, or interracial family.

It is essential that individuals working with DBFs become aware of their personal attitudes and beliefs about race, gender, interracial partnerships, biracial children, divorce, and gay and lesbian multiracial families. Individuals are encouraged to confront inaccurate perceptions. This may be accomplished by conducting an internal audit using the following questions as a guiding tool (Harris, 2009, 2013):

- What are my real thoughts and feelings towards DBFs?
- How do I feel about biracial children and how are my perceptions impacted by their gender?
- What thoughts do I have when I see a biracial family compared to a traditional family?
- Am I aware of how my own gender, race, and sexual orientation may impact my perceptions of DBFs?
- How much does the race of individuals from DBFs impact my perceptions? For example, am I more supportive of a biracial family consisting of an Asian and White parent compared to biracial family consisting of a Black and White parent?
- How do I feel about grandparents raising biracial grandchildren?
- Does the race or age of the grandparents impact my perceptions?
- How do I feel about same-sex biracial families?
- Am I aware of how my perceptions of biracial children may be influenced by their siblings and phenotype or physical appearance?
- How does the socioeconomic status of DBFs influence my perceptions of issues the families may encounter?
- Am I aware of the societal stressors that DBFs may encounter and how the stressors may be influenced by the uniqueness of the family structure?

This type of personal self-analysis and cultural audit may prove challenging; however, it is a necessary first step (Harris, 2009, 2013).

It is essential that interracial stepfamilies establish and maintain a healthy family environment. This requires that parents (1) empathize and understand their children, (2) avoid speaking negatively about the other parent in front of children, (3) validate their child's experiences, (4) avoid making negative comments about the other parent that may intensify loyalty bonds from their children, (5) commit to improving communication with children in a safe and productive manner, and (6) approach children with love and affection (Jensen et al., 2015; Papernow, 2013).

Strengths of Diverse Biracial Families

When considering DBFs, given the social and cultural challenges that some of the families may encounter, it would be beneficial to help these families understand how their challenges and strengths intersect in a manner that creates unique opportunities. For example, many demonstrate strength as they learn new ways or modify traditional methods of managing family tasks while simultaneously blending their differing cultures, traditions, and values. DBFs may also have a unique advantage in their ability to remain open and flexible with family roles and rules. These families have a wide range of life and cultural experiences that offer options on how to develop as a multiracial family unit. Unique perspectives from each family, based on previous experiences, may allow the family to work together in a manner that helps them navigate conflicts and embrace other cultures more so than monoracial families.

Professionals working with DBFs should highlight the positive aspects of a multiracial background. Results from Pew Research Center (2015a) indicated that nearly 60% of multiracial adults indicated that their racial background helped them become more open to other cultures and more understanding of people from different racial backgrounds. Professionals working with DBFs are encouraged to identify strengths that include resiliency, understanding and dealing with racism, and resisting racism (Laszloffy, 2005).

Future Directions

The research on DBFs is virtually nonexistent. For example, Charmaraman, Woo, Quach, and Erkut (2014) conducted a content and methodological review of research from 1990 to 2009 with a specific focus on how researchers have studied multiracial populations. A total of 133 studies were included in this analysis and the results indicated that 41% of the studies did not report a gender breakdown and 70% of the studies focused on high school adolescents or young college-aged adults. The major constructs explored focused on racial identity (55%); impact of physical appearance and phenotype (43%); exposure to ethnic, racial, and cultural diversity within the community (33%); influence of peers (32%); and a sense of exclusion or belonging to a specific racial group. The only family characteristic studied was family racial socialization (26%). Noticeably missing were constructs specifically focused on DBFs. Additional analysis of multiracial research has further confirmed that the exclusion of DBFs continues to routinely occur (Gaither, 2015).

Given the improved racial climate towards interracial dating and marriage (see Chaps. 4 and 5 for more information) we most likely will continue to see an increase in the number of DBFs. As a result of this societal transformation, more research is needed to provide empirical evidence that will increase our understanding of the experiences of DBFs. This research is needed to develop approaches to better support biracial families and their children (Lambert, 2005).

With regard to biracial stepfamilies, future studies should explore the relationships among family variables, including race of couple, length of their relationship prior to marriage, size of combined family, number of children brought into the marriage, and racial background of children brought into the marriage. Additionally more research is needed on single-parent biracial families to better understand the unique challenges they may encounter. Some variables worthy of exploration include the race of the parent, physical appearance of the child and parent, type of family support received, gender of child, level of contact with other parent, extended family, sibling relationships, how the single parent understands and deals with racism, and how identity development is supported. A better understanding of the role of each family member, age of children, sexual orientation, how the DBF originated, how cultural conflicts are managed, and how cultural values and traditions are celebrated are factors that will help understand the challenges DBFs encounter along with the strengths they possess.

Given the number of grandparents raising their grandchildren, more research is needed on all elements of the family including variables such as family socioeconomic status, specific biracial heritage of the grandchild, gender of grandchild, specific reasons that led to this family formation, level of extended family involvement, and race of grandparents.

Conclusion

Diverse biracial families comprise a unique segment of our evolving society and will likely continue to increase. Projections from the Census Bureau have suggested that by 2060, the multiracial population will triple as a result of increased divorce rates, declining number of monoracial marriages, and an increase in the number of interracial marriages and partnerships (Pew Research Center, 2015a). A sharper focus is therefore needed to better understand the unique family culture of DBFs. For example, a grandparent raising a biracial grandchild may experience a different set of challenges and possess different strengths compared to a single female raising a biracial child. The same may also be stated for same-sex biracial families compared to biracial stepfamilies. Regardless of the family structure, given the history associated with biracial children, interracial partnerships, interracial marriages, sexual orientation, and single-parent families, it is imperative these factors be taken into consideration. While social stigma associated with DBFs remains a challenge these families must guard against, it is equally imperative to recognize the unique strengths of these families.

References

AARP. (2011). *Grandfact Sheets*. Retrieved from http://www.aarp.org/relationships/friends-family/grandfacts-sheets

Bachay, J. B., & Buzzi, B. M. (2012). When grandma and grandpa become mom and dad: Engaging grandfamilies in clinical practice. *Kriminologija & Socijalna Integracija, 20*(1), 63–70.

Barajas, M. S. (2011). Academic achievement of children in single parent homes: A critical review. *The Hilltop Review, 5*, 13–21.

Bratter, J., & Damaske, S. (2010). *What about these children? Assessing poverty among the 'hidden population' of multiracial children in single-mother families*. University of Kentucky Center for Poverty Research Discussion Paper Series, DP2010-09. Retrieved from http://www.ukcpr.org/Publications/DP2010-09.pdf

Bratter, J., & Damaske, S. (2013). Poverty at a racial crossroads: Poverty among the multiracial children of single mothers. *Journal of Marriage and Family, 75*, 486–502. https://doi.org/10.1111/jomf.12012

Chan, R. W., Brooks, R. C., Raboy, B., & Patterson, C. J. (1998). Division of labor among Lesbian and heterosexual parents: Associations with children's adjustment. *Journal of Family Psychology, 12*(3), 402–419.

Chancler, L. M. L. (2014). *Role of Black grandmothers in the racial socialization of their biracial grandchildren*. Unpublished doctoral dissertation, Kansas State University, Manhattan, KS.

Chapman, A. (2014). Single-parent families. In M. J. Coleman & L. H. Ganong (Eds.), *The social history of the American family: An encyclopedia* (pp. 1188–1193). Thousand Oaks, CA: Sage Publications.

Charmaraman, L., Woo, M., Quach, A., & Erkut, S. (2014). How researchers studied multiracial populations: Content analysis and methodological review of 20 years of research. *Cultural Diversity and Ethnic Minority Psychology, 20*(3), 336–352. https://doi.org/10.1037/a0035437

Crenshaw, K. (1991). Mapping the margins: Intersectionality, identity politics, and violence against women of color. *Stanford Law Review, 43*(6), 1241.

Dhooper, S. S. (2003). Social work response to the needs of biracial Americans. *Journal of Ethnic and Cultural Diversity in Social Work, 12*, 19–47. https://doi.org/10.1300/J051v12n04_02

Dunifon, R., Ziol-Guest, K., & Kopko, K. (2014). Grandparental co-residence and family well-being: Implications for research and policy. *Annals of the American Academy of Political and Social Science, 654*, 110–126.

Dunn, J. (2002). The adjustment of children in stepfamilies: Lessons from community studies. *Child and Adolescent Mental Health, 7*(4), 154–161.

Fields, J. (2003). Children's living arrangements and characteristics: March 2002. In *Current population reports* (pp. 20–547). Washington, DC: U.S. Census Bureau.

Gaither, S. E. (2015). "Mixed" results: Multiracial research and identify exploration. *Current Directions in Psychological Science, 24*(2), 114–119. https://doi.org/10.1177/0963721414558115

Gartrell, N., Banks, A., Reed, N., Hamilton, J., Rodas, C., & Deck, A. (2000). The National Lesbian Family Study: 3. Interviews with mothers of five year-olds. *American Journal of Orthopsychiatry, 70*, 542–548.

Gates, G. J. (2011). *How many people are lesbian, gay, bisexual, and transgender?* Los Angeles, CA: The Williams Institute.

Gates, G. J., Badgett, M. V. L., Macomber, J. E., & Chambers, K. (2007). *Adoption and foster care by gay and lesbian parents in the United States*. Retrieved from http://williamsinstitute.law.ucla.edu/wp-content/uploads/Gates-Badgett-Macomber-Chambers-Final-Adoption-ReportMar-2007.pdf

Gladding, S. T. (2015). *Family therapy: History, theory, and practice* (6th ed.). Boston, MA: Pearson.

Goldenberg, I., Stanton, M., & Goldenberg, H. (2017). *Family therapy: An overview* (9th ed.). Boston, MA: Cengage Learning.

Haleman, D. L. (2004). Great expectations: Single mothers in higher education. *International Journal of Qualitative Studies in Education, 17*, 769–784.

Harris, H. L. (2009). Counseling multiple heritage children. In R. C. Henriksen Jr. & D. A. Paladino (Eds.), *Counseling multiple heritage individuals, couples, and families* (pp. 45–64). Alexandria, VA: American Counseling Association.

Harris, H. L. (2013). Counseling single-parent multiracial families. *The Family Journal: Counseling and Therapy for Couples and Families, 21*(4), 386–395.

Jensen, T. M., Shafer, K., & Holmes, E. K. (2015). Transitioning to stepfamily life: The influence of closeness with biological parents and stepparents on children's stress. *Child & Family Social Work, 22*, 275–286. https://doi.org/10.1111/cfs.12237

Johnston, M. P., & Nadal, K. L. (2010). Multiracial microaggressions: Exposing monoracism in every-day life and clinical practice. In D. W. Sue (Ed.), *Microaggressions and marginality: Manifestation, dynamics, and impact* (pp. 123–144). New York: Wiley & Sons.

Kaplan, M., & Perez-Porter, M. (2014). Support for grandfamilies: A mosaic of intervention strategies. *Journal of Intergenerational Relationships, 12*(2), 99–112. https://doi.org/10.1080/15350770.2014.901076

Kelley, S. J., Whitley, D. M., & Campos, P. E. (2011). Behavior problems in children raised by grandmothers: The role of caregiver distress, family resources, and the home environment. *Children and Youth Services Review, 33*(11), 2138–2145.

Kerwin, K., & Ponterotto, J. G. (1995). Biracial identity development. In J. G. Ponterotto, J. M. Casas, L. A. Suzuki, & C. M. Alexander (Eds.), *Handbook of multicultural counseling* (pp. 199–217). Thousand Oaks, CA: Sage.

King, V., Boyd, L. M., & Thorsen, M. L. (2015). Adolescents' perceptions of family belonging in stepfamilies. *Journal of Marriage and Family, 77*, 761–774.

Lambert, S. (2005). Gay and lesbian families: What we know and where to go from here. *The Family Journal: Counseling and Therapy for Couples and Families, 13*, 43–51. https://doi.org/10.1177/1066480704270150

Laszloffy, T. A. (2005). Multiracial families. *Family Therapy Magazine, 2*, 39–43.

McIntyre, D. H. (1994). Gay parents and child custody. A struggle under the legal system. *Mediation Quarterly, 12*, 135–149.

Meichenbaum, D. (1977). *Cognitive-behavior modification*. New York: Plenum.

Minkler, M., & Fuller-Thomson, E. (2005). African American grandparents raising grandchildren: A national study using the Census 2000 American Community Survey. *Journal of Gerontology: Psychological Sciences, 60B*(2), S82–S92. https://doi.org/10.1093/geronb/60.2.S82

Mitchell, Y. T. (2014). *"My daughter is a White girl in a mixed body that wishes she were Black:" Monoracial parents perceptions of mixed-race children and racial identity development.* Unpublished doctoral dissertation, Kansas State University, Manhattan, KS.

Onwuachi-Willig, A., & Willig-Onwuachi, J. (1990). A house divided: The invisibility of the multiracial family. *Harvard Civil Rights-Civil Liberties Law Review, 44*, 231–253.

Papernow, P. L. (2013). *Surviving and thriving in stepfamily relationships: What works and what doesn't*. New York: Routledge.

Park, R. E. (1928). Human migration and the marginal man. *American Journal of Sociology, 33*, 881–893.

Patterson, C. J. (2000). Family relationships of lesbians and gay men. *Journal of Marriage and the Family, 62*, 1052–1069.

Patterson, C. J. (2005). *Lesbian and gay parents and their children: Summary of research findings*. Washington, DC: American Psychological Association.

Pew Research Center. (2015a). *Multiracial in America: Proud, diverse, and growing in numbers*. DC: Washington.

Pew Research Center. (2015b). *Parenting in America: Outlook, worries, aspirations are strongly linked to family situation*. DC: Washington.

Pew Research Center. (2016). *On views of race and inequality, Blacks and Whites are worlds apart*. DC: Washington.

Pilkauskas, N. V., & Dunifon, R. E. (2016). Understanding grandfamilies: Characteristics of grandparents, nonresident parents, and children. *Journal of Marriage and Family, 78*, 623–633.

Powell, B., Hamilton, L., Manago, B., & Cheng, S. (2014). Implications of changing family forms for children. *Annual Review of Sociology, 42*, 301–322.

Rauktis, M. E., Fusco, R. A., Goodkind, S., & Bradley-King, C. (2016). Motherhood in liminal spaces: White mothers' parenting Black/White children. *Journal of Women and Social Work, 31*, 434–449. https://doi.org/10.1177/0886109916630581

Ray, V., & Gregory, R. (2001). School experiences of the children of lesbian and gay parents. *Family Matters, 59*, 28–35.

Reich, J. A. (2002). Building a home on a border: How single White women raising Multiracial children construct racial meaning. In C. Levine-Rasky (Ed.), *Working through Whiteness: Internation perspective* (pp. 179–208). Albany, NY: State University of New York Press.

Richards, M. A., Rothblum, E. D., Beauchaine, T. P., & Balsam, K. F. (2017). Adult children of same-sex and heterosexual couples: Demographic "thriving". *Journal of GLBT Family Studies, 13*, 1–15. https://doi.org/10.1080/1550428X.2016.1164648

Root, M. P. P. (2003). Multiracial families and children: Implications for educational research and practice. In J. A. Banks & C. A. McGee Banks (Eds.), *Handbook of research on multicultural education* (pp. 110–124). San Fransciso, CA: Jossey-Bass.

Ross, M. E. T., Kang, D.-H., & Cron, S. (2015). Psychological profile, salivary cortisol, C-reactive protein, and perceived health of grandmothers with childrearing responsibility. *Journal of Family Issues, 36*, 1904–1927.

Scommegna, P. (2012). More U.S. children raised by grandparents. *Population Reference Bureau*. Retrieved from http://www.prb.org/Publications/Articles/2012/US-children-grandparents.aspx

Smith, G. C., & Palmieri, P. A. (2007). Risk of psychological difficulties among children raised by custodial grandparents. *Psychiatric Services, 58*, 1303–1310.

Stanley, F., Richardson, S., & Prior, M. (2005). *Children of the lucky country?* Sydney: Macmillan.

Stonequist, E. V. (1937). *The marginal man: A study in personality and culture and conflict*. New York: Russell & Russell.

Sue, D. W., Capodilupo, C. M., Torino, G. C., Bucceri, J. M., Holder, A. M., Nadal, K. L., et al. (2007). Racial microaggressions in everyday life: Implications for counseling. *American Psychologist, 62*, 271–286. https://doi.org/10.1037/0003-066X.62.4.271

U.S. Census Bureau. (2002). *Grandparents living with own grandchildren under 18 years and responsibility for own grandchildren*: Table PCT015 of the Census 2001 Supplementary Survey. Retrieved from http://factfinder.census.gov/servlet/BasicFactsServlet

U.S. Census Bureau (2011a): (2005–2009 American Community Survey). *Selected social characteristics in the United States*, Miami-Dade County, Florida. Retrieved from http://factfinder.census.gov/servlet/ADPTable?_bm=y&-geo_id=050

U.S. Census Bureau. (2011b). *America's families and living arrangements: 2010*. Retrieved from http://www.census.gov/population/www/socdemo/hh-fam/cps2010.html

Vanorman, A. G., & Scommegna, P. (2016). Understanding the dynamics of family change in the United States. *Population Bulletin, 71*(1). Retrieved from www.pbr.org

Wang, W. (2012). *The rise of intermarriage*. Washington, DC: Pew Research Center.

Warnock-Graham, O. (Producer & Director). (2006). *Silences*. Blooming Grove, NY: New Day Films.

Racial Identity: Choices, Context, and Consequences

Annamaria Csizmadia and Susan White

Corinne, a 14-year-old Black-White biracial girl, was born in a predominantly White, Midwestern college town. She spent her first 5 years in university housing with her family, which exposed her to a rich array of highly educated people of diverse ethnic-racial, cultural, linguistic, and religious backgrounds. She attended preschool with children of faculty and students where her best friends were Black and Asian-American children. Her family attended a church with graduate students from Asia, South America, and Africa, as well as White and interracial American families from the community. Family, friends, and those familiar with her family background identified her as biracial. Strangers identified her as Black. At this age, she did not identify herself in terms of race, although she understood that her mother and father differed in ethnic origin and skin color.

At the age of 5, she moved to an ethnically-racially diverse urban area in the Northeast where her mother became a college professor. Corinne attended an ethno-racially and socio-economically diverse public school and an after-school program with a predominantly low-income, Black, Latino, and immigrant student body. Despite the diverse social environment, here she encountered a different set of experiences. Peers' questions such as "Are you adopted?" and "Is this really your mom?" made Corrine ask her mother whether she was indeed adopted. She would explain to her that children who asked these questions were not used to families with members who looked different. At other times, an adult would speak to her in Spanish assuming that she was a Latina. Since sixth grade, Corrine has been attending an independent school with children, most of whom come from wealthy White American families. With a keen interest in diversity and social justice, she became

A. Csizmadia (✉)
Human Development and Family Studies, University of Connecticut, Stamford, CT, USA
e-mail: Annamaria.Csizmadia@uconn.edu

S. White
Clinical Mental Health Counseling, Southern Connecticut State University,
New Haven, CT, USA

R. Nazarinia Roy, A. Rollins (eds.), *Biracial Families*,
https://doi.org/10.1007/978-3-319-96160-6_11

a leader in the school diversity club. Her best friend in school is White, and she remains close with two friends whom she has known since she first moved to the East Coast. Both girls are children of color, from well-educated immigrant-origin families. Over the years, Corinne has had open conversations about her ethnic-racial background and other race-related issues with her family. She has been encouraged to choose her own racial identity instead of being forced or expected to identify as monoracial or biracial. She identifies as a biracial person of color.

Racial Identity: Choices, Context, and Consequences

Greater public visibility, growing social acceptance, and institutional recognition have opened up the opportunity for many contemporary biracial individuals to choose from a variety of racial identity options. Although macro-level (e.g., legal) barriers have all but disappeared, microlevel challenges (e.g., multiracial microaggressions) persist (Nadal, Sriken, Davidoff, Wong, & McLean, 2013). Some of Corinne's experiences with identity questioning and misidentification described in the opening story illustrate these microlevel challenges. Thus, it is important to understand how racial identity choices are exercised differently within and across social contexts, and how these options in turn affect development. The purpose of this chapter is to elucidate the considerable developmental diversity that exists in the multiracial population by highlighting the role that variation in racial self-understanding and identification plays in tandem with individual characteristics and environmental influences in positive and negative psychosocial adjustment, academic adjustment, and health behaviors.

Research on the multiracial population has increased impressively since 2000 when the US Census for the first time in its history allowed respondents to mark more than one racial category in response to the race question (Jones & Bullock, 2013). The focus of this scholarship has been primarily on racial identity, its individual and contextual predictors, and to a lesser extent its developmental correlates and consequences (for a review, see Csizmadia, Brunsma, & Cooney, 2012). Comparisons of biracial youth to their monoracial majority and minority peers on a variety of adjustment indicators have yielded mixed results. These between-group comparisons do not address within-group variation. In contrast, recent research suggests considerable developmental diversity in the multiracial population, and that the developmental consequences of racial identity may be context dependent. In other words, how racial identity impacts developmental adjustment depends on the social, cultural, ethnic-racial, or geographic context within which multiracial people grow up and live. For example, Black-White biracial adolescents who identify as biracial may feel accepted in ethnically and racially diverse peer groups. However, in ethnically and racially homogenous peer groups, they may feel less acceptance and experience anxiety or depression associated with (perceived or actual) peer rejection.

In this chapter, drawing on the ecological approach (Rockquemore, Brunsma, & Delgado, 2009), we review the literature on racial identity among biracial people, and we discuss select individual and contextual factors that shape their racial identity choices. We then review research in which multiracial youth are compared to their monoracial counterparts on indicators of positive and negative psychosocial adjustment, health behaviors, and academic adjustment. We also summarize existent research on associations between different multiracial youth's racial identity choices (e.g., biracial, monoracial, and situationally changing identity) and diverse developmental outcomes (e.g., depression). Given the heterogeneous nature of the multiracial population (Binning, Unzueta, Huo, & Molina, 2009), we review, where available, research on specific biracial subgroups. We end with strategies to support biracial youth's racial identity and developmental adjustment and conclude with a discussion of gaps and directions for future research.

Racial Identity: Choices in Context

Historically, hypodescent rules relegated biracial people to a racial identity that reflected the minority race of their family background. Black-White biracial individuals' racial identity in particular was determined by the one-drop rule, which ascribed a Black identity to anyone with a traceable amount of African ancestry (Davis, 1991). As described in the opening story, during her early years in a Midwestern small town, strangers tended to identify Corinne as Black, which illustrates the enduring effect of the one-drop rule in this region.

The beginning of the twenty-first century ushered in an era of greater public recognition and visibility for biracial people, and with that decreasing structural constraints on and greater agency for racial identity (e.g., Csizmadia et al., 2012). However, "the influence (including removal) of structural constraints is filtered through the social microcosm within which multiracial youth live their daily lives" (Csizmadia et al., 2012, p. 37), which contributes to developmental diversity in this population. Despite the fact that anti-miscegenation laws, which prohibited interracial marriages, were declared unconstitutional in 1967, and that social acceptance of interracial families has increased, some interracial families and multiracial children still experience social ostracism in their hometown or neighborhood. Thus, racial identity theories must reflect an *ecological approach* (Rockquemore et al., 2009).

Two particularly relevant assumptions of the ecological approach for understanding developmental diversity in the contemporary multiracial population are that for biracial people: (a) racial identity development does not follow a linear path, and thus there is no psychologically ideal racial identity type, and (b) racial identity is context dependent (Rockquemore et al., 2009). Therefore, "race is not an entirely structurally imposed status for mixed-race people but instead is characterized by fluidity and constrained choice" (Rockquemore et al., 2009, p. 30). Contemporary biracial people can choose from various racial identities, and they negotiate their racial identity in consideration of salient contextual influences (e.g., Csizmadia et al., 2012). For example, in order to be accepted, a Black-White adolescent may identify as Black in a school whose student body is predominantly or exclusively

Black American. In contrast, Black-White teens who attend ethno-racially diverse schools whose population includes numerous multiracial students may opt to identify as biracial given that they belong to a visible multiracial group. Consequently, we argue that the dynamic interaction of a chosen racial identity and concomitant contextual constraints powerfully shapes multiracial youth's developmental adjustment.

In this chapter, we distinguish between the overlapping constructs of *racial identity* (i.e., racial self-understanding), *racial identification* (i.e., how others identify biracial people), and *racial category* (i.e., racial identity choices available and exercised in a particular context) (Rockquemore et al., 2009). The majority of biracial young adults tend to embrace either a biracial or a monoracial (specifically minority) identity (e.g., Brunsma, 2006; Lusk, Taylor, Nanney, & Austin, 2010). In non-representative samples of Black-White young adults, when given the choice, about two-thirds of respondents chose a *border identity*, which is a biracial identity that represents a unique blend (not just the sum total) of two racial backgrounds (Rockquemore & Brunsma, 2002).

Some biracial people experience acceptance of their chosen border identity (*validated border identity*); others perceive their biracial identity unaccepted (*unvalidated border identity*). Black-White young adults who had an unvalidated border identity felt that they identified as biracial, although they experienced the world as a Black person (Rockquemore, 1998).

Of those Black-White individuals who embrace a *singular racial identity*, i.e., they identify with one racial group, more tend to identify as Black than as White (Rockquemore & Brunsma, 2002). Only a small percentage of Black-White young adults embrace a White identity (Brunsma, 2006), and compared to their Latino-White and Asian-White counterparts they are the least likely to choose this identity (Davenport, 2016). Instead of identifying with one or more racial groups, some biracial individuals embrace a *transcendent* or an "*aracial*" *identity*, which means that they refuse to be confined by extant racial categories, and choose not to define themselves in racial terms (e.g., Lou, Lalonde, & Wilson, 2011; Rockquemore, 1998). Others exercise agency in their racial self-understanding by deploying a contextually variant racial identity, i.e., a racial identity that shifts from one context to another. For example, a Latino-White biracial college student may identify as a Latina when she is spending time with her family, but she may choose to identify as White when she is in class at the predominantly White college she attends. A number of terms are used in the literature to refer to this type of racial identity. These include "*situational*" (Rockquemore, 1998), "*protean*" (Rockquemore & Brunsma, 2002), "*malleable*" (Sanchez, Shih, & Garcia, 2009), or "*chameleon identity*" (Miville, Constantine, Baysden, & So-Lloyd, 2005). Parents too may identify their biracial offspring in a number of ways (Brunsma, 2005): Two-thirds of parents identified their children's race as biracial, 23% as Black, and 12% as White (Csizmadia, Rollins, & Kaneakua, 2014).

Biracial individuals may vary their racial identity not only across context (Brunsma, 2006; Burke & Kao, 2013; Harris & Sim, 2002), but also over time (e.g., Doyle & Kao, 2007; Terry & Winston, 2010). Although the racial identity shifts found in these studies were not interpreted in terms of a particular racial identity type, they are in line with the conceptual definition of a situationally variant (i.e., protean) racial identity. Fluidity in racial identity is much more characteristic of biracial youth than it is of monoracial youth (Doyle & Kao, 2007). Biracial youth are more likely than monoracial youth to switch identities, rather than maintaining the same racial identity from early adolescence to young adulthood. They may take several pathways over time: shifting from a monoracial to a biracial identity (i.e., "diversifiers"), which is prevalent among Asian-White youth; changing a biracial to a monoracial identity (i.e., "consolidators"); switching between monoracial identities; trading one type of biracial identity for another; and maintaining the same monoracial identity, or the same biracial identity (Hitlin, Brown, & Elder Jr., 2006).

Racial identity seems to be a particularly fluid concept for Native American-White youth. Using data from 371 biracial adolescents enrolled in the National Longitudinal Study of Adolescent Health (Add Health), 81% of Native American-White youth (vs. 45% of Asian-White and 41% of Black-White youth) shifted their racial identity during the transition from adolescence to young adulthood (Doyle & Kao, 2007). For Black-White youth, racial identity is especially variable during adolescence. For instance, Terry and Winston (2010) found that 73% of Black-White adolescents changed their racial identity from 7th through 11th grades.

Fluidity in biracial youth's racial identity also manifests across context. For example, Brunsma (2006) compared Black-White college students' responses on the Survey of Biracial Experience (private identity) to the racial category they chose on the 2000 Census form (public identification). He found that two-thirds of those identified as biracial on the Survey of Biracial Experience self-identified as Black on the Census form. Furthermore, biracial adolescents may identify differently at home and in school: They are more likely to choose a multi-race identity in school than at home, and less than 2% of these youth identify themselves as biracial in both contexts (Harris & Sim, 2002). Finally, relative to Black-White youth, a smaller proportion of Asian-White youth identify consistently across these contexts (Burke & Kao, 2013).

Although biracial individuals today have a greater level of human agency, with which they can approach their racial identity than in the past, their agency depends on environmental constraints. Hence, racial identification is a highly contextualized process for contemporary biracial youth (Csizmadia et al., 2012). Their racial identity has been found to vary among other factors as a function of gender (e.g., Davenport, 2016) and phenotype (Brunsma & Rockquemore, 2001; Townsend, Markus, & Bergsieker, 2009). Socioeconomic status (SES, Campbell, 2007), parent race (e.g., Herman, 2004), its combination with gender, parent education, immigrant background (e.g., Roth, 2005), type of school (Brunsma, 2005), racial composition of the preadult social environment (Brunsma & Rockquemore, 2001) including neighborhood (Rockqemore and Brunsma 2002) and school (Brunsma, 2005; Burke & Kao, 2013), geographic locale (e.g., Brunsma, 2006; Csizmadia et al., 2014), racial socialization (e.g., Brittian, Umaña-Taylor, & Derlan, 2013), and racial discrimination (e.g., Lou & Lalonde, 2015) also play significant roles.

Geographic regions vary in the composition of and relations between racial groups across the United States, which influences the level of agency that biracial people can exercise in their racial identity in a given geographic location. In support of this idea, research revealed that Black-White individuals were more likely to identify as Black in the South (e.g., Khanna, 2010). However, they were more likely to embrace a biracial identity or a protean identity in the Northeast than in the South (Brunsma, 2006). This finding is born out in the story of Corinne who now resides in New England and identifies as biracial. The racial composition of proximal environments such as neighborhood and school has also been linked with variation in biracial individuals' racial identity. For instance, for Black-White youth, living in a predominantly Black neighborhood is associated with a higher likelihood of identifying as Black (Brunsma, 2006), whereas living in a predominantly White neighborhood is associated with a higher likelihood of identifying as White (Rockquemore & Brunsma, 2002). Likewise, Black-White and Asian-White youth who attend an overwhelmingly White school are more likely to identify as White than their peers in schools whose student body has a smaller percentage of Whites (Burke & Kao, 2013). Finally, biracial youth also experience discrimination (Lou & Lalonde, 2015); in fact for Black-White youth who had negative experiences with Blacks, Whites, or members of both groups, skin color was associated with racial identification (Brunsma & Rockquemore, 2001). These findings indicate that macro- and microlevel differences in racial composition and concomitant negative race-related experiences shape biracial youth's racial identity choices.

Racial Identity Choices and Developmental Diversity

The literature does not bear out the existence of a psychologically ideal racial identity for biracial youth. Instead, it suggests that the developmental implications of a given racial identity should be understood relative to other racial identity alternatives and in consideration of social influences. Different racial identity choices have been linked with varying levels of adjustment, although the exact nature of these relationships is unclear. Racial identity among biracial individuals has been examined in relation to indicators of (a) *positive adjustment*: self-esteem/self-evaluation (e.g., Bracey, Bamaca, & Umaña-Taylor, 2004; Townsend et al., 2009), life satisfaction, perceived physical attractiveness, social acceptance (Suzuki-Crumly & Hyers, 2004), overall psychological well-being, and positive affect (Binning et al., 2009); (b) *negative adjustment*: depression (e.g., Lusk et al., 2010; Sanchez, 2010; Sanchez et al., 2009) and anxiety (Coleman & Carter, 2007; Fisher, Reynolds, Hsu, Barnes, & Tyler, 2014); (c) *health behaviors*: attitude and use of drugs (Zapolski, Fisher, Banks, Hensel, & Barnes-Najor, 2016); and (d) *academic adjustment*: performance, motivation, citizenship behavior, school problems, and belonging (Binning et al., 2009; Burke & Kao, 2013; Herman, 2009).

Positive adjustment: Understanding clearly the meaning of one's membership in an ethnic-racial group (i.e., ethnic identity resolution) (Umaña-Taylor, Alfaro, Bámaca, & Guimond, 2009) has psychosocial benefits. For instance, it has been positively linked with self-esteem and self-acceptance among Asian-White and

Latino-White college students (Brittian et al., 2013). In contrast, non-identification (relative to a biracial and monoracial minority identity), a forced monoracial identity (i.e., a monoracial identity that biracial individuals adopt because they feel social pressure to do so, or because biracial or multiple racial categories are not available to them), an unvalidated biracial identity (relative to a validated one), and a White identity (relative to identifying Hispanic, Black, or Asian) have been associated with lower self-esteem (and with lower perceived social acceptance) among biracial youth (Phillips, 2004; Suzuki-Crumly & Hyers, 2004; Townsend et al., 2009). Among Asian-White and Black-White individuals, biracial and monoracial minority identity predicted higher self-esteem (and life satisfaction) than did non-identification (Suzuki-Crumly & Hyers, 2004). Relative to those with an unvalidated biracial identity, those with a validated identity (i.e., they perceived their chosen biracial identity to be socially accepted) had greater identity integration and self-concept clarity (Lou et al., 2011).

Findings regarding the psychosocial implications of specific racial identity types are mixed. Self-esteem did not significantly differ among Black-White individuals with a biracial border, singular, protean, or transcendent identity. However, young adults with a biracial identity relative to those individuals with the other three identity types together reported higher self-esteem (Lusk et al., 2010), and they also reported higher self-esteem than those with a transcendent or singular identity (Townsend et al., 2009). Furthermore, biracial individuals with a protean identity reported higher self-esteem than those with a transcendent or singular identity (Townsend et al., 2009), but a protean identity was also linked with lower psychological well-being for those who exhibited less tolerance for an inconsistent self (Sanchez et al., 2009). Biracial people with a multigroup identity reported higher positive affect than those with a low-status identity, but no difference from those with a high-status identity (Binning et al., 2009).

While these studies do not provide a clear picture of the exact role that particular racial identity types play in multiracial youth's social-emotional adjustment, collectively they point to developmental diversity among multiracial youth. They also suggest that a biracial identity might have positive implications for certain areas of multiracial youth development, and that in a racialized society identifying in racial terms (for example as monoracial, biracial, or varying these identities) might be better than not considering race in one's identity (i.e., transcendent identity). They also suggest that a situationally shifting racial identity (i.e., protean identity) can be beneficial (at least in some areas of development), provided that a biracial person has a personality disposition with tolerance for ambiguity. Albeit absent in these studies, individual characteristics and contextual influences might explain the mixed findings. For instance, for a biracial college student on an ethno-racially diverse college campus or at a college with a critical mass of multiracial students, a biracial identity might lead to higher self-esteem. Likewise, some biracial college students might have a higher self-esteem when they feel comfortable shifting their racial identity depending on the ethnic-racial makeup of their peer group. However, the self-esteem of those biracial young adults for whom changing racial identity from context to context engenders feelings of discomfort and ambiguity might suffer.

Negative adjustment: Lower levels of depression have been found among Asian-White and Latino-White college students who scored higher on ethnic identity resolution (Brittian et al., 2013) and among Black-White young adults who embraced a biracial identity (compared to all other identity types together) (Binning et al., 2009). Biracial individuals with a biracial identity compared to those with a high-status (i.e., White or Asian) or a low-status (e.g., Black or Hispanic) identity also reported lower stress (Binning et al., 2009). However, depression did not differ among individuals with a biracial border, singular, protean, or transcendent identity, respectively (Lusk et al., 2010). A closer examination revealed nuanced differences among biracially identifying Black-White individuals. Those who felt validated in their racial identity by their environment (i.e., they felt people in their social context accepted their identity choice) reported lower levels of depression (and anxiety) relative to those with an unvalidated biracial identity (i.e., they did not feel that their social environment embraced their biraciality) (Coleman & Carter, 2007). For example, a Black-White young woman who identifies as biracial, but with her friends' questioning of her Blackness resulting in her feeling that her chosen racial identity is not accepted, would be described as having an unvalidated border identity.

Higher levels of depression have also been linked with a forced monoracial identity (indirectly through perceived racial identity autonomy and public regard) (Sanchez, 2010), and a protean (i.e., situationally variant) identity (indirectly through unstable racial regard and for those with less tolerance for inconsistency and contradiction in self) (Sanchez et al., 2009).

Somatic symptoms of depression are prevalent among Black-White adolescent girls who identify as White (e.g., Phillips, 2004). Among Asian-White youth non-identification (relative to biracial or minority identification) has been associated with increased depression (Suzuki-Crumly & Hyers, 2004). The implications of a singular Asian identity are less clear: whereas Asian-White adolescent girls with a singular Asian identity reported the highest level of depression (Phillips, 2004), Asian-White individuals in general who embraced an Asian (or a biracial) identity reported feeling less anxious in interactions with Whites than their non-identified Asian-White peers (Suzuki-Crumly & Hyers, 2004). Finally, the role of racial identity in biracial youth's health behaviors is not well understood. In one study stronger ethnic identity was linked with less drug use, although not related to drug-use attitudes (Zapolski et al., 2016).

Academic adjustment: Research on the role of racial identity in biracial youth's school adjustment suggests that biracial (or multigroup) identification has some academic and cognitive benefits compared to a monoracial identification, but that a White identity has negative consequences for biracial youth's school success. For instance, although White-identifying biracial youth as a group did not differ from other biracial peers in school engagement (Burke & Kao, 2013), biracial youth who identified with multiple groups or with a lower status group (e.g., Black) compared to White-identifying youth reported higher levels of school belonging, higher GPA (Burke & Kao, 2013), and lower levels of school alienation (Binning et al., 2009). Biracial youth who identified with multiple groups also reported more citizenship behaviors than biracial youth with a low-status (i.e., minority) identity, although they did not differ from youth with a high-status identity (Binning et al., 2009). These findings suggest that whereas biracial youth report similar levels of school involvement regardless of the racial identity they embrace, their feelings around school involvement do vary depending on how they identify racially. Although not examined in these studies, context might explain why the school-related feelings of biracial youth with one type of racial identity differ from the feelings of biracial youth with a different type of racial identity. For instance, biracial youth who identify as biracial or as a monoracial minority in a predominantly White or less diverse school might exhibit school engagement behaviors similar to those of their peers, yet they may feel less accepted, and therefore report lower levels of school belonging and higher levels of school alienation.

In terms of specific biracial subgroups, research suggests that Black-White youth who identify as Black rather than White report feeling stronger school belonging, whereas Asian-White adolescents who identify as White and Asian in school tend to engage less in school than their biracial peers (Burke & Kao, 2013). Some researchers found that Black-identifying Black-White youth have higher grades than White-identifying biracial youth (Burke & Kao, 2013); another work suggests that a part-Black (and a part-Hispanic) identification is linked with lower grades than a part-White (or a part-Asian) identification (Herman, 2009). These findings suggest that a White identity incurs more psychosocial and academic penalties, and that in a racialized society in which biracial people have historically been forced to identify with their minority background (Davis, 1991), White identification may still be considered to be an attempt to pass as White, and interpreted as a social-cultural transgression.

Biracial Youth Development: A Comparative Perspective

Historically, biracial people were viewed as "tragic mulattos" (e.g., Kerwin & Ponterotto, 1995) and "marginal" people (Park, 1928). However, recent reviews of the literature do not consistently support this deficit view (Csizmadia et al., 2012). A review of 28 qualitative and 16 quantitative studies revealed maladjustment primarily in studies of clinical samples (Shih & Sanchez, 2005). While unequivocal support for the claim that biracial people are maladjusted is lacking, research suggests that they have challenges in some areas of development.

Positive Adjustment

Biracial youth have been compared to their monoracial peers on several self-related constructs (e.g., self-esteem/self-worth, and self-assessment/evaluation); racial affect and identity (e.g., racial-ethnic centrality, exploration, and affirmation); and social functioning (e.g., social acceptance, popularity, association, communication, and parental closeness).

Self-esteem: Self-esteem has been the focus of multiple studies, which produced mixed findings. No significant differences were found between biracial and monoracial adolescents in general (e.g., Phillips, 2004). However, when biracial youth were compared to specific subgroups of their monoracial peers, they reported significantly lower self-worth than White and minority (Milan & Keiley, 2000), specifically Black youth, but higher self-esteem than Asian youth (Bracey et al., 2004). Further differences emerged in studies in which subgroups of biracial youth were compared to their monoracial peers: Asian-White adolescent girls who identified as White reported lower self-esteem than their White peers; Latino-White adolescent girls who identified as non-White reported higher self-esteem than their Latino peers (Phillips, 2004).

Although not examined in these studies, social context such as the ethnic-racial composition of these adolescents' peer environment and cultural ideas around Whiteness, colorism, and gendered views of physical appearance may explain the nuanced differences in biracial adolescents' self-esteem in and across specific biracial subgroups. For instance, given that colorism, i.e., preferential treatment of lighter skinned individuals, is prevalent in Latino communities, Latino-White adolescent girls who identify as non-White may report higher self-esteem than their Latino peers if they are perceived to have "White" physical features (e.g., lighter skin, straight hair, and "European" facial features).

Racial identity: In studies of 9th and 12th graders in public schools located in urban areas of the Northeast and in the Midwest, biracial adolescents reported lower levels of racial-ethnic centrality (i.e., salience of race and ethnicity to one's identity) (Charmaraman & Grossman, 2010) and lower levels of exploration (i.e., learning about one's ethnicity-race) and affirmation (i.e., understanding what it means to be a member of an ethnic-racial group) relative to Black youth, but they scored higher on these constructs than White youth (e.g., Fisher et al., 2014).

Social functioning: Biracial adolescents as a group do not differ from monoracial peers in emotional closeness, contact, or talking with their mothers (Radina & Cooney, 2000), and popularity (Quillian & Redd, 2009). However, biracial adolescent girls reported talking with their mothers significantly more than minority girls, and they had more behavioral contact with their mothers than minority and White girls. In contrast, biracial boys did not differ on contact; they reported less emotional closeness and communication with their fathers than their monoracial (including White) peers, but they engaged in more activities with their fathers than minority boys (Radina & Cooney, 2000). Biracial youth as a group including Native American-White and Black-White youth also reported feeling less socially accepted than White youth (Campbell & Eggerling-Boeck, 2006). Although Asian-White youth as a group do not significantly differ from their White peers in perceived social acceptance (Campbell & Eggerling-Boeck, 2006), Asian-White girls *do*: They perceive themselves to be less socially accepted than White girls (Phillips, 2004). In contrast, Hispanic-White girls report higher perceived physical attractiveness and social acceptance than Hispanic girls (Phillips, 2004).

Collectively, these findings highlight the importance of considering within-group variation in multiracial adolescents' self-development. Multiracial youth do not represent a homogeneous population (Binning et al., 2009). They vary in specific biracial background and in their (actual and perceived) social acceptance by people in and outside of their racial groups. Comparisons of multiracial youth to their monoracial peers in general appear to gloss over important developmental nuances that arise from gendered and culture-specific influences. For instance, White beauty standards (e.g., fair skin, straight hair, "European" facial and body features) may favor Latino-White adolescent girls' social status, but they may or may not enhance Black-White or Asian-White adolescent girls' (perceived or actual) peer status. A Black-White biracial teen girl may perceive to be accepted in a racially diverse peer group, but she may experience or perceive less acceptance by Black peers if these peers exhibit internalized colorism (i.e., they see her as a light-skinned biracial girl who is trying to be prettier than them). In the opening story, Corinne encountered questioning of her racial identity in her after-school program mostly comprised of (Black) students of color, which provides a real-life illustration.

Negative Psychological Adjustment

Biracial youth have been compared to their monoracial peers on internalizing problems (e.g., depression, anxiety, somatic symptoms, and suicidal ideation) and externalizing problems (e.g., aggression, behavioral adjustment, violence, and delinquency).

Internalizing problems: Among college students, biracial participants as a group did not report significantly more depressive symptoms than their monoracial peers (Cheref, Lane, Polanco-Roman, Gadol, & Miranda, 2015). In studies of adolescents, however, significant differences have emerged. In some studies, biracial youth as a group reported higher levels of depression relative to only White youth (only boys after controlling for demographic characteristics such as age and parental education, Cooney & Radina, 2000; boys and girls, e.g., Campbell & Eggerling-Boeck, 2006); in others they reported higher levels of depression than minority and majority youth and greater somatization and anxiety than their monoracial (e.g., Black) peers (Fisher et al., 2014).

When looking at biracial subgroups, Asian-White (girls) and Native American-White, but not Black-White or Hispanic-White, youth reported higher levels of depression than White youth (Campbell & Eggerling-Boeck, 2006; Phillips, 2004). Findings on suicidal ideation are somewhat mixed: Biracial college students as a group did not report significantly higher levels of suicidal ideation than their monoracial peers (Cheref et al., 2015), but biracial adolescents as a group did. Relative to White youth, Native American-White youth were 2.5 times more likely to consider suicide, but not Native American-Black youth (Campbell & Eggerling-Boeck, 2006).

Externalizing problems: Biracial youth did not differ in antisocial behaviors from monoracial youth as a group (Choi, He, Herrenkohl, Catalano, & Toumbourou, 2012).

Relative to White youth, however, they reported significantly more conduct problems (Milan & Keiley, 2000), higher delinquency (girls only) (Cooney & Radina, 2000), and violent behaviors (e.g., ever threatening to beat someone up, or being hurt badly in a fight) (Choi, Harachi, Gillmore, & Catalano, 2006). With peer risks controlled, no difference was found; violence rates were higher only for youth with more antisocial friends (Choi et al., 2012).

Collectively, these studies indicate that multiracial youth as a group may experience more problems than their White peers; however, they also suggest nuanced differences across biracial subgroups, particularly in internalizing problems. This research also points to adolescence as a vulnerable developmental period for multiracial youth. Greater importance of peer acceptance, increased identity exploration (with little commitment), and adolescent egocentric thinking might explain the greater prevalence of depressive, somatic, and anxiety-related symptoms among multiracial youth in adolescence. By young adulthood, the intensity of these influences lessens as the importance of peer relations changes, identity advances, and egocentrism becomes much less pronounced, which may explain lower levels of depression among biracial college students.

School Adjustment

Relative to White peers, biracial adolescents as a group reported significantly more behavioral conduct and school problems (Milan & Keiley, 2000), including grade retention (only for boys) and school suspension and expulsion (only for girls) (Cooney & Radina, 2000). Relative to minority peers, however, biracial girls reported significantly lower levels of grade retention and school suspension (Cooney & Radina, 2000). Findings on school closeness are more mixed: Some studies revealed that relative to White youth, biracial adolescents reported feeling less close to people at school and not feeling part of their school (Campbell & Eggerling-Boeck, 2006), and others found no significant differences after controlling for background characteristics (Cooney & Radina, 2000). There were also no significant differences between biracial and monoracial adolescents in club participation (Campbell & Eggerling-Boeck, 2006), and in self-reported grades between biracial and White adolescent girls, although biracial girls did report significantly higher grades than monoracial minority girls (Cooney & Radina, 2000).

Collectively, these findings suggest that between-group comparisons may mask considerable within-group variation and important gender differences in biracial adolescents' school adjustment. For instance, biracial adolescents may experience more school problems because of added social-emotional challenges such as multiracial microaggressions from peers and teachers, teacher bias towards students of color, and elevated racial identity struggle, particularly in schools whose student body is homogenous or lacks a critical mass of multiracial youth. Furthermore, although biracial adolescent girls do academically well, this is not the case for many biracial adolescent boys. Stereotype consciousness (i.e., awareness of the stereotypes others hold about them) and stereotype threat (e.g., awareness of negative stereotypes relating to their academic abilities leads to poor performance under high-stakes testing conditions or to failure to try hard out of fear of confirming existing stereotypes; see McKown & Strambler, 2009) may compromise some biracial adolescent boys' school success.

Health Behaviors

Tobacco use: Using data collected in 1990s, some research revealed that biracial youth were significantly more likely to have ever smoked than single-race White, Black, and Asian youth (Choi et al., 2006). Studies of data collected in the early 2000s revealed mixed findings: Some found no significant differences in tobacco use (Choi et al., 2012), and others found that biracial adolescents were significantly more likely to ever have smoked regularly than Black, Latino, and Asian/Pacific Islander youth, but less likely to do so than White youth (Chavez & Sanchez, 2010). When comparing specific subgroups of biracial youth to monoracial youth, studies revealed that Black-White youth reported lower lifetime cigarette use than White youth, but higher than Black youth (Goings, Butler-Bente, McGovern, & Howard, 2016a; Goings, Hidalgo, & McGovern, 2016b); Native-American-White and Asian-White youth began smoking earlier than White youth; and Black-American-Indian youth began smoking earlier than Black youth (Clark et al. 2013a). Biracial Hispanic youth smoked more than monoracial Hispanic and non-Hispanic biracial youth (Whaley & Francis 2016), although Hispanic-Asian youth began smoking later than Hispanic youth (Clark et al. 2013b). Longitudinal research revealed that in general, biracial youth in preadolescence and adolescence are less likely to smoke than their White peers, but by their mid-20s the difference either narrows or becomes nonsignificant, and by their early 30s, in several biracial subgroups (e.g., Hispanic-White and Black-American-Indian), smoking becomes more prevalent (Clark, Nguyen, & Coman, 2015).

Alcohol use: Some studies revealed that biracial youth as a group were more likely to have ever drunk alcohol than monoracial youth (Choi et al., 2006); however, they did not significantly differ from White youth in binge drinking (Chen, Balan, & Price, 2012) and in alcohol use after controlling for background characteristics (Choi et al., 2012). In terms of specific biracial subgroups, Black-White adolescents' reported lifetime alcohol use was higher than Black youth's, but lower than White youth's, and Black-American-Indian youth reported lower alcohol use than American-Indian youth and White youth although the difference in the mean number of drinks reported by Black-American-Indian and White individuals decreased over time (Goings, Butler-Bente, et al., 2016a; Goings, Hidalgo, et al., 2016b). Further, relative to Black-White youth, Black-Hispanic youth of all ages were more likely to report not drinking, but less likely to do so than Black youth. Black-American-Indian youth (and Black youth) were the least likely, whereas White youth and Black-White youth were the most likely, to report heavy drinking. Drinking increased over time, occurring at a faster rate for Black-White young men than any other groups between ages 23 and 35 (Clark et al. 2013a). Black-American-Indian (vs. Black), Hispanic-Asian (vs. Hispanic), and Hispanic-American-Indian (vs. American-Indian) youth reported later alcohol initiation; White-American-Indians began drinking at the same age as Whites; White-Asians did earlier than Asians (Clark et al. 2013b).

Drug use: Biracial youth reported higher substance use rates than White youth (Chen et al., 2012) and minority youth (only boys) (Cooney & Radina, 2000). Specifically, they reported more frequent past-month drug use than Black youth, but less frequent drug use than Hispanic youth (Zapolski et al., 2016). They were more likely to report having tried marijuana, ever having gotten high on drugs (relative to White and Asian-American youth only), and ever having used crack or cocaine (compared to Asian youth only) (Choi et al., 2006). White-American-Indian and Black-American-Indian youth reported trying marijuana earlier than their non-American-Indian monoracial peers. White-Asian youth also smoked marijuana earlier than Asian youth and White youth did. However, Hispanic-Asian youth relative to Hispanic youth and Hispanic-American-Indian youth relative to American-Indian youth tried marijuana later (Clark et al. 2013b). Black-White youth had higher lifetime marijuana use than White and Black youth (Goings, Hidalgo, et al., 2016b).

It is clear from this research that multiracial youth's substance use has received considerably more scholarly attention than other developmental areas did. Collectively, these studies revealed a mixed pattern of findings: Some found no differences between biracial and monoracial youth (e.g., Choi et al., 2012); others found differences (e.g., Phillips, 2004), although findings varied by substance type, biracial background, and monoracial comparison group.

Peer influences, increasing exposure to and awareness of racial discrimination and microaggressions, family SES and neighborhood, as well as psychological distress (e.g., depression and anxiety) might explain the higher rates of substance use found among biracial adolescents. Biracial youth reported a significantly higher rate of yielding to peer pressure (relative to Latino youth), and more substance-using and antisocial friends (relative to their White peers) (Choi et al., 2012). Furthermore, biracial adolescent boys and girls with friends who used tobacco, alcohol, and marijuana were more likely to use over-the-counter drugs than biracial youth who did not associate with substance-using peers (Vidourek & King, 2013). Depending on their residential location and family SES, some biracial youth might be exposed to race and economic stressors that would increase their likelihood of substance use. Finally, it is also possible that some biracial youth who struggle with depression and anxiety turn to substance use to cope with feelings of sadness, a sense of not belonging, and not being accepted.

Conclusion

In this chapter, we reviewed the literature on racial identity, some of its contextual correlates, and associated developmental outcomes in the multiracial population. We discussed research that compared biracial youth to their monoracial peers and studies that examined associations between racial identity and various psychosocial, academic, and health behavioral outcomes among biracial youth. Our review suggests that biracial people, overall, can and do exercise greater agency in their racial identity choices, although the extent to which contextual influences constrain their choices varies across biracial subgroups. We also argued that a chosen racial identity and co-occurring contextual factors powerfully shape biracial youth's adjustment and lead to developmental diversity in the multiracial population.

Biracial individuals today may choose from multiple monoracial identities; a distinct biracial identity; a monoracial minority identity; a White identity; a situational (i.e., contextually variant) identity; or a "transcendent" identity. Relative to their monoracial counterparts, they are also more likely to vary their racial identity across contexts and over time. Variability in their racial identity is common during the transition from adolescence to young adulthood, with important differences among biracial subgroups. Whereas Black-White individuals still experience more constraints around their racial identity, perhaps in part due to persisting discrimination, more agency is afforded to Asian-White and Native American-White individuals; that is, they have more freedom to choose a racial identity that they psychologically identify with.

Developmental comparisons do not consistently indicate that biracial people as a group are more maladjusted than their monoracial peers, although they do suggest that adolescence is a vulnerable developmental period for biracial youth with a greater likelihood of problems for some subgroups (e.g., Asian-White and Native American-White) relative to White youth. When biracial youth as a group are compared to monoracial youth, often no significant differences emerge. When specific biracial subgroups are compared to monoracial youth as a group or to specific monoracial subgroups, significant group differences are detected in positive and negative psychosocial adjustment and school outcomes. To develop a more nuanced understanding of these between-group differences, it is important to consider the role of gender. Findings on substance use differences between monoracial and biracial youth vary by substance type, biracial subgroup, and monoracial comparison group. Finally, the literature on the role of racial identity in psychosocial and academic adjustment does not confirm that biracial identity is the developmentally ideal racial identity choice for all biracial youth, but it does suggest that an unvalidated biracial identity, a forced monoracial identity, a White identity, and nonracial identification have negative developmental consequences.

Implications for Practice

Our review of the literature has several important practical implications. Given that biracial youth negotiate their racial identity in response to contextual constraints, which in turn shapes their adjustment, schools have the potential to significantly enhance or compromise their development. School administrators must recognize biracial youth in their student body. They must work with teachers, school counselors, and social workers to create a school culture that recognizes them as an important part of the school population. To this end, professional development activities should include information about the multiracial population and experience. It is important that there is an understanding of the heterogeneity in this population, which means that biracial students may differ in their racial background, identity choices, experiences, family environment, and psychosocial and academic development. It must also be understood that although their multi-race background is an important factor in their development, it does not necessarily doom them for developmental problems. School racial composition and climate can make racial identity more or less salient for biracial students, and racial identity shapes their self-esteem, depression, problem behaviors, school belonging, and performance.

A forced racial identity has negative consequences for biracial youth development; thus it is important that they are encouraged, rather than being forced, to choose their racial identity. For instance, teachers and school social workers should not assume, question, or (in)advertently deny biracial students' racial identity. Because adolescence is a vulnerable developmental period for biracial youth, and they are likely to experience racial identity changes, schools' sensitivity to their increased need for support at this life stage is essential.

An inclusive curriculum can also aid biracial students' development by educating students on interracial families, biracial scientists, historians, writers, and artists, for instance, through book discussions. In a culture where biracial matters are rarely included in discussions on race, a curriculum that incorporates information on biracial people and their experience will create the opportunity to have open discussions about and normalize the biracial experience (Williams, 2015). Teachers often avoid talking about race due to discomfort with the topic and conversation (Williams, 2015); therefore, they must be trained to openly discuss racial diversity and inequality in the classroom to support (biracial) student development. Such discussions can increase biracial youths' social acceptance and school belonging and peers' cultural sensitivity.

Finally, family-school partnerships can benefit biracial youth in important ways. Teachers and school counselors who are knowledgeable about research on biracial child development and interracial families can inform and support parents of biracial students. When they understand that biracial youth may face microaggressions in their own families (e.g., isolation, favoritism, questioning of authenticity, denial of biracial identity and experiences, and negative feelings about their lack of knowledge about family heritage or culture) (Nadal et al., 2013), or be told how to identify racially (Gaither, 2015), teachers and counselors can inform and work with parents to develop parenting and racial socialization strategies that support biracial youth's healthy (racial identity) development. Finally, therapists should encourage parents to be mindful of and resolve potential conflicts that may arise between their chosen family identity and their biracial child's racial self-understanding (Csizmadia, Leslie, & Nazarian, 2015).

Implications for Future Research

Although existent research enhances current understanding of the multiracial (youth) population in important ways, several gaps remain in this literature. Much work has been done to understand racial identity and its individual and contextual predictors, but much less is known about other aspects of psychosocial development (as well as health behaviors and academic adjustment) among biracial youth. The number of developmental studies in which biracial youth's developmental outcomes are evaluated relative to those of their monoracial peers still far outweighs the number of studies that examine the role that specific racial identity options play in psychosocial, academic, and behavioral adjustment within and across subgroups of multiracial youth. For instance, whereas numerous studies compared biracial youth to their monoracial peers on tobacco, alcohol, and drug use, to our knowledge only Zapolski et al. (2016) studied the role of racial identity in biracial youth's substance use. More of this research is needed on biracial youth, given that racial identity has been identified as a protective factor that promotes healthy development among youth of color (Neblett, Rivas-Drake, & Umaña-Taylor, 2012).

Furthermore, findings regarding biracial youth's adjustment are often inconsistent across studies because (a) some studies examined biracial youth as a group, which can mask important within-group variation, and others focused on specific biracial subgroups; (b) although a variety of adjustment indicators have been examined, many of these indicators were the focus of single studies; and (c) studies also varied in their focal age group. Additionally, scholarly attention has heavily tilted towards some biracial subgroups (i.e., Black-White) with little attention to others such as part-Hispanic biracial youth, although people of Hispanic origin contribute considerably to current population growth in the United States. Moreover, because biracial adolescents and young adults have been the primary focus of past research, the developmental antecedents of adolescent and young adult outcomes in this population are poorly understood. Considering that biracial children begin to develop a sense of their "racial otherness" by the time they enter kindergarten (Kerwin & Ponterotto, 1995), it is important for future work to examine young biracial children. Finally, while we know that biracial youth may shift their racial identity over time, longitudinal research is needed to understand how these changes relate to patterns of change in other areas of their development, and across developmental periods.

References

Binning, K. R., Unzueta, M. M., Huo, Y. J., & Molina, L. E. (2009). The interpretation of multiracial status and its relation to social engagement and psychological well-being. *Journal of Social Issues, 65*, 35–49. https://doi.org/10.1111/j.1540-4560.2008.01586.x

Bracey, J. R., Bamaca, M. Y., & Umaña-Taylor, A. J. (2004). Examining ethnic identity and self-esteem among biracial and monoracial adolescents. *Journal of Youth and Adolescence, 33*(2), 123–132. https://doi.org/10.1023/B:JOYO.0000013424.93635.68

Brittian, A. S., Umaña-Taylor, A. J., & Derlan, C. L. (2013). An examination of biracial college youths' family ethnic socialization, ethnic identity, and adjustment: Do self-identification labels and university context matter? *Cultural Diversity and Ethnic Minority Psychology, 19*(2), 177–189. https://doi.org/10.1037/a0029438

Brunsma, D. L. (2005). Interracial families and the racial identification of mixed-race children: Evidence from the Early Childhood Longitudinal Study. *Social Forces, 84*, 1131–1157.

Brunsma, D. L. (2006). Public categories, private identities: Exploring regional differences in the biracial experience. *Social Science Research, 35*, 555–576.

Brunsma, D. L., & Rockquemore, K. A. (2001). The new color complex: Appearances and biracial identity. *Identity: An International Journal of Theory and Research, 1*, 225–246.

Burke, R., & Kao, G. (2013). Bearing the burden of whiteness: The implications of racial self-identification for multiracial adolescents' school belonging and academic achievement. *Ethnic and Racial Studies, 36*(5), 747–773. https://doi.org/10.1080/01419870.2011.628998

Campbell, M. E. (2007). Thinking outside the (Black) box: Measuring Black and multiracial identification on surveys. *Social Science Research, 36*, 921–944.

Campbell, M. E., & Eggerling-Boeck, J. (2006). 'What about the children?' The psychological and social well-being of multiracial adolescents. *Sociological Quarterly, 47*(1), 147–173.

Charmaraman, L., & Grossman, J. M. (2010). Importance of race and ethnicity: An exploration of Asian, Black, Latino, and multiracial adolescent identity. *Cultural Diversity and Ethnic Minority Psychology, 16*(2), 144–151. https://doi.org/10.1037/a0018668

Chavez, G. F., & Sanchez, D. T. (2010). A clearer picture of multiracial substance use: Rates and correlates of alcohol and tobacco use in multiracial adolescents and adults. *Race and Social Problems, 2*(1), 1–18. https://doi.org/10.1007/s12552-010-9023-1

Chen, H.-J., Balan, S., & Price, R. K. (2012). Association of contextual factors with drug use and binge drinking among White, Native American, and mixed-race adolescents in the general population. *Journal of Youth and Adolescence, 41*, 1426–1441.

Cheref, S., Lane, R., Polanco-Roman, L., Gadol, E., & Miranda, R. (2015). Suicidal ideation among racial/ethnic minorities: Moderating effects of rumination and depressive symptoms. *Cultural Diversity and Ethnic Minority Psychology, 21*(1), 31–40.

Choi, Y., Harachi, T. W., Gillmore, M. R., & Catalano, R. F. (2006). Are multiracial adolescents at greater risk? Comparisons of rates, patterns, and correlates of substance use and violence between monoracial and multiracial adolescents. *American Journal of Orthopsychiatry, 76*(1), 86–97. https://doi.org/10.1037/0002-9432.76.1.86

Choi, Y., He, M., Herrenkohl, R. F., Catalano, R. F., & Toumbourou, J. W. (2012). Multiple identification and risks: Examination of peer factors across multiracial and single-race youth. *Journal of Youth and Adolescence, 41*, 847–862. https://doi.org/10.1007/s10964-012-9750-2

Clark, T. T., Corneille, M., & Coman, E. (2013a). Developmental trajectories of alcohol use among monoracial and biracial Black adolescents and adults. *Journal of Psychoactive Drugs, 45*(3), 249–257. https://doi.org/10.1080/02791072.2013.805980

Clark, T. T., Doyle, O., & Clincy, A. (2013b). Age of first cigarette, alcohol, and marijuana use among U.S. biracial/ethnic youth: A population-based study. *Addictive Behaviors, 38*, 2450–2454. https://doi.org/10.1016/j.addbeh.2013.04.005

Clark, T. T., Nguyen, A. B., & Coman, E. (2015). Smoking trajectories among monoracial and biracial Black adolescents and young adults. *Journal of Drug Issues, 45*(1), 22–37.

Coleman, V. H., & Carter, M. M. (2007). Biracial self-identification: Impact on trait anxiety, social anxiety, and depression. *Journal of Theory and Research, 7*, 103–114.

Cooney, T. M., & Radina, E. M. (2000). Adjustment problems in adolescence: Are multiracial children at risk? *American Journal of Orthopsychiatry, 70*(4), 433–444.

Csizmadia, A., Brunsma, D. L., & Cooney, T. M. (2012). Racial identification and developmental outcomes among Black-White multiracial youth: A review from a life course perspective. *Advances in Life Course Research, 17*, 34–44.

Csizmadia, A., Leslie, L., & Nazarian, R. (2015). Understanding and treating interracial families. In S. Browning, K. Pasley, S. Browning, & K. Pasley (Eds.), *Contemporary families: Translating research into practice* (pp. 89–107). New York, NY: Taylor & Francis.

Csizmadia, A., Rollins, A., & Kaneakua, J. P. (2014). Ethnic-racial socialization and its correlates in families of Black-White biracial children. *Family Relations, 63*, 259–270.

Davenport, L. D. (2016). The role of gender, class, and religion in biracial Americans' racial labeling decisions. *American Sociological Review, 81*(1), 57–84.

Davis, J. F. (1991). *Who is Black? One nation's definition*. University Park, PA: The Pennsylvania State University Press.

Doyle, J. M., & Kao, G. (2007). Are racial identities of multiracials stable? Changing self-identification among single and multiple race individuals. *Social Psychology Quarterly, 70*(4), 405–423.

Fisher, S., Reynolds, J. L., Hsu, W.-W., Barnes, J., & Tyler, K. (2014). Examining multiracial youth in context: Ethnic identity development and mental health outcomes. *Journal of Youth and Adolescence, 43*, 1688–1699. https://doi.org/10.1007/s109064

Gaither, S. E. (2015). 'Mixed' results: Multiracial research and identity explorations. *Current Directions in Psychological Science, 24*(2), 114–119. https://doi.org/10.1177/0963721414558115

Goings, T. C., Butler-Bente, E., McGovern, T., & Howard, M. O. (2016a). Prevalence and correlates of substance use in Black, White, and biracial Black-White adolescents: Evidence for a biracial intermediate phenomenon. *American Journal of Orthopsychiatry, 86*(5), 527–539. https://doi.org/10.1037/ort0000166

Goings, T. C., Hidalgo, S. J. T., & McGovern, T. (2016b). Similarities and differences in alcohol trajectories: Testing the catch-up effect among biracial black subgroups. *Addictive Behaviors, 60*, 13–17.

Harris, D. R., & Sim, J. J. (2002). Who is multiracial? Assessing the complexity of lived race. *American Sociological Review, 67*(4), 614–627.

Herman, M. (2004). Forced to choose: Some determinants of racial identification in multiracial adolescents. *Child Development, 75*(3), 730–748.

Herman, M. (2009). The Black-White-Other achievement gap: Testing theories of academic performance among multiracial and monoracial adolescents. *Sociology of Education, 82*(1), 20–46.

Hitlin, S., Brown, J. S., & Elder Jr., G. H. (2006). Racial self-categorization in adolescence: Multiracial development and social pathways. *Child Development, 77*(5), 1298–1308.

Jones, N. A., & Bullock, J. J. (2013). Understanding who reported multiple races in the U.S. Decennial Census: Results from Census 2000 and the 2010 Census. *Family Relations: Interdisciplinary Journal of Applied Family Studies, 62*, 5–16.

Kerwin, C., & Ponterotto, J. G. (1995). Biracial identity development: Theory and research. In J. G. Ponterotto, J.M. Casas, L.A. Suzuki, and C. Alexander (Eds.), Handbook of multicultural counseling (pp. 199–217). Thousand Oaks, CA: Sage.

Khanna, N. (2010). "If you're half Black, you're just Black:" reflected appraisals and the persistence of the one-drop rule. *The Sociological Quarterly, 51*, 96–121.

Lou, E., & Lalonde, R. N. (2015). Signs of transcendence? A changing landscape of multiraciality in the 21st century. *International Journal of Intercultural Relations, 45*, 85–95.

Lou, E., Lalonde, R. N., & Wilson, C. (2011). Examining a multidimensional framework of racial identity across different biracial groups. *Asian American Journal of Psychology, 2*, 79–90.

Lusk, E. M., Taylor, M. J., Nanney, J. T., & Austin, C. C. (2010). Biracial identity and its relation to self-esteem and depression in mixed Black-White biracial individuals. *Journal of Ethnic & Cultural Diversity in Social Work, 19*, 109–126.

McKown, C., & Strambler, M. J. (2009). Developmental antecedents and social and academic consequences of stereotype-consciousness in middle childhood. *Child Development, 80*, 1643–1659.

Milan, S., & Keiley, M. K. (2000). Biracial youth and families in therapy: Issues and interventions. *Journal of Marital and Family Therapy, 26*, 305–315.

Miville, M. L., Constantine, M. G., Baysden, M. F., & So-Lloyd, G. (2005). Chameleon changes: An exploration of racial identity themes of biracial people. *Journal of Counseling Psychology, 52*, 507–516. https://doi.org/10.1037/0022-0167.52.4.507

Nadal, K. L., Sriken, J., Davidoff, K. C., Wong, Y., & McLean, K. (2013). Microaggressions within families: Experiences of multiracial people. *Family Relations: An Interdisciplinary Journal of Applied Family Studies, 62*(1), 190–201.

Neblett, E. W., Rivas-Drake, D., & Umaña-Taylor, A. J. (2012). The promise of racial and ethnic protective factors in promoting ethnic minority youth development. *Child Development Perspectives, 6*(3), 295–303. https://doi.org/10.1111/j.1750-8606.2012.00239.x

Park, R. (1928). Human migration and the marginal man. *American Journal of Sociology, 33*, 881–893.

Phillips, L. (2004). Fitting in and feeling good: Patterns of self-evaluation and psychological stress among biracial adolescent girls. *Women & Therapy, 27*(1/2), 217–236.

Quillian, L., & Redd, R. (2009). The friendship networks of multiracial adolescents. *Social Science Research, 38*(2), 279–295. https://doi.org/10.1016/j.ssresearch.2008.09.002

Radina, E. M., & Cooney, T. M. (2000). Relationship quality between multiracial adolescents and their biological parents. *American Journal of Orthopsychiatry, 70*(4), 445–454.

Rockquemore, K. A. (1998). Between Black and White: Exploring the "biracial" experience. *Race & Society, 1*(2), 197–212. https://doi.org/10.1016/S1090-9524(99)80044-8

Rockquemore, K. A., & Brunsma, D. L. (2002). *Beyond Black: Biracial identity in America*. Thousand Oaks, CA: Sage Publications.

Rockquemore, K. A., Brunsma, D. L., & Delgado, D. J. (2009). Racing to theory or retheorizing race? Understanding the struggle to build a multiracial identity theory. *Journal of Social Issues, 65*(1), 13–34. https://doi.org/10.1111/j.1540-4560.2008.01585.x

Roth, W. D. (2005). The end of the one-drop rule? Labeling of multiracial children in Black intermarriages. *Sociological Forum, 20*, 35–67. https://doi.org/10.1007/s11206-005-1897-0

Sanchez, D. T. (2010). How do forced-choice dilemmas affect multiracial people? The role of identity autonomy and public regard in depressive symptoms. *Journal of Applied Social Psychology, 40*, 1657–1677. https://doi.org/10.1111/j.1559-1816.2010.00634.x

Sanchez, D. T., Shih, M., & Garcia, J. A. (2009). Juggling multiple racial identities: Malleable racial identification and psychological well-being. *Cultural Diversity and Ethnic Minority Psychology, 15*, 243–254. https://doi.org/10.1037/a0014373

Shih, M. J., & Sanchez, D. T. (2005). Perspectives and research on the positive and negative implications of having multiple racial identities. *Psychological Bulletin, 131*, 569–591.

Suzuki-Crumly, J., & Hyers, L. (2004). The relationship among ethnic identity, psychological well-being, and intergroup competence: An investigation of two biracial groups. *Cultural Diversity and Ethnic Minority Psychology, 10*(2), 137–150.

Terry, R. L., & Winston, C. E. (2010). Personality characteristic adaptations: Multiracial adolescents' patterns of racial self-identification change. *Journal of Research on Adolescence, 20*, 432–455.

Townsend, S. S. M., Markus, H. R., & Bergsieker, H. B. (2009). My choice, your categories: The denial of multiracial identities. *Journal of Social Issues, 65*(1), 185–204.

Umaña-Taylor, A. J., Alfaro, E. C., Bámaca, M. Y., & Guimond, A. B. (2009). The central role of familial ethnic socialization in Latino adolescents' cultural orientation. *Journal of Marriage and Family, 71*, 46–60. https://doi.org/10.1111/j.1741-3737.2008.00579.x

Vidourek, R., & King, K. A. (2013). Parent, teacher, and school factors associated with over-the-counter drug use among multiracial youth. *American Journal of Health Education, 44*, 306–315. https://doi.org/10.1080/19325037.2013.838889

Whaley, A. L., & Francis, K. (2016). Behavioral health in multiracial adolescents: The role of Hispanic/Latino ethnicity. *Public Health Reports, 121*, 169–174.

Williams, R. M. F. (2015). When gray matters more than Black or White: The schooling experiences of Black-White biracial students. *Education and Urban Society, 45*, 175–207.

Zapolski, T. C. B., Fisher, S., Banks, D. E., Hensel, D. J., & Barnes-Najor, J. (2016). Examining the protective effect of ethnic identity on drug attitudes and use among a diverse youth population. *Journal of Youth and Adolescence, 46*, 1–14. https://doi.org/10.1007/s10964-016-0605-0

New Directions

Alethea Rollins and Roudi Nazarinia Roy

When I was in graduate school, a colleague and I shared a taxi at a professional conference. The driver asked me if I was half-and-half. My colleague was offended on my behalf. She berated the driver and then looked at me and said, "You don't have to answer that question." I was surprised by her response. I had been asked this question countless times. It didn't offend me. While she sat indignant, I simply answered, "Yes." In truth, that is exactly how I had always seen myself: half Black and half White.

When I turned 40, I decided to explore my ancestral DNA with a popular testing company. I never thought about how it might impact my identity; in truth, I was mostly interested to see to which African countries my ancestry would be traced. The test results suggest that I am 65% European American (mostly French and German), 33% Sub-Saharan African (mostly West African), and 2% unassigned. I, apparently, am not half-and-half.

This technological fact surprised me and delighted me and puzzled me. I have never thought of or referred to myself as White. I knew my grandfather was German, but I never thought of myself as German; I never considered my European ancestors. It was exciting to examine the world map of my ancestral background. It gave me great pleasure (and some pain) to think of the distance my ancestors had traveled and to feel a greater connection to my personal family history. It also

A. Rollins (✉)
Child and Family Development Program, School of Human Services,
Harmon College of Business and Professional Studies, University of Central Missouri,
Warrensburg, MO, USA
e-mail: arollins@ucmo.edu

R. N. Roy
Department of Family and Consumer Sciences, California State University Long Beach,
Long Beach, CA, USA
e-mail: Roudi.Roy@csulb.edu

R. Nazarinia Roy, A. Rollins (eds.), *Biracial Families*,
https://doi.org/10.1007/978-3-319-96160-6_12

> *challenged how I thought about myself, my family, and who I am. I found myself considering and reconsidering how I racially identify and the circumstances and historical experiences that influence how I see myself and how I am seen by others. Ultimately, it lent support for an idea that I had struggled to articulate. I am not half-and-half. I cannot be divided into percentages. I am not half-Black and half-White. I am Black and White. I am biracial.*
>
> —Alethea Rollins

Biracial families are formed and develop in many of the same ways as other families. Two people develop a mutual affection, establish a partnership, and choose to be parents. They may marry or not, stay married or not, live together or not; they may adopt or have biological children. They experience the same developmental stages and life trajectories as any other individuals do. Yet, biracial families have the added challenge of crossing racial boundaries and blurring color lines in ways that many people are afraid to do. Although formal legal barriers have been rescinded, societal discord and racial inequities remain; thus, cross-race relationships are more complex than same-race relationships. The layers of complexity can be viewed as opportunities for growth and can lead us into a more comprehensive understanding of race, prejudice, and bias. These same layers of complexity can become a heavy burden, consuming energy and ruffling resolve to blaze an important path forward. One cannot comprehend the experience of biracial families without interrogating the layers of intersections that yield complex, contradictory, and complementary relationships. Intersectionality has been, and will always be, the only way to describe and understand the experiences of biracial families and individuals. Evaluating intersections (e.g., of race and class, colorism and bias, exposure, and ideology) is necessary to gain a more nuanced understanding of how and why individuals partner across race; how they create family and think about parenting biracial children; how they choose to identify themselves, their family, and their children; and how identity impacts (among other things) the health and well-being of biracial people.

A New Perspective

Understanding these intersections and being able to evaluate them with theoretical principles are important and necessary to move beyond our current understanding of biracial families. We need theoretical models that help us understand the complexities of interracial partnering and marriage (for more information, see Chaps. 4 and 5). We need racial identity models (for more information, see Chap. 3) that move beyond stages to capture a biracial or multiracial identity that allows for fluidity and self-identifications that might not currently exist. Further, we need theoretical models that help us consider universal biracial experiences (things that are true of biracial families and people regardless of racial heritage) and individual mixed-race experiences (including unique racial combinations: Korean/Black or Mexican/White or Puerto Rican and Chinese). As reported by the Pew Research Center (2015a), "Only about a third (34%) of all multiracial Americans think they have a lot in common with other adults who are the same racial mix that they are, while only half as many (17%) think they share a lot with multiracial Americans whose racial background is different from their own" (The Multiracial Experience section, para. 6). There is very little research to help us understand the within-group variability among biracial families and individuals.

Beyond Black-White

Almost every author in this book noted a need to look beyond Black-White mixed families. Given the sociohistorical experiences in the United States, much of the research has focused on the experiences of Black-White partners and their offspring. Truly, crossing the Black-White racial divide is unique and particularly relevant, but it is only part of the biracial story. Among biracial adults, the most prevalent biracial heritage is American-Indian and White (Pew Research Center, 2015a). Thus, as noted in Chaps. 4 and 5, the generalizability of the current research on partnering across race and interracial marriage is greatly limited by its narrow focus on Black-White relationships, diminishing our understanding of the majority of cross-race romantic relationships. Likewise, investigations of parenting, racial socialization, and racial identity among biracial families and individuals have often narrowly focused on the Black-White subgroup (see Chaps. 7, 8, and 11).

It was our intention to explicate universal biracial experiences. However, with so little understanding of heritage-specific biracial groups, authors found it difficult to identify universal truths about biracial families and mixed-race individuals. Being able to make these types of theoretical leaps and have more generalizable findings will push our understanding further and allow us to look at both universal and heritage-specific experiences.

Parenting Biracial Youth

Becoming a parent changes everything. It intensifies your passions and ideals. It challenges your worldview. It heightens your capacity for understanding and love. It is a challenging and life-altering experience for anyone who chooses to embark on the journey. When biracial couples transition to parenthood, the burden of being an interracial couple increases and has a lasting impact on the relationship (see Chap. 6 for more information). Yet, empirically, we know very little about this important, life-altering time in a biracial couple's relationship. More work is needed to understand how biracial couples integrate their racial and cultural differences and interact with their extended families. Further, we know very little about their experiences as parents. Interestingly, much of the available information consists of anecdotal experiences of White mothers raising biracial children. More research is needed to understand the experiences of parents of color, fathers' experiences, and coparenting experience in biracial families.

Because parenting doesn't occur in a vacuum, it is also important to consider school experiences, peer relationships, siblings (including monoracial siblings), and, as children get older, adolescent world of dating. Our understanding would be greatly enhanced by investigations that include the family system. The inclusion of siblings, both parents (most research includes only one parent), and extended-family dynamics would aid us in understanding and supporting biracial families (see Chap. 7 for more information).

Beyond identity development, we know very little about how biracial youth navigate their duality. They develop racial awareness from many socializing agents, including parents, siblings, extended family, neighborhoods, schools, teachers, peers, and media. They are inundated with messages about race and identity and often have very few peers or role models to help them navigate their everyday experiences. More research is needed to explicate racial socialization in biracial families (see Chap. 8 for more information). Investigations should look at parental racial ideologies and family processes. We know very little about who decides what racial messages are being taught, who takes the lead in these discussions, and how parents negotiate racial socialization in biracial families. Further, we know that racial socialization is bidirectional; however, we know little about how specific biracial heritage, individual social experiences, and biracial children's own questions affect parental racial socialization strategies.

According to a Pew Research Center (2017) analysis of 2015 Census Bureau data, 14% of infants living with two biological parents were multiracial or multiethnic. Among them, 22% have at least one parent who is multiracial or multiethnic. If demographic predictions hold true, the multiracial population will triple by 2060 (Pew Research Center, 2015a). These mixed-race parents and second-generation mixed-race children will increasingly be the norm in the US society. Biracial individuals tend to be young, proud, and tolerant, and the majority report being subject to racism and discrimination (Pew Research Center, 2015a), but they are not a monolithic group. They do not all identify as biracial, and they report varying attitudes and experiences. It is imperative that we consider this group when designing investigations and find ways to capture their experiences in small- and large-scale studies.

Lastly, biracial families are often formed through adoption. While much research has examined transracial adoption, it has primarily focused on Asian children adopted by White parents in the United States (see Chap. 9 for more information). Few investigations have considered domestic cross-race adoptions, including the adoption of biracial youth by monoracial families. Moreover, we know even less about minority families adopting cross-racially, especially those adopting White children. Further research should include investigations of the many ways biracial families are formed through adoption. These investigations would benefit from using a systems theory approach to examine the impact on the couple's relationship and on siblings (adopted and biological). A life-course perspective might also aid in better understanding the adopted child's needs and challenges at different developmental stages.

Racial Identity and Outcomes

Minority youth who report greater levels of racial/ethnic identity also report higher levels of self-esteem, optimism, and happiness; cope more effectively with stress; and report higher academic achievement and fewer emotional and behavioral problems. Typically, racial/ethnic identity is measured by asking questions about feelings of closeness and connection with one's ethnic group. For biracial youth, whose identity is naturally more fluid, measuring racial/ethnic identity can be difficult. Traditional measurement techniques make it impossible to know if biracial youth are answering survey questions about racial "group" or "identity." Further, researchers have not been able to clearly identify to which racial/ethnic group the biracial participant is referring, or if their responses are referencing a biracial or multiracial group. Further still, they could be referencing something we have not yet fully understood or articulated: an identity space that is beyond our current understanding. More research is needed to understand racial identity development, levels of racial identity, and their antecedents and consequences (e.g., impact on dating) for biracial individuals. Moreover, much of the current research focuses on adolescents and young adults and compares biracial youth to monoracial peers (see Chap. 11 for more information). Future investigations should include younger participants and within-group analyses.

Some biracial youth may experience dissonance as they consider their racial self-identification. However, unlike early deficit-model perspectives that consider negative emotional stability the likely cause, the research presented in this book suggests that this reaction is more likely the result of societal expectations and limitations that do not fit their lived biracial experience. Further, identifying as biracial is sometimes considered a rejection or denial of one's minority status. In reality, it is more likely a proclamation that *biracial* is a unique racial category, a recognition of duality. Social constructions of race embolden us to assign racial categories based on phenotype (skin, hair, nose, lips), but racial group membership and identity are not merely based on external features; it is a shared cultural experience, encompassing beliefs, history, cultural expressions, art, and more. Identity is a result of social interactions; thus, identity is a personal choice. This recognition may be particularly relevant as we consider the impact of one's self-identification relative to society's interpretive categorization. Historically, "passing" was discussed in relation to light-skinned Black persons living their lives and identifying as White to avoid the negative impact of being Black in America. Many of those "passing" would today be considered biracial. We know very little about biracial passing in our current racial context. How do we think about biracial people passing as monoracial minority versus monoracial White? What about biracial people who identify as being biracial or minority but are viewed by others as White? How does the notion of passing change in this context?

Biracial youth more often choose a biracial or minority label (Rollins and Hunter, 2008). A societal prohibition against biracial people taking on a White racial self-label persists and limits their freedom to choose. Biracial youth are often racially isolated in their homes, as their parents do not share their duality, and may lack personal biracial role models. However, with more prominent representations of biracial people (e.g., Jesse Williams, Meghan Markle) and greater numbers of second-generation biracial youth being raised by biracial parents, we may see a shift in identity and self-identifications in the years to come.

Diverse Biracial Family Structures

Families in the United States are more diverse than ever (Pew Research Center, 2015b). Two-parent households are no longer the norm; divorce, remarriage, and cohabitation have all increased; single-parent households are typical; and same-sex parents can legally marry. Children are more likely than ever to experience familial fluidity, living in diverse family arrangements and experiencing multiple transitions. Much research has been conducted to explore diverse family structures among monoracial families, yet we know very little about diverse family structures among biracial families. More research is needed to explore biracial family structures and processes, including transitions and fluidity, queer families, stepfamilies, single-parent families, cohabitation, and grandparents raising biracial grandchildren (see Chap. 10 for more information). As the number of interracial relationships and biracial offspring continues to increase, more research is needed to better understand and support these biracial families.

Conclusion

As illustrated in the opening story and throughout this book, technological advances, changing demographics, and a more socially (and physically) connected world have resulted in the most diverse multiethnic, multiracial, and multinational society in history. Although biracial people may have some universal experiences, they are far from a monolithic group. Because of this inherent diversity, more research is needed to explore variations in their personal and familial experiences, identity processes and trajectories, and impact of these variations on the well-being of this population. We hope that further research will lead to better understanding of the familial and relational experiences in biracial families, an awareness of the complex nature of biracial identity, and greater recognition of the diversity among biracial families. As we move toward a deeper understanding of biracial families, our society will be better positioned to support our increasingly diverse American families.

References

Pew Research Center. (2015a). *Multiracial in America: Proud, diverse and growing in numbers.* Retrieved from http://www.pewsocialtrends.org/2015/06/11/multiracial-in-america/

Pew Research Center. (2015b). *Parenting in America: Outlook, worries, aspirations are strongly linked to financial situation.* Retrieved from http://www.pewsocialtrends.org/2015/12/17/1-the-american-family-today/

Pew Research Center. (2017). *The rise of multiracial and multiethnic babies in the U.S.* Retrieved from http://www.pewresearch.org/fact-tank/2017/06/06/the-rise-of-multiracial-and-multiethnic-babies-in-the-u-s/

Rollins, A. & Hunter, A. G. (2008, November). *Deconstructing race: Biracial adolescents' fluid racial self-labels.* Poster presented at the annual conference of the National Council on Family relations, Little Rock, AR.

Index

R. Nazarinia Roy, A. Rollins (eds.), *Biracial Families*,
https://doi.org/10.1007/978-3-319-96160-6

CPSIA information can be obtained
at www.ICGtesting.com
Printed in the USA
LVHW081935050120
642560LV00001B/8/P

9 783319 961590